New York

ADVENTURES IN TIME AND PLACE

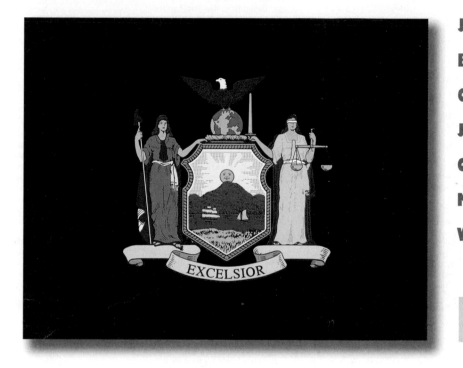

James A. Banks

Barry K. Beyer

Gloria Contreras

Jean Craven

Gloria Ladson-Billings

Mary A. McFarland

Walter C. Parker

NATIONAL GEOGRAPHIC SOCIETY

ADOPTED IN 1909, OUR STATE'S FLAG SHOWS THE OFFICIAL SEAL OF NEW YORK ON A BLUE BACKGROUND. A BRIGHT SUN RISES ABOVE MOUNTAINS AND A RIVER WITH SAILING SHIPS. A BALD EAGLE, THE SYMBOL OF THE UNITED STATES, PERCHES ON TOP OF A GLOBE. ON THE LEFT IS A FIGURE OF A WOMAN WHO REPRESENTS LIBERTY; ON THE RIGHT IS A FIGURE OF JUSTICE. THE WORD "EXCELSIOR," NEW YORK'S MOTTO, IS LATIN FOR "EVER UPWARD."

THE PRINCETON REVIEW

McGraw-Hill School Division

New York   Farmington

PROGRAM AUTHORS

Dr. James A. Banks
Professor of Education and Director of the Center for Multicultural Education
University of Washington
Seattle, Washington

Dr. Barry K. Beyer
Professor Emeritus, Graduate School of Education
George Mason University
Fairfax, Virginia

Dr. Gloria Contreras
Professor of Education
University of Northern Texas
Denton, Texas

Jean Craven
District Coordinator of Curriculum Development
Albuquerque Public Schools
Albuquerque, New Mexico

Dr. Gloria Ladson-Billings
Assistant Professor of Education
University of Wisconsin
Madison, Wisconsin

Dr. Mary A. McFarland
Instructional Coordinator of Social Studies, K–12, and Director of Staff Development
Parkway School District
Chesterfield, Missouri

Dr. Walter C. Parker
Professor and Program Chair for Social Studies Education
University of Washington
Seattle, Washington

NATIONAL GEOGRAPHIC SOCIETY
Washington, D.C.

SENIOR CONSULTANTS

Ann K. Fronckowiak
Associate Director of Programs
Buffalo Public Schools
Buffalo, New York

John Paul Bianchi
Social Studies Coordinator
New York City Community School District 08
New York, New York

Nancy Murinka
Fourth Grade Teacher
Arthur A. Gates Elementary School
Port Byron, New York

Gloria Harris
Assistant Professor of Education
Queens College of City University of New York
New York, New York

GRADE-LEVEL CONSULTANTS

Henry Mueller
Former Supervisor Niskayuna Schools
Niskayuna, New York

Robert Pierce
Professor of Geography
State University of New York, Cortland
Cortland, New York

Janice Finger
Fourth Grade Teacher
Martin Van Buren Elementary
Kinderhook, New York

Paul Scudiere
Former New York State Historian
Delmar, New York

Elizabeth Coene
Fourth Grade Teacher
Hosea Rogers Middle School
Rochester, New York

Bruce Reinholdt
New York Historical Society
Cooperstown, New York

John Mohawk
Professor of American Studies
State University of New York, Buffalo
Buffalo, New York

Joan W. Casterline
Former Fourth Grade Teacher
Rush-Henrietta Central School District
Henrietta, New York

CONSULTANTS FOR TEST PREPARATION

THE PRINCETON REVIEW

The Princeton Review is not affiliated with Princeton University or ETS.

ACKNOWLEDGMENTS

The publisher gratefully acknowledges permission to reprint the following copyrighted material:
From *Riverkeeper* by George Ancona. Copyright ©1990 George Ancona. Reprinted with the permission of Simon & Schuster Books for Young Readers, an imprint of Simon & Schuster Children's Publishing Division. From *The Blizzard* by Robert Bahr. Copyright © 1980 by Robert Bahr. From *The Historical Atlas of New York City* by Eric Homberger. Copyright © 1994 by Eric Homberger. Reprinted by permission of Henry Holt & Co., Inc. From "Foundation Stones of Western New York" by Dennis Nichols. Copyright © 1990 by the New York State Department of Environmental Conservation. Article published in *The Conservationist*, January-February 1990. From brochure *Doing Business in the New Empire State*, Empire State Development. From *Seneca Indian Stories* by Ha-yen-doh-nees (Leo Cooper). Copyright © 1995 by Marion G. Cooper. The Greenfield Review Press, NY. From *White Roots of Peace: The Iroquois Book of Life* by Paul A. W. Wallace. Copyright © 1994 by Clear Light Publishers. From *The Revolutionary War* by Gail B. Stewart. Copyright © 1991 by Lucent Books. From *Shh! We're Writing the Constitution*. Text © 1987 by Jean Fritz, reprinted by permission of G. P. Putnam's Sons. From *My House of Life* by Jessie B. Rittenhouse. Copyright © 1934, ©1961. Reprinted by permission of Houghton Mifflin Company. All rights reserved. From "Toward America" in *World of Our Fathers*. Copyright ©1976 by Irving Howe, reprinted by permission of Harcourt Brace & Company. From *World of Our Mothers* by Sydney Stahl Weinberg. Copyright © 1988 by the University of North Carolina Press. Used by permission of the publisher. From *How the Other Half Lives*, Jacob A. Riis. Copyright © 1970 by the President and Fellows of Harvard College. Reprinted by permission of Harvard University Press. From *Collected Poems* by Langston Hughes. Copyright © 1994 by the Estate of Langston Hughes. Reprinted by permission of Alfred A. Knopf, Inc. "It Don't Mean a Thing (If It Ain't Got That Swing)" by Duke Ellington and Irving Mills. Copyright © 1932 (Renewed) EMI Mills Music, Inc. and Famous Music Corporation in USA. All rights outside USA controlled by EMI Mills Music, Inc. All rights reserved. Used by permission of Warner Bros. From *A Choice of Weapons* by Gordon Parks. Copyright © 1965, 1966 by Gordon Parks. Copyright renewed 1994 by Gordon Parks. Reprinted by permission of HarperCollins Publishers, Inc. From *Letter 9-9-30*, From *The Roosevelt Reader*, edited by Basil Rauch. Copyright © 1957 by Basil Rauch. Reprinted by permission of Henry Holt & Co., Inc. From "The Home Front in Upstate New York" by Josephine E. Case. Published by *Yorker Magazine*, Summer 1995. By courtesy of the New York State Historical Association. From *Diaries of Mario M. Cuomo* by Mario M. Cuomo. Copyright © 1984 by Mario M. Cuomo. Reprinted by permission of Random House. "I Love New York" by Steve Karmen. Copyright © 1977 by Elsmere Music, Inc. From the poem "On Our Avenue of the World" in *Street Music: City Poems* by Arnold Adoff. Text Copyright © 1995 by Arnold Adoff. Used by permission of HarperCollins Publishers. "Walter" by Christopher Alden Shaw. Copyright © 1987 Christopher Alden Shaw, Hotel Silly Publishing, BMI.

McGraw-Hill School Division

A Division of The McGraw·Hill Companies

McGraw-Hill School Division
Two Penn Plaza
New York, New York 10121
Printed in the United States of America
ISBN 0-02-149194-1 / 4
3 4 5 6 7 8 9 071 04 03 02 01

Handbook
for Reading
Social Studies

One important thing you will do this year is read this textbook. In order to understand important facts and ideas it is necessary to read in a certain way. This Reading Handbook will show you some helpful ways to read Social Studies.

Main Idea and Supporting Details

As you read, look for the **main idea** and **supporting details**. The main idea is what a paragraph or section is mostly about. The details support or expand the main idea. Keeping track of the main idea and details will help you remember what you read.

- The first sentence or two of a paragraph often—but not always—contains the main idea.

- Use titles and subheads in your book as a guide in identifying the main idea.

- Make an outline of the main ideas and supporting details of a lesson to help you review.

To Find the Main Idea
Ask yourself:
- What is this paragraph or section mostly about?

To Find the Supporting Details
Ask yourself:
- What words give more information about the main idea?

In your book, you will read about World War II. Many New Yorkers fought in the war or worked in factories, making war supplies. Read this paragraph to find the main idea and details.

Main Idea:
New York industries played an important role in the war.

Supporting Details:
New York factories made telescopes, switchboards, and airplanes.

New York played an important role in the war effort. Industries were busy making war goods for the United States government. Factories in Rochester built telescopes and telephone switchboards. In the Buffalo-Niagara area one aircraft company built about 10,300 airplanes. In Bethpage another company built more than 17,000 fighter planes. That was more than any other factory in the country made.

from page 252

TRY IT!

Read the paragraph below about Buffalo, New York. Copy and complete the chart below to find the main idea and supporting details.

> Buffalo is an important manufacturing city. Factories in Buffalo make iron and steel parts for automobiles and airplanes. The city's chemical factories make medicines and other chemical products. Other manufacturers make flour and animal feed from the grain grown in New York and other states.
>
> *from page 278*

Factories make iron and steel parts for cars and planes.	Factories make medicines and chemicals.	

- How did you find the main idea and details?

Keep in Mind...

For more help in reading social studies, try these strategies:

☑ **Reread**
Review each sentence carefully. Make sure you understand what each sentence means.

☑ **Form the big picture**
As you read, think about the topic and the most important information in each paragraph or section.

☑ **Look up unknown words**
Use a dictionary or the glossary in your book to find the meanings of any words or terms you do not know.

Practice Activities

 1 READ Read the second paragraph under "Farm Families" on page 102. Identify the main idea and details.

2 WRITE Write a paragraph describing a business in your community. Be sure to include a main idea and supporting details.

Context Clues

As you read a sentence or paragraph in your book, you may find words or terms you do not know. One way to find the meaning of a new word or term is to look for **context clues**. Context clues are the words and sentences around the unfamiliar term. Using context clues helps you become a better reader.

To Use Context Clues

Ask yourself:

- What word is new to me?

- What might the word mean?

- What other words, phrases, and sentences in this paragraph help me figure out the meaning of the word? What information do these other words provide?

Read the following selection from your book about New York. What context clues would you use to identify the meaning of the word *hamlet*?

TIP!

- Have you heard this word before? How was it used?

- Write down the context clues you used to find the meaning of the new word.

- Use the new word in a sentence of your own to help you remember it.

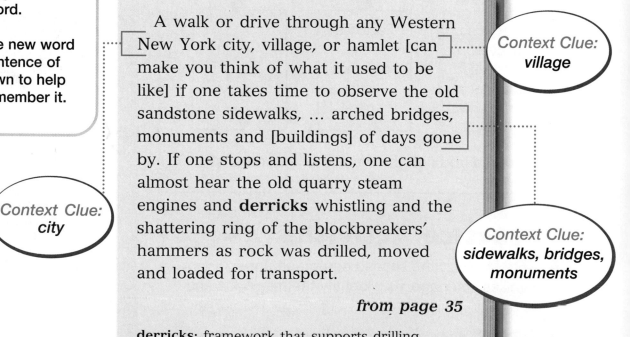

A walk or drive through any Western New York city, village, or hamlet [can] make you think of what it used to be like] if one takes time to observe the old sandstone sidewalks, ... arched bridges, monuments and [buildings] of days gone by. If one stops and listens, one can almost hear the old quarry steam engines and **derricks** whistling and the shattering ring of the blockbreakers' hammers as rock was drilled, moved and loaded for transport.

from page 35

derricks: framework that supports drilling machinery

Context Clue: *village*

Context Clue: *city*

Context Clue: *sidewalks, bridges, monuments*

TRY IT!

Read the paragraph below about transportation along the Hudson River. Copy and complete the chart to find context clues for *routes*.

In a way, the Hudson River is like a very old highway. It is one of the transportation routes that people have used for thousands of years.... Native Americans of our area used this route to transport goods to trade with one another. Later, the Dutch and the English who came here used this long waterway to trade with Native Americans. The Hudson is more than 300 miles long.

from page 19

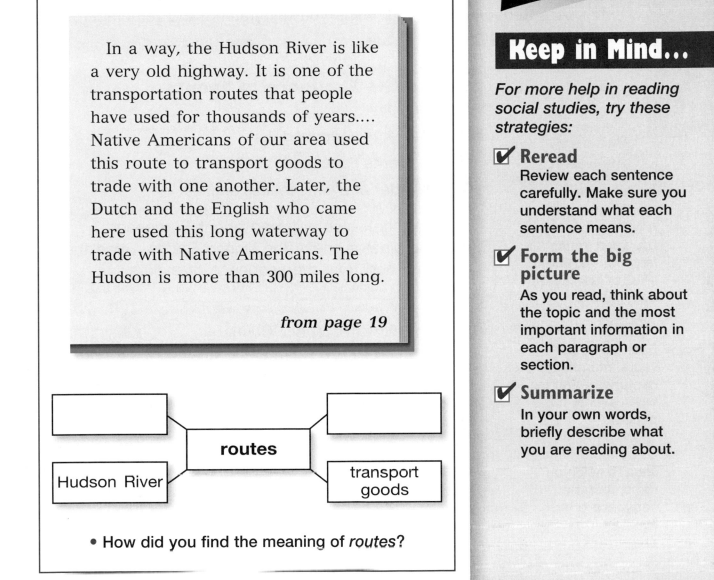

routes

Hudson River

transport goods

• How did you find the meaning of *routes*?

Keep in Mind...

For more help in reading social studies, try these strategies:

☑ **Reread**
Review each sentence carefully. Make sure you understand what each sentence means.

☑ **Form the big picture**
As you read, think about the topic and the most important information in each paragraph or section.

☑ **Summarize**
In your own words, briefly describe what you are reading about.

Practice Activities

1 READ Read the first paragraph under "The Young State" on page 137 of your book. What context clues helped you find the meaning of *challenge*?

2 WRITE Write a paragraph using a new word from the dictionary. Include context clues.

Sequencing

As you read, look for the order in which things happen. **Sequencing** events is listing them in the order in which they happen. Sequencing events helps you understand and remember what you read.

- Look for clue words such as *first, next, then, finally, by, when, until, last, before,* and *after* to identify the sequence of events.

- Look for dates—years, months, or centuries—that tell when events happened.

- Use chapter time lines to help you remember the sequence of events.

To Find the Sequence of Events
Ask yourself:

- Which events happened first?

- Which events happened next?

- Which order of events makes sense?

In your book, you will read about Europeans exploring what is today the United States. Read the paragraph and note the sequence of events.

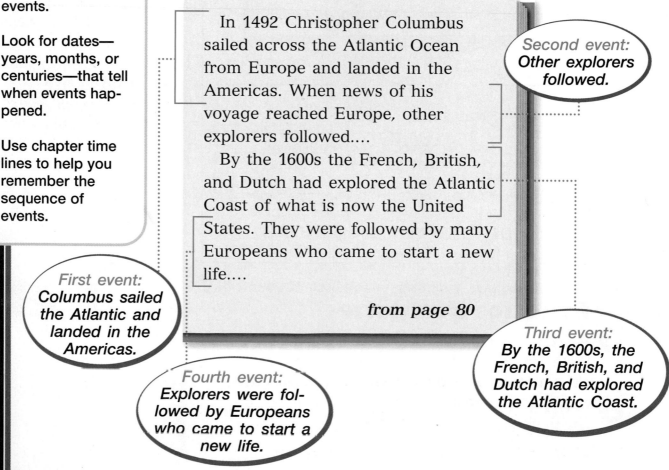

In 1492 Christopher Columbus sailed across the Atlantic Ocean from Europe and landed in the Americas. When news of his voyage reached Europe, other explorers followed....

By the 1600s the French, British, and Dutch had explored the Atlantic Coast of what is now the United States. They were followed by many Europeans who came to start a new life....

from page 80

Second event:
Other explorers followed.

First event:
Columbus sailed the Atlantic and landed in the Americas.

Third event:
By the 1600s, the French, British, and Dutch had explored the Atlantic Coast.

Fourth event:
Explorers were followed by Europeans who came to start a new life.

TRY IT!

Read below about Renee Mancino's baking business. Then copy and complete the chart.

Many people start up businesses to make a product that consumers need. Renee Allen Mancino is the owner of Carrot Top Pastries in New York City. Her mother and grandmother taught her how to bake. Renee started cooking as a way to earn money. She began selling carrot cakes to families in the late 1970s. In 1980 she was selling cakes from the back of a truck on Wall Street. Today, Renee owns two cafes and one large bakery. Her carrot cakes are now sold to New York City's best restaurants.

from page 277

▼

In the late 1970s, Renee sold cakes to families.

▼

In 1980, she sold cakes from a truck on Wall Street.

▼

• How did you determine the sequence of events?

Keep in Mind...

For more help in reading social studies, try these strategies:

☑ **Look up unknown words**
Use a dictionary or the glossary in your book to find the meanings of any unfamiliar words.

☑ **Form the big picture**
As you read, think about the topic and the most important information in each paragraph or section.

☑ **Summarize**
In your own words, briefly describe what your reading is about.

Practice Activities

1 READ Read the section titled "A Business Center" on page 152. List the events of the beginnings of The Bank of New York in sequence.

2 WRITE Write about the events of your day. Include words such as *first, then, next,* and *finally.*

Make Predictions

As you read a paragraph or section in your book, think about what might come next. What you think will happen is your **prediction**. A prediction does not have a correct or incorrect answer. Making predictions helps you to carefully consider what you are reading.

- Think about other things you know that will help you make an "educated guess."

- Test your prediction: read further to see if you were correct.

- Revise your prediction: read further to see if more information changes your prediction.

To Make a Prediction
Ask yourself:

- What happened in this section?
- What background knowledge do I already know about the events in the text?
- What similar situations do I know of?
- What do I think might happen next?

In your book, you will read about *climate*. Climate is the pattern of weather of a certain place over many years. The climate of a place is affected by its geographical location. Read these paragraphs below to see how a prediction might be made. Do you agree or disagree with this prediction?

Whiteface Mountain [in the Adirondacks] is about 360 miles north of Freeport [on Long Island]. This means that Whiteface Mountain is farther from the equator than Freeport is. Usually, the farther from the equator you go, the colder the temperature is.

What do you expect the weather to be like in Canada?

from page 24

Text Information:
The farther from the equator, the colder the temperature.

Background Knowledge:
I know that Canada is farther from the equator than New York.

Prediction:
Canada will be colder than New York.

TRY IT!

In your book you will read about New York City in the early 1900s. Read the following and copy and complete the prediction chart below.

In the early 1900s, New York City had almost 4 million people. It had new bridges and new businesses. Manhattan was very crowded. There was not much land to spread out on. The streets were filled with horses, carriages, and trolleys. Traveling around the city was slow. As the population and businesses grew, New Yorkers had to look beneath the ground and up toward the sky to solve their "space" problems.

from page 244

Text Information

Manhattan was crowded in early 1900s. People looked underground and skyward for space.

My Prediction

New Yorkers built subways and tall buildings to solve their space problems.

Background Information

• On what did you base your prediction?

Keep in Mind...

For more help in reading social studies, try these strategies:

☑ **Sequencing**
As you read, think about the order in which things happened.

☑ **Form the big picture**
As you read, think about the topic and the most important information in each paragraph or section.

☑ **Relate to personal experience**
Think about how what you are reading about relates to your own life.

Practice Activities

1 **READ** Read the *Read Aloud* under "New Netherland" on page 90. Predict how Henry Hudson and his crew would influence others in Europe.

2 **WRITE** Write a paragraph predicting what you will do after high school. Give reasons why.

Compare and Contrast

This book often **compares** and **contrasts** people or events. To compare things is to show how they are alike. To contrast things is to show how they are different. Comparing and contrasting helps you understand the relationship between things.

To Compare

Ask yourself:

• What are the things being compared?
• How are they alike?

To Contrast

Ask yourself:

• What are the things being contrasted?
• How are they different?

In your book, you will read about the Erie Canal. Read below to compare and contrast the canal when it was first built with the canal today.

■ To compare, look for clue words such as: *like, similar, in common, both, same,* and *resemble.*

■ To contrast, look for clue words such as: *before, after, different from, unlike, however,* and *by contrast.*

Compare:
The canal served people then and serves us now.

Contrast:
The canal is wider and deeper than it used to be.

The Erie Canal has changed quite a bit from the time it was first built. It has been widened from 40 feet at the top to 75 feet. It is deeper than it was, too. It used to be only 4 feet deep, and now it is 12 feet deep.

Today canal boats usually have motors. The biggest change, though is how people use the canal. Old towpaths have been made into bicycle paths and parks. People now use the Erie Canal more for having fun than for transporting goods...

from page 174

Contrast:
Today, boats move by motors instead of mules.

Contrast:
Towpaths are now parks used for fun.

TRY IT!

Read the paragraph and copy and complete the diagram.

Before the canal, shipping goods over land between Buffalo and New York City took 20 days and cost $100 a ton. The Erie Canal brought the price down to $10 a ton and cut travel time to 8 days.

With the Erie Canal, trade boomed. Eastern merchants sold their iron and trade goods to settlers in the West. Settlers in the West shipped products such as wheat and lumber to cities in the East. New York City quickly became the country's most important port and city.

from page 170

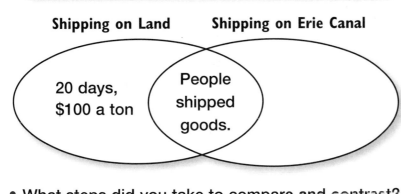

Shipping on Land   Shipping on Erie Canal

20 days, $100 a ton

People shipped goods.

- What steps did you take to compare and contrast?

Keep in Mind...

For more help in reading social studies, try these strategies:

☑ **Sequencing**

As you read, think about the order in which things happened.

☑ **Summarize**

In your own words, briefly describe what your reading is about.

☑ **Form the big picture**

As you read, think about the topic and the most important information in each paragraph or section.

☑ **Look up unknown words**

Use a dictionary or the glossary in your book to find the meanings of any words or terms you do not know.

Practice Activities

1 READ Read the first paragraph under "George Eastman" on page 216. Compare and contrast photography before and after Eastman's invention.

2 WRITE Compare and contrast the weather in your community in July and December.

Summarize

After you read a paragraph or section of this book, you can **summarize** what you have read. In a **summary**, you briefly tell in your own words about the most important information in that section. Summarizing is one way to help you understand what you read.

To Summarize

Ask yourself:

• What is this paragraph or section about?

• What information is most important?

• How can I say this in my own words?

In your book, you will read about farming in our state. Read the paragraph and summary below.

■ Look for titles, headings, and key words that identify important information.

■ Keep your summary brief, and organize the information in a clear way.

■ Don't include information and facts that are not important.

Sample Summary:
Agriculture is very important to New York State, where much of the land is ideal for farming.

The Hoffmans are one of thousands of families in New York who raise animals and crops to feed you and your family. <u>Farming is very important in New York.</u> Much of the land in our state is covered with <u>rich soil</u> and <u>low, rolling hills that make it ideal for farming</u>. In fact, <u>over one quarter of New York's land is used for agriculture</u>. Agriculture is the business of growing crops and raising animals. <u>The sale of crops and cattle is important to the state's economy</u>. <u>Around 70,000 New Yorkers make their living on farms</u>. You can find food from New York farms on dinner tables all over the country.

from page 272

Important information is underlined.

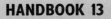

TRY IT!

Read the following paragraph. Then copy and complete the diagram.

The Adirondack Park covers one-fifth of New York State's land. It contains six million acres. That is as big as the state of Vermont! Some of Adirondack Park is public land—land owned by the government. Over half the parkland is privately owned. Its owners include more than 100,000 people who live in the park all year. About 200,000 other people own land on which they have summer homes. Other private owners include lumber companies and people who run hotels, restaurants, and tourist spots.

from page 232

Keep in Mind...

For more help in reading social studies, try these strategies:

☑ **Reread**
Review each sentence carefully. Make sure you understand what each sentence means.

☑ **Form the big picture**
As you read, think about the topic and the most important information in each paragraph or section.

☑ **Make an outline**
As you read, write an outline of the topic and the main ideas of the reading.

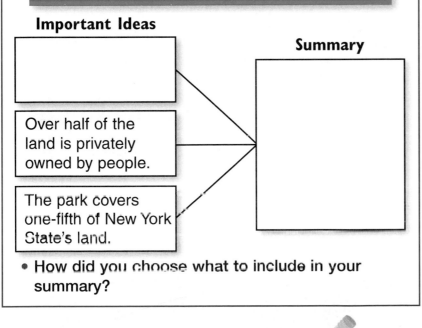

Important Ideas

Summary

Over half of the land is privately owned by people.

The park covers one-fifth of New York State's land.

• How did you choose what to include in your summary?

Practice Activities

1 **READ** Read the last paragraph under "The Industrial Revolution" on page 179. Make a summary.

2 **WRITE** Write a summary of a book you have recently read.

Use Visuals

One way to learn from your reading is to use **visuals**. Visuals are the graphs, charts, pictures, and maps in your book. Visuals provide useful information in a clear, easy-to-study form.

To Use Visuals

Look closely at the visual. Ask yourself:

- What does the graph, chart, picture, or map show?
- How does it help me to understand what I have read?
- How does it add to the information I have read?
- What information do the visual's caption or label provide?

In your book, you will read about an aqueduct built in 1837 to supply New York City with water from the Croton River, miles away. Study this diagram showing how an aqueduct works.

- Read the caption and labels for information they provide.

- Look for objects in the picture that might give additional information.

- When looking at graphs, maps, or charts, be sure to read the legend or key to find the meanings of special symbols.

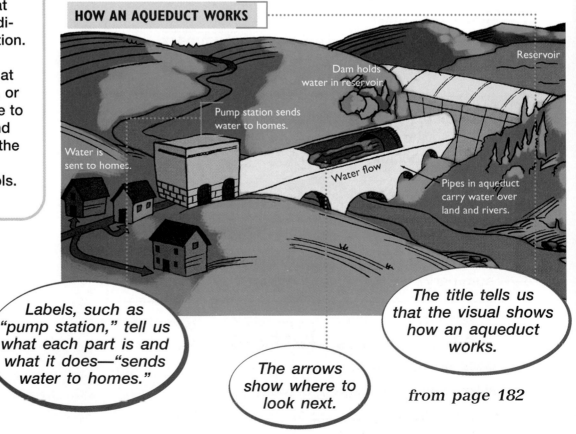

HOW AN AQUEDUCT WORKS

Reservoir

Dam holds water in reservoir.

Pump station sends water to homes.

Water is sent to homes.

Water flow

Pipes in aqueduct carry water over land and rivers.

Labels, such as "pump station," tell us what each part is and what it does—"sends water to homes."

The arrows show where to look next.

The title tells us that the visual shows how an aqueduct works.

from page 182

TRY IT!

Study this diagram showing a hydroelectric plant. Then copy and complete the chart below.

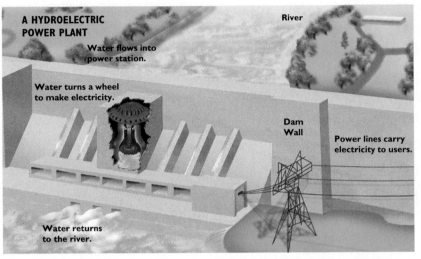

A HYDROELECTRIC POWER PLANT

River

Water flows into power station.

Water turns a wheel to make electricity.

Dam Wall

Power lines carry electricity to users.

Water returns to the river.

from pages 230-231

Label Information:

Visual Information:

Visual: diagram showing a hydro-electric plant

Label information: electricity comes from plant, through power lines, to homes

Title: Hydroelectric Power Plant

• What steps did you take to use the visual?

Practice Activities

1 **USE VISUALS** Make a chart similar to the one above. Fill in the chart using information from the diagram on page 273.

2 **WRITE** Find a photograph that interests you. Write a paragraph based on information in the photo. Add labels, captions, and a title.

Keep in Mind...

For more help in reading social studies, try these strategies:

✔ **Reread**
Review each sentence carefully. Make sure you understand what each sentence means.

✔ **Sequencing**
As you read, think about the order in which events happened.

✔ **Look up unknown words**
Use a dictionary or the glossary in your book to find the meanings of any words or terms you do not know.

CONTENTS

UNIT ONE A Place Called New York

4

UNIT TWO
Settlement of a New Land

54

Thaw Collection, Fenimore House Museum, Cooperstown, N.Y. Photo by John Bigelow Taylor, N.Y.C.

Albany Institute of History and Art

Sophia Smith Collection, Smith College

Griffith Bailey Coale, On the Erie Canal, Canajoharie
Library and Art Gallery, Canajoharie, N.Y.

v

UNIT FOUR   *Building the Empire State*

Lewis W. Hine, Courtesy of George Eastman House

UNIT FIVE
New York Today
266

REFERENCE SECTION

STANDARDIZED TEST SUPPORT

THE PRINCETON REVIEW

FEATURES

LOCAL CONNECTIONS

SKILLS LESSONS

CITIZENSHIP

Used with permission. I♥NY is a
registered trademark and service mark of
the New York State Department of Economic Development.

CHARTS, GRAPHS, & DIAGRAMS

TIME LINES

TIME LINES

1807
HUDSON RIVER
Robert Fulton's steamboat travels up the Hudson River to Albany

1825
NEW YORK HARBOR
The Erie Canal opens with the "Wedding of the Waters"

MAPS

YOUR TEXTBOOK
at a glance

Your book is called *New York: Adventures in Time and Place*. It has thirteen chapters. Each chapter has two or more lessons. There are also many special features for you to study and enjoy.

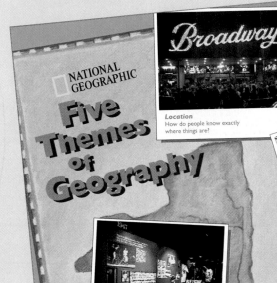

NATIONAL GEOGRAPHIC

Five Themes of Geography

Location
How do people know exactly where things are?

Place
What special places can you visit in New York that you can't find in any other state?

Movement
How can pe[...] place to an[...]

▲ Special pages bring you ideas in geography from **National Geographic**.

LESSON 2

1720   1740   1760   1775 1783   1800

REVOLUTION IN NEW YORK

READ ALOUD
Three weeks after New Yorkers had pulled down the statue of King George III in 1776, thousands of British soldiers landed on Long Island. For four days, the American militia and the British soldiers battled each other near what was then the village of Brooklyn. The American Revolution had come to New York.

THE BIG PICTURE
In Lesson 1, you learned that in 1775 the colonial militia and the British fought each other at Lexington and Concord. This was the start of the American Revolution.

Within a year New York became a key state in the war for independence. Think about why this might have been. One reason was its location. New York was about halfway between the New England colonies and the Southern colonies.

General George Washington was commander of the Continental, or American, Army. He knew what would happen if the British controlled New York. The New England colonies would then be separated from the Southern colonies. It would be much more difficult for the colonies to send messages and supplies to each other. It would also be much harder to send soldiers back and forth. He had to try to stop the British!

Focus Activity

READ TO LEARN
What happened to the British plan to capture New York?

VOCABULARY
surrender
retreat
Battle of Saratoga
Battle of Yorktown

PEOPLE
Sarah Jay
Sybil Ludington
John Burgoyne
Joseph Brant
Horatio Gates

PLACES
Saratoga
Oriskany

122

---

air-conditioned tractors and listen to a radio or their favorite CDs. Besides raising food for the livestock, the Hoffmans plant vegetables for themselves.

In summer the hay is cut and then stored in the barns. This is also the time when Jeremy and Valerie show their cows at the Chemung County fair.

In the fall the [...] and the cows are [...] barn. This must b[...] the first snowfall [...]

All the work th[...] on the farm is im[...] might pour the m[...] on your breakfast [...]

WHY IT [...]
Fa[...]re in New [...] fruits and vegeta[...] raise animals for [...] and meat. They [...] people all over th[...]

Reviewing

SUM IT UP
- The business o[...] and raising ani[...] agriculture.
- One quarter of [...] York is used for [...]
- Apples, grapes, [...] and dairy prod[...] New York's mo[...] cultural produc[...]
- Farmers now u[...] other machines [...]

DO KNOW?
How many eggs does New York make?

New York chickens lay about 2 billion eggs a year. That's more than 100 eggs for every person in our state! With that many eggs you could make an omelet taller than the Empire State Building!

NEW LIFE IN A NEW LAND
For most immigrants New York City was a strange and fantastic place. "The city dazzled us. We had never seen such buildings, such people, such activity," said one young immigrant from Slovenia, in Eastern Europe. "Maybe the stories were [...], Maybe everything was possible in America."

However, most i[...] many difficult years[...] Most arrived with li[...] of them lived in ten[...] built apartment buil[...] ments were cramped [...] or six people would [...] sleep in one tiny ro[...] [...]ep were few wi[...] dows for light o[...] a[...]

Some people tri[...] make life better for [...] these newcomers. I[...] 1895, nurse Lillian [...] Wald began to visi[...] homes of poor imm[...] grant families and [...] vide basic health c[...] By 1913, under W[...] leadership, over 90[...] es worked in poor [...] A newspaper re[...] Jacob Riis (REES) [...]

MANY VOICES LITERATURE

Excerpt from *How the Other Half Lives*, written by Jacob Riis in 1890.

In a miserable tenement in Cherry Street . . . the man, his wife, and three children [were] shivering [from] winds of winter . . . The room was [...]

Infographic
Dutch Life in New York
Many Dutch settlers in New York farmed land in the Hudson River Valley. Today you can see how they lived at the Luykas Van Alen House Museum in Kinderhook.

The Van Alen house (above) was built of bricks in 1737. Luykas, his wife Elizabeth, and their three sons farmed 500 acres of land.

◄ Special features called **Infographics** inform you with pictures and maps. **Did You Know** has interesting information to share. Enjoy **Many Voices**—writings and songs from many sources.

Look for a variety of lessons and features. Each chapter has a **Local Connection**—a link to local communities. You will build **Skills**, learn about **Legacies** that connect us to the past, and meet people who show what **Citizenship** is.

CITIZENSHIP
VIEWPOINTS

HOW SHOULD WE USE THE LAND OF THE ADIRONDACKS?

Three DIFFERENT Viewpoints

PETER SAUER
Director of an environmental organization, North Creek
Excerpt from interview, 1996

The future . . . health of the park depends both on our resource-based economy, which harvests trees on private land to make paper, lumber, and furniture, and on the tourist industry. People up and down the East Coast come to the Adirondacks for outdoor recreation and wilderness experiences that are disappearing in many other places. We have a success story of people living with nature without destroying it.

MICHAEL MARTIN

a success story of people living with nature

Legacy
LINKING PAST AND PRESENT
BASEBALL

THINKING SKILLS

Decision Making

recycled. Sometimes products are recycled in surprising ways. A factory in Ronkonkoma (rahn KAHN kuh muh), New York, makes picnic tables from

TRYING THE SKILL
Imagine that there is a forest area near your community. A company has asked to build

HELPING yourself
• A decision is a choice about what to do.
• Identify the choices

REVIEW THE SKILL
1. What is a decision?
2. Look at the section called Trying the Skill. If your

LOCAL CONNECTIONS
BRENTWOOD: LEARNING FROM BUILDINGS

"We can learn about early settlers on Long Island by studying their buildings," Christine Finn said to students in her fourth-grade class at Twin Pines Elementary School. "Did you know that Old Bethpage Vill-

The students then went inside the house. They noticed the large stone fireplace at the end wall. "Why is the fireplace so big?" Ms. Finn asked them.

"The fireplace was where they cooked all their food," Jessica replied.

"I'll bet they used the fire to stay warm," said Gualberto.

"That's right," Ms. Finn told him. "They didn't have radiators or furnaces in their houses like we do."

As they continued on their tour, the students could see how the buildings and the materials used to build them changed over time. The Noon Inn was built in the 1850s. It is a two-story house made from wood. It has a wide front porch. The Manetto Hill Church is made from brick. It was built in the middle of the 1800s.

Ms. Finn had the students form groups. The students in each group selected one of the buildings at Old Bethpage Village. They made careful drawings of the building they selected. When the class returned to school, each group built a cardboard model of its building. The students arranged their buildings in a village and then shared what they had learned with others.

MAKE your LOCAL CONNECTION

What historic houses or buildings are located in your community? What can these buildings tell you about the history of your community? Make your own model village and share it with others.

After visiting Old Bethpage Village, students worked together to make models of the historic buildings.

107

THE BATTLES ON LONG ISLAND AND MANHATTAN

The battle that was fought on Long Island in August 1776 did not go well for the American soldiers. They were beaten badly. The British stopped firing their rifles and cannons and waited for the Continental Army to surrender, or give up. However, General Washington had other plans. When a heavy fog moved in, Washington and his troops escaped by rowing boats across the East River to Manhattan.

New York City Is Captured

A few weeks later the Americans and British fought each other in Manhattan. Once again, the Continental Army lost. In November, Washington and his soldiers left the city and went to New Jersey. Now New York City was under British control. It stayed that way until the end of the war.

When the British took over New York, Loyalists poured into the city. They knew they would be safe there. On the other hand, many Patriots fled the city. They went to places where they would be safe from the British.

At about the same time the British captured New York City, they also landed at Peekskill, north of New York City. Sarah Jay, the wife of patriot John Jay, was visiting near there. She wrote to her husband:

I am determined to . . . prepare for the worst and hope for the best. . . . Not less than twelve hundred of the enemy landed at Peekskill . . . and . . . they had been firing sometime.

The British later turned back from Peekskill, but Sarah Jay had a narrow escape from the battle!

A Continental soldier had to fill his rifle with gunpowder.

Links to MUSIC

Yankee Doodle

The patriotic song "Yankee Doodle" was first sung during the American Revolution. The British sang it to make fun of the Continental Army's sloppy clothing:

*Yankee Doodle came to town,
Riding on a pony.
He stuck a feather in his hat,
And called it macaroni.*

But the Continental Army liked the song anyway. Riding on a pony was a sign of importance. Having a feather in one's hat was a sign of honor. And macaroni did not mean a noodle. It meant a British man who liked fancy clothes and showed off.

Sing "Yankee Doodle" as a class. Identify other songs that became popular during other wars.

123

The end of your book has a **Reference Section** with many types of information. Use it to look up words, people, and places.

Biographical Dictionary

The Biographical Dictionary tells you about the people you have learned about in this book. The

Burgoyne, John (bar gŏyn"), 1722–1792 British general whose defeat at the Battle of Saratoga was . . .

Dictionary of GEOGRAPHIC TERMS

GULF (gulf) Part of an ocean that extends into the land; larger than a bay.

PLATEAU (pla tō"), A high, flat area that rises steeply above the surrounding land

DAM (dam) A wall across a river, creating a lake used to store water.

RESERVOIR (rez"ər vwär) A natural or artificial lake used to store water.

ESCARPMENT (e skärp"mənt) A steep cliff

CANYON (kan"yən) A deep, narrow valley with steep sides.

PEAK (pēk) A hill or small mountain that stands alone.

HILL (hil) A rounded, raised landform; not as high as a mountain.

BUTTE (byōot) A flat-topped, four-stepped small mountain; smaller than a mesa or plateau.

DESERT (dez"ərt) A dry environment with few plants and animals

VALLEY (val"ē) An area of low land between hills

BAY (bā) Part of an ocean or lake that extends deeply into the land

COAST (kōst) The land along an ocean.

Lessons begin with a **Read Aloud** selection and **The Big Picture**. Study with the **Read to Learn** question and a list of words, people, and places. Some lessons have features called **Links** with activities to try.

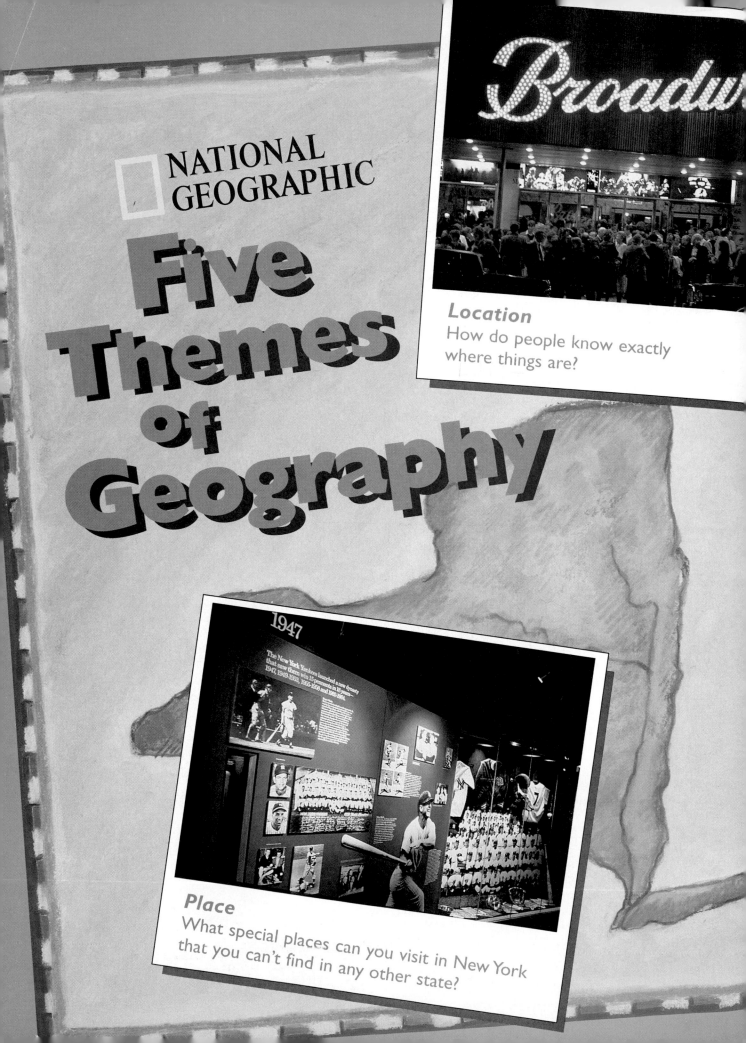

NATIONAL GEOGRAPHIC

Five Themes of Geography

Location
How do people know exactly where things are?

Place
What special places can you visit in New York that you can't find in any other state?

Human-Environment Interaction
How do people use and shape the environment in New York?

Movement
How can people get from one place to another in New York?

Region
What makes each region of New York special?

G3

GEOGRAPHY SKILLS

PART 1
Using Globes

VOCABULARY
ocean
continent
hemisphere
equator

What does a globe show?

- A globe is a small copy of Earth. Like Earth, a globe is a round object, or sphere.

- Globes show the parts of Earth that are land and the parts that are water. Earth's largest bodies of water are called oceans. There are four oceans—the Atlantic, Arctic, Indian, and Pacific oceans. Look at the globe shown here. What color is used to show oceans?

- Globes also show the seven large bodies of land called continents. The continents are Africa, Antarctica, Asia, Australia, Europe, North America, and South America. Find North America and South America on the globe below. Which oceans are shown bordering these continents?

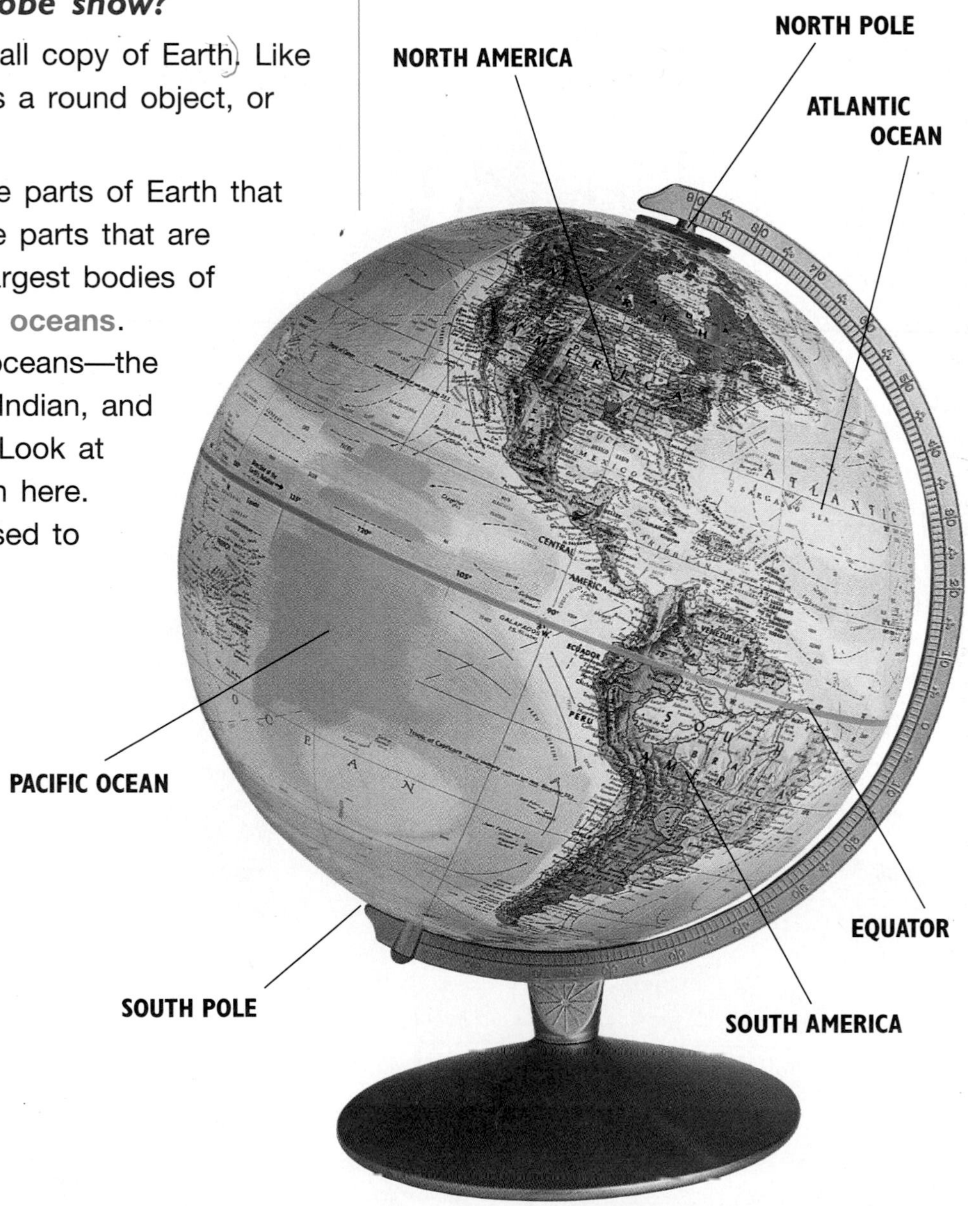

NORTH POLE

NORTH AMERICA

ATLANTIC OCEAN

PACIFIC OCEAN

EQUATOR

SOUTH POLE

SOUTH AMERICA

What are the four hemispheres?

- Look again at the globe on the previous page. Can you see the whole globe? You can see only half of a globe or sphere at any one time. A word for half a sphere is hemisphere. The word *hemi* means "half."

- Earth is divided into the Northern Hemisphere and Southern Hemisphere by the equator. The equator is an imaginary line that lies halfway between the North Pole and the South Pole. Look at the maps below. What continents are located on the equator?

- Earth can also be divided into two other hemispheres. What are the names of these hemispheres? In which hemispheres do you live?

More Practice

There are more maps in this book that show the equator. For example, see pages 61, 86, and 88.

THE HEMISPHERES

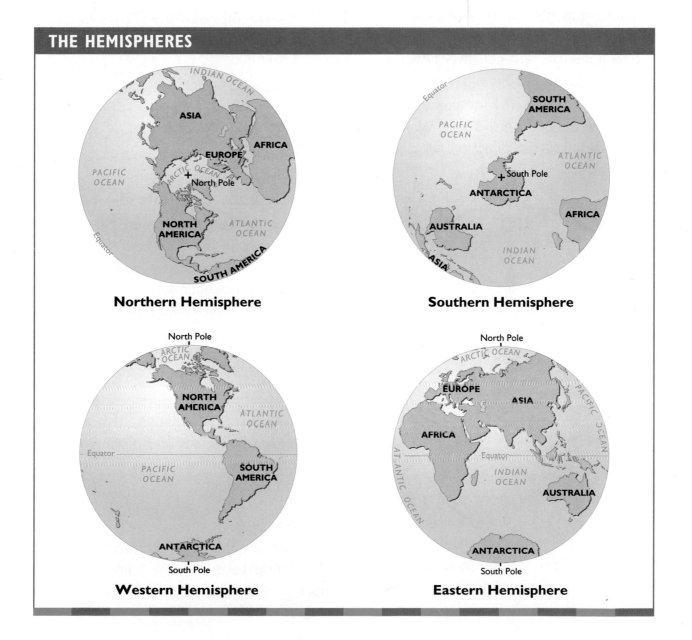

Northern Hemisphere

Southern Hemisphere

Western Hemisphere

Eastern Hemisphere

PART 2
Using Maps

VOCABULARY
cardinal directions
compass rose
intermediate directions
symbol
map key
scale
locator

What are cardinal directions?

- Directions describe the way you face or move to get somewhere. North, east, south, and west are the main directions, or cardinal directions.

- If you face the North Pole, you are facing north. When you face north, south is directly behind you. West is to your left. What direction will be to your right?

How do you use a compass rose?

- A compass rose is a small drawing on a map that can help you find directions. You will see a compass rose on most maps in this book.

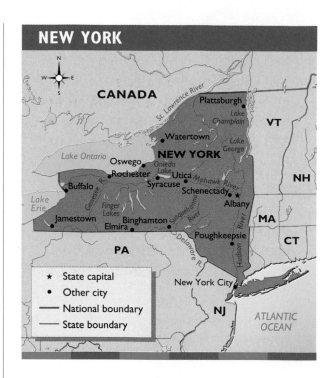

NEW YORK

- The cardinal directions are written as **N**, **E**, **S**, and **W**. Find the compass rose on the map above. In which direction is Syracuse from Watertown?

What are intermediate directions?

- Notice the spikes between the cardinal directions on the compass rose. These show the intermediate directions, or in-between directions.

- The intermediate directions are northeast, southeast, southwest, and northwest. The direction northeast is often written as **NE**. What letters are used for the other intermediate directions? Which intermediate direction lies between south and east? Which intermediate direction lies between north and west?

More Practice

You can practice finding directions using a compass rose on most maps in this book. For examples, look at the maps on pages 17, 83, and 168.

Why do maps have titles?

- When using a map, first look at the map title. The title names the area the map shows. It may also tell you the kind of information shown on the map. Look at the maps on this page. What is the title of each?

Why do maps include symbols?

- A **symbol** is something that stands for something else.

- On a map common symbols include dots, lines, triangles, and colors. Many maps use the color blue to stand for water. What do dots sometimes stand for?

- Maps also often use symbols that are small drawings of the things they stand for. A drawing of a tent, for example, might stand for a campground. What might an airplane stand for?

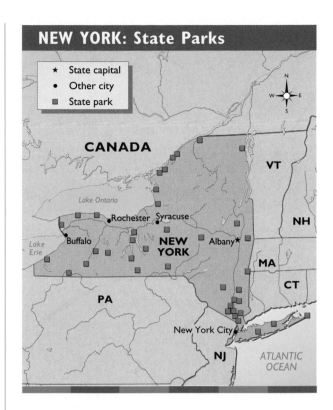

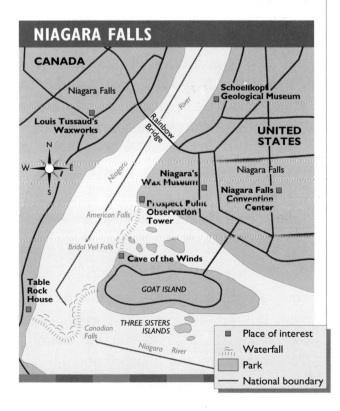

How can you find out what map symbols stand for?

- Often the same symbol stands for different things on different maps. For this reason many maps include a **map key**. A map key gives the meaning of each symbol used on the map.

- When you look at a map, you should always study the map key. Look at the maps on this page. What symbol marks places of interest on the map of Niagara Falls? How many places of interest are shown? What does the same symbol stand for on the map of New York parks? What other symbols are used on the parks map?

More Practice

There are many maps with symbols and map keys in this book. For examples, see pages 61, 125, and 168.

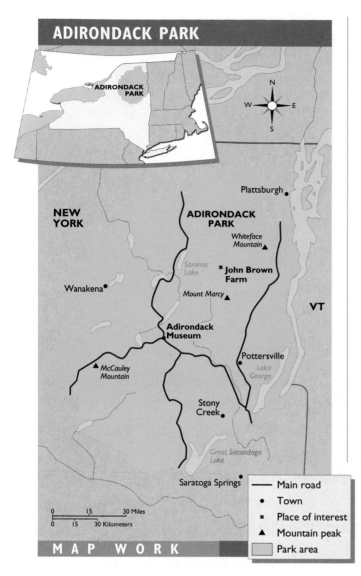

ADIRONDACK PARK

NEW YORK

ADIRONDACK PARK

Plattsburgh

Whiteface Mountain ▲

Saranac Lake

■ John Brown Farm

Wanakena ●

Mount Marcy ▲

VT

Adirondack Museum ■

Pottersville ●

Lake George

▲ McCauley Mountain

Stony Creek ●

Great Sacandaga Lake

Saratoga Springs ●

0   15   30 Miles
0   15   30 Kilometers

M A P   W O R K

—— Main road
● Town
■ Place of interest
▲ Mountain peak
  Park area

What is a map scale?

- All maps are smaller than the real area that they show. How can you figure out the real distance between places? Most maps include a scale. The scale shows the relationship between distances on a map and real distances.

- The scales in this book are drawn with two horizontal lines. The top line shows distance in miles. What unit of measurement does the bottom line of the scale use? Which is longer, 100 miles or 100 kilometers?

How do you use a map scale?

- You can use a ruler to measure distances on a map. You can also make a scale strip like the one shown on this page. Place the edge of a strip of paper under the scale lines on the map of Adirondack Park. Mark the distances in miles. Slide your strip over and continue to mark miles until your strip is long enough to measure the whole map.

- Use your scale strip to measure the distance between Stony Creek and Pottersville. Place the edge of the strip under the two points. Line the zero up under Stony Creek. What is the distance to Pottersville?

0   2   4   6   8
                   miles

What do locators show?

- A locator is a small map set onto the main map. It shows where the area of the main map is located. Where is the the locator on the map of Adirondack Park?

- The area shown by the main map is highlighted in green on the locator. Look at the map of Adirondack Park. What area does the locator show?

More Practice

You can find scales and locatators on many in this book. For examples of scales, see pages 20, 101, and 168. For examples of locators, see pages 8 and 11.

PART 3
Different Kinds of Maps

VOCABULARY
political map
physical map
landform map
transportation map
historical map

What is a political map?

- A political map shows information such as cities, capitals, states, and countries. What symbol is used to show state capitals on the map below? What city is the capital of our state? What is the symbol for our national capital?

- Political maps use lines to show borders. The states or countries are also often shown in different colors. Look at the map below. What color is used to show our state? How many different colors are used to show the states? What color are the other countries on the map?

More Practice

There are other political maps in this book. For examples, see pages 161, 197, and 258.

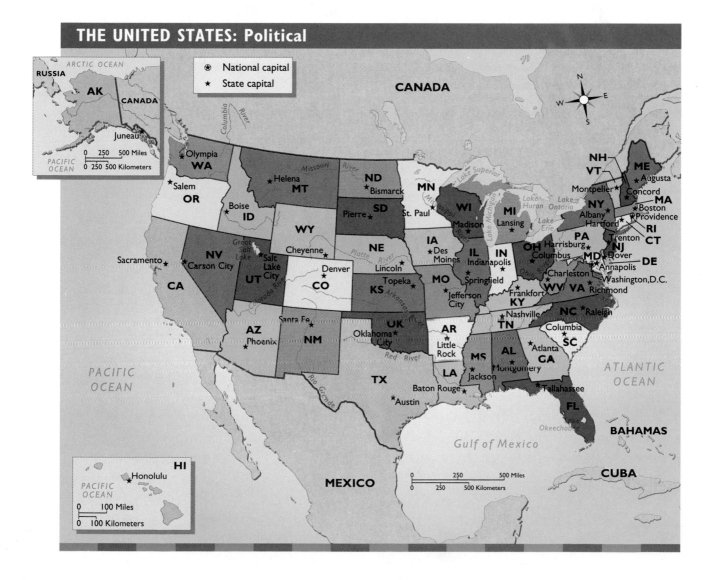

THE UNITED STATES: Political

⊛ National capital
★ State capital

What are physical maps?

- Maps that show the natural features of Earth are called physical maps. There are different kinds of physical maps in this book.

- One kind of physical map shows landforms, or the shapes that make up Earth's surface. These maps are called landform maps. Mountains, hills, and plains are all examples of landforms. Landform maps also show bodies of water such as lakes, rivers, and oceans.

- Look at the map of the United States. What kinds of landforms are found in the United States? What is the name of the plains area that is to the east of the Rocky Mountains? What large bodies of water are shown? Which ocean borders the Coast Ranges?

- Find New York on the map. Which different landforms are shown in New York? What bodies of water lie along the northern border of New York? What ocean borders New York?

More Practice

For other physical maps, see pages 17 and 20.

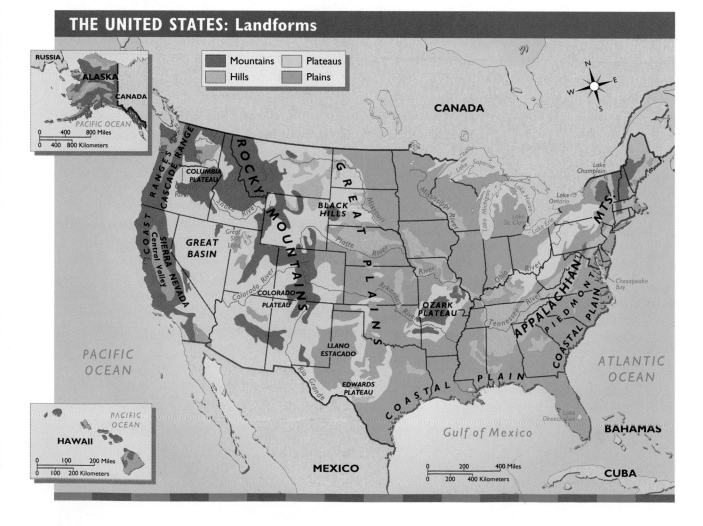

THE UNITED STATES: Landforms

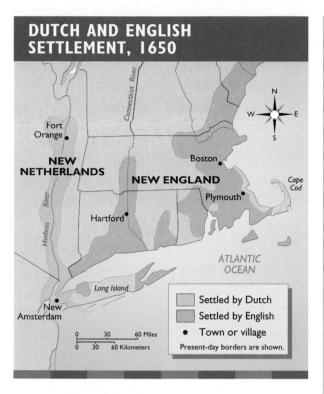

DUTCH AND ENGLISH SETTLEMENT, 1650

Fort Orange

NEW NETHERLANDS

Boston

NEW ENGLAND

Cape Cod

Plymouth

Hartford

Hudson River

Connecticut River

ATLANTIC OCEAN

Long Island

New Amsterdam

0   30   60 Miles
0   30   60 Kilometers

Settled by Dutch
Settled by English
● Town or village
Present-day borders are shown.

What is an historical map?

- An **historical map** is a map that shows information about past events and where they occurred. Historical maps often show places and political boundaries that are different from those that exist today.

- When you look at an historical map, first study the map title. What does the title tell you about the historical map on this page?

- Historical maps often show dates in the title or on the map. Study the map on this page. What time period does it show?

- Next look at the map key. The map key tells you what information is shown on the map. Along which river did the Dutch build settlements?

What is a transportation map?

- A **transportation map** is a kind of map that shows you how you can travel from one place to another.

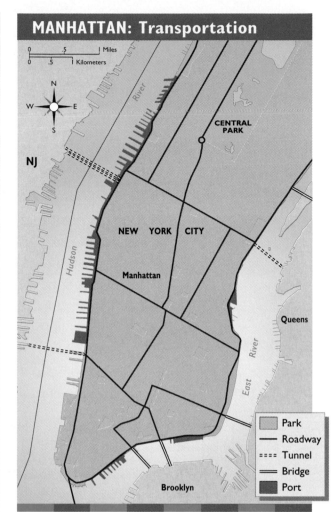

MANHATTAN: Transportation

0   .5   1 Miles
0   .5   1 Kilometers

CENTRAL PARK

NJ

NEW YORK CITY

Manhattan

Hudson River

East River

Queens

Brooklyn

Park
— Roadway
==== Tunnel
═ Bridge
Port

- Some transportation maps show roads for traveling by car, bus, train, ship, or airplane. The map above shows how to reach the island of Manhattan from across the East River or the Hudson River. What are two ways that cars can use to cross over to the island? What kind of transportation would you expect to find in the areas shown by the color purple?

More Practice

There are other historical and transportation maps in this book. For examples of historical maps, see pages 83 and 125. For examples of transportation maps, see pages 161 and 168.

LOCAL CONNECTIONS

LEARNING FROM OUR COMMUNITIES

This book tells the story of the state of New York and the people who make it such a great place to live. As you read, you will learn about the different parts of our state. You will discover how people lived in these places in the past and how they live there today.

As you read, think about how your community fits into the picture. What were people in your community doing during the Revolutionary War, or when the Erie Canal was built? How does geography help shape the way people in your

Students in Sleepy Hollow made a book (right) of stories and songs about their community. The newspaper (below) taught Elmira students about their government. Salamanca students learned about the Iroquois by studying artifacts (below right).

Our History in Story and Song

STAR-GAZETTE
FRIDAY
tober 4, 1996
.Y. EDITION
Elmira, New York
t Gannett newspaper

New chief plans changes

Elmira likely to see more officers walking beats, volunteers in of

By JIM PFIFFER
Star-Gazette

Elmira's new police chief wants to see more officers walking beats, more community volunteers and more cooperation with other law enforcement agencies.

Michael Ciminelli, a former Rochester police sergeant, outlined his plans for the 83-member police force as he made his debut Thursday during a special Elmira City Council meeting at City Hall.

The 41-year-old Ciminelli is scheduled to start his $62,000-a-year police chief job on Nov 2, said Elmira City Manager Samuel F. traci Jr., who appointed him to the post. The appointment does not need city council approval.

Ciminelli, who works in the criminal law section of the U.S. Drug Enforcement Administration in Washington, D.C., replaces former chief Joseph Michalko, who retired in May.

After Thursday's meeting, Ciminelli met with reporters to outline his plans. He said he hopes to:

■ Take more officers out of patrol cars and put them on walking beats, to get closer to the people they serve.
■ Develop a volunteer citizens

Seneca-Iroquois
National Museum

2

community make a living, or what they do to enjoy themselves? What do citizens do to help govern your community?

At the end of each chapter, you will find a feature called Local Connections. Each Local Connection shows you how students in different communities in New York learned about the places where they live. You will explore with them as they visit historic sites, do in-depth research, and brainstorm ideas. Then you will see the interesting ways they put their knowledge to use.

After you have read each feature, you and your teacher might want to explore the community you call home. You will find questions or suggestions to help guide you in a box like the one on the right.

MAKE Your LOCAL CONNECTION

What can you learn about your community by studying a map? What kinds of features can you identify on the map? When looking at the map, can you tell why roads are located where they are? Can you tell where most of the people live? How can you share this information with others?

▌Brentwood students made models of colonial
▌buildings (below). A class in Watertown made
▌a report (below right) on jobs in Watertown.
▌At a library (right), students learned more
▌about Buffalo's history.

The Number of Workers at Companies in Our Community

Businesses in Our Community

3

A BOAT TRIP IN THE ATLANTIC
OCEAN (ABOVE)
LAKE PLACID (TOP LEFT)

NEW YORK CITY'S TALL BUILDINGS (ABOVE)
CAMPING IS A FAVORITE WEEKEND PASTIME
IN NEW YORK (LEFT)
GRAPES GROWN IN NEW YORK (RIGHT)

A Place Called New York

"The land is excellent and agreeable . . ."

from a description of New York by Johan de Laet, 1625
See page 32.

WHY DOES IT MATTER?

Where is New York? What does New York look like? Are all parts of New York the same? How do New Yorkers make use of our state's land and water?

Our state offers great riches, both in land and in resources. New York has rivers and lakes, rolling hills, amazing waterfalls, beautiful mountains, and sandy beaches.

How does the land affect the way people live? How do people change the land? Read on. Unit 1 introduces the geography and resources that make New York the special state it is.

CHEESE IS ONE OF THE MOST IMPORTANT PRODUCTS FROM NEW YORK FARMS

5

Adventures with

NATIONAL GEOGRAPHIC

Natural New York

You sigh. There's just too much to do outdoors in New York. What would you like to try? Surf fishing off Fire Island? Snowshoeing or hiking in the frosty Adirondacks? Diving into the cool Finger Lakes? Biking country roads or quiet paths? Canoeing calm lakes? There are adventures waiting for you in every part of New York State. Why not try them all?

GEO JOURNAL

In your Geo Journal, describe an outdoor adventure that you would like to take in New York State.

CHAPTER 1

The Geography of New York

THINKING ABOUT GEOGRAPHY AND CULTURE

Have you ever been to a place in New York that is very different from where you live? New York is very special. It has many different types of land, bodies of water, and weather. Look at the photographs on the next page. Using the colored squares, match each photograph to its location on the map. What do they tell you about New York?

CANADA

Adirondack
Mountains

Buffalo

NEW YORK

Schoharie

Long Island

ATLANTIC
OCEAN

UNITED
STATES

Adirondack Mountains

The high peaks of the Adirondack Mountains are often covered with snow during winter.

Schoharie

Dairy cattle graze on the rolling hills near Schoharie. They help make New York a leading state in producing milk and cheese.

Buffalo

A view of the Buffalo skyline from the Erie Basin Marina. People use the marina to dock their boats. A boat ride on Lake Erie is a great way to spend a summer afternoon.

Long Island

These sand dunes lie on the South Fork of Long Island. Some of New York's most beautiful beaches are on this island in the Atlantic Ocean.

THE LAND OF NEW YORK

Focus Activity

READ TO LEARN
What kind of landforms make up New York?

VOCABULARY
landform
plain
geography
border
plateau
valley
Ice Age
glacier
moraine
till
drumlin

PLACES
Adirondack Mountains
Appalachian Plateau
Genesee River
Finger Lakes
Catskill Mountains
Hudson River Valley
Taconic Mountains
Long Island Sound
Montauk Point
Allegany State Park
Lake Oneida

READ ALOUD

In 1903, Marjorie Hudnut went on a hike with her family in the Adirondack Mountains in the northern part of New York. Marjorie and her family climbed up Bald Top Mountain. There Marjorie saw "magnificent mountains" as far as the eye could see. Below her lay a "little valley amidst meadows of soft velvety green through which ran our little river sparkling like a silver thread."

THE BIG PICTURE

You can see the same breathtaking scenery in the Adirondack Mountains today. These mountains are just one of the landforms of New York. Landforms are shapes that make up the surface of Earth.

Besides mountains, our state has many other kinds of landforms. For example, it also has hills and plains. A plain is a large area of nearly flat land. What does the land look like near where you live?

Landforms such as mountains, hills, and plains are part of geography. Geography is the study of Earth. It includes the way people, plants, and animals live on and use the land. Geography is a tool for exploring the world. Earth's geography matters to us all. It affects how we live and where we live.

10

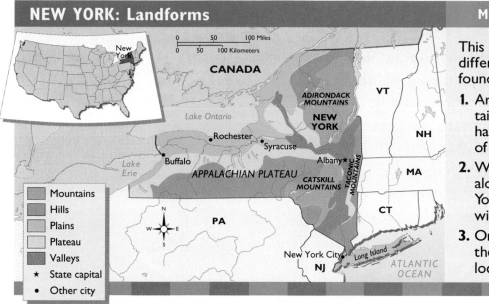

0   50   100 Miles
0   50   100 Kilometers

CANADA

Lake Ontario

ADIRONDACK MOUNTAINS

VT

NEW YORK

NH

Rochester

Syracuse

Lake Erie

Buffalo

Albany ★

MA

APPALACHIAN PLATEAU

CATSKILL MOUNTAINS

TACONIC MOUNTAINS

CT

PA

N
W   E
S

Mountains
Hills
Plains
Plateau
Valleys
★ State capital
• Other city

New York City

Long Island

NJ

ATLANTIC OCEAN

This map shows where different landforms are found in New York.

1. Are New York's mountains found in the eastern half or the western half of the state?

2. What landform is found along most of New York's southern border with Pennsylvania?

3. On which landform is the city of Rochester located?

WHERE IS NEW YORK?

Where do we live, anyway? If Marjorie Hudnut had looked through a telescope, she could have seen Vermont. Vermont is one of the states that shares a border with New York. A border is a line that people agree on that divides one place from another. Vermont, Massachusetts, and Connecticut all border New York on the east.

Look at the map on this page. You can see that other states also share New York's borders. What states lie along New York's southern border?

Often a river or an ocean forms a border between two places. Look at the map again. What lakes form borders between New York and the country of Canada?

Niagara Falls lies on the border between New York and Canada. Thousands of visitors come to see this natural wonder every year.

A TRIP ACROSS NEW YORK STATE

One exciting way to learn about New York's geography is to take a plane ride across our state. Suppose you take a plane from Buffalo on Lake Erie and head southeast to Long Island in the Atlantic Ocean. This trip will take you a little over an hour. On the way you are sure to see different landforms from the air.

Fasten your seatbelt. You're on your way. Looking out your window as the plane takes off, you see towns, roads, and farms on the flat plain that borders Lake Ontario. Wave goodbye!

The land becomes hilly as you fly east. Soon you are looking out over the Appalachian (ap uh LAY chee un) Plateau. A plateau is a large area that rises steeply above the surrounding land. Sometimes a plateau is flat, but sometimes it is hilly. The Appalachian Plateau covers nearly half of New York State. Looking down, you can see the dark-green forests below.

A few minutes later, you cross over the Genesee River. It winds through what Native Americans called "the beautiful valley." A valley is low land between hills or mountains. Usually a valley has a river

flowing through it. Some time after, you see some of the Finger Lakes lying between high rocky ridges. They are shaped like the fingers of a hand. Soon you fly over the Catskill Mountains. Here some mountaintops reach 4,000 feet.

The mountains end as you come to the wide Hudson River Valley. In the distance are the steep-sided Taconic Mountains. The pilot guides the plane south by following the Hudson River Valley. Little villages dot the landscape.

Soon you recognize the tall buildings of New York City. Long Island stretches ahead of you. As you fly over Long Island, you can see the Long Island Sound on the north side and the Atlantic Ocean on the south. The North Shore of Long Island is jagged and rocky. The South Shore is sandy beach.

Finally, you have come to the end of your trip. Your plane lands near Montauk Point, the easternmost place in New York.

On your plane trip, you might see a farm on the Appalachian Plateau (left), the Genesee River winding through a steep-walled valley, Ashokan Lake in the Catskills (top, center), the towering World Trade Center buildings in New York City, and the beaches of Long Island.

13

ICE AGES AND GLACIERS

Many landforms in New York were formed long before people lived there. At this time, Earth was much colder than it is today.

Scientists believe that Earth has had several periods of very cold weather. Such a period is an Ice Age. The most recent Ice Age probably ended about 10,000 years ago. During that Ice Age, a huge glacier (GLAY shur), or thick sheet of ice, moved across most of New York.

Glacier Power

Just how thick was the ice that coated New York? Close your eyes for a few seconds and picture a mountain of ice. Scientists think that parts of the glacier may have been more than one mile thick.

New York's glacier moved like a giant

Water from a melting glacier helped form the Mendon Ponds (right). Trees cover the smooth slopes of this drumlin near Rochester (below).

bulldozer, pushing tons of soil and rock along in its path. It rounded off high hills, filled in deep valleys, and cut huge holes into the land.

The glacier crawled as far south as Long Island. A line of low hills marks where the glacier stopped. These hills are called a moraine. They were formed by the rocks pushed at the front of the glacier.

Only one small part of New York was *not* covered by the glacier. Found in southwestern New York, this piece of land is where Allegany State Park is located. Here the steep valleys and pointed hills look different from the land outside the park.

The Ice Age Ends

For reasons scientists still don't understand, Earth warmed up around 10,000 years ago. The glacier began to melt. Water from the melting glacier filled many of the deep holes dug by the glacier's rough rocks. Lakes, such as Lake Oneida (oh NĪ dah), were filled with water this way.

As the ice melted, the glacier dropped soil and rocks it had picked up hundreds of miles away. This mix of soil and rocks is called till. Some of New York's best farmland is in areas covered with a thick layer of till.

All over New York, you can see smoothly rounded hills that look like an egg sliced in half along its length. These hills, called drumlins, were formed by the melting glacier. In the area between the cities of Rochester and Syracuse, there are about 10,000 of these drumlins. Everywhere you look, you can see signs of the long-gone glaciers.

WHY IT MATTERS

Our state has mountains that seem to touch the sky. It has rolling hills and beautiful valleys. It has wide-open plains. In studying New York's geography, we realize how special our state is.

Links to MATHEMATICS

Glaciers on the Move

Glaciers usually form in valleys where snow stays on the ground all year. Each new layer of snow packs the snow beneath it tighter and tighter. Over time, the snow turns to ice. Eventually the ice and snow become so heavy that the bottom of the glacier is squeezed forward.

Then the huge glacier begins to ooze down the valley.

Even the fastest glaciers move only about half an inch per minute. How many inches would the fastest glacier move in an hour? How many feet is that? How long would it take a glacier to move 10 feet?

✓// Reviewing Facts and Ideas

SUM IT UP

- Geography is the study of Earth and everything on it.
- New York shares borders with five states and the country of Canada.
- Many of New York's landforms were formed by glaciers during the last Ice Age.
- As you go from one part of the state to the other, you see many different kinds of landforms.

THINK ABOUT IT

1. What is a landform?
2. What part of our state was not covered by the glacier?
3. **FOCUS** Name three types of landforms found in New York.
4. **THINKING SKILL** Explain the _cause_ and _effect_ of glaciers in New York.
5. **GEOGRAPHY** Find the place where you live on the map on page 11. On what kind of landform is it located?

GEOGRAPHY SKILLS

Reading Elevation Maps

VOCABULARY
elevation

WHY THE SKILL MATTERS

Much of New York State is covered with mountains and rolling hills. The Appalachian Plateau and the Catskill Mountains are in the southern part of the state. The Adirondack Mountains are found in the north. The Taconic Mountains are in the east, bordering Vermont. Which mountains are higher, the Adirondacks or the Taconics? You could use an **elevation** (el uh VAY shun) map to find out. Elevation is the height of the land above the level of the sea. Elevation at sea level is 0 feet.

An elevation map uses different colors to show different elevations. Look at the map key on this page. All the places shown on the map in light green are between 700 feet and 1,600 feet above sea level.

USING THE SKILL

Elevation maps show us many things. One example is the important information they show about rivers. Have you ever wondered why the water in a river moves? The answer is simple: water runs downhill. Every river begins at a higher elevation than where it ends. The water naturally flows downhill toward a lower elevation. Let's say the land slopes down toward the east. Then the river will flow from west to east. If the land slopes downhill toward the south, the river will flow south. That is why an elevation map can help you understand a river's course.

Let's try using the elevation map on the next page to trace the path of a river. Locate the Hudson River. As you can see, it begins in the Adirondack Mountains. What color is the area where the river begins? Check the map key to find out what elevation this color represents. You can see that the river begins at an elevation of 3,300 feet above sea level or higher.

Follow the Hudson River's path. It winds through areas of lower and lower elevation to Albany. From Albany the river flows south through a fairly level valley to New York City. Eventually, it

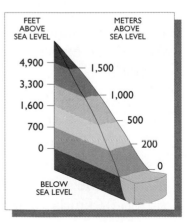

FEET ABOVE SEA LEVEL / METERS ABOVE SEA LEVEL

4,900 — 1,500
3,300 — 1,000
1,600 — 500
700 — 200
0 — 0

BELOW SEA LEVEL

empties into the Atlantic Ocean. What is the elevation of the ocean?

TRYING THE SKILL

You have just used the map to trace the path of the Hudson River. Now use the elevation map to trace the path of the Raquette River, which also starts in the Adirondack Mountains.

Does the Raquette River start at a higher or lower elevation than the Hudson River? In which direction does the Raquette River flow? What does that show you about the elevation in that direction? Into what other body of water does the Raquette River flow?

REVIEWING THE SKILL

Use the elevation map to answer the following questions. Use the Helping Yourself box for hints.

1. What is elevation?
2. What is the elevation of the highest Adirondack peak? Where is the lowest elevation found in New York?
3. On this map, what color would you use to show that a plateau is 2,000 feet above sea level?
4. How does an elevation map tell us which way a river flows?
5. How does an elevation map help us learn about geography?

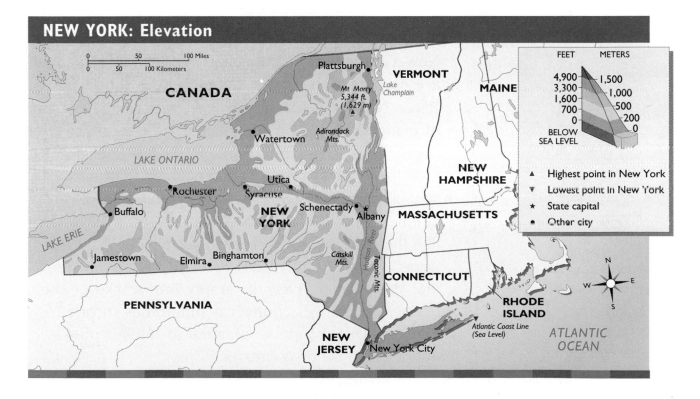

NEW YORK: Elevation

THE WATERS OF NEW YORK

READ ALOUD
The book Riverkeeper *explains that a person who takes care of a river is called a riverkeeper. John Cronin is a riverkeeper on the Hudson River. The Hudson is different from many other rivers because part of it is very deep—deep enough for very big ships to sail on. "Out on the river, John is sometimes tossed about in his boat as it wobbles over the [waves made by] giant ships, including tankers. . . . River pilots navigate [sail] cargo vessels from all over the world up to Port Albany."*

THE BIG PICTURE

New York is lucky! It has many bodies of water that are deep enough for big ships. Besides the Hudson River, New York has other large rivers and a number of giant lakes. New York touches on one of the four oceans. It also has many smaller rivers and lakes.

Is there a stream or brook near your home or school? Where does it lead? It probably leads to another body of water. New York's waterways are like the branches of a tree. Small brooks flow into larger streams and rivers. Streams and rivers flow into even larger rivers or empty into a lake or the ocean. Waterways connect communities to one another. They connect our state to other states—and even to other countries.

Focus Activity

READ TO LEARN
What are some of New York's most important bodies of water?

VOCABULARY
transportation
source
tributary
mouth
coast
bay
harbor

PLACES
Hudson River
Mohawk River
Niagara River
Lake Erie
Niagara Falls
Lake Ontario
Saint Lawrence River
Lake Champlain
New York Bay

THE HUDSON "HIGHWAY"

In a way, the Hudson River is like a very old highway. It is one of the transportation routes that people have used for thousands of years. Transportation means moving goods or people from one place to another. Native Americans of our area used this route to transport goods to trade with one another. Later, the Dutch and the English who came here used this long waterway to trade with Native Americans. The Hudson is more than 300 miles long.

At the Source

Like all rivers, the Hudson has a beginning called a source. The source of the Hudson is high in the Adirondacks. The huge Hudson begins as a tiny trickle of water in a place called Indian Pass.

As the river makes its journey south, it grows wider and deeper. Why is this? Smaller rivers and streams called tributaries (TRIB yoo tair eez) flow into it. The Mohawk River is the largest tributary of the Hudson. After the Mohawk joins the Hudson, the Hudson becomes deep enough to allow large ships to navigate it.

Like all rivers, the Hudson has an end, called a mouth. The mouth is a place where a river empties into a larger body of water. At New York City, the Hudson River empties into the Atlantic Ocean.

People have used canoes and sailboats on the Hudson River for hundreds of years.

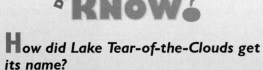

DID YOU KNOW?

How did Lake Tear-of-the-Clouds get its name?

Lake Tear-of-the-Clouds is a small pond near the top of Mount Marcy, the highest mountain in our state. At one time people believed that Lake Tear-of-the-Clouds was the source of the Hudson River, but it is not. Lake Tear-of-the-Clouds is the source of the Opalescent (oh pul ES sent) River, which joins the Hudson as a tributary.

In 1872, Verplanck Colvin, who explored the Adirondacks, came upon this tiny pond. He described it as a tiny "tear of the clouds . . . a lonely pool shivering in the breezes of the mountains . . ." That's how it got its name.

RIVERS AND LAKES OF ALL SIZES

New York has rivers and lakes of all sizes, from small to large. One of the smaller rivers is the Niagara.

The Niagara River

The Niagara River is only about 35 miles long. But what a wonderful journey it makes! Find the Niagara River on the map on this page.

The Niagara River starts peacefully at its source, Lake Erie. Past the halfway point, the river picks up speed. Now racing along, the river thunders down a cliff as far as 180 feet to the rocks below. The spray rises all the way to the top of Niagara Falls. Soon the river flows calmly on its way, emptying into Lake Ontario.

Why Are the Great Lakes Great?

You just read about Lake Erie and Lake Ontario. These are two of the five Great Lakes. The others are Lakes Superior, Michigan, and Huron. Put together, the five Great Lakes are larger than the state of Texas.

The Great Lakes are part of a great transportation route. You can travel from the city of Buffalo on Lake Erie, through Lake Ontario, through the Saint Lawrence River, all the way to the Atlantic Ocean. Once on the ocean, you can travel to any of the continents. Goods from New York can be shipped all over the world this way.

Lake Champlain

Long, skinny Lake Champlain forms part of the border between New York and the state of Vermont. You can take a ferry across it to get from one state to the other. In the summer, Joe Bombard often rides along with his father. His father is the captain of the ferry called the *Adirondack*. "The last trip of the day is my favorite," Joe said. "You get to see the sunset."

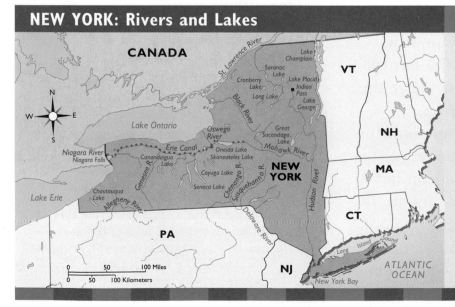

NEW YORK: Rivers and Lakes

MAP WORK

Rivers drain water from all parts of New York and carry it to the Great Lakes, the Saint Lawrence River, or the Atlantic Ocean.

1. Name a **tributary** of the Susquehanna River.
2. Where is the **mouth** of the Black River?
3. What lake forms part of the border with Vermont?

Watching whales off Long Island (above) is fun! A ship arrives in New York Harbor (right).

world can dock here. These ocean-going ships can also continue up the Hudson River—which is where this lesson began!

WHY IT MATTERS

New York has many rivers and lakes. Some of these waterways are important routes of transportation. Many of them are fun to swim in and sail on.

ALONG THE COAST

"There she blows!" A humpback whale coming to the surface is an incredible sight. Where in New York can you watch whales swimming? You can sometimes see them in the waters at the tip of Long Island. Long Island and New York City are part of the Atlantic Coast that stretches from Maine to Florida. A coast is the land next to an ocean or a large lake.

On Long Island, miles of white, sandy beaches lie along the Atlantic Ocean. The Hudson River flows into the Atlantic at New York Bay. A bay is a part of an ocean or lake that cuts deeply into the coast or shore.

New York Bay is an excellent harbor. A harbor is a sheltered place where ships can dock. Glaciers dug out this area and made it deep so large ships from all over the

Reviewing Facts and Ideas

SUM IT UP

- The Hudson is a waterway that has been used for thousands of years.
- Ships from all over the world can carry goods to and from the Great Lakes.
- Large ocean-going ships can transport goods to and from New York harbor.

THINK ABOUT IT

1. What is the difference between the mouth of a river and its source?

2. What makes the Mohawk River a tributary?

3. **FOCUS** What are some bodies of water in New York?

4. **THINKING SKILL** _Compare_ the Hudson River with the Niagara River.

5. **WRITE** Write a letter to a friend, describing a body of water near where you live.

OUR STATE'S CLIMATE

Focus Activity

READ TO LEARN
Why is the climate different in different parts of our state?

VOCABULARY
weather
climate
temperature
precipitation
hurricane
blizzard

PLACES
Freeport
Whiteface Mountain

READ ALOUD

This is how writer John Burroughs described a spring day in the Catskill Mountains: "This was a typical March day, clear, dry, and windy, the river rumpled and crumpled, the sky intense, distant objects strangely near; a day full of strong light. . . . At night . . . the stars all seemed brighter than usual, as if the wind blew them up like burning coals." How would you describe a typical spring day in the place where you live?

THE BIG PICTURE

John Burroughs lived in the Catskill Mountains for many years. He loved to study nature. In the passage you just read, John Burroughs described weather on a March day. Weather is the condition of the air at a certain time and place. It may be hot or cold, rainy or dry, sunny or cloudy, windy or calm. The weather changes from day to day. Sometimes it changes from hour to hour, like when a spring rainstorm suddenly blows through.

Every place has a pattern of weather over many years. This pattern is called climate (KLĪ mit). What is the difference between weather and climate? Weather affects how you live day to day. Do you need to take an umbrella to school? Climate affects long-range plans. Will you buy a light jacket or a heavy overcoat for the winter?

22

TWO PARTS OF CLIMATE

Different parts of our state have different climates. Some people choose to live in a certain place because summers are generally cool there or because there is less snow in winter than in other parts of the state.

What questions would you ask to find out about the climate of a certain place in New York? You might start by asking, "How hot is the summer? How cold is the winter?" These questions ask about temperature (TEM pur uh chur). Temperature measures how hot or cold the air is. The usual afternoon temperature in Albany may be 84°F in July. In January, the afternoon temperature may only reach 30°F.

Another question you would want to ask is, "How much precipitation (prih sihp ih TAY shun) falls?" Precipitation is the moisture that falls to the ground. It may be in the form of rain, snow, sleet, or hail. The precipitation map shows how much precipitation to expect during one year. Some places in New York get a lot of rain. Other places get little. For example, Rochester gets less rain than most other big cities in the eastern United States.

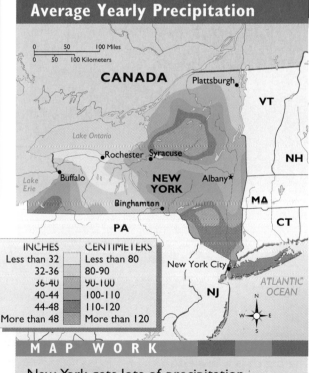

Lightning (right) signals a storm in New York skies.

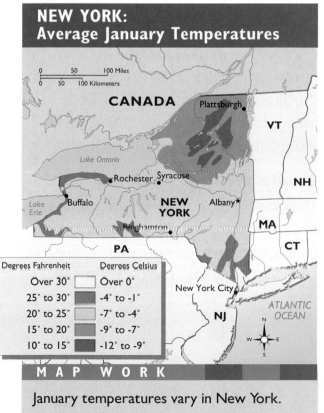

NEW YORK: Average January Temperatures

Degrees Fahrenheit	Degrees Celsius
Over 30°	Over 0°
25° to 30°	-4° to -1°
20° to 25°	-7° to -4°
15° to 20°	-9° to -7°
10° to 15°	-12° to -9°

MAP WORK

January temperatures vary in New York.

1. Which city is warmer in January, Binghamton or Plattsburgh?

NEW YORK: Average Yearly Precipitation

INCHES	CENTIMETERS
Less than 32	Less than 80
32-36	80-90
36-40	90-100
40-44	100-110
44-48	110-120
More than 48	More than 120

MAP WORK

New York gets lots of precipitation.

1. Where is the driest part of New York?

INVESTIGATING CLIMATE

Suppose you leave your home in Freeport on Long Island and travel to the top of Whiteface Mountain in the Adirondacks. You notice that it is much cooler there, even in the summer. Luckily you brought an extra sweater! Why is it cooler in the Adirondack Mountains than in Freeport? There are three questions you can ask to find the answer.

How Far North?

Whiteface Mountain is about 360 miles north of Freeport. This means that Whiteface Mountain is farther from the equator than Freeport is. Usually, the farther from the equator you go, the colder the temperature is.

What do you expect the weather to be like in Canada?

The beach is a favorite destination (right). Many people go skiing on Whiteface Mountain during the winter.

How High?

On the highest peaks of the Adirondacks, the snow may not completely melt, even in the summer. This happens because of the high elevation. The higher a place is above sea level, the colder the climate usually will be. Whiteface Mountain is 4,867 feet above sea level, so it can get pretty cold!

How Far from Water?

Did you ever go swimming on a hot summer day and find your teeth chattering? The water is colder than the air around you. That is because water heats up more slowly than air. Breezes that blow off the ocean and other large bodies of water bring cooler air to the land nearby during the summer.

Water also gets cold more slowly than air. In winter, breezes from the ocean and lakes bring warmer air to the land. Freeport is cooler in summer and warmer in winter than it would be if it were not on the coast.

Severe Weather

Sometimes our state gets strong storms. Huge, windy rainstorms called hurricanes form over the ocean. They can strike Long Island and cause damage.

A blizzard is a snowstorm with very strong winds. In January 1977, a terrible blizzard

Blizzards in New York can make driving impossible.

plowed across western New York. Robert Bahr describes what some people saw at the start of the blizzard from their office window in downtown Buffalo. Why do you think they could no longer see the Ellicott Square building across the way?

MANY VOICES
LITERATURE

Excerpt from *The Blizzard*, written by Robert Bahr in 1980.

Everyone turned to the windows. They heard a roar an instant before the wind struck the building. . . .

Sixteen floors below, shoppers and businessmen staggered into the wind. Some clung to streetlight poles and traffic signs; others ducked for shelter. A man's hat soared high above traffic. . . .

A few seconds later, the Ellicott Square building was blotted out, along with the cars, people and lights below.

WHY IT MATTERS

Our state has high mountains and low plains. It has coasts along the Atlantic Ocean and the Great Lakes. This means that the three factors of climate affect different parts of the state in different ways. As you read about our state, think about how people live in their surroundings.

✔️ Reviewing Facts and Ideas

SUM IT UP

- Climate is the pattern of weather a place has over a long time.
- Temperature and precipitation are two key parts of climate.
- Elevation, distance from the equator, and distance from large bodies of water affect the climate of our state.

THINK ABOUT IT

1. What is the difference between climate and weather?

2. As you move away from the equator, what happens to the climate?

3. **FOCUS** Why is the climate different in different parts of our state?

4. **THINKING SKILL** *Predict* whether or not Buffalo will usually have a lot of snow in the winter.

5. **GEOGRAPHY** Describe the climate of your area. How do the three factors of climate affect it?

LOCAL CONNECTIONS
GLOVERSVILLE:
LEARNING FROM MAPS

Stan and his grandfather John live in Gloversville. One day they were fishing on the Great Sacandaga Lake. John turned to Stan and said, "My father, your great-grandfather, grew up on a farm right here on this spot."

"You're kidding, grandpa," Stan said. "How could anyone live here?"

John explained that the Great Sacandaga Lake is a reservoir, or a lake that has been made by people. It was built in 1930 to prevent the Sacandaga River from flooding towns downstream. Before that, people lived on the land that is now covered by water.

People enjoy fishing in the Great Sacandaga Lake.

The next day, Stan told his classmates and Mrs. Stevens, his teacher, what he had learned about the lake. Mrs. Stevens asked the class how they could learn more about the lake. Rebecca suggested that they look at a physical map. "In which direction is Gloversville from the lake?" asked Mrs. Stevens.

"Northwest," Zach answered, "about five miles away."

"That's right, Zach," said Mrs. Stevens. "What else does the map tell us?"

"It tells us how big the lake is," said Lisa.

"Yes, it does, Lisa. If we look at the scale, then measure the length of the lake on the map, we find that the lake is about 29 miles long," Mrs. Stevens said.

Mrs. Stevens then asked, "What body of water does the Great Sacandaga Lake flow into?"

"The Hudson River," answered Stavros.

"Good, Stavros," said Mrs. Stevens. "In what direction does the water in the lake flow on its way to the Hudson River?"

The students looked at the map's compass rose. They agreed that the water flows in a northerly direction, toward the dam at Conklingville.

26

Mrs. Stevens then asked the students to name some of the towns located on the edge of the lake. They identified Mayfield, Cranberry Creek, Munsonville, Benedict, and Batchellerville.

"How has the lake changed life for people in our community?" Mrs. Stevens asked.

"We can go boating and fishing in the same place that people used to farm. People also like to camp, backpack in the mountains, and swim in the lake," said Judy.

After studying the map, the students realized that there was much more to learn about the lake and its importance to the community. They did more research and then drew their own maps of the ways people use the Great Sacandaga Lake. They displayed their maps under a banner that said, "Great Sacandaga Lake: A Resource for Our Community."

MAKE your LOCAL CONNECTION

What can you learn about your community by studying a map? What kinds of features can you identify on the map? When looking at the map, can you tell why roads are located where they are? Can you tell where most of the people live? How can you share this information with others?

Boating is a favorite activity of people who live near Great Sacandaga Lake. Students made maps that show how people in the community use the lake.

27

CHAPTER 1 REVIEW

THINKING ABOUT VOCABULARY

Number a sheet of paper from 1 to 5. Next to each number, write the letter of the definition that best matches the word.

1. landform
   a. An area where plants and animals live
   b. One of the shapes that make up the surface of Earth
   c. An area affected by weather and climate
   d. An area of high elevation

2. geography
   a. The people who live in a place
   b. The transportation used in a place
   c. The way people live
   d. The study of Earth and all the things that live on it

3. Ice Age
   a. A long period of very cold weather
   b. An unusually cold winter
   c. The weather in very cold places, like the North Pole
   d. A year with a lot of snow

4. transportation
   a. Keeping something in one place for a long time
   b. The movement of glaciers across the Earth
   c. Moving goods or people from one place to another
   d. A river and its tributaries

5. climate
   a. The day-to-day weather of an area
   b. The change in temperature during one month
   c. Distance from the equator
   d. The pattern of weather of an area over a long period of time

THINKING ABOUT FACTS

1. Name three different types of landforms that are found in New York.

2. What mountains cover much of northern New York?

3. What event in Earth's past helped shape New York's land?

4. Name three things left by glaciers.

5. What is the source of a river?

6. What bodies of water does the Niagara River connect?

7. How far does the Atlantic Coast stretch in the United States?

8. What three factors affect climate?

9. How is climate different from weather?

10. What are two parts to climate?

THINK AND WRITE

WRITING A DESCRIPTION
Write a paragraph that describes the area in which you live. Include landforms and information about climate in your description.

WRITING AN ADVERTISEMENT
Suppose you want people to visit a vacation spot in your area. Write and design an advertisement highlighting the landforms and bodies of water of this area.

WRITING AN EXPLANATION
Write an explanation of how the climate in different parts of the state is affected by distance from the ocean, distance from the equator, and elevation.

APPLYING GEOGRAPHY SKILLS

ELEVATION MAPS

Answer the following questions about the map of New York on this page to practice your skill at reading elevation maps.

1. How do you know that this is an elevation map?

2. What area of New York has the highest elevation?

3. In what color would this map show a plateau that is 1,700 feet above sea level?

4. At about which elevation is the city of Albany?

5. People have used the Mohawk River Valley to travel across the state for hundreds of years. Look at the map. Why do you think this was the easiest way to travel?

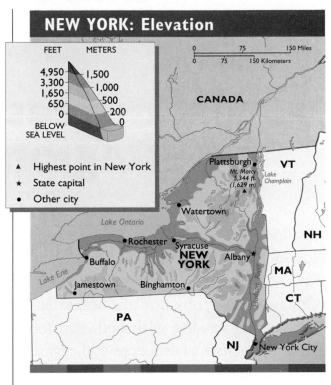

NEW YORK: Elevation

FEET	METERS
4,950	1,500
3,300	1,000
1,650	500
650	200
0	0
BELOW SEA LEVEL	

▲ Highest point in New York
★ State capital
• Other city

Summing Up the Chapter

Use the following spider map to organize information from the chapter. Copy the map on a sheet of paper. Then write at least one piece of information in each blank circle. When you have filled in the map, use it to help you write a paragraph that answers the question, "How do the land, water, and climate of New York affect how you live?"

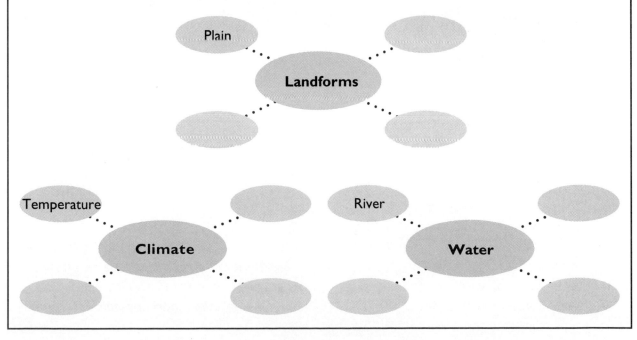

CHAPTER 2

Resources and Regions

THINKING ABOUT GEOGRAPHY AND ECONOMICS

How do New Yorkers make their livings? In what ways do we use the land and water of our state? What useful things does our state offer us? Geography isn't just something you learn about in school. It is something you live with everyday. You will discover many things about New York's resources and regions as you read Chapter 2.

CANADA

Connery Pond

Pultneyville

Letchworth State Park

NEW YORK

New York Harbor

UNITED STATES

ATLANTIC OCEAN

Pultneyville

Fruit orchards are important for farmers in the region near Lake Ontario. Farmers grow crops such as apples, cherries, peaches, and pears.

Connery Pond

In the Adirondacks, Connery Pond is one home of the loon. Loons migrate to the Adirondacks from New York coastal waters in late April or May.

New York Harbor

The South Street Seaport in New York Harbor provides jobs for people. Tourists visit museums, galleries, and the historic ships.

Letchworth State Park

This is one of three waterfalls that flow through Letchworth State Park. The Letchworth Falls are formed by the Genesee River.

31

NEW YORK'S NATURAL RESOURCES

Focus Activity

READ TO LEARN
In what ways are New York's natural resources important?

VOCABULARY
environment
natural resource
renewable resource
fertilizer
nonrenewable resource
population
economy
quarry
conservation

READ ALOUD

In 1625, Johan de Laet (YO han du LAHT) wrote a geography book about what is now New York. "The land is excellent and agreeable," he wrote, "full of noble . . . trees and grapevines, and [it could become] one of the finest and most fruitful lands in that part of the world."

THE BIG PICTURE

De Laet wrote this passage almost 375 years ago. Yet it describes the environment (en VĪ run munt) found in New York today. Environment is the surroundings in which people, animals, and plants live. We depend on our environment for clean air, water, food, and countless other things.

To meet these needs we use and shape our environment. For example, we cut down forests for wood. We take useful materials like coal and iron out of the ground. We grow food in the soil. We drink water that comes from lakes and rivers. Things in the environment that we can use are natural resources. Through the years, people have fed their families, built their homes, and earned their livings with our state's resources. Our businesses grew because of resources. Look around your classroom. How does your school use natural resources?

USING RESOURCES

Today, New York's people and businesses are working together to preserve, or protect, our environment. We want our natural resources to last into the future.

Renewable Resources

There are two kinds of natural resources. One kind is renewable (rih NOO uh bul). Renewable resources can be renewed or replaced. For example, when water in rivers and lakes gets low, water from rain or melting snow can fill them up again.

People as well as nature can renew resources. When a lumber company cuts down trees in a forest, foresters can plant new trees to take their place.

Farmers plant crops in the same soil year after year. So soil is also a renewable resource. But it can be worn out. Farmers renew the soil by adding fertilizer (FUR tih li zur), the "food" that helps plants grow.

Nonrenewable Resources

The second kind of natural resource is nonrenewable. When we have used up a nonrenewable resource, it is gone forever. Oil and natural gas are examples of nonrenewable resources. Workers drill for them in Cattaraugus (cat TAH raw gus) and Chautauqua (shu TAH kwah) counties. Metals such as titanium (ti TAY nee um) and iron, found in St. Lawrence County, are also nonrenewable resources.

The Most Important Resource

Have you ever shaped clay into a pot? If you hadn't shaped it, that piece of clay would never have become a useful product. People dig the clay. Then they run the machines that form it into bricks or tile. Without people, clay would not really be a resource.

New Yorkers are New York's greatest resource because of their skills and knowledge. The population, or number of people, in New York is about 18 million. That is a lot of resources!

This furniture maker uses wood, an important renewable resource (above). Drilling for oil (left) makes use of a nonrenewable resource.

WORKING WITH OUR RESOURCES

New York has many natural resources. Every natural resource in New York creates jobs. Jobs help create a strong economy. An economy is the way people use or produce goods and services. How do our resources create jobs for so many people?

Consider a few of the jobs created by just one resource—water. Hundreds of New Yorkers work at water treatment plants to make sure our drinking water is safe. Park rangers patrol our lakes, while dock workers load goods onto boats. Clerks sell tickets at water amusement parks, and boat captains take travelers for a day of fishing on Lake Ontario.

DID YOU KNOW?

What is a Herkimer diamond?

A Herkimer diamond is a kind of rock called quartz. Quartz is a common natural resource. Even though it's not a real diamond, it looks a lot like one. These clear, bright crystals are found underground. Rock hounds are people who search for rocks as a hobby. They hunt for Herkimer diamonds in the Mohawk Valley around Herkimer, Middleville, and Little Falls.

New York Building Stones

Did you ever see a wall made of stone or a path made of pebbles? Many people do not know that stone can be an important resource.

About 100 years ago, many buildings were built out of stone from Western New York. Stone cutters found that sandstone and limestone from Orleans County were good for building. A place where stone is cut out and removed from the ground is called a quarry. By 1905, there were 48 quarries in Orleans County alone. Stone from these quarries was used as far away as Boston, Philadelphia, and Detroit.

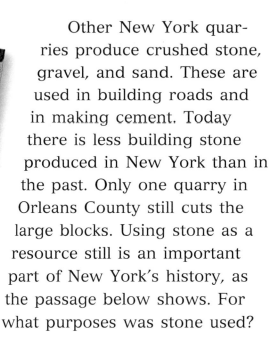

Other New York quarries produce crushed stone, gravel, and sand. These are used in building roads and in making cement. Today there is less building stone produced in New York than in the past. Only one quarry in Orleans County still cuts the large blocks. Using stone as a resource still is an important part of New York's history, as the passage below shows. For what purposes was stone used?

Excerpt from an article written by Dennis G. Nichols in 1990.

A walk or drive through any *Western New York city, village, or hamlet [can make you think of what it used to be like] if one takes time to observe the old sandstone sidewalks, . . . arched bridges, monuments and [buildings] of days gone by. If one stops and listens, one can almost hear the old quarry steam engines and* **derricks** *whistling and the shattering ring of the blockbreakers' hammers as rock was drilled, moved and loaded for transport.*

---

derricks: framework that supports drilling machinery

A stone worker is hard at work in a quarry (top left). This boat captain uses one of New York's most important natural resources—water (top right). Many New Yorkers use their skills and knowledge in laboratories (bottom).

MAKING OUR RESOURCES LAST

People once thought our natural resources would last forever. Some, like stone, are in no danger of running out. However, today we know that many natural resources can be used up or damaged. Conservation is the careful use of our natural resources.

When people use only as much of a resource as they need, they are practicing conservation. Conservation helps make our resources last longer. When you turn off the water while brushing your teeth, you're conserving water. What are other ways of conserving resources?

WHY IT MATTERS

New York's resources help make our lives comfortable. For hundreds of years people have started businesses that use New York's natural resources. These businesses improved our state's economy by providing thousands of jobs for people.

✓✓ Reviewing Facts and Ideas

SUM IT UP

- Natural resources are things people can use in the environment.
- Some natural resources can be replaced or renewed, but others cannot.
- People are New York's most important resource.
- Practicing conservation makes our resources last longer.

THINK ABOUT IT

1. Name three of New York's natural resources.

2. In what ways do people conserve resources?

3. **FOCUS** How do people in New York use their natural resources?

4. **THINKING SKILLS** _Compare_ and _contrast_ renewable and nonrenewable resources. Give examples of each kind.

5. **WRITE** Write a paragraph that tells how you use one of New York's natural resources. In what ways would your life be different without this resource?

Careful use of water at home helps to conserve an important resource.

Riverkeeper of the Hudson

GARRISON, NEW YORK—John Cronin grew up along the Hudson River. So did his parents and grandparents. "When I was young," John Cronin remembers, "the Hudson River was a place you stayed away from." It was very dirty. Factories dumped their wastes directly into the water.

The river had not always been that way. "I knew my parents and grandparents used to go boating and swimming and have family picnics there."

When John grew older, he wanted to make the Hudson a place for families again. He became a volunteer for a group working to clean up the river. His first job was helping to put out an environmental newsletter.

Today John Cronin is the "Riverkeeper of the Hudson." He works closely with volunteers and government officials to protect the river. His chief weapon is a law called the Clean Water Act. This law sets up rules about how much waste can be poured into the river.

Cronin and his staff make sure that companies obey this law. "More than half the cases we work on start as complaints from citizens. Hikers, fishermen, and boaters are our eyes and ears. They call us to report problems."

From his boat, Cronin looks for oil, sewage, or chemical wastes dumped into the river. He contacts state or local governments to report problems. Sometimes law students from a nearby college help him take these cases to court.

Thirty years ago the Hudson River was very dirty. But today it is once again a place where families can swim, boat, and picnic. As Riverkeeper of the Hudson, John Cronin has helped bring about that change. Cronin is proud of the work he and others are doing. "We found bad things and made them better," Cronin says. "We've made a difference in the water quality of the Hudson River and in the lives of people who live along the Hudson River."

"We found bad things and made them better."

John Cronin

Maple Syrup

Do you like maple syrup on your pancakes? Did you know that it comes from one of our natural resources—trees? Maple syrup is made from the sap of the sugar maple tree. Sap is a watery liquid that contains sugar.

Maple syrup is a legacy from the early Iroquois (EER ah koy). A legacy is something that has been handed down from people in the past and is valued by people today. Long ago the Iroquois learned how to collect the sap and cook it until it turned into maple syrup or maple sugar. When Europeans came to New York, the Iroquois taught them how to collect and cook the maple sap.

Today, New Yorkers make about 300,000 gallons of maple syrup every year, especially in Adirondack counties such as Warren, Lewis, and Fulton. The next time you pour on some maple syrup made in New York, remember that you are enjoying one of our state's sweeter legacies.

A bucket (below) catches the sap that is dripping from a spout "tapped" into the tree. It takes about 42 gallons of sap to make 1 gallon of maple syrup.

38

This painting shows people collecting and making maple syrup. It was painted by Grandma Moses, a famous painter from New York.

These Native Americans are making maple syrup (right). To make maple syrup, you can cook the sap until most of the water boils away. The thick, sweet liquid that is left is maple syrup.

THINKING SKILLS

Decision Making

VOCABULARY
decision

WHY THE SKILL MATTERS

Decision making is a skill people use every day. Making a decision is the same as making a choice. You have to make up your mind what to do. Decisions may be simple, like deciding what clothes to wear, or more difficult, like deciding where to live. To make a good decision, you have to know what your goal is.

People must make decisions about how they use Earth's resources. They decide which resources to use and the best ways to use them. Should a house be built of wood, stone, or brick?

Another decision people must make is how to conserve, or carefully use, their resources. Using too much of a resource can make it difficult to get more of that resource. Using more of a resource than needed can also waste money.

One way of conserving a resource is to recycle. Recycling is when you use something again instead of throwing it away. Sometimes recycling means turning old, used products into new and different products.

People must decide the best ways to recycle. What can be reused? What can be thrown away? Plastic bottles, metal cans, and newspapers can all be recycled. Sometimes products are recycled in surprising ways. A factory in Ronkonkoma (rahn KAHN kuh muh), New York, makes picnic tables from recycled plastic bottles.

USING THE SKILL

In one community, people are making a decision that will affect our resources. There already is a recycling center in town where people can bring their trash. Not everyone uses it, though. Some people in the community want a better recycling program. They want sanitation workers to pick up their recyclables. More workers will have to be hired. Hiring workers means that more people will have jobs. However, it will cost the community money to pay new workers.

Each citizen needs to ask, "What is my goal?" One goal might be to recycle more things. That will help to conserve resources. Another goal might be to save the community's money.

After you state your goal, you should predict what the results of your choices will be. This will help you know what decision is likely to meet your goal. Here are some possible results of each choice.

- A new recycling program would help to conserve resources.

- Keeping the program the same would save the community's money.

- A new program will create jobs.
  If your goal was to conserve more resources, what decision would you make?

TRYING THE SKILL

Imagine that there is a forest area near your community. A company has asked to build a factory there. Building a new factory will mean cutting down some of the forest. A nearby river might get dirty from factory wastes. But the factory would create jobs for people. The owners of the factory would also pay taxes that could be used to build a new school or park.

The citizens will have to decide whether to have a new factory. Use the Helping Yourself box for hints. What is your goal for your community? What are your choices? What do you think the results of each choice might be?

REVIEW THE SKILL

1. What is a decision?
2. Look at the section called Trying the Skill. If your goal was to create new jobs, how would you have voted?
3. How will predicting possible results help you make a good decision?
4. Why is it important to know how to make a good decision?

Citizens must sometimes make difficult decisions about our economy and our environment.

THE REGIONS OF NEW YORK

READ ALOUD

In 1996, Governor George Pataki described our state this way: "Not only is New York a great place to work . . . it's also a great place to live . . . from the cultural centers of New York City to the wild forests of the Adirondack and Catskill parks, and from the beaches of Long Island to the . . . Finger Lakes and the majesty of Niagara Falls."

THE BIG PICTURE

From one end to the other, New York is filled with interesting and beautiful sights. New Yorkers hike in hills and mountains. We play in the waves at the ocean. We sail on lakes and rivers. We gaze at marvelous waterfalls. We tour large cities and small towns. Perhaps you have a favorite part of the state to do things in. What do you like about that part of the state? What makes it different from other parts?

Focus Activity

READ TO LEARN
What different regions does New York have?

VOCABULARY
region
history
port
gorge

PLACES
Western New York
Finger Lakes
Watkins Glen Gorge
Northern New York
Central New York
Helderberg Escarpment
Thousand Islands
Hudson River Valley and
   Catskill Mountains
New York City and Long
   Island

REGIONS

When we talk about a "part" of our state, we are probably talking about a **region**. A region is an area that has features that set it apart from others. One region may have lots of mountains, small towns, and heavy snowfalls in winter. Another may have flat land, large cities, and rainy springs. In this lesson you will read about regions in our country and regions in our state.

Regions of the United States

New York is one of the 50 states that make up the United States of America. Some geographers divide the United States into five regions. Look at the map below. Name the five regions. In which region is our state? What other states are located in that region?

Each region is shaped by the people who have lived there. Each region has its own environment. Each region also has a **history**, a story of the past. The Northeast has long been the home of the Iroquois and Algonkian Native Americans. Many places in New York, like Seneca Falls and Montauk Point, are named after Native American groups.

The foods of New York also show the region's history. When the Dutch arrived in New York, they brought many of their foods with them. When you eat doughnuts and waffles, you are eating foods brought to us by the Dutch.

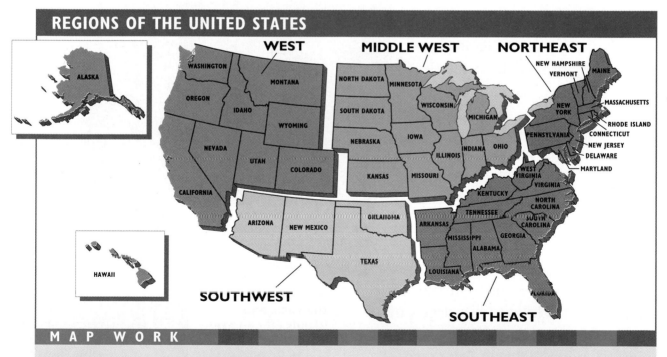

REGIONS OF THE UNITED STATES

ALASKA

WEST · WASHINGTON · OREGON · MONTANA · IDAHO · WYOMING · NEVADA · UTAH · COLORADO · CALIFORNIA

MIDDLE WEST · NORTH DAKOTA · SOUTH DAKOTA · MINNESOTA · WISCONSIN · MICHIGAN · IOWA · NEBRASKA · ILLINOIS · INDIANA · OHIO · KANSAS · MISSOURI

NORTHEAST · NEW HAMPSHIRE · VERMONT · MAINE · NEW YORK · MASSACHUSETTS · RHODE ISLAND · CONNECTICUT · NEW JERSEY · PENNSYLVANIA · DELAWARE · MARYLAND

WEST VIRGINIA · VIRGINIA · KENTUCKY · NORTH CAROLINA · TENNESSEE · SOUTH CAROLINA · ARKANSAS · GEORGIA · MISSISSIPPI · ALABAMA · LOUISIANA · FLORIDA

SOUTHWEST · ARIZONA · NEW MEXICO · OKLAHOMA · TEXAS

HAWAII

SOUTHEAST

MAP WORK

New York is part of the Northeast region.

1. How many states make up the Northeast region?
2. Is New York closer to the Middle West region or the Southeast region?
3. Have you ever visited another state? What region is it in? Did you notice any differences between that state and New York?

NEW YORK'S REGIONS

New York can be divided into six regions. Each region has certain common features. The Infographic on pages 46–47 gives you an idea of what these features are.

Western New York

Remember your plane ride across the state in Chapter 1? You started in the Western New York region, where much of the land is flat. Many people in this region live in Buffalo, a major port on Lake Erie. A port is a place where ships load and unload their goods.

Farther east, the land becomes more hilly. The Genesee River runs through Letchworth State Park. The cliffs, or sharp drops, along the river valley are spectacular. In fact, this area is called the "Grand Canyon of the East," after the famous cliffs in Arizona.

Finger Lakes Region

Farther east is the Finger Lakes region. It gets its name from the 11 lakes that lie in a row across the center of the region. They are long and thin, like fingers.

South of these lakes, in the Appalachian Plateau, hundreds of gorges dot the land. Gorges are narrow, deep valleys with steep, rocky sides. The most famous gorge in New York is the Watkins Glen Gorge. There are 19 waterfalls in this area. Each one has a different name. Olivia Lopez visited the gorge with her family. When she saw a rainbow by a waterfall, she smiled and said, "I bet I know what this waterfall is called!" Can you guess the name? It's called Rainbow Falls.

Northern New York

The plains turn into hills as you enter the Northern New York region. The hills grow to become the Adirondack Mountains. About 2,500 mountains cover 11,000 square miles. Mount Marcy, the highest mountain in New York, is located here.

The Thousand Islands (above) are located at the mouth of the St. Lawrence River. Watkins Glen (right) is a beautiful gorge in the Finger Lakes region.

The Helderberg Escarpment is filled with caves. They are fun to explore.

To the north of the Adirondacks is the Saint Lawrence River and the Canadian border. Near its mouth, the river is dotted with so many small islands that early explorers called the area the Thousand Islands. Actually, there are more— about 1,700!

Central New York

When you travel south, you enter the Central New York region. In this region, the Mohawk River meets the Hudson River near three cities: Albany, Schenectady, and Troy.

Southwest of Albany is the Helderberg Escarpment. An escarpment is a line of steep cliffs. Thousands of feet of tunnels and caves dig into these rocks. Some caves are only a few feet tall, and are filled with bats.

The Hudson River Valley and Catskill Mountains

If you follow the Hudson River south, you enter the Hudson River Valley and Catskill Mountains region. The Catskill Mountains rise on the west side of the valley. The book *Rip van Winkle* takes place in the Catskill Mountains. The story says that on a clear day the Catskills look like "they are clothed in blue and purple." In fact, these mountains used to be called the Blue Mountains.

On the east side of the Hudson River are the Taconic Mountains. While these mountains are smaller than the Catskills, they are much steeper.

New York City and Long Island

Farther south is the New York City and Long Island region. How would you describe New York City? Most people would say that New York City is a land of tall buildings. It is. The hard rock that lies under much of the city makes a very good "floor" for these buildings.

However, the region is more than just tall buildings. Even though almost 7 million people live on Long Island, many farms and pine forests cover the coastal plain. This region is the most southern and the most eastern part of New York.

Infographic

A Tour of New York's Regions

You have learned about the special features of New York's six regions. Some of these features are shown below. What other features can be found in these regions?

Dear Mom & Dad,
This is a great place.
There's so much to
see! I'll be home
soon.

Love,
Me

PLACE
STAMP
HERE

Mom & Dad
7210 Schiller Street
Bath, New York
14810

Lake Canandaigua is one of the many beautiful lakes in the Finger Lakes region.

The *Maid of the Mist* shows visitors Niagara Falls in Western New York.

This man fishes in a river in the Catskill Mountains.

I ♥ NY

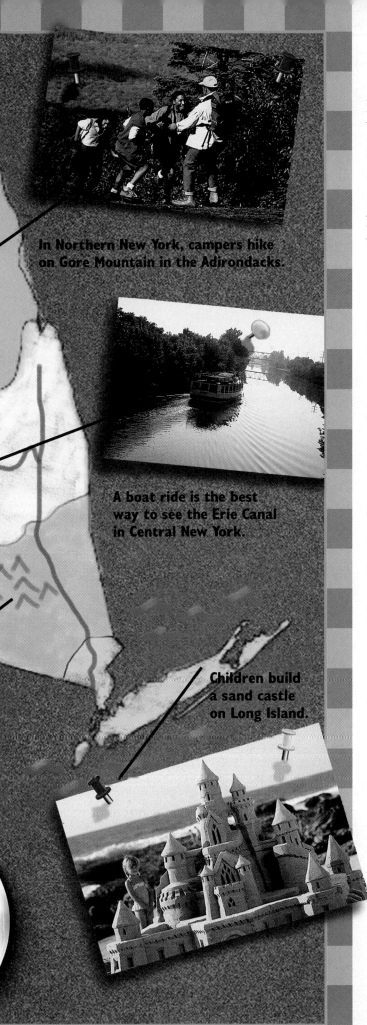

In Northern New York, campers hike on Gore Mountain in the Adirondacks.

A boat ride is the best way to see the Erie Canal in Central New York.

Children build a sand castle on Long Island.

WHY IT MATTERS

In studying the regions of New York, we realize how special our state is. The different regions in our state make it a good place to work and to have fun. In the pages ahead, you will learn more about the things that make our state special.

✓✓ Reviewing Facts and Ideas

SUM IT UP

- A region is an area with common features that set it apart from other areas.
- New York is located in the Northeast region of the United States.
- New York can be divided into six regions.

THINK ABOUT IT

1. What is a region?

2. Which New York regions contain mountains?

3. **FOCUS** What are some of the features that make the six regions of New York different from one another?

4. **THINKING SKILL** _Compare_ and _contrast_ the land of Western New York with the land of Northern New York.

5. **WRITE** Write a poem or a song that tells about the beauty of the region in which you live.

LOCAL CONNECTIONS

SALINA:
LEARNING FROM PLACE NAMES

The children in Mrs. Murphy's class at the Nate Perry School looked up at their teacher. Andrew raised his hand. "Mrs. Murphy," Andrew asked, "how did our school get its name?"

Mrs. Murphy answered, "It was named after Nate Perry. He used to be a principal at this school." Mrs. Murphy's answer made the students in the class think more about the place names in their community.

Cyeara spoke next. "We live in the town of Salina," she said. "Is Salina somebody's name, too?"

"How do you think we might find out?" asked Mrs. Murphy.

Roderick thought someone should look up the name in the dictionary.

"Give it a try," Mrs. Murphy told him.

Roderick checked the dictionary and reported to the class what he found. "There is no word salina, but there is a word spelled almost like it—saline. It means salty."

"Hey!" said Paige. "That makes me think of a place nearby that my family and I visited—the Salt Museum in Liverpool. We learned that salt was an important resource around here."

"That's right, Paige," said Mrs. Murphy. "People once

Nate Perry Elementary School is located in the Liverpool Central School District.

boiled the water from nearby salt marshes until only salt remained. Then they sold the salt," she added.

Mrs. Murphy then showed the class a map of Syracuse which included nearby Salina and Liverpool. The students looked at the list of street names in these cities and found many that had to do with salt. Besides Salina Street, there were Salt Lane, Saltbox Lane, Salt-makers Road, Saltwell Road, and three roads named Salt Springs.

The students continued to look at the map. They saw the word *Onondaga* in several different places and wondered about that name. Mrs. Murphy explained that many places in our country have Native American names. She told the class that Onondaga is the name of a Native American group that live in the area. The Onondaga, too, used salt as a resource.

Together the students began to realize that places get their names in many ways. They also learned that names could tell them a lot about their community. The class formed small groups. After doing research, each group made a poster telling about five place names in their community. With the help of their principal, Mrs. Fields, the students hung their posters in the display case for all to see.

MAKE *your* LOCAL CONNECTION

What are the names of places in your community? How can you find out how these places got their names? Make your own posters to share your knowledge with others.

Place Names

1. Salina
2. Salt Springs Road
3. Saltbox Lane
4. Saltmakers Road
5. Onandaga

Reasons for Names

Means "Saltmarsh"
Leads to salt springs
"Saltbox" is a kind of house
People who made salt lived here
Name of Native American group who live nearby

Students display a poster (left) of place names in Salina.

CHAPTER 2 REVIEW

THINKING ABOUT VOCABULARY

Number a sheet of paper from 1 to 10. Beside each number write **C** if the underlined word or phrase is used correctly. If it is not, write the word or phrase that would correctly complete the sentence.

1. Water from a lake that is refilled by rainwater is an example of a <u>renewable</u> resource.

2. The careful use of our natural resources is called <u>environment</u>.

3. Replanting forests is an example of replacing a <u>nonrenewable</u> resource.

4. A <u>history</u> is a place where stone is cut.

5. Many jobs help create a strong <u>economy</u>.

6. A <u>gorge</u> is a place where ships load and unload their goods.

7. A <u>region</u> is an area where people live and work.

8. <u>Fertilizer</u> means the number of people living in a place.

9. A <u>port</u> is a deep, narrow valley with straight, rocky sides.

10. <u>Population</u> is the "food" in the soil that helps plants grow.

THINKING ABOUT FACTS

1. What natural resource is used to make bricks or tile?

2. Name the two counties from which most of the oil and natural gas in New York comes.

3. How many people live in New York?

4. Name three jobs that deal with natural resources.

5. What is one good way to conserve water?

6. In which region of the United States is New York located?

7. Why are natural resources important?

8. What are the six regions of New York?

9. How do natural resources help make a strong economy?

10. What is our most important resource?

THINK AND WRITE

WRITING A PARAGRAPH

Suppose you are living in New York 100 years in the future. Write a paragraph explaining why you are glad that people in the 1990s cared about conservation.

WRITING A TRAVEL BROCHURE

Write a travel brochure for your town or community. Describe the land and resources of the area and explain why people should visit there.

WRITING A PARAGRAPH

Write a paragraph describing the importance of New York's resources, such as water, trees, and people.

APPLYING THINKING SKILLS

DECISION MAKING

Suppose that you and your friends enjoy riding your bikes in your neighborhood. You notice that one of the stop signs on your street has disappeared. You have to decide whether or not to try and get another one. Answer the following questions to practice your skill at making decisions.

1. What is your goal?
2. What are the choices you can make to reach your goal?
3. What do you think the results might be of each choice you make?
4. Which choice will you make?
5. Do you think you made a good decision? Why?

Summing Up the Chapter

Use the horizontal organization chart below to organize information from the chapter. Copy the chart on a sheet of paper. Use the words in the box below to fill in the blanks in the columns. When you have filled in the chart, use it to help you write a paragraph that answers the question "How do New York's resources provide jobs for New Yorkers?"

farmer	oil
stone cutter	trees

NEW YORK'S MOST IMPORTANT RESOURCE

Natural Resource		Jobs in New York
water	+ People =	boat captain
	+ People =	forester
	+ People =	driller
soil	+ People =	
sandstone	+ People =	

UNIT 1 REVIEW

THINKING ABOUT VOCABULARY

Number a sheet of paper from 1 to 10. Next to each number, write the word or term from the list that best fits the description.

border

conservation

economy

environment

glacier

mouth

natural resource

plain

population

port

1. Something found in the Earth that people can use

2. A place where ships load and unload goods

3. The surroundings in which people live

4. A huge, moving sheet of ice

5. A type of landform that is nearly flat

6. The place where a river empties into a larger body of water

7. The careful use of natural resources

8. The number of people living in an area

9. An imaginary line on a map that divides one place from another

10. The way people use or produce goods and services

THINK AND WRITE

WRITING A LETTER
Suppose you have a pen pal in another state. Your pen pal knows very little about New York. Write a description of your state. In your description include information about the environment, people, resources, and regions.

WRITING A PARAGRAPH
Write a paragraph that explains why temperatures during the summer months are cooler in the Adirondacks than on Long Island.

WRITING AN EXPLANATION
Design and draw a commemorative stamp showing one of New York's many resources. On the back explain what your stamp represents.

BUILDING SKILLS

1. **Elevation maps** Suppose you are planning a bicycle trip in New York. Explain why it would be important to have an elevation map with you on your trip.

2. **Elevation maps** Look at the map on page 17. Which city is at a higher elevation, Plattsburgh or Elmira?

3. **Elevation maps** Using the map on page 17, find the approximate elevation of the area where you live.

4. **Decision making** What is a good first step when making a decision?

5. **Decision making** Why is it important for you to learn how to make decisions?

YESTERDAY, TODAY &
TOMORROW

In this unit you have read about the geography and resources of our state. You have seen how the environment has changed since the Ice Age. How do you think the environment of New York will change in the future?

READING ON YOUR OWN

These are some of the books you could find at the library to help you learn more.

THE MAGIC SCHOOL BUS INSIDE THE EARTH
by Joanna Cole
Ms. Frizzle and her class take a trip to study the rocks they find under the Earth.

PADDLE-TO-THE-SEA
by Holling Clancy Holling
A young Native American boy makes a toy carving and sends it on a journey that takes it all the way to the Atlantic Ocean.

WEATHER FORECASTING
by Gail Gibbons
This book describes how people predict the weather and why weather forecasting is important.

UNIT PROJECT

Make a Natural Resources Mobile

1. Think about the geography and the natural resources of New York.
2. Work in a group. Have each group member choose one natural resource or a feature.
3. Then cut a shape from a piece of construction paper. You might draw a square, circle, or star.
4. Draw on each shape a picture of the natural resource that you chose.
5. Then color each picture and write a caption beneath it.
6. Punch a hole in the top of each shape and attach it to a piece of string.
7. Cut 3 rectangles of cardboard. Punch holes at the ends and tie the rectangles together to form a triangle.
8. Next, punch a hole in the center at the top of each piece of cardboard. Attach a piece of string to each one and tie the strings together at the top.
9. Finally, tape each natural resource picture to the cardboard.

US Army Center of Military History

MRS. WILLIAM WALTON OF NEW YORK CITY, A BRITISH COLONIST (RIGHT)

Detail from: Mrs. William Walton by John Wollaston
Collection of The New-York Historical Society

GEORGE WASHINGTON AWARDING A MEDAL TO A CONTINENTAL SOLDIER (ABOVE) MOHAWK CHIEF JOSEPH BRANT (RIGHT)

Thaw Collection Fenimore House Museum Cooperstown NY Photo by John Bigelow Taylor, N.Y.C.

Albany Institute of History and Art

SILVER BOWL MADE BY A BRITISH SILVERSMITH

Clinton County Historical Museum, Plattsburgh, N.Y.

5000-YEAR-OLD SPEAR POINT FOUND NEAR LAKE CHAMPLAIN (ABOVE)

DUTCH SETTLERS BOWLING IN NEW NETHERLAND (RIGHT)

North Wind Pictures

54

Settlement of a New Land

"We must unite ourselves. . . ."

from a speech by Hiawatha
See page 71.

WHY DOES IT MATTER?

Who were the first people to live in New York? Why did they come here? What was New York like hundreds or even thousands of years ago? How did it become part of the United States?

Unit 2 will answer these questions. It begins with the first people to come to the land that is now New York— bands of hunters following wild animals. It ends with a war that made the United States a country, and New York a state. What happened in between? What is the story of how New York was settled?

Thaw Collection, Fenimore House Museum, Cooperstown, N.Y. Photo by: John Bigelow Taylor, NYC.

**FIRST UNITED STATES FLAG (TOP)
SENECA WOOL-AND-BEAD
CEREMONIAL SCARF**

REDCOATS & PATRIOTS

B lam! The cannon roar their defiance, as muskets erupt in a wall of flame, smoke, and noise. But there's no need to take cover. It's just a reenactment. The real Battles of Saratoga were fought and won more than two hundred years ago. It was in 1777 that British general John Burgoyne surrendered his 5,900 troops to American general Horatio Gates at Saratoga. Today you can sightsee, picnic, hike, and bike in the battlefield park. Or visit a nearby historic fort: star-shaped Fort Ticonderoga still guards Lake Champlain. The British fort, captured by American forces in 1775, surrenders to tourists everyday. Be one of them. Do something revolutionary!

GEO JOURNAL

After doing some research, describe in your Geo Journal what daily life was like for a soldier in the Revolutionary War.

CHAPTER 3

First People of New York

THINKING ABOUT HISTORY AND GEOGRAPHY

Chapter 3 tells the story of the Native Americans in the land that became New York. Different groups, from the Senecas in Western New York to the Montauks in the east, all developed their own ways of life. Some of these groups joined together in a powerful union. Follow the story of these people by linking the colored squares on the map to the colored boxes on the time line.

PACIFIC OCEAN

40,000 YEARS AGO

ALASKA

Land bridge allows people to come from Asia to North America

15,000 YEARS AGO

DUTCHESS QUARRY CAVES

Hunter-gatherers settle in what is now New York

1,000 YEARS AGO

HUDSON RIVER VALLEY

Farming groups plant pumpkins, squash, and sunflowers

Alaska

CANADA

NEW YORK

Onondaga
Lake

Hudson
River Valley

Dutchess
Quarry Caves

UNITED
STATES

AROUND 1570

ONONDAGA LAKE

**Hiawatha works to form
Iroquois Confederacy**

Gulf of
Mexico

MEXICO

Courtesy of the New York State Museum, Albany, N.Y.

EARLY PEOPLE OF THE AMERICAS

Focus Activity

READ TO LEARN
Who were the first people to come to New York?

VOCABULARY
artifact
archaeologist
prehistory
hunter-gatherer

PLACES
Dutchess Quarry Caves

READ ALOUD

Wearing animal skins to keep them warm, the people moved silently over the land. They watched and listened. They were searching for animals they could kill for food and clothing. These were some of the first people to set foot in North America.

THE BIG PICTURE

The story of New York begins with the story of North America. Many scientists think that people began to arrive in North America about 40,000 years ago.

These people were probably hunters from Asia. They were following herds of giant elephant-like animals called mammoths. Over time, these hunters moved from Asia to North America. How did they cross the Pacific Ocean? Scientists think that during the last Ice Age, a wide strip of land connected Asia and what is today Alaska. Look at the map on the opposite page to see what paths they followed. When the Ice Age ended, glaciers melted. The water caused the ocean levels to rise, which flooded the land bridge.

Clinton County Historical Museum, Plattsburgh, NY.

EXCITING DISCOVERIES IN NEW YORK

Over a long period, these hunters moved from Alaska through North America. By about 11,500 years ago, some had made their way to what is now New York. Some began to live in the Dutchess Quarry Caves. These caves are in southeastern New York, near present-day Middletown.

How do we know they lived there? Scientists found remains of a fireplace in the caves. Here early people cooked their food over fires. Nearby the scientists found stone tools and weapons.

Discoveries like these are one way we trace the story of the earliest New Yorkers. Weapons, tools, pottery, jewelry, and even trash give us clues about people who lived long ago. An object made by people in the past is called an artifact (AHR tuh fakt).

Clues to the Past

A scientist who studies artifacts to learn about the past is an archaeologist (ahr kee AHL uh jihst). Sometimes artifacts are the only clues we

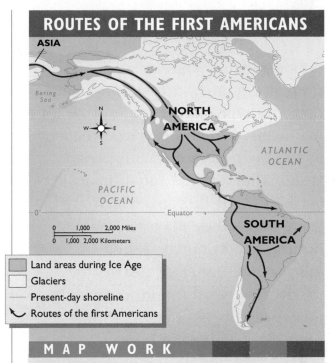

ROUTES OF THE FIRST AMERICANS

ASIA
Bering Sea
NORTH AMERICA
ATLANTIC OCEAN
PACIFIC OCEAN
Equator
SOUTH AMERICA

0   1,000   2,000 Miles
0   1,000 2,000 Kilometers

Land areas during Ice Age
Glaciers
Present-day shoreline
Routes of the first Americans

MAP WORK

During the Ice Age, hunters crossed the land bridge.

1. Which continents did the land bridge connect?
2. Which body of water now covers the land bridge?

have about life long ago. That is because early people did not leave written records. They lived in a time called prehistory. Prehistory is the period of time before people left written records.

The stone ax (left) and the slate spear (below) were used by hunters in what is now New York. Both artifacts were found near Lake Champlain.

Clinton County Historical Museum, Plattsburgh, N.Y.

61

LIFE IN PREHISTORIC NEW YORK

Archaeologists know that people in prehistoric times dressed in animal furs and wore boots made from animal skins. Hunters carried wooden spears with points of sharpened stone. They hunted big animals like caribou (KAR ih boo), which are large deer. They may also have hunted giant animals called mastodons. Bones of nearly 100 mastodons were found at one site near present-day Batavia. Stone points lay under the bones.

Hunter-Gatherers

These early people moved from place to place in search of food. They traveled in bands of about 20 people. They sometimes slept in caves or under cliffs. Some made tents from branches and animal skins.

Sometimes bands set up camp on top of a hill near a river valley. Why do you think they would camp on a hill? That way hunters could look down into the river valley and watch for animals to pass.

Hunting was not the only way early New Yorkers got food. They also gathered plants, fruit, and nuts from the forests. Because these people both hunted and gathered food, we call them **hunter-gatherers**.

When they were not hunting or gathering, people met to share food or to trade things they made. Sometimes they visited with families from other camps.

Early Farmers

With the end of the Ice Age, about 12,000 years ago, the climate grew warmer. The ice sheet no longer covered North America. Many of the large Ice Age animals died out.

As the environment changed, people's lives changed too. Hunter-gatherers learned new ways to get food and provide shelter. They discovered new skills that made their lives easier.

One of the new skills that people learned was farming. More than 1,000 years ago, people in New York grew pumpkins, squash, and sunflowers in the rich soil of the river valleys.

Farming brought many changes to people's lives. Growing their own food meant that people could stay in the same area rather than move from place to place.

As people became more skilled at farming, they were able to raise more food for the group. That way not everyone had to spend time growing food. Some people could work at other tasks. For example, some people learned how to make pottery from clay, a soil that hardens when it is dried or baked.

Courtesy of the New York State Museum, Albany, N.Y.

This diorama at the
New York State Museum in Albany
shows how early people in North America
hunted mastodons and other animals (above).
They also wore fur and skins for warmth (left).

Courtesy of the New York State Museum, Albany, N.Y.

WHY IT MATTERS

The early people of New York hunted and gathered for food. In time they discovered how to make tools and grow food. Our lives still depend on these skills.

✓ Reviewing Facts and Ideas

SUM IT UP

- Scientists think the first people to come to North America were hunters who came from Asia.
- Archaeologists use artifacts to find out what life was like in the past.
- Early New Yorkers got food by hunting animals and gathering fruit, plants, and nuts. More than 1,000 years ago, early New Yorkers started farming.

THINK ABOUT IT

1. How do archaeologists learn about the past?
2. What is prehistory?
3. **FOCUS** Who were the first people to come to New York?
4. **THINKING SKILL** _Compare_ and _contrast_ hunter-gatherers and early farmers.
5. **GEOGRAPHY** Give two reasons why early people settled near rivers.

THINKING SKILLS

Identifying Cause and Effect

VOCABULARY
cause
effect

WHY THE SKILL MATTERS

You have read how large animals like mammoths moved across the land bridge between Asia and North America. Many scientists believe that some early people followed these large animals across the land bridge to hunt them. The animals moving across the land bridge was a **cause**. A cause is an event that makes something else happen. The early people coming across the land bridge was an **effect**. An effect is what happens as a result of something else.

Understanding cause and effect allows you to put facts together in a meaningful way. It helps explain why things happen.

It makes connections between one event and another. Use the Helping Yourself box for some word clues that may help you find causes and effects.

USING THE SKILL

As you read in Lesson 1, after the Ice Age ended, early people learned how to plant seeds and grow their own food. As a result, their lives changed. They no longer had to spend all their time hunting and gathering food. They could now live in one place more easily. People began to settle in small communities and build long-lasting homes.

In this case, learning to farm is a cause. It caused people to settle in communities. Settling in communities is an effect. It took place *as a result* of people learning to farm.

People learned how to grow and harvest corn (left and above). We know that mastodons once lived on Earth because scientists have found mastodon skeletons (right).

64

Often, an effect becomes the cause of something else. If you think of early people settling in one place as a cause, what was one effect?

TRYING THE SKILL

Mammoths and mastodons lived during the Ice Age. When the Ice Age ended, the climate grew warmer. The giant animals could not survive in the new environment. As a result, most of these animals died out.

Is the end of the Ice Age a cause or an effect of the death of these animals? How can you tell? How could the change in the environment be both a cause and an effect?

REVIEWING THE SKILL

1. What is a cause? What is an effect?

2. When the large animals died off, what effect did this have on early people's hunting?

3. When the glaciers melted and water flowed into the sea, the sea level rose. As a result, the land bridge disappeared. Identify the causes and effects.

4. How might identifying cause and effect help you to understand history?

Cleveland Museum of Natural History

Iroquois Indian Museum, Howes Cave, N.Y.

PEOPLE OF THE EASTERN WOODLANDS

Focus Activity

READ TO LEARN
How did the Algonkian and Iroquois live in the land that became New York?

VOCABULARY
heritage
longhouse
ancestor

READ ALOUD

"My father told us many stories years ago when we were children growing up. . . . His father had told him the stories and his father before him." Leo Cooper, a Seneca (SEH neh kuh) storyteller, was talking about how he learned the stories he told. The stories were never written down because people *"depended on remembering things, storing them in their heads so they could be told and enjoyed every now and then."*

THE BIG PICTURE

Leo Cooper lived in Western New York from 1909 through the early 1970s. The stories he told had been passed down for hundreds of years. They explained "how things came to be and why things are as they are." In this way, the Seneca learned about their environment and their heritage. Heritage is the history, beliefs, and customs that a group of people share.

The Seneca were one of many groups of Native Americans who lived in the Eastern Woodlands. The Eastern Woodlands was an area that covered most of the land east of the Mississippi River. This area was given the name *Woodlands* because it was covered with forests. The people who lived in the Eastern Woodlands made use of the resources they found around them.

66

THE ALGONKIAN AND THE IROQUOIS

By 1300 many groups of Native Americans lived in the Eastern Woodlands of New York. Look at the map on this page to see where the groups lived. The people who lived on Long Island and in the Hudson River Valley included the Mahican (ma HEE kahn), Shinnecock (SHIH nuh kahk), and Lenni Lenape (LEH nee LEN nah pee). They are called Algonkian (al GAHNG kee un) groups because they all spoke an Algonkian language. For example, the language that a Mahican spoke was similar to what a Lenni Lenape spoke.

Many Iroquois groups lived in Central and Western New York. They included the Mohawk, Oneida (oh NĪ duh), Onondaga (ahn un DAH guh), Cayuga (kah YOO guh), and Seneca. All these groups spoke an Iroquois language.

These people did not call themselves Iroquois. In fact *Iroquois* is what their Algonkian enemies called them. It means "rattlesnakes." They called themselves the Hodenosaunee (ho den oh SAH nee). That means "people of the longhouse." A longhouse is a wooden building that housed many families.

The Seneca carved moose or elk antlers into objects like this animal comb (left). Older men among the Mahicans carved wooden spoons like this one (right) for feasts.

Thaw Collection, Fenimore House Museum, Cooperstown, N.Y. Photo by John Bigelow Taylor, N.Y.C.

Courtesy of the New York State Museum, Albany, N.Y.

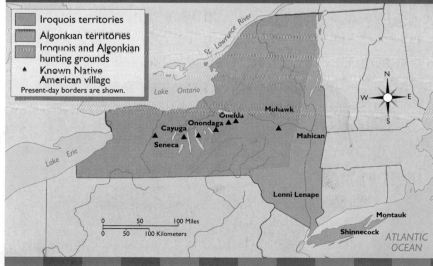

NATIVE AMERICANS OF NEW YORK, 1500s

Legend:
- Iroquois territories
- Algonkian territories
- Iroquois and Algonkian hunting grounds
- ▲ Known Native American village

Present-day borders are shown.

St. Lawrence River
Lake Ontario
Lake Erie

Cayuga
Seneca
Onondaga
Oneida
Mohawk
Mahican
Lenni Lenape
Montauk
Shinnecock
ATLANTIC OCEAN

0   50   100 Miles
0   50   100 Kilometers

MAP WORK

New York was home to both the Iroquois and the Algonkians.

1. Which group lived farthest west?
2. Which group lived farthest east?
3. What types of geographical features are the Native American villages located near?

AN EASTERN WOODLAND VILLAGE

The Iroquois and most Algonkian in New York lived in longhouses. Look at the diagram on this page, and you can see how the longhouse got its name. Some were as long as 200 feet. They were wide, too. Some were as wide as 36 feet, which is about the length of a school bus. They were made out of wooden poles and branches, and covered with sheets of bark.

Up to 20 families lived in a longhouse. Each family lived in its own part. A village of several longhouses was surrounded by a tall wooden fence called a palisade.

Life in the Eastern Woodlands

The different groups of Eastern Woodlands people had a similar way of life. The women of the village planted and cared for the crops in fields that were close to the village. They used pointed sticks to dig holes in each row. Then they planted the seeds.

Their main crops were corn, beans, and squash. The Iroquois called these three crops the Three Sisters. These crops were an important part of the diet of people in the Eastern Woodlands.

The women also picked the crops when the crops were ready. Every village had special buildings for storing food for the coming winter.

The men helped clear the fields for planting. They also fished, hunted, traded, and made canoes from logs.

Children helped get water and wood for the fire. Boys learned to shoot a bow and arrow, and to build traps for bear, deer, turkey, rabbits, and other animals. Girls learned to cook, make pottery, and make clothing, mostly of deerskin.

IROQUOIS LONGHOUSE

Smoke Hole

dorm

Cooking Fire

One Family's Living Space

Storytelling

Suppose you are a Seneca child who lived in a village in Central New York. You and the other children gather around the storyteller. The storyteller tells about the land and animals around you. He also tells about your history and your **ancestors**. Ancestors are the people in your family who lived before you. You enjoy listening to the storytellers tell wonderful stories. Here is a Seneca tale you might have heard if you were a child long ago. In what ways is it similar to or different from stories you have been told?

MANY VOICES LITERATURE

From _Seneca Indian Stories_ by Ha-yen-doh-nees (Leo Cooper), published in 1995.

One day Dah-go-geeh, the cat, caught a mouse and made ready to eat it, but just as he was about to take his first bite, the mouse said, "Wait!" "Why should I wait?" said Dah-go-geeh, "I've waited long enough and I'm very hungry."

The mouse answered, "No brave warrior ever eats until after he has first washed his hands and face." Dah-go-geeh then put the mouse down and began to wash his face. The mouse jumped up and scampered away and Dah-go-geeh lost his dinner. . . . [He] said, "This has taught me a lesson, I will never wash until after I have eaten."

WHY IT MATTERS

The Algonkian people and the Iroquois people were the largest Native American groups in the part of the Eastern Woodlands that became New York. They had much in common because they used the forests of the Eastern Woodlands to meet their needs. In the 1600s the Iroquois became very powerful. You will read more about them in the next lesson.

✓✓ Reviewing Facts and Ideas

SUM IT UP

- Native Americans who lived in the Eastern Woodlands used the resources around them to meet their needs.
- There were two major Native American groups in New York—the Algonkian and the Iroquois.
- Children of the Eastern Woodlands often learned about their past and the environment from storytellers.

THINK ABOUT IT

1. Where are the Eastern Woodlands?
2. What is a longhouse?
3. **FOCUS** How did the Algonkian and Iroquois use their environment to live?
4. **THINKING SKILL** _Compare_ and _contrast_ your life with that of a child from the Eastern Woodlands.
5. **GEOGRAPHY** Look at the map on page 67. Why do you think the Algonkian and the Iroquois needed canoes?

Detail from: Ki-on-twog-ky the Seneca chief known as Cornplanter by F. Bartoli, Collection of the New-York Historical Society

| 15,000 YEARS AGO | 10,000 YEARS AGO | 5,000 YEARS AGO | 1570 | 1722 |

THE IROQUOIS CONFEDERACY

Focus Activity

READ TO LEARN
What events led to the forming of the Iroquois Confederacy?

VOCABULARY
Iroquois Confederacy
confederacy
clan
clan mother
council
sachem
wampum

PEOPLE
Hiawatha
Deganawida

READ ALOUD

The Iroquois believe that more than 400 years ago, a leader by the name of Deganawida (day gahn uh WEE duh) urged his people to form "a circle so strong that if a tree should fall upon it, it could not shake or break it." This circle was the beginning of the Great Peace, a time when the Iroquois people joined together and became strong.

THE BIG PICTURE

Before the Great Peace, the Iroquois groups constantly fought among themselves and with the other Eastern Woodlands peoples. Wars became a part of daily life, and many people were killed.

At the time of the Great Peace, around 1570, five Iroquois groups joined together. They were the Cayuga, Mohawk, Oneida, Onondaga, and Seneca. The union they formed is called the Iroquois Confederacy. A confederacy is a group of people who join together to help each other. The Iroquois Confederacy added one more group in about 1722. In that year the Tuscarora, who had come to New York from North Carolina, joined it. As you will read, the Iroquois Confederacy became one of the most powerful groups of people in the Eastern Woodlands.

HIAWATHA

Sometime in the late 1550s an Onondaga chief named Hiawatha (hi uh WAH thuh) lived in one of the Onondaga villages in what became Central New York. He felt sad and alone because his wife and daughters had died. According to Iroquois tradition, he left his village and lived in the forest.

At about the same time, Deganawida, a Huron, was traveling from one village to another, trying to get the Iroquois to make peace with each other. During his travels, he met Hiawatha.

A United People

Hiawatha listened to what Deganawida was saying. He believed Deganawida was right. Together the two men worked to bring peace to the Iroquois.

Hiawatha called the five groups of the Iroquois together. They met on a hilltop near Onondaga Lake. Hiawatha spoke:

We must unite ourselves into one common band of brothers. We must have but one voice. Many voices makes confusion. We must have one fire, one pipe, and one war club. This will give us strength.

Hiawatha and Deganawida convinced the Seneca, Cayuga, Onondaga, Oneida, and Mohawk that joining together would bring them strength and peace. Together, these nations formed the Iroquois Confederacy.

This 350-year-old Dutch map (below) shows Iroquois villages protected by palisades. The Iroquois made a short style of pipe (below) and used wooden war clubs (right).

Courtesy of the New York State Museum, Albany, N.Y.

Modus muniendi apud Mahikane
Maniere van woonplaetsen ofte Dorpen der Mahicans ende andre Natien haer geburen

Armeomec

Sennecaas   t'

Sennecas

Gacheos

Gachoy   Matan

Capitannasses
Capitanasses

The Granger Collection, New York

The Buffalo and Erie County Historical Society

ONE BODY, ONE HEAD, ONE HEART

How would the Confederacy work? Deganawida had a plan. The Iroquois Confederacy, he said, "shall in [the] future have only one body, one head, and one heart."

People of the Longhouse

At the meeting on the hilltop, Deganawida began to speak to the five Iroquois groups. His words that day became known as the Great Laws. They were rules that showed how the Confederacy would work and allow people to live together in peace. Deganawida became known as the Peace Maker.

Deganawida described the Iroquois Confederacy as a great longhouse that stretched across the lands. Why do you think Deganawida compared the Confederacy to a longhouse?

The words of Deganawida, in an excerpt from *White Roots of Peace*, written by Paul Wallace in 1994.

It [the Confederacy] will take the form of the longhouse in which there are many fires, one for each family, yet all live as one household [family] under one chief mother. . . . They shall have one mind and live under one law. Thinking shall replace killing.

IROQUOIS VILLAGE COUNCIL

Council Leaders
-made plans and decisions

Respected Older People
-gave their advice

Clan Mothers
-appointed council leaders

Village Members
-attended councils and had a right to speak

Laws for Everyone

The Confederacy protected the Iroquois from other groups that might attack them. It also protected the rights of each Iroquois.

All Iroquois had the right to speak freely and give their views at village meetings. They had a right to the food, clothing, and shelter that they needed. For this reason, the hunting grounds and the forests of the Iroquois were open to everyone. The Great Laws also made it clear that people had the right to worship in their own way.

Deganawida said that the Iroquois "shall live together as one household in peace." He planted a pine tree called the Tree of the Great Peace. The tree symbolized the Great Laws. Beneath the tree he threw away war clubs and hatchets. Above the tree, said Deganawida, an eagle watched for enemies.

Choosing Leaders

Iroquois women held a great deal of power. They decided how the land would be used and who would use it. They owned the longhouses and everything in them. They were also the leaders of the clans. A clan is a group of families who share the same ancestor. The head of each clan was called a clan mother.

Each Iroquois group had several clans. They were named for animals, such as wolf, turtle, and bear. A picture of the clan animal was carved above the doorway of every longhouse. The clans played an important part in the way the Iroquois governed, or ruled, themselves. Men representing each of the clans made decisions at village councils. A council is a group of people who meet to talk about and solve problems.

No important council decision could be made without the permission of the clan mothers. They chose the council leaders of each village. If a leader failed in his duties, the clan mothers also decided who would replace him.

Courtesy of the artist: Arnold Jacobs/IROQUOIS

Iroquois Indian Museum, Howes Cave, N.Y.

This painting (above), called *The Gathering of Clans*, is by Onondaga artist Arnold Jacobs. It shows the clan animals meeting under the Tree of the Great Peace. Mohawk artist Stan Smith also placed the Tree and the eagle watching for enemies on this pot (left).

MEETING IN THE LAND OF THE "FIREKEEPERS"

Thinking of their land as a long-house, the Iroquois had a special name for each group. The Seneca, as you see on the map, lived in the west. They were the "Keepers of the Western Door." The Mohawk, who lived in the east, were the "Keepers of the Eastern Door." The Onondaga were the "Firekeepers." Their land was in the center, where a fireplace would be in a longhouse.

Sitting at the Council Fire

As you read, each village governed itself by a council. Leaders of the different Iroquois groups also came together to discuss matters that were important to all of them, such as peace, war, or trade. They met each year in the land of the Firekeepers.

Every year, 50 members gathered in a council house around a large fire. This meeting was called the Grand Council. Its members were called **sachems** (SAY chumz). Only men could be sachems, and only women could choose them. Each group had more than one sachem on the Council. Everyone had to agree before any decision was made.

Detail from: Tee Yee Neen Ho Ga Row by John Verelst, National Archives of Canada

Cranbrook Institute of Science

The Buffalo and Erie County Historical Society

MAJOR IROQUOIS PEOPLES

Present-day boundaries are shown.

Lake Ontario

MOHAWK

ONEIDA

ONONDAGA

SENECA

CAYUGA

Mohawk River

Hudson River

0   50   100 Miles
0   50   100 Kilometers

M A P   W O R K

The Iroquois thought of their land as a longhouse.

1. Which Great Lake did the Iroquois live near?
2. The Seneca, Onondaga, and Mohawk were called the Elder Brothers. Who were the Younger Brothers?

Wampum

Sachems would rise to their feet when it was their turn to speak at a council. As one speaker finished, he would pass the wampum to the next speaker. Wampum was a string or belt of small, polished beads. If it was accepted, people would know the words that were spoken were true.

The wampum beads were usually made from white shells. The word *wampum* in the Algonkian language means "strings of white." The beads were sewn onto deerskin belts in special designs. The designs were sometimes used to record information. The Hiawatha belt tells about the start of the Iroquois Confederacy. Wampum was also given as a gift, or used in exchange for furs.

The Confederacy Today

Today more than 60,000 Iroquois live in the Northeastern United States. Most of them live in New York. Each year, the Grand Council meets in Onondaga to vote on important decisions. Most Iroquois live in houses like those of other Americans. Longhouses are used, however, for ceremonies and community meetings. The Iroquois are still Hodenosaunee, the people of the longhouse.

A cane of maple wood (far left) was used to call the names of chiefs. It is carved with the symbols for the Confederacy's 50 sachems. Tee Yee Neen Ho Ga Row was a Mohawk sachem in the early 1700s (left center). A wampum belt is made of many small, polished beads (left).

WHY IT MATTERS

The Iroquois agreed to make the Great Peace and built a strong Confederacy. This Confederacy made the Iroquois the most powerful Native American group in the Eastern Woodlands. Their enemies came to fear the Iroquois. In the next chapter, you will read about the Europeans who soon challenged their power in New York.

Reviewing Facts and Ideas

SUM IT UP

- Deganawida and Hiawatha helped the Iroquois set up the Confederacy.

- The Confederacy protected the rights of each Iroquois to have enough food, clothing, and shelter and to speak and worship freely.

- Members of the Confederacy came together at the Grand Council to discuss war, peace, and trade.

THINK ABOUT IT

1. Who were Deganawida and Hiawatha?

2. What groups were part of the Iroquois Confederacy?

3. **FOCUS** How did the Confederacy help the Iroquois?

4. **THINKING SKILL** *Predict* what might have happened if the five Iroquois groups had decided not to form a confederacy.

5. **WRITE** What would you have said to convince the Iroquois to stop fighting and form a confederacy? Write the speech you might give supporting this idea.

LOCAL CONNECTIONS
SALAMANCA:
LEARNING FROM ARTIFACTS

The Iroquois made musical instruments and headdresses that they used during celebrations and festivals (below).

Seneca-Iroquois
National Museum

Seneca-Iroquois National Museum

Students in Salamanca were learning about how the Iroquois lived long ago. Many Iroquois still live nearby. Ms. Hynes, their teacher, suggested that one way to learn about history was to study artifacts, the things people in the past made and used. "Where would we find artifacts?" she asked the students.

Juyong raised her hand. "We could go to a museum! It has all kinds of things from the past."

"You're right, Juyong," said Ms. Hynes.

The students decided to visit the Seneca-Iroquois National Museum in their community. When they got to the museum, Holly, their guide, explained that one of the jobs of the museum is to protect artifacts. "By studying artifacts, people will continue to learn about people who lived in the past," she explained.

Then she held up an Iroquois drum. Holly told them that the drum was made of deer hide stretched over a hollow log. She asked the students to look closely and guess what kind of drum it is.

Kinetha said, "It has a plug, and it sounds like it is full of water. It's a water drum!" she exclaimed.

"That's right. The sound of the drum depends on the amount of water in it," said Holly.

After all the students looked at the water drum, Holly showed them another artifact. "This is a gourd rattle," she said. "A gourd is a kind of squash that gets hard when it is dried. This gourd was dried and then filled with small pebbles. A stick was used for the handle."

The students saw other instruments like wrist and ankle jinglers or bells. Holly asked them how all these artifacts might have been used.

"People made music with them," said Diana.

"Yes," said Holly. "These artifacts were used to make music at ceremonies and dances." Holly explained that the

76

Iroquois held about eight major ceremonies a year where they sang, danced, told stories, played games, and gave thanks. For example, corn was an important food crop for the Iroquois. They celebrated when the corn was planted, when the young corn was green, and when the corn was harvested. In the early spring, the Iroquois danced to bring on the maple sap. Later they held a feast to celebrate the ripening of wild berries.

The students also learned that some of the Iroquois ceremonies were stories that were acted out like plays. These stories told about Iroquois life and included music, singing, and dancing.

When the students returned to school, they decided to make musical instruments like those of the Iroquois. One group made rattles from plastic bottles and soda cans that they filled with pebbles, dried beans, and unpopped corn kernels. Another used large cans with plastic lids to make drums. The groups decorated their instruments. Then they held a concert for other students and explained the importance of such artifacts to New York's Iroquois. The Iroquois still make these items today to use in religious ceremonies and celebrations.

MAKE Your LOCAL CONNECTION

What kinds of artifacts were made by people who once lived in your community? How were these artifacts used? What do they tell you about how those people lived? Make your own artifacts and share them with others.

Students made musical instruments from objects they had at home (left).

77

CHAPTER 3 REVIEW

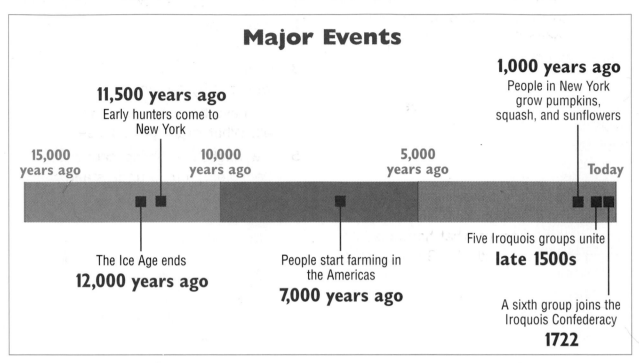

Major Events

1,000 years ago
People in New York grow pumpkins, squash, and sunflowers

11,500 years ago
Early hunters come to New York

15,000 years ago
10,000 years ago
5,000 years ago
Today

The Ice Age ends
12,000 years ago

People start farming in the Americas
7,000 years ago

Five Iroquois groups unite
late 1500s

A sixth group joins the Iroquois Confederacy
1722

THINKING ABOUT VOCABULARY

Number a sheet of paper from 1 to 10. Next to each number write the term from the list that best fits the description.

archaeologist
artifact
clan
confederacy
heritage

hunter-gatherer
longhouse
prehistory
sachem
wampum

1. A member of the Grand Council
2. A string of small, polished beads
3. An object made by people long ago
4. A group of people who join together to help each other
5. The history, beliefs, and customs a group of people share
6. The period of time before people left written records
7. Type of house the Iroquois lived in
8. A person who hunts animals and gathers plants for food
9. A group of families who share the same ancestor
10. A scientist who studies artifacts

THINKING ABOUT FACTS

1. When did people begin to live in the Dutchess Quarry Caves?
2. How do scientists think hunters came from Asia to North America?
3. How did people's lives change when many Ice Age animals died out?
4. What is one difference between the Algonkians and Iroquois?
5. What was the role of women in choosing Iroquois leaders?
6. Name five Iroquois groups.
7. Why were storytellers important?
8. Who chose the sachems?
9. What did it mean when wampum was passed in the Grand Council?
10. What rights did the Iroquois Confederacy protect?

THINK AND WRITE

WRITING A REPORT

Suppose you were the archaeologist who discovered the remains of a cooking fire in New York's Dutchess Quarry Caves. Write a report about your discovery.

WRITING A PARAGRAPH

Write a paragraph that describes the everyday life of an Iroquois boy or girl long ago.

WRITING A DIARY

Suppose you were just chosen to be a sachem for the Iroquois Confederacy. Write a diary entry of what happened at your first meeting with the Grand Council.

APPLYING STUDY SKILLS

CAUSE AND EFFECT

1. What is a cause? What is an effect?
2. Name one cause of the Iroquois Confederacy forming.
3. Name one effect of the Iroquois Confederacy forming.
4. You have been handed a wampum belt. What might be a cause of this?
5. How might identifying cause and effect help you to understand history?

Summing Up the Chapter

Write at least two pieces of information in each blank in the word map below. When you have filled in the blanks, use what you have written to help you write a paragraph that answers the question "How did different people of New York use resources to live?"

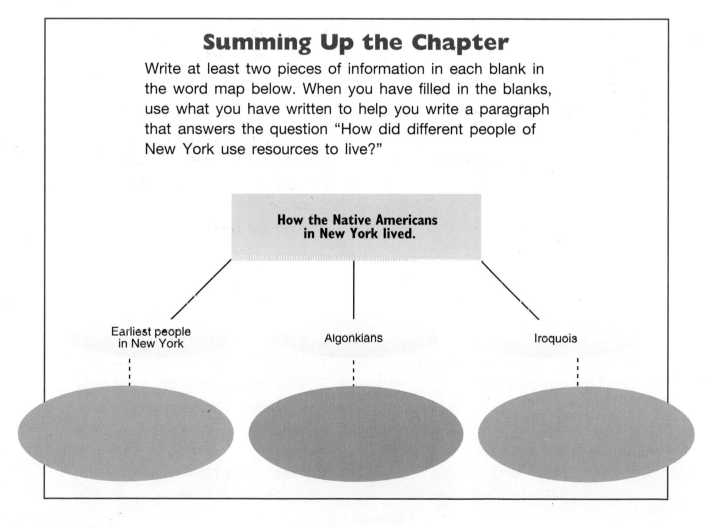

How the Native Americans in New York lived.

Earliest people in New York

Algonkians

Iroquois

CHAPTER 4

Colonial New York

THINKING ABOUT GEOGRAPHY AND HISTORY

In 1492 Christopher Columbus sailed across the Atlantic Ocean from Europe and landed in the Americas. When news of his voyage reached Europe, other explorers followed. Countries in Europe wanted to control the natural resources of North and South America.

By the 1600s the French, British, and Dutch had explored the Atlantic Coast of what is now the United States. They were followed by many Europeans who came to start a new life. Read on to discover the events that made New York a colony of a country far away.

1609

HUDSON RIVER

Henry Hudson claims land for the Netherlands

1609

LAKE CHAMPLAIN

Samuel de Champlain explores Lake Champlain

1625

NEW AMSTERDAM

People from the Netherlands start new lives in the Dutch Colony

CANADA

Lake Champlain

NEW YORK

Hudson River

New Paltz

New Amsterdam

New York City

UNITED STATES

ATLANTIC OCEAN

1685

NEW PALTZ

French Huguenots seek religious freedom in New York

1740s

NEW YORK CITY

Craftsworkers help make New York City the major port in British New York

The Granger Collection, New York

EUROPEAN EXPLORERS

Focus Activity

READ TO LEARN
Why did European explorers come to New York?

VOCABULARY
ally

PEOPLE
Christopher Columbus
Giovanni da Verrazano
Jacques Cartier
Samuel de Champlain
Henry Hudson

PLACES
New York Bay
St. Lawrence River
Quebec
Lake Champlain

READ ALOUD

In 1492, an Italian ship captain set off on a voyage across an unknown ocean. "I, Columbus," he wrote, "decided to write down everything I might do, see, and experience on this voyage, from day to day, and very carefully." His journey would change the lives of people all over the world.

THE BIG PICTURE

Christopher Columbus believed he could find Asia by sailing west from Europe across the Atlantic Ocean. Columbus believed he would discover a route to trade for silks, spices, and gold in Asia. That trade could make him a rich man.

He set sail from Spain with three small ships—the *Nina*, the *Pinta*, and the *Santa Maria*. One night after weeks at sea, Columbus thought he saw a small light far off in the distance. Columbus wrote, "At two hours after midnight, the *Pinta* fired a cannon, my signal for the sighting of land."

On October 12, 1492, Columbus waded ashore on one of the Bahama Islands. He called the people he met there "Indians," because he thought he was close to India.

Columbus was wrong. India was on the other side of Earth. The people he met were Native Americans. He had stumbled onto a continent, North America, that Europeans did not know existed.

FIRST CONTACT IN NEW YORK

News of Columbus's discovery quickly spread across Europe. Yet no one was sure exactly what he had discovered. If this was Asia, where were the silks and spices? If this land was not Asia, then what was it?

Spain sent more people to explore the land Columbus had reached. Then France, England, Portugal, and the Netherlands sent their ships. The king of France wanted to know what lay north of where Columbus sailed. So in 1524 he sent an Italian explorer named Giovanni da Verrazano (joh VAHN nee duh vair uh ZAHN oh) to find out.

Verrazano Reaches New York

Verrazano reached the Atlantic coast of what is now South Carolina. Then he began to go north. In April 1524, Verrazano sailed into New York Bay. He saw "a very wide river, deep at its mouth" that flowed into the sea.

Verrazano anchored his ship in the bay. Then he and a few of his men went out in a small boat to

Scala/Art Resource, N.Y.

Giovanni da Verrazano was the first European explorer to visit New York.

explore. Many Native Americans who lived near the shore came to look at these newcomers.

This first meeting between Europeans and Native Americans in New York was short. The wind caused Verrazano to return to his ship and sail out of New York Bay.

At the end of his voyage, Verrazano knew that the land he had explored was not Asia. For him this was a "new land" that was "beautiful and delightful."

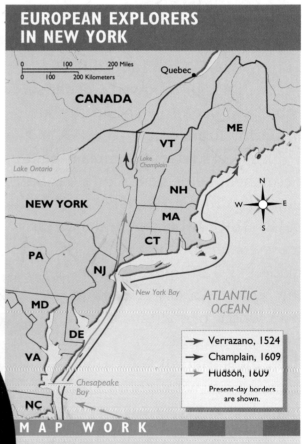

EUROPEAN EXPLORERS IN NEW YORK

Quebec
CANADA
ME
VT
Lake Ontario
Lake Champlain
NH
NEW YORK
MA
CT
PA
NJ
New York Bay
ATLANTIC OCEAN
MD
DE
VA
Chesapeake Bay
NC

→ Verrazano, 1524
→ Champlain, 1609
→ Hudson, 1609
Present-day borders are shown.

MAP WORK

The explorers came to New York from two different directions.

1. Which explorer came to New York from the north?
2. Which explorers came to New York from the south?
3. Which explorer traveled up the Hudson River?

EXPLORING NEW YORK

Twelve years after Verrazano's voyage, the French explorer Jacques Cartier (ZHAHK kahr TYAY) traveled from the Atlantic up the St. Lawrence River. The French became interested in the area around the St. Lawrence because they wanted to trade with Native Americans in the area for furs. There was a great demand in Europe for furs to make clothing such as hats and coats.

Samuel de Champlain

In 1603, another French explorer, Samuel de Champlain (duh sham PLAYN), followed Cartier's route. He began to set up the fur trade for France.

Five years later, Champlain built a permanent settlement along the St. Lawrence River. He called it Quebec (kwih BEK). It became a major fur trade center for the French. He made allies of the Algonkians in the region. An ally is a friend with whom one is united for a common purpose.

In the spring of 1609, Champlain set out with a group of Algonkians. Their goal was to explore the region south of Quebec—what is now New York. They arrived at a large lake. Champlain called it Lake Champlain, after himself. He said, "There are many pretty islands here, low, and containing very fine woods and meadows." He described snow-capped mountains, tall trees,

and many kinds of fish and animals.

While traveling along the lake's shore, Champlain joined his Algonkian allies in an attack on a group of Iroquois. His guns helped the Algonkians to win. From that time on, the Iroquois considered the French to be enemies.

The Voyage of the *Half Moon*

At almost the same time that Samuel de Champlain was exploring Lake Champlain, another European explorer had arrived in New York. Henry Hudson was an English sea captain who worked for a Dutch trading company. He set sail from the Netherlands in his small ship, the *Half Moon*.

In September 1609, Henry Hudson sailed into New York Bay. Unlike Verrazano, Hudson sailed up the deep Hudson River. He hoped

Courtesy of Clinton County Historical Society

Fort Ticonderoga Museum

that this river might be a passage through the continent. If it was, he could sail all the way to Asia. As the *Half Moon* traveled up the river, Hudson met many Native Americans. Hudson and his crew traded beads, knives, and hatchets with them for food and furs.

The *Half Moon* sailed as far north as present-day Albany. Here, the river became too shallow for his ship, and Hudson was forced to turn back. The *Half Moon* returned to Europe.

No route to Asia was found. The Dutch, however, learned of an excellent harbor and a river leading from New York Bay far inland. The Dutch claimed this land in North America.

The Granger Collection, New York

Samuel de Champlain (far left) named Lake Champlain (left) after himself. Henry Hudson (top) sailed the *Half Moon* (above) on the Hudson River. He traded beads like these (right) to the Native Americans.

WHY IT MATTERS

The first explorers who came to North America were trying to find an easier way to reach the rich markets of Asia. Instead, they found a continent with great riches and people of its own. These people, the Native Americans, were rich in furs. Later, Europeans set up trading posts for furs and settlements in these lands.

✓ Reviewing Facts and Ideas

SUM IT UP

- After Columbus reached America, European countries began sending people to explore them. Giovanni da Verrazano was the first European to reach New York.

- In 1609 the French explorer Samuel de Champlain traveled from Canada into New York, reaching Lake Champlain.

- As a result of Henry Hudson's voyage, the Dutch claimed all the land along the Hudson River.

THINK ABOUT IT

1. What was the goal of Columbus's voyage?

2. What did Champlain find when he explored the area south of Quebec?

3. **FOCUS** Why did European explorers come to New York?

4. **THINKING SKILL** *Predict* what might have happened if Columbus had turned back before he reached land.

5. **GEOGRAPHY** How could Columbus have reached Asia by sailing west from Europe? Use the Atlas map on page R12 for help.

GEOGRAPHYSKILLS

Using Latitude and Longitude

VOCABULARY

latitude
parallel
degree
longitude
meridian
prime meridian
global grid

WHY THE SKILL MATTERS

The explorers you just read about in Lesson 1 crossed the Atlantic Ocean from Europe to North America. They explored lands that were unknown to them.

Mapmakers in Europe needed a way to give any place on Earth an "address." They drew a grid of imaginary lines on the globe. Points along these lines provided an "address"—even for places in the middle of an ocean. Now other ships could use the maps and follow the routes the explorers had taken.

The grid of imaginary lines is still used today. It helps ship captains and airline pilots to figure out exactly where they are going. And you can locate a place on a map by looking up its "address" in a gazetteer (ga zuh TEER) like the one starting on page R36.

USING LATITUDE

Let's study these imaginary lines. Look at the map on this page and place your finger on the equator. This is the starting point for measuring latitude. Latitude is a measure of how far north or south a place is from the equator.

Lines of latitude are also called **parallels** because they are parallel lines. Parallel lines always remain the same distance apart.

Each line of latitude has a number. You can see on the map below that the equator is labeled 0°, meaning zero **degrees**. Degrees are used to measure the distance on Earth's surface. Look again at the map. The symbol ° stands for degrees. What is the latitude of the equator?

Now look at the lines of latitude north of the equator. Notice that these parallels are labeled N for north. The North Pole

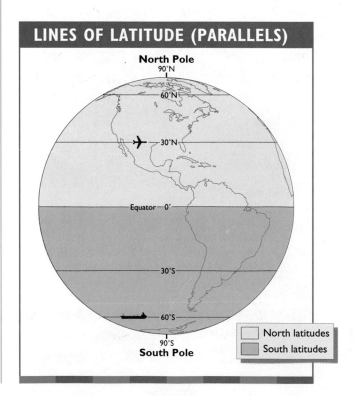

LINES OF LATITUDE (PARALLELS)

North Pole
90°N
60°N
30°N
Equator—0°
30°S
60°S
90°S
South Pole

North latitudes
South latitudes

has a latitude, too, which is 90°N. The parallels south of the equator are labeled S for south. The latitude of the South Pole is 90°S.

Find the ship on the map. It is located at 60°S. Now find the airplane on the map. Along which parallel is it flying? Next find the United States. Between about which two parallels does most of the country lie?

USING LONGITUDE

Now look at the map on this page. It shows lines of **longitude**. Lines of longitude are also called **meridians**. Like parallels, meridians are imaginary lines on a map or globe. But instead of measuring distance north or south, they measure the distance east or west of the **prime meridian**. Prime means "first." The prime meridian is the first line, or starting place, for measuring lines of longitude. That's why the prime meridian is marked 0° on the map. Put your finger on the prime meridian. It runs through the western parts of Europe and Africa.

Look at the meridians to the west of the prime meridian. These lines are labeled W for west. The lines east of the prime meridian are labeled E for east. Longitude is measured up to 180° east of the prime meridian and up to 180° west of the prime meridian.

Since 180° east and 180° west of the prime meridian fall on the same line, this line is marked neither E nor W. It runs through the Pacific Ocean.

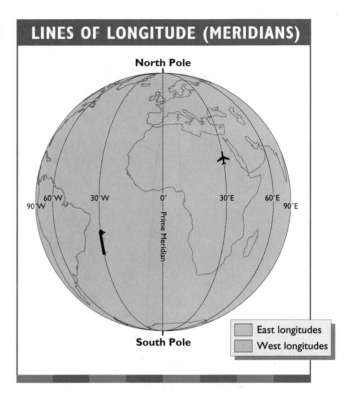

LINES OF LONGITUDE (MERIDIANS)

Unlike lines of latitude, meridians are not parallel to one another. Because Earth is round, meridians divide it into sections that look like orange slices. Look at the map on this page again. As you can see, the meridians are far apart at the equator. They all meet, however, at the North Pole and the South Pole.

Lines of longitude measure degrees east and west. Look at the ship on the map. It is sailing in the ocean at 30°W. Now look at the airplane on the same map. It is flying over the continent of Africa at 30°E. In which direction is the airplane traveling? Suppose a pilot is flying an airplane at 15°E. Between which two lines of longitude on the map would the plane be flying?

GEOGRAPHYSKILLS

GLOBAL GRID

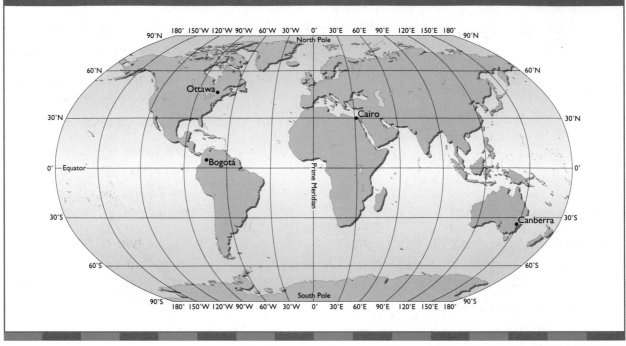

FINDING PLACES ON THE MAP

In order to use latitude lines and longitude lines to find places, you must combine them on the same map. Look at the world map on this page. You can see that the lines of latitude and longitude form a grid, or a set of crisscrossing lines.

The grid on this map is called a **global grid** because it covers the entire Earth. By using the global grid, you can find the "address" of any spot in the world.

Find Canberra, Australia, and Bogotá, Colombia, on the map above. Which of these two cities is closer to the equator? How can you tell?

Now find Ottowa, Canada. Is this city east or west of the prime meridian? Find

Cairo, Egypt. Is Cairo east or west of the prime meridian? Is it north or south of the equator?

Look at the map of New York on the right. Find Syracuse. As you can see, it is located at 43°N latitude. It is also located at about 76°W longitude. So we say that its location is 43°N, 76°W.

Remember that when you locate a place on a map, you always give latitude first and longitude second. You also must remember to give north or south for latitude and east or west for longitude. To describe a place that is not exactly at the point where two lines cross, you must use the closest lines.

TRYING THE SKILL

Try to locate a city on the map of New York from its "address." This city is located near 43°N, 79°W. What city is it? Now describe the location of Binghamton, New York, using latitude and longitude. Is it exactly on those lines?

Suppose that you have found a buried-treasure map. It points the way to a huge chest of gold. The map has an X with the following numbers: 41°N, 72°W. What town is closest to the buried treasure? Do you live near there? Start digging!

REVIEWING THE SKILL

Use the New York map to answer these questions.

1. What are lines of latitude and longitude? How can they be helpful?

2. Are there any cities on the map located exactly on 74°W? What part of New York is this?

3. Name two cities on the map that share the same latitude. Name two cities that share the same longitude.

4. How did you find the answer to the last question?

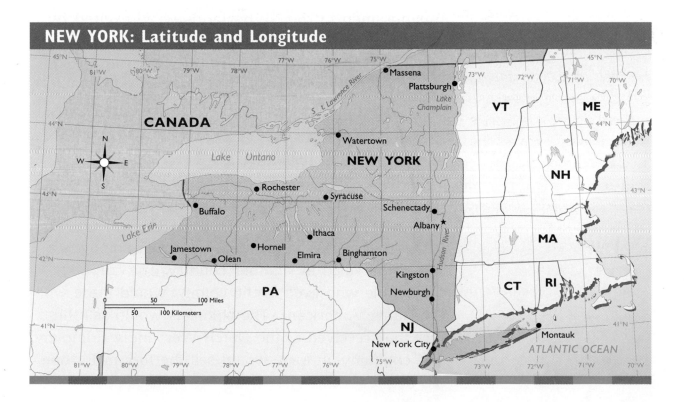

NEW YORK: Latitude and Longitude

The Granger Collection, N.Y.

Focus Activity

READ TO LEARN
Why did the Dutch settle New Netherland?

VOCABULARY
Dutch West India
  Company
colony
colonist
governor
patroon

PEOPLE
Peter Minuit
Peter Stuyvesant

PLACES
New Netherland
Fort Orange
New Amsterdam

NEW NETHERLAND

READ ALOUD

When Henry Hudson and his crew returned to Europe, they reported what they had seen. They described the trees and the animals, the rivers, and even the air! They said the air smelled sweet. They talked about the Native Americans they met. One crew member said that the Native Americans were a "friendly and polite people, who had an abundance [large amount] of provisions [food], skins and furs."

THE BIG PICTURE

Businessmen in the Netherlands were excited by the reports of North America. They listened to stories of beavers and otters living in the forest. Europeans loved to wear hats and clothing made from the fur of these animals. Native Americans, they heard, were eager to trade fur and animal skins for Dutch products.

In 1621, the Dutch government allowed a group of businessmen to set up the Dutch West India Company. The company's goal was to send settlers to North America to set up a colony. A colony is a settlement ruled by another country. The colonists, the people who lived in the colony, would trade with the Native Americans. The colonists would sell the furs they received to the Dutch West India Company. The company, in turn, would sell the furs in Europe.

THE NEW DUTCH COLONY

The new Dutch colony was called New Netherland. It included parts of present-day New York, New Jersey, and Delaware. In 1624, the first colonists sailed for New Netherland.

Thirty families made the trip. After eight long weeks at sea, the ship arrived. Some of the families stopped at the mouth of the Hudson River. Others sailed about 150 miles upriver to what is now Albany. There they built Fort Orange. This was the first permanent European settlement in New York.

Soon more settlers arrived from the Netherlands. They built a fort at the tip of Manhattan. The settlers called it Fort Amsterdam, after the city of Amsterdam in the Netherlands. Around the fort the city of New Amsterdam grew.

In 1626 a man named Peter Minuit (MIN yew it) arrived. He took over the job of governor, or person in charge, of the new colony. One of the first things he did was to buy Manhattan Island from the Lenni Lenape. He paid for it with tools, beads, and clothing worth $24.

The Lenni Lenape, however, did not understand that Minuit was trying to buy the land. They did not have the same idea about owning land. They believed that the land was for people to use and that they were being paid only for the resources used by the Dutch.

L. F. Tantillo, Nassau, N.Y.

L. F. Tantillo's painting (above) shows what Fort Orange looked like. Above the shield on the Seal of New Amsterdam (right) is a beaver, a symbol of the fur trade.

Museum of the City of New York

AMSTELODAMENSIS IN NOVO BELGIO

Infographic

Dutch Life in New York

Many Dutch settlers in New York farmed land in the Hudson River Valley. Today you can see how they lived at the Luykas Van Alen House Museum in Kinderhook.

The Van Alen house (above) was built of bricks in 1737. Luykas, his wife Elizabeth, and their three sons farmed 500 acres of land.

The Van Alens cooked their meals in an open fireplace in the kitchen (above). Dutch waffles could be cooked with this iron waffle maker (left).

Museum of the City of New York

A wealthy farmer or merchant might own things from all over the world. This plate (right) was made in China. Local artists painted portraits, like that of Magdalena Gansevoort of Albany (right), for many families.

LIFE IN NEW AMSTERDAM

The Dutch settlers in New Amsterdam built tall, narrow, brick houses like the ones in the Netherlands. In gardens behind the houses, they grew neat rows of vegetables. Businesses began to spring up—a sawmill here, a blacksmith shop there, a bakery across the street. Windmills were built to grind grain into flour. New Amsterdam was a busy town!

A Day in the Life of Peter and Katerina

What was life like as a child in New Amsterdam? Ten-year-old Peter and eight-year-old Katerina wake in their warm feather beds. Their beds are built into the wall, and doors close to hide the beds during the day. Once they are awake, Peter and Katerina sit next to the fireplace to keep warm.

Time for chores! Peter gets water from the well, and Katerina sweeps the floor. As their mother makes breakfast, their father chops wood. Katerina removes the table carpet, a large cover that keeps the table clean when no one is using it.

They all sit down for a breakfast of oatmeal and milk. After breakfast Peter and Katerina go to school. They study religion, reading, and arithmetic. Their reading, of course, is in Dutch. They pay to go to school—with two beaver skins a year. Children in New Amsterdam do not have summer vacation. They go to school all year long!

At lunchtime, the children return home to eat. Their mother makes a big lunch. She makes a thick soup made with vegetables and meat, like a stew. They also eat fish or pork at lunch. After a dessert of pie or pudding, everyone goes back to work or school.

After school, Peter and Katerina do more chores. One job is to feed the horses. Then the children can go out and play. Sometimes they play games. In the winter they go ice skating. After a dinner of bread, rice, salad, and applesauce, they open the doors to their beds and crawl in for a good night's rest.

Museum of the City of New York

Collection of The New-York Historical Society

Like many Dutch children, the Rapalje children (above) may have eaten their oatmeal and milk from a porringer (above left). The handle prevented burned fingers.

93

TRADE AND SETTLEMENT

New settlers came to the colony hoping to start a new life. Some settlers came to farm. Others came to trade furs. Look at the map on page G11 to see where people settled.

The Fur Trade

The area around Fort Orange was the most important area in New Netherland for fur trading. In the springtime, Native Americans would come to Fort Orange in canoes filled with deer, mink, and beaver skins. They traded with the Dutch for such items as cloth, knives, metal pots, metal axes, and guns.

The Patroon System

To get more people to settle in New Netherland, the Dutch West India Company had a plan. It promised large amounts of land to anyone who brought 50 settlers to the colony. The **patroon** was the person who would own the land. The 50 settlers had to give the patroon part of their crops and live-stock as a form of rent.

At first, only five patroons were allowed to own land. However, life on the patroon's land was often very hard. Settlers had to clear the land for crops, build houses, and defend them-selves from attacks by Native Americans. Soon, four of the patroons failed. In time, the laws changed, and more people were allowed to own land. People began to spread out in the colony.

Peter Stuyvesant

In 1647, Peter Stuyvesant (STĪ ves int) arrived in New Amsterdam. He was the new governor of the colony. Stuyvesant made new laws that made life safer.

Fire was a great danger. Some houses and barns were made of wood and caught on fire easily. Sometimes a chimney was built poorly and it caught on fire. Stuyvesant made laws to make sure that chimneys were built well and kept clean. He also started a kind of police

Peter Stuyvesant was the governor of the New York colony for 17 years.

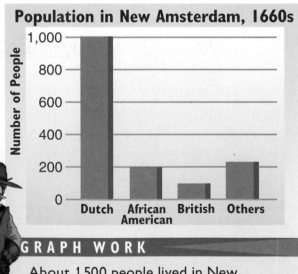

Population in New Amsterdam, 1660s

(bar graph showing Number of People from 0 to 1,000)
- Dutch: 1,000
- African American: 200
- British: 100
- Others: 230

GRAPH WORK

About 1,500 people lived in New Amsterdam in the 1660s.

1. What group made up the largest part of the population?
2. How much larger was the Dutch population than the African American population?

force called a "rattle watch." The "watchmen" walked the streets at night. If they saw a crime or fire, they used a wooden rattle to call for help.

Yet Stuyvesant treated some colonists unfairly—especially Jews and Quakers. He wanted them to leave the colony because he did not like their religions. The Dutch West India Company, however, told Stuyvesant they must stay. New Amsterdam became a place where people of many religions could settle. Look at the graph on page 94 to see what people settled in New Amsterdam.

WHY IT MATTERS

Henry Hudson's voyage led the Dutch to begin a colony called New Netherland. They wanted to gain riches from the fur trade. The colony began to grow as more settlers arrived.

DID YOU KNOW?

Who brought bowling to North America?

In the 1600s, people in the Netherlands enjoyed bowling. The early Dutch colonists brought the game with them when they came to North America.

The game they played then was a little bit different from the one we play now. The players used nine pins, not ten like today. And they played the game outside. They rolled the *bowls*, or balls, down a long strip of grass called a bowling green. But whether you bowl on a grass lane or a wooden one, the game is as much fun today as it was in Peter Minuit's day.

✓ Reviewing Facts and Ideas

SUM IT UP

- The Dutch government set up the Dutch West India Company to trade with Native Americans.

- In 1624 the Dutch built Fort Orange near what is now Albany. They also founded New Amsterdam on Manhattan island.

- Peter Stuyvesant passed new laws that made life in New Netherland safer.

THINK ABOUT IT

1. What was the first permanent European settlement in New York?

2. Who became governor of New Amsterdam In 1626?

3. **FOCUS** Why did the Dutch settle New Netherland?

4. **THINKING SKILL** What *effect* did reports of the Native Americans in New York have on business leaders in the Netherlands?

5. **WRITE** Suppose you live in New Amsterdam. Write a letter to a friend describing what life is like.

1450   1550   1650   1664 1745   1750   1850

A
Brief Description
OF
NEW-YORK:
Formerly Called
New-Netherlands.

With the Places thereunto Adjoyning.

Together with the
Manner of its Scituation, Fertility of the Soyle,
Healthfulness of the Climate, and the
Commodities thence produced.

ALSO
Some Directions and Advice to such as shall go
thither: An Account of what Commodities they shall
take with them; The Profit and Pleasure that
may accrew to them thereby.

Corbis-Bettmann

Focus Activity

READ TO LEARN
How did the British take control of New York?

VOCABULARY
tax
freedom of the press

PEOPLE
Richard Nicolls
John Peter Zenger
Martha Turnstall Smith
Samuel Townsend

PLACES
New York City

BRITISH NEW YORK

READ ALOUD

In 1664, a fleet of British warships sailed into the harbor of New Amsterdam. The commander of the British fleet sent a short message to Peter Stuyvesant. The message read, "His majesty [the king] of Great Britain . . . requires a surrender of all such forts, towns or places of strength, which are now possessed [held] by the Dutch."

THE BIG PICTURE

Many countries in Europe wanted the lands and resources of North America. The Spanish had settlements in Florida and Mexico. They also claimed a large part of what is today the Southwestern United States. The French had a busy fur trade with the Native Americans of the Great Lakes. They built forts and trading posts in Canada and along the Mississippi River. The British had settlements in New England and in Virginia. The Dutch colony of New Netherland lay between these British settlements.

The British wanted to take over New Netherland. That would give them control of the Atlantic Coast from Georgia into eastern Canada. In 1664, Great Britain was ready to make its move!

THE BRITISH TAKE OVER

The British king laid out a map of North America. He drew a circle around an area that included New Netherland. The king said that he would give the land to his brother James, Duke of York. Soon, James ordered a fleet of warships to New Netherland.

Not a Shot Was Fired!

The powerful British warships sailed into New Amsterdam. Aiming their guns at the crumbling walls of the harbor's fort, the British demanded that the Dutch surrender. The Dutch had almost no choice. Their cannons were rusty, and they had only a small supply of gunpowder.

Peter Stuyvesant did not want to give up the colony without a fight. He was ready to fire a cannon at the British ships when a group of citizens begged him to give up. One said, "What will our twenty guns do in the face of the sixty-two which are pointed toward us? . . ." Stuyvesant knew it was hopeless. On September 8, 1664, the British took over New Netherland without firing a shot!

New Netherland was renamed New York. New Amsterdam became New York City. They were named in honor of James, Duke of York. Britain now controlled most of the Atlantic Coast of North America. It was here that 13 British colonies formed. Look at the map on this page to see the names of these colonies.

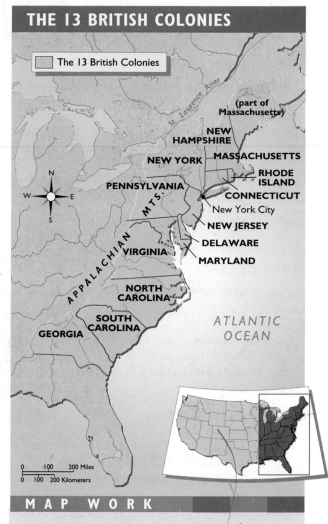

THE 13 BRITISH COLONIES

The 13 British Colonies

(part of Massachusetts)

NEW HAMPSHIRE

NEW YORK   MASSACHUSETTS

RHODE ISLAND

PENNSYLVANIA   CONNECTICUT

New York City

NEW JERSEY

DELAWARE

VIRGINIA   MARYLAND

NORTH CAROLINA

SOUTH CAROLINA

GEORGIA   ATLANTIC OCEAN

APPALACHIAN MTS.

St. Lawrence River

0   100   200 Miles
0   100   200 Kilometers

MAP WORK

This map shows the 13 British colonies in the 1770s.

1. Which colony does not border the ocean?
2. Which colony is the farthest south?
3. Which colony is the smallest?

Collection of The New York Historical Society

This painting, by an unknown artist, shows New York City in about 1756.

THE BRITISH COLONY GROWS

The first British governor of New York was Richard Nicolls. The Duke of York gave him the power to make laws and raise taxes. A tax is money people pay to the government so that it can perform services. Nicolls set up the new colonial government and treated the Dutch well.

More people came to settle in the colony. Trade grew as more ships arrived in New York Harbor. The first mail service in America was set up in 1673 between New York and Boston. Now people could receive letters and goods within days. Look at the graph to see how New York's population rapidly increased in the 1700s.

The Zenger Trial

In 1733, John Peter Zenger started to publish a newspaper called the *Weekly Journal*. Zenger's paper printed news stories that made fun of Governor William Cosby. Cosby threw Zenger in jail.

Zenger was put on trial. The governor expected to win the case. British law said that people could not print things that found fault with the government. Zenger's lawyer argued that the *Journal* stories were true. The *Journal,* he said, had a right to print the stories.

The court believed Zenger was not guilty. In the courtroom, people stood up and cheered! The Zenger trial was an important step toward freedom of the press. That is the right of people to print or tell the news.

Long Island's Heritage of the Sea

The Montauk and Shinnecock were Native Americans who lived on Long Island. They taught Europeans how to hunt the whales that swam close to shore. Whaling quickly became an important business on Long Island.

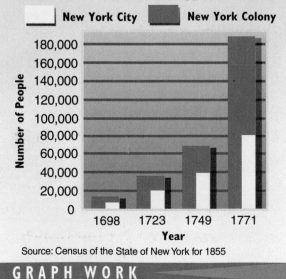

John Peter Zenger printed the *Weekly Journal* on a press like this one.

Population in New York City and New York Colony, 1698–1771

	New York City	New York Colony

Number of People

180,000
160,000
140,000
120,000
100,000
80,000
60,000
40,000
20,000
0

1698 1723 1749 1771

Year

Source: Census of the State of New York for 1855

GRAPH WORK

The graph shows the growth in population in New York while it was a British colony.

1. Between which years did the New York colony gain the most people?
2. In 1723, how many people lived in New York City? In the rest of the colony?

In 1683, Martha Turnstall Smith and her husband William began a whaling business on Long Island. After her husband's death in 1705, Martha ran the whaling company with the help of her sons and a Native American man named Harry. She sold the whale oil, which was burned in lamps. Whale bones were used to make buttons.

Whaling helped other businesses on Long Island. Many communities turned to shipbuilding. In turn, shipbuilding helped Long Island trade grow. In 1745, Samuel Townsend had a small fleet of ships built in Oyster Bay. He carried Long Island lumber, grain, and beef to be sold in New York City. He would return with molasses and sugar to be sold on Long Island.

Links to LANGUAGE ARTS

Early New York Newspapers

New York's first newspaper started in 1725. In the early colony, newspapers were short. For example, John Peter Zenger's *Journal* was only four pages. Before newspapers, people often got their news from broadsides. These were large sheets of paper with printing on only one side. They could be tacked up on walls or poles around the city. Broadsides offered news, political messages, and advertisements.

In small groups, design your own broadside to be posted on a bulletin board.

WHY IT MATTERS

By taking New Netherland and forming the colony of New York, the British gained firm control of the Atlantic Coast of North America. It was in this region that 13 British colonies formed. These 13 colonies were the start of what would become the United States.

✓ Reviewing Facts and Ideas

SUM IT UP

- In 1664 the British took over New Netherland without firing a shot.

- British leaders set out to make the New York colony grow.

- The trial of John Peter Zenger was an important step toward freedom of the press.

- Businesses such as whaling and shipbuilding helped Long Island communities grow.

THINK ABOUT IT

1. Why did the British want control of New Netherland?

2. Why was John Peter Zenger put in jail?

3. **FOCUS** How did the British take control of New York?

4. **THINKING SKILL** Why did the court *decide* that John Peter Zenger was not guilty?

5. **GEOGRAPHY** How did the location of New Netherland make it easy for the British to take over?

1450   1550   1650 1685   1775   1850

LIFE IN THE NEW YORK COLONY

READ ALOUD

Franklin D. Roosevelt of Hyde Park was President of the United States from 1933 to 1945. He said this about the early settlers along the Hudson River: "Their lives were the lives of pioneers, lives of hardship . . . and often of danger. Roads were few and rough, household belongings modest [plain], and the dwelling [house] that contained more than four rooms was an exception."

THE BIG PICTURE

Franklin D. Roosevelt's family was among the first settlers in New Netherland in the early 1600s. By 1700, more than 18,000 people lived in British New York. New York City and Albany were the two main towns. Most other New Yorkers lived in villages or on farms along the Hudson River Valley and on Long Island.

By the 1770s, settlement had pushed into the Mohawk River Valley. Look at the map on page 101 to see the land settled in the 1770s.

Not everyone who came to New York from Europe had money to buy land or set up a business. Some people came as indentured (in DEN churd) servants. Indentured servants promised to work for an employer in the colony for a period of time. In return, the employer paid for their boat trip to the colony. At the end of their service, they were free to find other jobs.

EUROPEAN SETTLEMENT IN NEW YORK, 1775

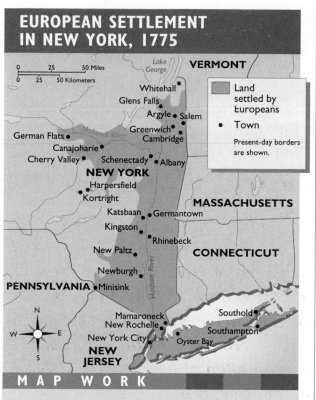

MAP WORK

By 1775, a number of settlements had begun in New York.

1. Along which river are the most settlements?
2. What river is Canajoharie near?

NEW YORK'S NEW PEOPLE

New arrivals from many different countries came to New York. Each brought their own culture with them. Culture is the way of life of a people, including their customs, beliefs, and language.

In 1685 a group of French Huguenots (HYOO guh nahtz) arrived. Their religion was Protestant. Because of their religion, the French government treated them poorly. In New York, the Huguenots could practice their religion freely. They set up communities such as New Paltz in the Hudson River Valley. There they built houses like the ones in Europe, with thick stone walls and steep roofs. Today, you can see Huguenot buildings in New Paltz and New Rochelle (roh SHEL).

One of the largest groups of people to come to New York was Germans. In 1710 many Germans settled along the Hudson River, where they founded towns such as Rhinebeck. They also settled along the Mohawk River in places such as German Flats near today's Herkimer.

African Americans in New York

By 1745 more than one fifth of the people in New York were African Americans. Some African Americans were free. Most, however, were either born into or brought to North America in slavery. Slavery is the practice of making one person the property of another. Some enslaved African Americans worked on farms. Some did housework. Others were skilled blacksmiths, tailors, carpenters, shoemakers, goldsmiths, and leatherworkers.

Many enslaved people were treated very poorly. None of them had the freedom to live as they wished.

New York's colonists cooked food in iron dutch ovens (below) and drank from pewter tankards (right).

Museum of the City of New York

Courtesy, the Henry Francis du Pont Winterthur Museum

LIFE IN THE HUDSON RIVER VALLEY

How do you think life was different on a farm in the New York colony than it is today? There was no running water or electricity. Roads were often poor, if they existed at all.

Farm Families

Farm families that settled a new area had to clear the land. They cut down trees and dug up rocks. Often they would use the rocks and trees to build their houses and fences. It was almost as important to put up fences as it was to build houses. Can you guess why? Fences kept animals from eating and trampling crops.

Everyone at the farm worked hard. The men did most of the hunting and fishing. They also made chairs, tables, and cradles. Sometimes they even made plates out of wood. Women spun thread, wove cloth, and made clothes for the family. They made soap and candles. Children often fed the animals and gathered berries until they were old enough to do other chores.

Wheat and corn were usually the main crops. If they could, the farmers would sell most of the wheat they grew. They used the corn to feed the farm animals and to make food for the family. Johnnycake, or cornbread, was one favorite food. Sometimes the family would cook their johnnycakes with maple sugar they had made. They might finish their meal with a drink of apple cider.

The Great Landowners

In the late 1600s, large pieces of land along the Hudson River were owned by a few powerful families. Some were Dutch landowners such as the Van Rensselaers (ren su LEERS), the Van Cortlandts, and the Philipses.

Frederick Philipse had been a landowner in New Amsterdam. His wife, Margaret Hardenbroeck Philipse, was a successful fur trader and ship owner. In 1661, she began a shipping line between New Amsterdam and Europe. The Philipses became one of the wealthiest families in British New York.

The Philipses bought a large amount of land near what is today Sleepy Hollow. Here they set up Philipsburg Manor. A manor is a large piece of land that the owner rents in smaller plots to a number

Pierre Van Cortlandt (top right) was one of the lords of the Van Cortlandt manor house (right). Farm skills such as milking cows are still demonstrated at Philipsburg manor (below).

of farmers. These tenant farmers gave part of what they grew to the owner in return for use of the land.

Frederick Philipse built a gristmill, which is a place where grain is ground into flour. Farmers brought their wheat to the gristmill to have it ground. Philipse also set up a sawmill, where logs were cut into boards.

A community of enslaved African Americans ran the mills. Philipse built a dock for boats to carry the farmers' grain and lumber to markets in New York City.

Historic Hudson Valley, Tarrytown, N.Y.

Courtesy Bronck Museum

People Who Lived on the Manor

Robert Livingston became a powerful landowner after the British took over the colony. In 1686, he was the owner of a 160,000-acre manor in the Hudson River Valley. An acre is a little bit smaller than a football field. Many of the German settlers you just read about settled on Livingston Manor. By 1750, about 220 tenant families lived on the manor.

On Livingston Manor, the size of a tenant farm was usually around 84 acres. The farmers grew wheat and planted vegetable gardens and fruit orchards. They also owned horses, cattle, and hogs. They went to a store owned by the manor to buy tools and supplies.

Farming was not the only activity that took place on Livingston Manor. In 1749, an ironworks was set up there. Here, skilled workers made iron nails, kettles, pots, and stoves that the Livingston family sold.

Tenant families often stayed on the same land for many years. Children would take over the farm as they grew up and their parents got older. These families helped to form strong communities.

TOWN LIFE

Albany and New York City were the two largest communities in the New York colony. They both were centers of business. They were important markets for the buying and selling of goods.

Portrait of Mrs. Roger Morris by John Singleton Copley, ca. 1771, Courtesy the Henry Francis du Pont Winterthur Museum

Wealthy women in New York, such as Mrs. Roger Morris (left), dressed in fine satin. Craftsworkers made utensils (below) of silver. The streets of New York City were bustling with people (right).

Teapot by Nicholas Roosevelt, ca. 1755–65, Yale University Art Gallery, The Mabel Brady Garvan Collection

Life in Albany

By 1750, about 11,000 people lived in Albany. Many were Dutch, but there were also English and Scottish. About one-tenth of Albany's population was African American. Most were enslaved people.

Albany was a busy town with many shops, two churches, a courthouse, and a town hall. Many houses were built of stone with roofs of white pine. Anne Grant visited Albany when she was a young girl in the 1760s. She wrote in her journal that each house had a garden, a well, and trees planted in front to shade the porch or front steps. Families would gather here on warm summer days to relax. She continued:

Each family had a cow, fed in a common pasture at the end of town. In the evening the herd all returned together . . . along the wide and grassy street.

Many **merchants**, or people who bought and sold goods, owned boats. The merchants would load their ships with goods such as grain, other farm products, lumber, and furs. They would ship the goods down the Hudson River to New York City.

Life in New York City

Over 13,000 people lived in New York City in 1750. The outer palisade of the city was near today's Chambers Street. The streets of the city were lined with buildings. There were many inns, with rooms for travelers. People and carriages bustled through the streets all day. Even then New York City was a lively place, as it is today.

Some of New York City's leading citizens were wealthy merchants. They lived near the harbor on Dock Street, Pearl Street, and Queen Street. They owned businesses that traded goods with people all over the world.

WHY IT MATTERS

Under British rule, the New York colony grew. People came from many countries to be a part of the new colony. As time passed, they began to think of themselves as New Yorkers. Eventually, they grew restless under British rule. You will read about this in the next chapter.

Most of the merchants were British and French, but a few were Dutch. After several years of living in British New York, they all thought of themselves as British colonists.

Many people owned shops or inns. Others were tailors, bakers, barrel makers, carpenters, or black-smiths. They often lived and worked in what were called **double houses**. These houses had a business on the ground floor and a home upstairs. The owners would work downstairs and eat and sleep upstairs. Why do you think these places were called double houses?

Most of the poor in New York City were workers and servants. They had to struggle to survive. Many lived in poorly made buildings in the back alleys of the city. Servants often lived in the homes of the people they worked for. They had very small rooms that they often shared with several other people.

Reviewing Facts and Ideas

SUM IT UP

- Many different people settled in New York, including French, Germans, and African Americans.
- Wealthy landowners lived in manors along the Hudson River. Tenant farmers paid them rent to use their land.
- New York City and Albany were the two largest communities in the colony.

THINK ABOUT IT

1. How did some people get their passage to New York?

2. What kinds of people lived on a manor?

3. **FOCUS** What was life like in the New York colony?

4. **THINKING SKILL** _Contrast_ life as a tenant farmer in the Hudson River Valley with life as a merchant in New York City.

5. **GEOGRAPHY** In what areas did the colonists settle after they arrived in the New York colony?

LOCAL CONNECTIONS

BRENTWOOD:
LEARNING FROM BUILDINGS

"We can learn about early settlers on Long Island by studying their buildings," Christine Finn said to students in her fourth-grade class at Twin Pines Elementary School. "Did you know that in Old Bethpage Village, near Brentwood, we can see one of the oldest Dutch farmhouses in the United States? This house was built around 1730. It is called the Schenck House."

Ms. Finn explained that Old Bethpage Village is a place that shows what life was like in a Long Island village long ago. She arranged for the class to visit the village.

"What do you see when you look at the Schenck House?" Ms. Finn asked the students.

"It's made from wood," said Melissa.

"The Dutch settlers must have had lots of trees to build with," observed Nicholas.

"You're both right," said Ms. Finn. "Many of the early Dutch houses were built with heavy wooden frames. The shingles that cover the roof and the sides of the houses are also made from wood. Each shingle was cut by hand."

The Schenck house is one of the oldest Dutch farmhouses in the United States.

"There are two doors in front of the house," said Jasmine.

Ms. Finn explained that early Dutch houses were built with two rooms. Each room had a separate entrance.

"What do you notice about the roof?" Ms. Finn asked.

"The roof comes down over the front of the house," answered Naphtalie.

"That would keep the rain and snow from falling on the front door of the house," Erik added.

106

The students then went inside the house. They noticed the large stone fireplace at the end wall. "Why is the fireplace so big?" Ms. Finn asked them.

"The fireplace was where they cooked all their food," Jessica replied.

"I'll bet they used the fire to stay warm," said Gualberto.

"That's right," Ms. Finn told him. "They didn't have radiators or furnaces in their houses like we do."

As they continued on their tour, the students could see how the buildings and the materials used to build them changed over time. The Noon Inn was built in the 1850s. It is a two-story house made from wood. It has a wide front porch. The Manetto Hill Church is made from brick. It was built in the middle of the 1800s.

Ms. Finn had the students form groups. The students in each group selected one of the buildings at Old Bethpage Village. They made careful drawings of the building they selected. When the class returned to school, each group built a cardboard model of its building. The students arranged their buildings in a village and then shared what they had learned with others.

MAKE your LOCAL CONNECTION

What historic houses or buildings are located in your community? What can these buildings tell you about the history of your community? Make your own model village and share it with others.

After visiting Old Bethpage Village, students worked together to make models of the historic buildings.

107

CHAPTER 4 REVIEW

Major Events

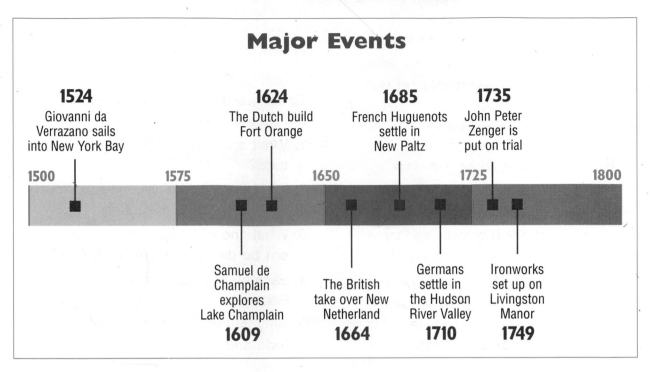

1524
Giovanni da Verrazano sails into New York Bay

1624
The Dutch build Fort Orange

1685
French Huguenots settle in New Paltz

1735
John Peter Zenger is put on trial

1500   1575   1650   1725   1800

Samuel de Champlain explores Lake Champlain
1609

The British take over New Netherland
1664

Germans settle in the Hudson River Valley
1710

Ironworks set up on Livingston Manor
1749

THINKING ABOUT VOCABULARY

Number a sheet of paper from 1 to 10. Beside each number write the word or words that best completes the sentence.

ally
colony
culture
governor
gristmill

indentured servant
manor
patroon
tax
tenant farmer

1. In 1647, Peter Stuyvesant became the _____ of New Netherland.

2. A _____ is a settlement ruled by another country.

3. An _____ worked for an employer in return for a boat trip to the colony.

4. A _____ is money paid to the government so that it can perform services.

5. Robert Livingston owned a large _____ in the Hudson River Valley in 1686.

6. Frederick Philipse built a _____ on his land to grind grain into flour.

7. A _____ was a Dutch person who was given land to start a settlement.

8. A _____ rents land from a landowner to grow crops on.

9. Samuel de Champlain was an _____ of the Algonkians.

10. The French Huguenots and the Germans brought their _____ with them when they came to New York.

THINKING ABOUT FACTS

1. Who was the first European to sail into New York Bay?

2. What did Henry Hudson hope to find when he sailed up the Hudson River?

3. Why were furs important to the Dutch?

4. What job did Peter Minuit take in 1626?

5. What items did the Native Americans trade with the Dutch?

6. When did Peter Stuyvesant give up New Netherland?

7. How did New York get its name?

8. Why was John Peter Zenger jailed?

9. Where did the Huguenots set up their communities?

10. Who lived on a manor?

THINK AND WRITE

WRITING A JOURNAL ENTRY

Write a journal entry that describes sailing into New York Bay with Verrazano.

WRITING A "HELP WANTED" AD

Suppose you were going to New York to trade furs. What kind of person would you want to go with you? Write a "help wanted" ad for the newspaper.

WRITING AN ARTICLE

Suppose you were a writer in New York during John Peter Zenger's trial. Write an article explaining why he's in jail.

APPLYING GEOGRAPHY SKILLS

USING LATITUDE AND LONGITUDE

To answer the following questions, use the map on page 89.

1. What are lines of latitude and longitude?

2. What line of longitude passes through New York City?

3. What line of latitude forms the southern border of western New York?

4. Estimate the latitude and longitude of Rochester.

5. Why is it important to understand latitude and longitude?

Summing Up the Chapter

Use the following cause-and-effect chart to organize information from the chapter. Fill in the blank spaces with causes or effects. When you have completed the chart, use it to write a paragraph titled "How did New York change after the Europeans arrived?"

CAUSE	EFFECT
European explorers searched for a route to Asia.	The explorers reached what is now New York.
The Dutch West India Company sent settlers to North America.	
	The British governor threw Zenger into jail.
Rich landowners set up large manors in New York.	

CHAPTER 5

The American Revolution

THINKING ABOUT
HISTORY AND GEOGRAPHY

Chapter 5 begins in the middle 1700s, when France and Britain were fighting over colonies in North America. It continues in 1776, when the 13 British colonies decided to break away from Great Britain. Follow these events on the time line and the map. You will learn much more about them as you read Chapter 5.

1759
FORT TICONDEROGA

The British defeat the French in the French and Indian War

1777
LUDINGTONS' MILLS

Sybil Ludington rides to warn of a British attack

1777
SARATOGA

The Continental Army defeats the British at the Battle of Saratoga

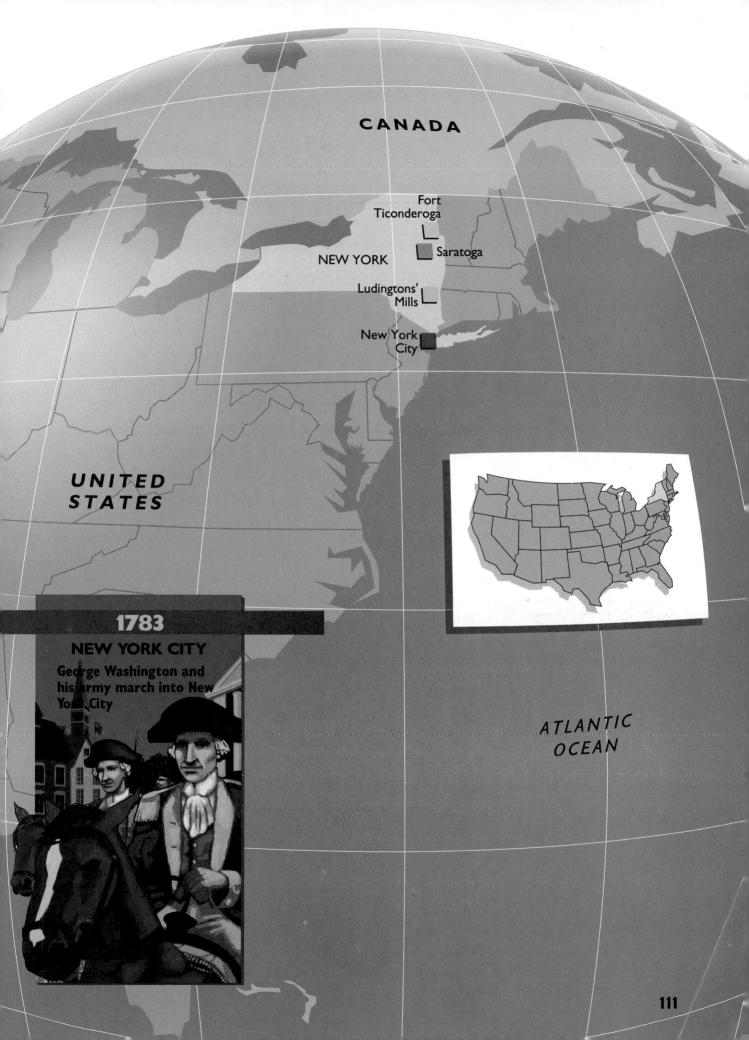

CANADA

Fort
Ticonderoga

Saratoga

NEW YORK

Ludingtons'
Mills

New York
City

UNITED
STATES

1783

NEW YORK CITY

George Washington and
his army march into New
York City

ATLANTIC
OCEAN

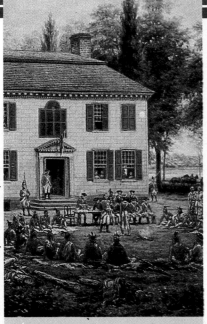

Focus Activity

READ TO LEARN
Why did colonists declare their independence from Great Britain?

VOCABULARY
government
French and Indian War
Stamp Act
Patriot
Loyalist
militia
American Revolution
Continental Congress
Declaration of Independence

PEOPLE
George Washington
William Johnson
Ethan Allen
John Jay
Thomas Jefferson

PLACES
Fort Niagara
Fort Ticonderoga

UNREST IN THE COLONIES

READ ALOUD

In 1752, British officials talked to Iroquois leaders about lands to the west. "Be assured that the king, . . . by purchasing your lands, had never any intention of taking them from you, but that we might live together as one people, and keep them from the French, who would be bad neighbors."

THE BIG PICTURE

In the middle 1700s, the French wanted to stop British colonists from moving into land west of the Appalachian Mountains. The French claimed this land belonged to them. The French built Fort Duquesne (doo KAYN) and several other forts in the region. This would lead to war.

Many British colonists became afraid for their safety. In 1754 leaders from eight colonies and the Iroquois Confederacy met in Albany. The colonies discussed how to protect themselves. This meeting was called the Albany Congress. At this meeting, the printer Benjamin Franklin from Pennsylvania had a plan. He thought that the colonies should join together under one government. Government is the laws and people that rule a country, state, or town. Many leaders agreed with Franklin's plan. But none of the colonies approved of it.

This was the beginning of a long period of unrest in New York and the other British colonies. Americans began to wish for independence.

THE FRENCH AND INDIAN WAR

In 1754, the British government sent George Washington with an army to take Fort Duquesne. The French defeated Washington. War broke out between Great Britain and France. This war is called the French and Indian War. The people the British were fighting were the French and their Native American allies.

The British Prepare for War

The British wanted to drive the French back into Canada. British leaders planned to capture Fort Duquesne and Fort Niagara. They also planned to build forts on Lake George and Lake Champlain to make it more difficult for the French to attack the 13 colonies.

The British worried that the Iroquois Confederacy would join the French side in the war. In 1755, British leader William Johnson asked the Iroquois to "stand by . . . the English . . . let not the French boastings or lies deceive you." The Iroquois agreed not to take sides.

British Victories

Many battles in the French and Indian War took place in New York. Look at the map on this page to see the location of these battles.

British soldiers led by William Johnson won the Battle of Lake George near Fort William Henry in 1755. Later, British troops captured Fort Niagara and Fort Ticonderoga.

In September 1759, the British soldiers captured Quebec. The war was over, and Great Britain won. France gave Canada to Britain.

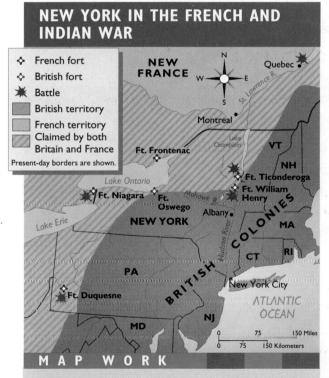

NEW YORK IN THE FRENCH AND INDIAN WAR

- ◆ French fort
- ◇ British fort
- ✳ Battle
- British territory
- French territory
- Claimed by both Britain and France

Present-day borders are shown.

NEW FRANCE

Quebec

Montreal

Lake Champlain

St. Lawrence R.

Ft. Frontenac

Lake Ontario

VT

NH

Ft. Ticonderoga

Ft. Niagara

Ft. Oswego

Ft. William Henry

Mohawk R.

Albany

NEW YORK

Lake Erie

MA

Hudson River

CT

RI

PA

BRITISH COLONIES

New York City

Ft. Duquesne

MD

NJ

ATLANTIC OCEAN

0   75   150 Miles
0   75   150 Kilometers

MAP WORK

Several battles in the French and Indian War were fought in New York.

1. Which areas of New York were claimed by both the French and British?
2. Which battle was fought in the French territory?

Both Iroquois warriors and colonial soldiers carried tomahawks (left). This powderhorn (right) was used to carry gunpowder for a soldier's gun.

Tilâw Collection, Fenimore House Museum, Cooperstown, N.Y. Photo by John Bigelow Taylor, N.Y.C.

McCord Museum of Canadian History

CONFLICTING LOYALTIES

After the French and Indian War ended, British colonists again began to move into lands west of the Appalachian Mountains. This upset many Native Americans. The colonists were moving into land that the Native Americans had long lived on.

To prevent fighting, the British government drew a line between the colonies and the Native American territory. No colonists were to live west of that line. In New York, the sources of the Mohawk River and the Hudson River marked this line. The British government's action angered many settlers. They were told to move back east of the mountains!

Patriots Fight Back

It had cost Great Britain a lot of money to fight the French and Indian War. Now it needed money to pay for its army in America. The British government in London thought the colonists should help pay. After all, the British soldiers were protecting the colonists. So the British decided to make the colonists pay taxes on certain goods.

The Stamp Act of 1765 placed taxes on items like newspapers and pamphlets. A stamp was put on them to show that the tax had been paid. The tax made many colonists angry. They didn't think it was fair. They also did not want the British to tell them what to do. These colonists who were against British rule were called Patriots. Some colonists remained loyal to Great Britain. They were called Loyalists.

Many Patriots refused to buy any items that needed a stamp. They marched in the streets demanding an end to the Stamp Act. In 1766, the British government ended the tax.

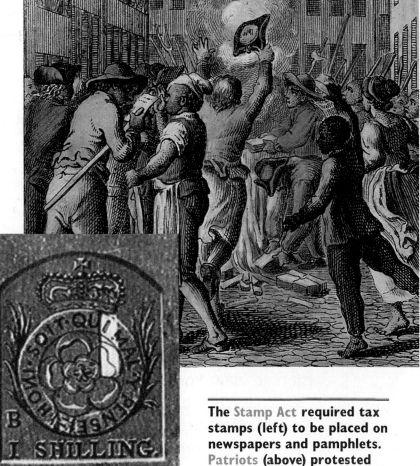

The American Revolution; A Picture Sourcebook, Dover Publications, Inc.

The Granger Collection, N.Y.

The **Stamp Act** required tax stamps (left) to be placed on newspapers and pamphlets. **Patriots** (above) protested the Stamp Act.

Colonial militia men often wore leather clothing to fight in the woods. This soldier was a Loyalist and fought on the British side.

A Tale of Two Tea Parties

In the next few years the British put taxes on more items. A tax on tea caused great anger.

In December 1773 a group of colonists disguised themselves as Mohawks. They crept toward the docks in Boston, Massachusetts. "Boston Harbor will be a teapot tonight!" they shouted. They then boarded a ship and dumped 342 chests of valuable tea into the harbor.

In 1774, Patriots in New York City followed Boston's lead. They boarded ships in New York Harbor and had their own "tea party." They dumped 18 boxes of tea into the harbor.

The Colonists Make a Stand

By 1775, many colonists had joined a colonial militia, or a volunteer group of soldiers. At this time both enslaved and free African Americans were allowed to join. Later, most colonial militias refused to accept African Americans.

Many people in the militias did not like British rule. British soldiers found out where the Massachusetts militia had stored weapons in Concord, Massachusetts, and they marched to take them.

The militia quickly gathered nearby at Lexington to stop the British. As the British began to drive them away, someone fired a shot. The battle that followed began the American Revolution. This was a war fought by the 13 colonies to gain their freedom from Great Britain.

DID YOU KNOW?

Who were the Redcoats?

Redcoats was another name for British soldiers. They were called Redcoats because of the red jackets they wore. The jackets were made of thick wool. They were warm in the winter, but they were hot and scratchy in the summer. The Patriots sometimes teased the soldiers by calling them "lobsterbacks." The red coats the soldiers wore made them easy to see and easy targets for the Patriots.

THE CHOICE OF FREEDOM

A militia leader named Ethan Allen planned to attack Fort Ticonderoga, on Lake Champlain. On May 10, 1775, Allen and his men, called the Green Mountain Boys, sneaked into the British fort. The attack went so well that the Green Mountain Boys were able to take over the fort quickly. The cannons they captured at Ticonderoga would help the Patriots win other battles.

The Declaration of Independence

Even as fighting was breaking out in May 1775, colonial leaders gathered in Philadelphia. This meeting was called the Continental Congress.

The Congress met to talk about how they should deal with Great Britain. Some of the people from

New York who attended were George Clinton, Robert Livingston, and John Jay. Jay was asked to write many of the important congressional papers. These included letters to the British government asking them to stop the fighting.

By 1776, the Continental Congress agreed that the colonies should become independent, or free, from British rule.

Thomas Jefferson of Virginia was asked to write a statement explaining the decision. This statement is known as the Declaration of Independence.

You can read part of this important document below. What were some of the rights the colonists had?

The cannons from Fort Ticonderoga were carried many miles to Boston, Massachusetts, to fight the British.

MANY VOICES PRIMARY SOURCE

Excerpt from the Declaration of Independence, approved by the Continental Congress in 1776.

*W*e hold these truths to be self-evident: That all men are created equal; that they are **endowed** by their Creator with certain **unalienable** rights; that among these are life, liberty, and the pursuit of happiness; that, to secure these rights, governments are **instituted** among men, **deriving** their just powers from the **consent** of the governed.

---
endowed: given
unalienable: basic
instituted: founded
deriving: getting
consent: agreement

116

General Washington had the Declaration of Independence read to his army in New York.

New York Gets the News

On July 4, 1776, the Continental Congress approved the Declaration. We celebrate this day as Independence Day. The Congress chose the publisher and printer Mary Goddard of Baltimore, Maryland, to print the official copy of the Declaration.

People in New York City heard about the Declaration of Independence several days later, when General George Washington brought the official copy to his troops. That evening, excited Patriots tore down a statue of British King George III. They melted down the metal statue. With the metal they made bullets to use against the British.

WHY IT MATTERS

Problems between the colonists and the British grew worse and worse. Each problem led them closer to war. Eventually, colonists began to fight a war for independence. You will read more about the American Revolution in Lesson 2.

✓✓ **Reviewing Facts and Ideas**

SUM IT UP

- The British fought the French and Native Americans in the French and Indian War.

- The colonists became angry with British laws and taxes that they thought were unfair.

- Fighting at Lexington and Concord started the American Revolution.

- The Declaration of Independence said that the colonies were independent from Britain.

THINK ABOUT IT

1. What was the Albany Congress?

2. Why was the Declaration of Independence an important statement for our country?

3. **FOCUS** Why did the colonists go to war with Britain?

4. **THINKING SKILL** Put these events in the correct _sequence_: the Declaration of Independence, the Stamp Act, the French and Indian War, and Ethan Allen captures Fort Ticonderoga.

5. **WRITE** Suppose you are a Patriot. Write a letter to a friend explaining why you think the colonies should be free from Britain.

The Granger Collection, N.Y.

Declaring independence and forming a new country, with a new flag, was an important decision for American colonists.

1774: WHAT DID PEOPLE THINK ABOUT THE AMERICAN REVOLUTION?

In the struggle over British rule in the 13 colonies, colonists in New York had different points of view. Some sided with the British. New York had more Loyalists than any other colony. Many Loyalists had family and friends in Great Britain or were shopkeepers or traders with strong business ties there. Some, like Samuel Seabury, were Anglicans, or members of the Church of England.

Other New Yorkers favored breaking all ties with Great Britain. Many were angered over the British government's tax policies. These Patriots, like John Jay, believed the British government did not have the right to tax the colonies. In fact, they thought that the British government did not have the right to rule the colonies at all. The Patriots wanted to make their own laws.

Some colonists wanted to avoid war between Britain and the colonies. Isaac Wilkins did not want to fight against British soldiers or against colonists. Read the three viewpoints on this issue. Then answer the questions that follow.

Three DIFFERENT Viewpoints

1 **JOHN JAY**
Lawmaker in New York
Excerpt from *Address to the People of Great Britain* in October 1774

We consider ourselves, and do insist that we are and ought to be, as free as our fellow subjects [citizens] in Britain, and that no power on earth has a right to take our property from us without our consent.

"No power on earth has a right to take our property . . ."

2 **SAMUEL SEABURY**
Anglican minister in New York
Excerpt from *A View of the Controversy Between Great-Britain and Her Colonies* written in December 1774

Upon the whole, liberty under . . . Great Britain is infinitely preferable to slavery under an American Congress. . . . The British government is the best scheme of government. . . . The rights and liberties of the people are better secured by it than by any other system.

"The British government is the best scheme of government."

3 **ISAAC WILKINS**
Lawmaker in New York
Excerpt from a letter in *Rivington's New-York Gazetteer,* May 1775

May . . . peace and liberty [return] to my unhappy country; may Great Britain and America be soon united in the hands of everlasting amity [friendship]; and when united, may they continue a free . . . and happy nation to the end of time.

I leave America and every endearing connection because I will not raise my hand against my sovereign [the king], nor will I draw my sword against my country [America].

"May Great Britain and America be soon united . . ."

BUILDING CITIZENSHIP

THINKING ABOUT VIEWPOINTS

1. What is the viewpoint of each person? Who strongly opposes independence for the colonies? Who probably favors it?
2. Why did Isaac Wilkins choose to leave America?
3. What other viewpoints might colonists have had on this issue?

SHARING VIEWPOINTS

Suppose you were a colonist in New York in 1774. Discuss what you might have agreed with or disagreed with about these and other viewpoints. Then, as a class, write three statements that all of you might have agreed with about the conflict over British rule.

STUDY SKILLS

Reading Time Line

VOCABULARY
time line

WHY THE SKILL MATTERS

In Lesson 1 you read about some events in New York while it was a British colony. How do these events fit into New York's history?

To understand history, you need to know when things happened. You also need to know in which order they happened. Did the protest over the tea tax take place before or after the John Peter Zenger trial? Did French Huguenots move to New York when it was under Dutch control or British control? To

help answer these questions, you can use a **time line**. A time line is a diagram that shows when events took place. It also shows the amount of time that passed between events. In this way a time line helps to give a sense of sequence, or order, to history. The time line below shows important events in New York's history.

USING THE SKILL

Look at the time line on this page. As you can see, the name of each event appears below or above the date it happened. The earliest event is on the left side. The most recent event is on the right.

Like most time lines, this one is divided into equal parts. Each part of New York's time line stands for 50 years.

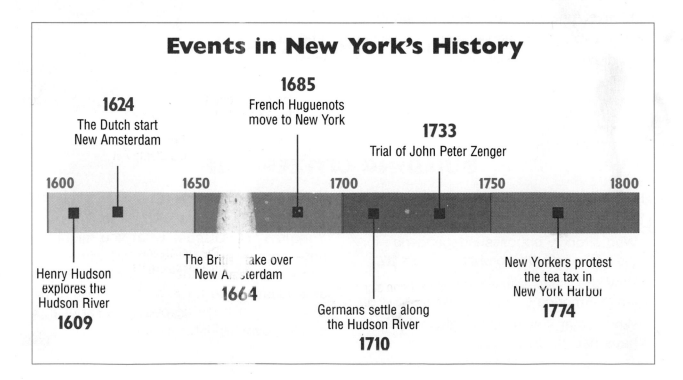

Events in New York's History

1624
The Dutch start New Amsterdam

1685
French Huguenots move to New York

1733
Trial of John Peter Zenger

1600 — 1650 — 1700 — 1750 — 1800

Henry Hudson explores the Hudson River
1609

The British take over New Amsterdam
1664

Germans settle along the Hudson River
1710

New Yorkers protest the tea tax in New York Harbor
1774

Now read the time line from left to right. The first event is Henry Hudson exploring the Hudson River. The last event is New Yorkers' protest of the tea tax. Which event took place between 1730 and 1740?

TRYING THE SKILL

Try reading this time line of events in the 13 colonies. Use the Helping Yourself box for hints.

What period of history does the time line cover? Which event on this time line happened last? In what year did the British order the Stamp Act? Which event happened in 1754? Did Georgia become the 13th colony before or after the French and Indian War?

HELPING Yourself

- A **time line** is a diagram that shows when events took place.
- Note how much time is represented by each part of the time line.
- Read the events from left to right.

REVIEWING THE SKILL

Look again at the time line of events in the 13 colonies. Use it to answer the following questions.

1. How does a time line help you to place events in the right order?
2. Which event took place in 1682?
3. How much time passed between the British ordering the Stamp Act and the meeting of the Continental Congress in Philadelphia?
4. Did the British start Jamestown before or after the start of Plymouth colony?
5. In what other subjects would a time line be useful?

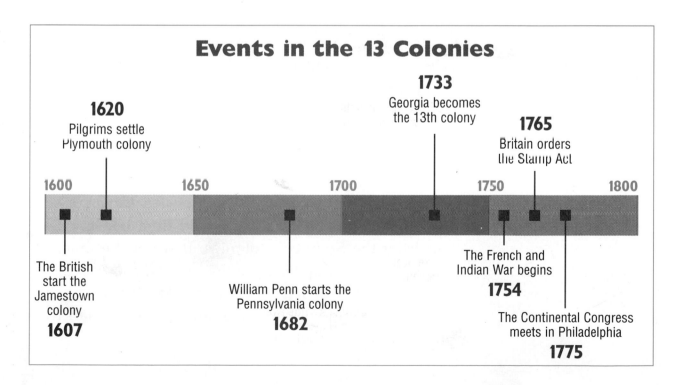

Events in the 13 Colonies

1733
Georgia becomes the 13th colony

1620
Pilgrims settle Plymouth colony

1765
Britain orders the Stamp Act

1600   1650   1700   1750   1800

The British start the Jamestown colony
1607

William Penn starts the Pennsylvania colony
1682

The French and Indian War begins
1754

The Continental Congress meets in Philadelphia
1775

REVOLUTION IN NEW YORK

READ ALOUD

Three weeks after New Yorkers had pulled down the statue of King George III in 1776, thousands of British soldiers landed on Long Island. For four days, the American militia and the British soldiers battled each other near what was then the village of Brooklyn. The American Revolution had come to New York.

THE BIG PICTURE

In Lesson 1, you learned that in 1775 the colonial militia and the British fought each other at Lexington and Concord. This was the start of the American Revolution.

Within a year New York became a key state in the war for independence. Think about why this might have been. One reason was its location. New York was about halfway between the New England colonies and the Southern colonies.

General George Washington was commander of the Continental, or American, Army. He knew what would happen if the British controlled New York. The New England colonies would then be separated from the Southern colonies. It would be much more difficult for the colonies to send messages and supplies to each other. It would also be much harder to send soldiers back and forth. He had to try to stop the British!

Focus Activity

READ TO LEARN
What happened to the British plan to capture New York?

VOCABULARY
surrender
retreat
Battle of Saratoga
Battle of Yorktown

PEOPLE
Sarah Jay
Sybil Ludington
John Burgoyne
Joseph Brant
Horatio Gates

PLACES
Saratoga
Oriskany

122

THE BATTLES ON LONG ISLAND AND MANHATTAN

The battle that was fought on Long Island in August 1776 did not go well for the American soldiers. They were beaten badly. The British stopped firing their rifles and cannons and waited for the Continental Army to **surrender**, or give up. However, General Washington had other plans. When a heavy fog moved in, Washington and his troops escaped by rowing boats across the East River to Manhattan.

New York City Is Captured

A few weeks later the Americans and British fought each other in Manhattan. Once again, the Continental Army lost. In November, Washington and his soldiers left the city and went to New Jersey. Now New York City was under British control. It stayed that way until the end of the war.

When the British took over New York, Loyalists poured into the city. They knew they would be safe there. On the other hand, many Patriots fled the city. They went to places where they would be safe from the British.

At about the same time the British captured New York City, they also landed at Peekskill, north of New York City. **Sarah Jay**, the wife of patriot John Jay, was visiting near there. She wrote to her husband:

I am determined to . . . prepare for the worst and hope for the best. . . . Not less than twelve hundred of the enemy landed at Peekskill . . . and . . . they had been firing sometime.

The British later turned back from Peekskill, but Sarah Jay had a narrow escape from the battle!

The Granger Collection, N.Y.

A Continental soldier had to fill his rifle with gunpowder.

Links to MUSIC

Yankee Doodle

The patriotic song "Yankee Doodle" was first sung during the American Revolution. The British sang it to make fun of the Continental Army's sloppy clothing:

Yankee Doodle came to town,
Riding on a pony.
He stuck a feather in his hat,
And called it macaroni.

But the Continental Army liked the song anyway. Riding on a pony was a sign of importance. Having a feather in one's hat was a sign of honor. And macaroni did not mean a noodle. It meant a British man who liked fancy clothes and showed off.

Sing "Yankee Doodle" as a class. Identify other songs that became popular during other wars.

123

THE BRITISH ON THE MARCH

After capturing New York City, the British chased Washington and the Continental Army through New Jersey. Then both armies went to their winter camps. The following spring the British troops began to attack the Patriots of upstate New York.

Sybil Ludington

In Ludingtons' Mills, Henry Ludington was a colonel (KUR nuhl) in the New York militia. He and some of the other men had come home in April 1777 to do the spring planting. Then they would go back to fight again.

Word reached Henry Ludington that British soldiers had arrived at Danbury, Connecticut, about 30 miles away. Henry Ludington feared that the British would march toward Ludingtons' Mills. Someone had to tell the other soldiers to gather at the Ludington farm. Ludington's daughter, 16-year-old Sybil Ludington, volunteered. "I will sound the alarm," she promised.

On her horse, Star, Sybil set out at night to spread the news. In the morning, Sybil's father and the other soldiers rode off to Danbury. They helped force the British to retreat, or turn back. Today, a statue of Sybil Ludington and Star stands in Carmel, New York, to honor her for her ride.

General Burgoyne's Plan

British General John Burgoyne (bur GOYN) had a plan to capture the entire New York colony. General Burgoyne and his soldiers would head south from Canada. A second group of British soldiers would march east from Oswego. A third group would come north from New York City. They would all march toward Albany. Once the British captured Albany, the New York colony would be in their hands.

These New Yorkers are re-enacting a British march at Fort Ticonderoga. The United States Postal Service honored Sybil Ludington with a stamp.

Contributors To The Cause...

U.S. 8c

Sybil Ludington   Youthful Heroine

Look at the map on this page to see the routes these British armies planned to travel.

General Burgoyne and his soldiers entered New York in June 1777. They defeated American forces near Fort Ticonderoga, and they captured Lake George. They then marched on to Saratoga.

The Battle of Saratoga

In early August, the British soldiers who had started from Oswego attacked American soldiers near Oriskany (aw RIS kuh nee).

Native American leader Joseph Brant fought at the Battle of Oriskany.

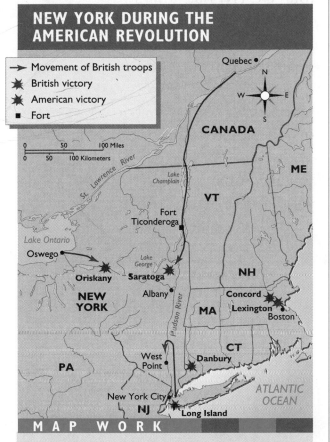

NEW YORK DURING THE AMERICAN REVOLUTION

→ Movement of British troops
✷ British victory
✷ American victory
■ Fort

0   50   100 Miles
0   50   100 Kilometers

Quebec •

CANADA

ME

Lake Champlain

VT

Fort Ticonderoga

Lake Ontario

Oswego •

Lake George

Oriskany   Saratoga

NEW YORK

Albany

NH

Concord

MA   Lexington •

Boston

Hudson River

CT

West Point   Danbury

PA

New York City

NJ   Long Island

ATLANTIC OCEAN

M A P   W O R K

Because of its location, New York was a key state in the American Revolution.

1. What victories by the Continental Army are shown on the map?
2. What victories by the British Army are shown on the map?

One of the leaders on the British side at Oriskany was Mohawk Chief Joseph Brant. Most Native Americans sided with the British. They believed they had been cheated out of their land by the Americans. The British were driven back at the Battle of Oriskany. They returned to Oswego.

At the Battle of Saratoga Burgoyne's troops were defeated by American soldiers led by General Horatio Gates. The Battle of Saratoga is really two battles that took place over three weeks. The British soldiers from New York City left the city too late to help General Burgoyne. On October 17, 1777, Burgoyne was surrounded by the Americans and surrendered. Look at the Infographic on page 126 to see more about the battle. This victory was very important because it helped convince France that the Americans could win the war. France decided to help the Americans by sending soldiers and money.

125

Infographic

Victory at Saratoga

At the second Saratoga battle, at Bemis Heights, the Americans broke through the British lines. Ten days later, on October 17, 1777, British General John Burgoyne surrendered to American General Horatio Gates. In the two Saratoga battles, about 1,700 British soldiers were killed, wounded, or captured. The remaining 6,000 British soldiers became prisoners! With the loss of so many troops, the British Army was weakened in New York.

British General John Burgoyne

Copyright The Frick Collection, NY. Detail from General John Burgoyne by Reynolds

American artilleryman, or gunner

To Saratoga

Third British retreat

Burgoyne's headquarters

Second British retreat

First British advance and retreat

First fighting

Second fighting

American advance

Mill Creek

Hudson River

American General Horatio Gates

Independence National Historical Park

Bemis Heights

Gates's headquarters

To Albany ↓

Legend

	Bemis Heights
	Road
	British lines
	American lines
→	**British movement**
→	**American movement**
☆☆☆	**Major fighting**

THE WAR ENDS

The Battle of Yorktown, in Virginia, was the final battle of the American Revolution. British General Charles Cornwallis surrendered to General Washington on October 19, 1781.

When the British soldiers left York-town, they played this song, called "The World Turned Upside Down":

> If ponies rode men and if grass ate cows,
> And cats should be chased into holes by the mouse,
> If summers were spring and the other way round,
> Then all the world would be upside down.

The British world had been turned upside down. After six long years of war, the Americans had won. New Yorkers fought hard for freedom.

The British signed a peace agreement on September 3, 1783. This marked the end of the American Revolution. On November 25, 1783, the last British soldiers left New York. After they left, General Washington and his soldiers entered the city. The 13 colonies were free to become the United States of America!

WHY IT MATTERS

The American Revolution made the 13 colonies a separate country. The Americans could now make their own laws. They began to build a country based on ideas of freedom.

✔ Reviewing Facts and Ideas

SUM IT UP

- New York's location was important to the American Revolution.
- Sybil Ludington was a New York Patriot who helped win the war.
- The Battle of Saratoga convinced the French to help the Americans.
- The American Revolution was won with the victory at Yorktown.

THINK ABOUT IT

1. What did Sybil Ludington do?
2. Who won the Battle of Saratoga?
3. **FOCUS** What happened to the British plan to capture New York?
4. **THINKING SKILL** *Predict* what might have happened if George Washington had not escaped to Manhattan.
5. **GEOGRAPHY** Look at the map on page 97. Why was New York in an important location for the British?

The Granger Collection, N.Y.

General Washington and his soldiers entered New York City after the British left.

127

West Point

The sun rises. A bugle sounds a wake-up call. The sleepy students, who are called cadets, file out of their barracks and form neat, straight lines. This is West Point, the United States Military Academy. West Point is a school that teaches young men and women to be officers in the Army.

West Point overlooks the Hudson River. During the American Revolution, a gigantic chain across the Hudson at West Point kept the British from sailing up the river. George Washington thought a military school would be a good way to train officers in the Army. The government created West Point Military Academy in 1802.

Today, West Point is a college as well as a military academy. So the cadets also learn about math, English, and history, just like you!

Religious services for the cadets are held in the beautiful Academy chapel (below).

The Academy teaches regular college subjects (above) as well as military ones. The cadet in battle dress (below) climbs rocks as a part of her combat training.

Cadets (above) learn to march in step. The gray and white uniform dates from the founding of the Academy. A statue of George Washington riding a horse (left) is on the Academy grounds.

129

LOCAL CONNECTIONS
ROME:
LEARNING FROM HISTORIC SITES

The students in Mr. Radnor's fourth-grade class in Rome were studying the Revolutionary War. "Fort Stanwix, which is near Rome, is a historic site, or place, where we can to learn about the Revolutionary War and how people who fought in it lived," he said. "We are going to visit the fort."

Mr. Radnor explained that it was important to prepare for the trip by studying about the fort's history. The students learned that the fort was built by the British in 1758. Then it was rebuilt by the Patriots in 1776 because it was near an important water route.

As part of their research, the students looked for pictures of soldiers who fought in the war. They learned that most soldiers wore regular clothes, not fancy uniforms. The students then made their own uniforms to wear when they visited the fort. They wore old work shirts and vests. They made breeches by rolling up their pants to the knees. They also wore knee socks and knitted hats.

A soldier at Fort Stanwix takes a break to eat his noon meal.

When the students arrived at Fort Stanwix, they saw many artifacts from the Revolutionary War period. Their guide told them all about the cannons and other weapons the soldiers used. The students got to see the quarters, or rooms, where the soldiers ate and slept.

The students also took part in the fort's Soldiers Day Program. They acted out the parts of Continental soldiers. Some students did fatigue duty, such as pulling weeds and picking up trash. Others joined in the drills. They marched and sang

"Yankee Doodle." A few students served as guards, or sentries. Their job was to watch for enemies. They also had to keep soldiers from deserting, or leaving the fort without permission.

At the end of the day, the students were given discharge papers that showed they had finished serving in the army. When they returned to school, the students talked about what they had learned.

"I liked marching and singing!" Cherise exclaimed. "But I can see how the drills could make soldiers really tired," she added.

The students agreed that the fort was an exciting place to visit. "How can we show other students how interesting Fort Stanwix is?" Mr. Radnor asked them. After discussing the question, the class decided to write a play about life at Fort Stanwix. Everyone would get a part. When they finished writing and rehearsing their play, they presented it to the younger students in their school. The younger students enjoyed the performance and looked forward to the time when they could visit the fort.

MAKE Your LOCAL CONNECTION

What historic site is located in or near your community? How can you learn about the history of this site and its importance to the community? How can you share this information with others?

▌Students visiting Fort Stanwix
▌learned about cannons from
▌a volunteer who plays the role
▌of a Continental soldier.

CHAPTER 5 REVIEW

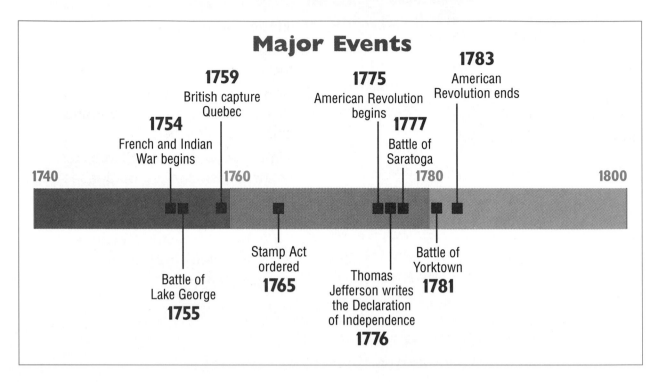

Major Events

1754 French and Indian War begins

1759 British capture Quebec

1775 American Revolution begins

1777 Battle of Saratoga

1783 American Revolution ends

1740 · 1760 · 1780 · 1800

Battle of Lake George **1755**

Stamp Act ordered **1765**

Thomas Jefferson writes the Declaration of Independence **1776**

Battle of Yorktown **1781**

THINKING ABOUT VOCABULARY

Write a sentence for each pair of words below. Include details that give clues to the meaning of the terms in each pair.

1. Loyalist, Patriot
2. Continental Congress, Declaration of Independence
3. militia, American Revolution
4. Battle of Saratoga, Battle of Yorktown
5. surrender, retreat

THINKING ABOUT FACTS

1. What did the Iroquois Confederacy do in the French and Indian War?
2. What did some people at the Albany Congress want the colonies to do?

3. Why did the British plan to build forts on Lake George and Lake Champlain during the French and Indian War?
4. Why did the British pass the Stamp Act?
5. How were Patriots different from Loyalists?
6. What battle started the American Revolution?
7. What happened when New Yorkers heard the Declaration of Independence?
8. Why was New York an important battleground in the American Revolution?
9. Why is there a statue of Sybil Ludington in Carmel, New York?
10. Why was the victory at Saratoga important?

THINK AND WRITE ◄▤▶

WRITING A PARAGRAPH

Write a paragraph that explains the British plan to capture the New York colony.

WRITING A POSTER

Write and illustrate a poster protesting the Stamp Act.

WRITING AN ESSAY

Write an essay that explains why you are a Patriot or a Loyalist.

APPLYING STUDY SKILLS

READING TIME LINES

1. How many years does the time line on the opposite page cover?
2. When did Thomas Jefferson write the Declaration of Independence?
3. How many years before the American Revolution started did the French and Indian War begin?
4. Which came first, the Stamp Act or the British capture of Quebec?
5. How are time lines useful for studying history?

Summing Up the Chapter

Use the vertical organization chart below to order information in the chapter. When you have filled in the blank spaces, use the chart to write a paragraph that answers the question "How did New York change in the 1700s?"

	THE FRENCH AND INDIAN WAR	THE REVOLUTIONARY WAR
Who was involved?		
Important battles		
Outcome		

UNIT 2 REVIEW

THINKING ABOUT VOCABULARY

Number a sheet of paper from 1 to 5. Next to each number write the letter of the definition that best matches the word.

1. prehistory
   a. the time before people lived in North America
   b. the time before people left written records
   c. the time before people left artifacts

2. confederacy
   a. separate groups of people
   b. a group of people ruled by one person
   c. a group of people who join together to help each other

3. ally
   a. a friend with whom one is united for a common purpose
   b. an enemy
   c. a person who refuses to help anyone

4. colony
   a. a settlement ruled by another country
   b. an independent country
   c. a settlement that rules itself

5. culture
   a. the way of life of a people
   b. what people say about themselves
   c. what people say about others

THINK AND WRITE

WRITING A DESCRIPTION
Write a paragraph that describes an artifact shown in Chapter 3. Tell what material it is made from and how the item may have been used.

WRITING AN INTERVIEW
Write an interview with a farmer or merchant who lived in British New York.

WRITING A NEWSPAPER ARTICLE
Suppose you are a newspaper reporter in New York during the American Revolution. Write a news report about one of the events. You might choose Sybil Ludington's ride, the Declaration of Independence, or the Battle of Saratoga.

BUILDING SKILLS

1. **Cause and effect** Name one cause and one effect of the Declaration of Independence.

2. **Cause and effect** Name one cause and one effect of Henry Hudson exploring what is now New York.

3. **Latitude and longitude** Look at the map on page 89. What New York cities lie along the 74°W meridian?

4. **Time lines** Draw a time line that begins with your birth year and ends with this year. Place three events on the time line.

5. **Time lines** How do time lines help you understand history?

YESTERDAY, TODAY &
TOMORROW

In this unit you read about the people scientists think came from Asia to North America thousands of years ago. You also read about European explorers like Henry Hudson and Samuel de Champlain. Today, people still explore the land and the oceans. What new places do you think people will explore in the future?

READING ON YOUR OWN

These are some of the books you could find at the library to help you learn more.

GEORGE WASHINGTON'S SOCKS
by Elvira Woodruff

Follow the adventures of 10-year-old Matt as he travels back in time to the American Revolution.

THE IROQUOIS
by Virginia Driving Hawk Sneve

Read about the history, beliefs, and daily life for the Iroquois of the past and present.

THE NEW YORK COLONY
by Dennis B. Fradin

This book tells what the New York Colony was like and how it became the eleventh state.

UNIT PROJECT

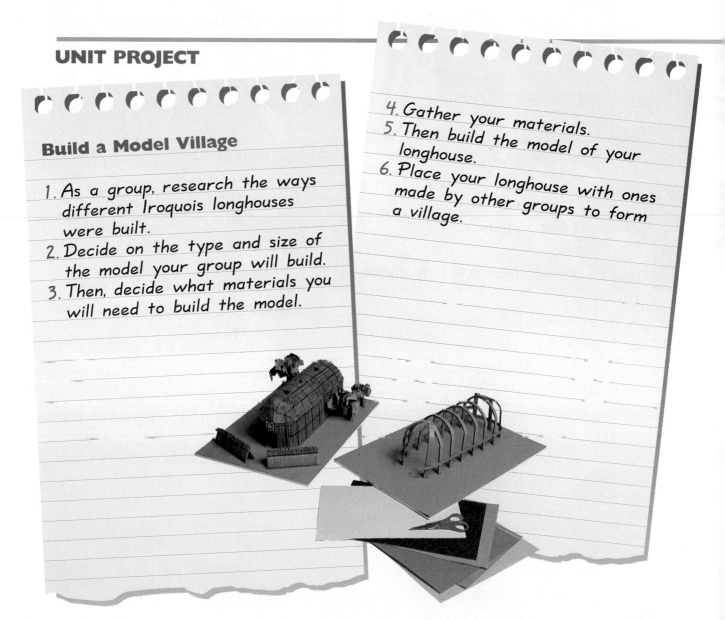

Build a Model Village

1. As a group, research the ways different Iroquois longhouses were built.
2. Decide on the type and size of the model your group will build.
3. Then, decide what materials you will need to build the model.
4. Gather your materials.
5. Then build the model of your longhouse.
6. Place your longhouse with ones made by other groups to form a village.

ASHER B. DURAND'S
PAINTING OF THE
HUDSON VALLEY (LEFT)
JOHN JAY (RIGHT)

Metropolitan Museum of Art

The Granger Collection, N.Y.

SUSAN B. ANTHONY
(LEFT)
NEW YORK
INFANTRY OFFICERS
IN THE CIVIL WAR
(ABOVE)
THE ERIE CANAL
(RIGHT)

Sophia Smith Collection, Smith College

Griffith Bailey Coale On the Erie Canal, Canajoharie Library and Art Gallery, Canajoharie, N.Y.

The Young State

"Let the shouts of triumph be heard."

from the Rochester newspaper *The Telegraph*
See page 170.

Detail from *The Entrance to the Highlands*, by Currier & Ives 1864.
The Harry Peters Collection, Museum of the City of New York

WHY DOES IT MATTER?

After the American Revolution the United States became its own country. New York and the other 12 colonies became states. The young state of New York had many different challenges to meet. One challenge was the need to improve transportation. Another challenge was the growth of cities and businesses. A third challenge was the issue of women's rights and the abolition of slavery.

New forms of transportation and expanding industry changed the face of much of New York from rugged forests to farms and cities. It was an exciting time to live in New York!

FREDERICK DOUGLASS (LEFT) BOATS ON THE HUDSON RIVER (ABOVE)

The Granger Collection, N.Y.

137

Adventures
with
NATIONAL GEOGRAPHIC

Waterway to the West

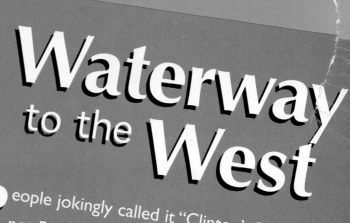

People jokingly called it "Clinton's Ditch." No, not President Bill Clinton. In 1817 it was New York Governor De Witt Clinton who had a plan to build a 363-mile-long canal linking the Great Lakes to the Hudson River. The Erie Canal proved to be very profitable. Mules pulled barges laden with passengers and freight. Elaborate locks raised barges over rough terrain. Grain from farms went east, people and goods went west, and towns grew up along the canal.

Today, motorized barges still ferry freight along the Erie Canal, and a mule or two still shows tourists how work was done in the 1800s. But much of the great waterway is quiet today, a haven for walkers and runners, bikers and bird-watchers.

GEO JOURNAL

Imagine yourself to be a traveler on the Erie Canal in the 1800s. In your Geo Journal, describe your trip from Buffalo to Albany.

139

CHAPTER 6

From Colony to State

THINKING ABOUT HISTORY AND GEOGRAPHY

Chapter 6 begins as New York becomes a state. Soon New York became part of a new country—the United States. The story continues with the opening of banks and other businesses, making New York City one of the leading cities of the new country. Follow these events on the time line and the map. You will learn more about them as you read Chapter 6.

1777
KINGSTON
New Yorkers write a state constitution

1789
NEW YORK CITY
George Washington becomes the first President of the United States

1792
NEW YORK CITY
A stock exchange is started on Wall Street

CANADA

NEW YORK

Albany

Kingston

New York City

UNITED
STATES

ATLANTIC
OCEAN

1797

ALBANY

**Albany becomes the new
state capital**

The Granger Collection, N.Y.

1770   1776   1797 1800   1810

A NEW STATE, A NEW NATION

READ ALOUD

As you read in Chapter 5, Americans broke their ties with the British government in 1776. John Jay said, "The first thing . . . to be done is to [build] good and well ordered governments in all the colonies."

THE BIG PICTURE

Once the 13 colonies had declared their independence on July 4, 1776, they no longer thought of themselves as colonies. Each one was now its own state. The states had certain rights and had to make decisions about them. For example, each state had to decide what kind of government it would have. In order to do this a state might hold a convention, or formal meeting held for a special purpose. The states also decided to unite and become one nation (NAY shun), or country. This country is the United States of America. This meant the states had to choose what kind of government the new nation would have.

Some of the decisions were very difficult. Each state wanted to be independent, almost like its own country. However, the states wanted to join together to defend themselves if another country attacked. It took years before the states solved the problem of how much power the states and the national government should have.

Focus Activity

READ TO LEARN
Why was writing a state constitution an important step for New Yorkers?

VOCABULARY
convention
representative
capital
constitution
ratify

PEOPLE
John Jay
George Clinton
Alexander Hamilton
George Washington
Martha Washington

PLACE
Kingston
Albany

142

SETTING UP THE STATE GOVERNMENT

A group of 106 representatives from different parts of New York met in 1776. A representative is someone chosen to speak or vote for others. The group was called the Convention of Representatives of the State of New York. Their goal was to set up the new state government.

The convention met during the American Revolution. The representatives had to meet in hiding. If they were captured by the British, they would have lost their lives. The British government did not want any of the colonies to have its own government.

The convention first met in New York City. To keep from being captured, the representatives moved from place to place. Soon they moved to White Plains, then to Fishkill, and then to Kingston. Each of these places became the capital of New York. A capital is the place where the government meets.

Writing the New York Constitution

The first thing the convention set out to do was to write a constitution (kahn sti TOO shun). A constitution is a plan of government. It explains how a government is set up. It also outlines the most important laws.

The convention chose a committee of 14 members to write the constitution. John Jay was one of the committee members. Jay was a lawyer. He had worked hard to make sure the Declaration of Independence was passed. It was his idea to make the Declaration of Independence part of New York's constitution. It was important, he believed, to show that New York was free from Great Britain's rule.

On April 20, 1777, the New York Constitution was signed in Kingston. It became the law of New York State.

Both the outside (left) and the inside (right) of New York's capital at Kingston have been restored to look like they did when the New York Constitution was signed.

THE YOUNG STATE

Now that New York had a constitution, its people had to choose the members of the new government. In June 1777, voters chose George Clinton to be the governor of New York. Clinton was a lawyer and a general in the Continental Army. Philip Schuyler, a state representative, said Clinton is "virtuous [honest] and loves his country, has abilities and is brave." New Yorkers elected Clinton governor again and again, for the next 18 years.

Representatives

Every year, voters from each New York county elected men to represent them in the state government. These representatives would make the laws for New York. Some representatives were farmers. Others were bakers, lawyers, silversmiths, barrel makers, and merchants.

Many representatives were American soldiers fighting against the British. Do you remember reading about Sybil Ludington in the last chapter? In 1779, her father was elected a representative.

In 1797 New Yorkers moved the capital from Kingston to Albany. Since then the governor and the state representatives have met in that city. One reason they moved the capital was Albany's location. Look at the map on page G6 and you can see why. Albany was easy to get to from the new farms in Western New York and from downstate.

Collection of The New-York Historical Society

This 1814 painting by Ezra Ames shows Governor George Clinton.

Forming a National Government

In 1776, New York and the other 12 states joined together to be a country, the United States of America. No state wanted to give up much of its power, however. This made the new country's government weak. For example, it had no power to collect taxes. It could only ask the states for money. The states never gave enough, so the new government could not pay all its bills.

Alexander Hamilton

After the American Revolution ended in 1783, the country's weak government caused many problems. As a result, many Americans began to believe that the United States needed a stronger government. One of them was a young lawyer from New York named Alexander Hamilton.

In May 1787, Hamilton and other representatives met in Philadelphia, Pennsylvania. They began to hammer out the Constitution.

It was hot in Philadelphia that summer. Even so, the representatives met in a room with the door closed and the windows shut tight. That way, no one else could hear what they were discussing. They could talk about their ideas without worrying about what other people would say. The chart shows some freedoms they discussed.

They had so many things to decide in setting up a new government. What might you have decided if you had to vote on who should head the new government?

Excerpt from
Shh! We're Writing the Constitution,
written by Jean Fritz in 1987.

Should there be just one person? If so, would he seem like a king? Why not three people, each representing a different part of the country? But what if they fought among themselves? What if they couldn't reach an agreement? Should the executive be paid a salary? . . . But who should pay the salary—the states or the government of the United States? How should the executive be chosen? By the people? By the states? By a branch of the United States legislature?

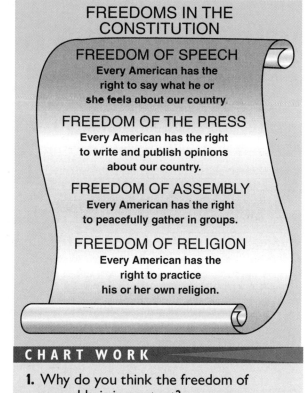

FREEDOMS IN THE CONSTITUTION

FREEDOM OF SPEECH
Every American has the right to say what he or she feels about our country.

FREEDOM OF THE PRESS
Every American has the right to write and publish opinions about our country.

FREEDOM OF ASSEMBLY
Every American has the right to peacefully gather in groups.

FREEDOM OF RELIGION
Every American has the right to practice his or her own religion.

CHART WORK

1. Why do you think the freedom of assembly is important?
2. Which freedom would have been important to John Peter Zenger?

The Constitution Becomes Law

On September 17, 1787, the representatives in Philadelphia signed the Constitution. However, before the Constitution could become our country's law, it had to be approved, or **ratified**, by at least 9 of the 13 states. New Hampshire was the ninth state to ratify the Constitution on June 21, 1788. The Constitution became law for the United States.

New Yorkers were still divided over whether or not to approve. If they did not, they would not be part of the new country. On July 26, 1788, New York voted for ratification. The vote was close—30 for and 27 against. New York became the eleventh state in the United States.

145

Infographic

New Yorkers and the United States Constitution

Three New York representatives went to the meeting in Philadelphia in May 1787. They were Alexander Hamilton, John Lansing, and Robert Yates. Hamilton wanted to ratify the Constitution. The other two did not, and they went home in July. Alexander Hamilton was the only New Yorker to sign the United States Constitution.

The representatives at Philadelphia used this pen (above) to sign the Constitution. As each representative signed, Hamilton (left) wrote the name of the person's state next to the signature.

This painting by Howard Chandler Christy (above) shows George Washington as head of the meeting for the Constitution. John Lansing (left) was against the Constitution and left the meeting early. New Yorker Gouverneur Morris (right), representing Pennsylvania, helped to finish writing the Constitution.

Charles Peale Polk painted George Washington (left), and John Trumbull painted Martha Washington (right).

THE FIRST PRESIDENT

In 1789, George Washington was elected the first President of the United States. At that time, New York City was the nation's capital.

On April 30, people lined the streets of New York City and cheered as Washington went by. In Federal Hall on Wall Street, Washington repeated the oath of office—the words that made him President. "[I] will to the best of my ability, preserve, protect and defend the Constitution," he said.

The First "First Lady"

After Washington became President, First Lady Martha Washington joined her husband in New York. *First Lady* is the term used to describe the President's wife.

Martha Washington hosted gatherings at their house at 39 Broadway. Government leaders came there to talk about important problems. In 1790 the government moved the country's capital from New York City to Philadelphia. As the Washingtons left New York, people crowded around to say goodbye.

WHY IT MATTERS

When New York became a state in 1776, New Yorkers wrote a constitution and elected a governor. The 13 states also formed the United States. Later, Americans wrote the United States Constitution and elected a President.

✓✓ Reviewing Facts and Ideas

SUM IT UP

- New York formed its own state government in 1777.
- The 13 states joined together to become the United States of America.
- Representatives from each state met in Philadelphia in 1787 and wrote the United States Constitution.
- George Washington was the first President of the United States.

THINK ABOUT IT

1. Who was George Clinton?
2. Why did George and Martha Washington live in New York?
3. **FOCUS** Why was writing a state constitution an important step for New Yorkers?
4. **THINKING SKILL** *Predict* what might have happened if the states had not ratified the United States Constitution.
5. **GEOGRAPHY** Why did Albany's location make it a better choice for the state capital than New York City?

147

THINKING SKILLS

Identifying Fact and Opinion

VOCABULARY
fact
opinion

WHY THE SKILL MATTERS

You have just read about how the governments of New York and the United States were formed. Suppose somebody told you that the United States Constitution was written in 1789. This statement is a **fact**. You can make sure it is true by checking the information in a book. A fact is a statement that can be proven true.

Suppose, however, somebody told you that she thinks Alexander Hamilton would have been a good governor. This statement cannot be proven, and so it is not a fact. It is an **opinion**. An opinion expresses one person's belief or feeling. One person might believe that George Clinton was a good governor. Another person might say George Clinton was a bad governor.

Facts and opinions are very different kinds of statements. It is important to be able to tell them apart because decisions we make should be based on facts. Use the Helping Yourself box to guide you in identifying these two kinds of statements.

The Granger Collection, N.Y.

Was George Clinton (above) a good governor? Is your answer a fact or an opinion?

USING THE SKILL

Read this passage from a magazine article. Then identify which statements are facts and which are opinions.

Every 20 years the New York government has a chance to rewrite the constitution. The one we have today was written in 1894. This is the best constitution for New Yorkers so far. I think it will be very exciting when a new constitution is written.

Which statements in the article are facts? Which are opinions? The first two sentences are facts. They could be proven true. You could check the information in a book.

Sometimes you can tell opinions by the use of such word clues as *I think, I believe, the best,* or *should.* Some of these word clues appear in the last two sentences. These sentences could not be proven true. However, opinions do not always have word clues.

TRYING THE SKILL

You have practiced identifying facts and opinions in a passage about the New York Constitution. Now read this passage about the United States Constitution. When you are done, figure out which statements are facts and which express the author's opinions.

The United States Constitution can be changed by adding new laws called amendments. Three fourths of the states must ratify an amendment for it to be added to the Constitution. The first ten amendments are called the Bill of Rights. People should know what each amendment means. I believe the Bill of Rights contains the most important amendments to the Constitution.

Which of these statements do you think could be proven true? How? Which statements do you think are opinions? What did you do to identify the facts and the opinions?

REVIEWING THE SKILL

1. In what ways is a fact different from an opinion?

2. Why does a word clue like *the best* often tell you that the speaker is expressing an opinion?

3. How would the library help you to decide if certain statements were facts or opinions?

4. Why is it useful to be able to tell a fact from an opinion?

5. Write down a statement that provides both a fact and an opinion.

The Granger Collection, N.Y.

The Federalist Papers were opinions written to persuade people to vote for the United States Constitution.

149

BUSINESS ON WALL STREET

Focus Activity

READ TO LEARN
How did New York business and trade grow after the American Revolution?

VOCABULARY
trade
entrepreneur
free enterprise
bank
stock
Buttonwood Agreement
New York Stock Exchange

PEOPLE
Alexander Hamilton
Elkanah Watson

PLACES
Wall Street

READ ALOUD

On May 11, 1785, a ship called the Empress of China *sailed into New York Harbor. It was the first American ship to sail almost 27,000 miles to China and back. It carried a cargo of tea, silk, cinnamon, and dishes.*

THE BIG PICTURE

The *Empress of China* opened trade between the United States and Asia. Trade is the buying and selling of goods. By 1790, twenty-eight American ships had set sail for China. They traded a cargo of furs and ginseng (JIN sing), an herb highly valued in China, for the goods from Asia.

Traders and shopkeepers in New York City made money by selling goods from Asia. Most of the traders and the shopkeepers were entrepreneurs (ahn tru pru NURZ). An entrepreneur is someone who starts and runs his or her own business.

People who started sawmills and potteries were entrepreneurs. So were shipbuilders, and barrel-makers. These people worked in a free enterprise system. "Enterprise" is another word for "business." In a free enterprise system, people make their own decisions about running their businesses.

New York City in the 1780s was bustling with entrepreneurs. Wall Street, near the southern tip of Manhattan Island, became the center for business.

This early view of Wall Street shows the New York city hall in the distance.

WALL STREET

What did Wall Street look like then? On one end were the docks of the East River. Here ships such as the *Empress of China* landed. The west end of the street led to docks on the Hudson River. Wall Street was lined with shops, coffee houses, elegant homes, and offices.

Business and government leaders met daily at coffee houses. Coffee houses were places where people met to talk and do business. One of the most popular was the Merchant's Coffee House.

Suppose you could go back in time and listen to people talking at the Merchant's Coffee House. What do you think they might be saying? Someone asks about a safe place to keep money. Someone else is trying to borrow money to start a new company.

"I've just shipped some tea to a shopkeeper in Albany," a trader says. "Now I have to wait two weeks before the shopkeeper sends me his payment. But I need the money now to buy tea from a ship that's just arrived!"

A **bank** could help solve these problems. A bank is a business that helps people save and borrow money. It also makes paying bills easier.

With the help of a bank, a shopkeeper could place an order and include a note promising to pay the trader. The trader could take the note to a bank. The banker will pay the trader. Then the bank will collect the money from the shopkeeper and keep a little for itself.

DID YOU KNOW?

How did Wall Street get its name?

In the early 1600s, Dutch settlers built a wall of mud and sticks along a path at the edge of New Amsterdam. The wall was to keep unwelcome visitors out and to keep animals such as cattle from wandering away. Although the wall was torn down soon after it was built, the name Wall Street has remained to this day. Thousands of New Yorkers go to work on Wall Street every day.

151

A BUSINESS CENTER

A notice in a New York City newspaper announced a meeting at the Merchant's Coffee House on February 24, 1784. The notice called on "gentlemen in this city, to establish a bank." Some of the state's most important traders and lawyers, including Alexander Hamilton, were at the meeting.

Under Hamilton's leadership, these New Yorkers decided to start a bank. They each took some of their own money and put it together. This gave the bank a large amount of money to work with.

The Bank of New York opened its doors on June 9, 1784. Traders of goods such as tea and sugar used the bank to handle their money. Even the United States government used it. In 1789, the government borrowed $200,000 from the bank to help pay the country's debts. In 1797, the Bank of New York built its headquarters at 48 Wall Street. The bank is still there.

Albany's First Bank

The success of the Bank of New York interested people in other cities. In 1802, Elkanah Watson dreamed one night of setting up a bank in Albany. "I started from my bed, lighted a candle, and committed [wrote down] the project to paper," he later explained. In September 1803, the New York State Bank opened its doors in Albany. Its first loan was a "sum of four thousand dollars for the use of the Great Western Turnpike Company." The road this company built would later become U.S. Route 20.

Stocks on Wall Street

In 1791, the Bank of New York wanted to raise more money. It did this by putting stocks for the bank up for sale. Stocks are shares of ownership in a business.

The money that buyers paid for stock allowed the bank to give more and larger loans. The bank divided the money it made among all the people who owned stock. These people are called stockholders.

The painting (above) shows the signing of the Buttonwood Agreement. The clock (right) is from the Bank of New York.

HOW STOCKS WORK

1 A company sells stock.

2 Money from stock is used to make products or offer services.

3 People buy products or use services.

4 The company uses money from sales to pay workers. Profit, or money left over, is returned to stockholders.

The stocks of many businesses were bought and sold on Wall Street everyday. Soon there were people called brokers whose job was buying and selling stocks. On May 17, 1792, twenty-four brokers met under the shade of a buttonwood tree on Wall Street. There they discussed rules for buying and selling stocks. The agreement they signed became known as the Buttonwood Agreement.

By the next year, brokers were buying and selling stock in an upstairs room of the Tontine Coffee House. Because the brokers carried out business seated in chairs, the right to buy and sell stocks at the meeting became known as a "seat."

These developments were the beginning of the New York Stock Exchange. The Exchange is still located on Wall Street. Each day

thousands of stocks are bought by and sold to people all over the world. Dozens of newspapers print the results of the day's trading at the New York Stock Exchange. The eyes of the world are on Wall Street.

WHY IT MATTERS

With the help of Alexander Hamilton, New York State built a good banking system. This helped make New York a leader in business and trade. Banks and stock trading are still two of New York City's most important kinds of businesses.

✓ Reviewing Facts and Ideas

SUM IT UP

- In the 1780s, people met on Wall Street to do business.
- Banks helped New York trade, start businesses, and build roads.
- Selling stock lets businesses raise money to grow.

THINK ABOUT IT

1. What are two things that a bank does?

2. What was the Buttonwood Agreement?

3. **FOCUS** How did New York business and trade grow after the American Revolution?

4. **THINKING SKILL** What was the *effect* of the *Empress of China*'s return on business in New York?

5. **GEOGRAPHY** How did the location of Wall Street make it a business center in New York?

LOCAL CONNECTIONS

BUFFALO:
LEARNING FROM LIBRARIES

Many libraries use computers to store information. Computers are a great way to do research.

"How old is our city?" Roseann asked Mrs. Hess, her fourth-grade teacher in Buffalo.

"How do you think we can we find the answer to Roseann's question?" Mrs. Hess asked the class.

"We could look in books," said Emanuel. "Maybe we could go to the library and find the information we need."

"That's the best place to go. We'll need to do some research!" said Mrs. Hess.

"After we find out, maybe we could have a birthday party for Buffalo," said Sanjay.

"That will give us a terrific goal," said Mrs. Hess.

When the students visited the library, Mr. Coyner, the librarian, was there to greet them. He took them on a tour of the library.

On their first stop, he showed them how to use the computer and the card catalog to find books about Buffalo's history. Then Mr. Coyner took them to the area where microfilm was kept. Microfilm is a long, thin strip of tiny photographs. He let the students use

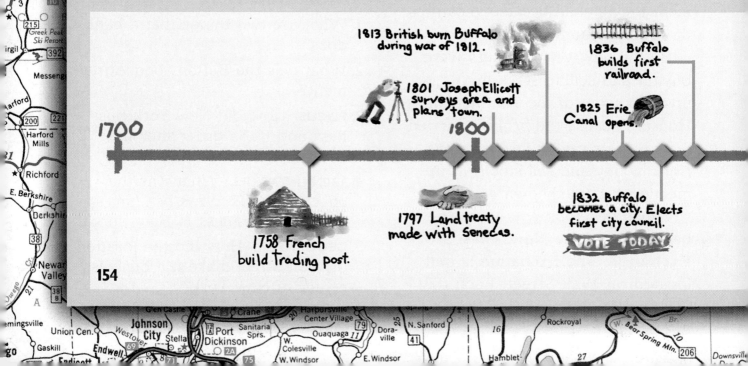

1700

1758 French build trading post.

1797 Land treaty made with Senecas.

1801 Joseph Ellicott surveys area and plans town.

1800

1813 British burn Buffalo during war of 1812.

1825 Erie Canal opens.

1832 Buffalo becomes a city. Elects first city council. VOTE TODAY

1836 Buffalo builds first railroad.

154

a special machine to look at some of the microfilm. It showed the *Buffalo Evening News* from 1882. That was the year that Buffalo celebrated its 50th birthday. The students also looked for articles about Buffalo's Centennial, or 100th birthday.

After they looked at the microfilm, Mr. Coyner told the students that the library keeps information about the city's history in special files. "Some of these files also have old photographs," he added.

During their tour, Mr. Coyner encouraged the students to ask the librarians for help, if they couldn't find what they were looking for. "We're always glad to help you find information," he said.

After their tour, the students stayed in the library and found more information about Buffalo's history. Then they shared their information with each other.

Everyone worked together to plan the birthday party. Emanuel's group made a time line of important events in Buffalo's past. Allison's group wrote speeches about the town's history. Kwami's group made posters and invitations for the celebration. The students were excited when the day came for them to present their celebration for other students in their school.

MAKE Your LOCAL CONNECTION

When is your town's birthday? Do people in your community celebrate this date? Research the history of your community. Then hold a celebration of your own.

Buffalo and Erie County Historical Society

BUFFALO CENTENNIAL

JULY 1-10 1932

❚ This magazine cover (right) tells
❚ us that Buffalo was 100 years
❚ old in 1932. Students displayed a
❚ time line of Buffalo's history
❚ (bottom) to share with others.

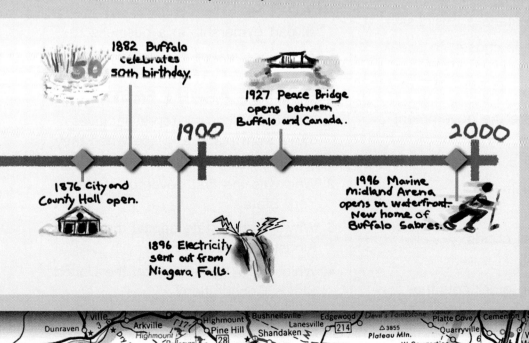

1882 Buffalo celebrates 50th birthday.

1927 Peace Bridge opens between Buffalo and Canada.

1900

2000

1876 City and County Hall open.

1996 Marine Midland Arena opens on waterfront. New home of Buffalo Sabres.

1896 Electricity sent out from Niagara Falls.

155

CHAPTER 6 REVIEW

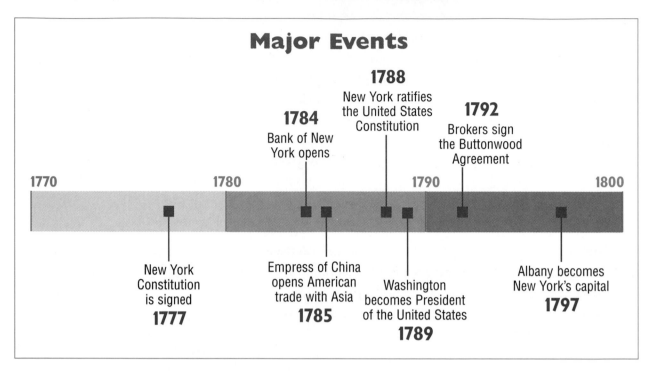

Major Events

1788
New York ratifies the United States Constitution

1784
Bank of New York opens

1792
Brokers sign the Buttonwood Agreement

1770   1780   1790   1800

New York Constitution is signed
1777

Empress of China opens American trade with Asia
1785

Washington becomes President of the United States
1789

Albany becomes New York's capital
1797

THINKING ABOUT VOCABULARY

Number a sheet of paper from 1 to 5. Next to each number write the letter of the definition that best matches the word or phrase.

1. representative

   a. a person who buys stocks

   b. a person who starts a business

   c. someone who is chosen to speak or vote for others

2. capital

   a. the place where the government meets

   b. a meeting hall

   c. a kind of agreement

3. trade

   a. to buy and sell goods

   b. to start a bank

   c. to sail ships to other countries

4. entrepreneur

   a. a person who works for someone else

   b. a person who manages a factory

   c. a person who starts and runs his or her own business

5. stock

   a. a kind of bank

   b. part ownership in a business

   c. a place where brokers meet

THINKING ABOUT FACTS

1. Why did New York representatives move from place to place when they were writing their constitution?

2. Who was the first governor of New York State?

3. Why was the state capital moved from Kingston to Albany?

4. Which New Yorker signed the United States Constitution?

5. Why did the new United States government have trouble paying its bills?

6. What goods did the *Empress of China* bring to New York?

7. Name three kinds of entrepreneurs in New York in the 1780s.

8. Where did New Yorkers meet to talk and do business?

9. What is a stock? Where do people buy and sell stock?

10. Who helped form the Bank of New York?

THINK AND WRITE

WRITING AN ARTICLE

Suppose you were a reporter in New York City the day that George Washington became President. Write an article that describes what you saw.

WRITING A MOVIE SCRIPT

Write a movie script of a conversation between the captain of the *Empress of China* and a group of traders at the Merchant's Coffee House.

WRITING A LETTER

Write a letter to Alexander Hamilton at the meeting in Philadelphia to write the United States Constitution. Describe to him what kind of leader you think the new country should have.

APPLYING STUDY SKILLS

IDENTIFYING FACT AND OPINION

1. What is the difference between a fact and an opinion? Identify items 2, 3, and 4 below as either fact or opinion. Explain your answer.

2. "George Washington was the best President of the United States."

3. "Alexander Hamilton helped start the Bank of New York."

4. "The Buttonwood Agreement set rules for buying and selling stocks."

5. Why is it important to know the difference between a fact and an opinion?

Summing Up the Chapter

Use the spider map below to organize information from the chapter. Copy the chart on a sheet of paper. Under each topic write at least two or more names, words, or phrases from the chapter that are related to that topic. When you have completed the chart, use it to write a paragraph that answers the question "How did New York government or business change when New York became a state?"

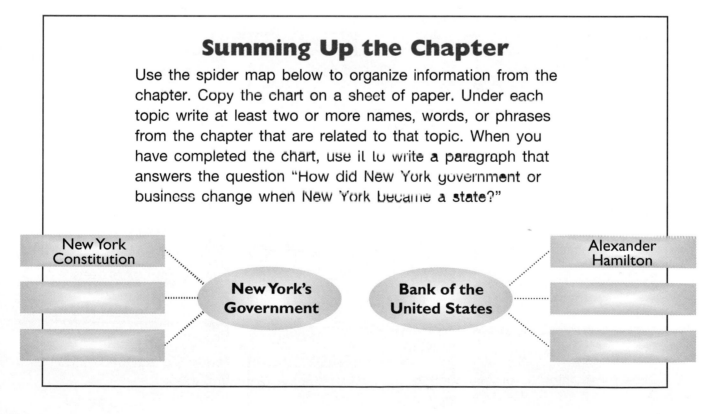

New York Constitution

New York's Government

Bank of the United States

Alexander Hamilton

CHAPTER 7

Early Years of Statehood

THINKING ABOUT HISTORY AND GEOGRAPHY

At the end of the American Revolution, more people came to New York from Europe and from the other states. Many of them started to move west. The United States soon fought another war with Great Britain. An American victory opened the door for New York to grow. Follow the time line below to trace some of the other major events of this period.

1797
GENESEE RIVER VALLEY

Mary Jemison and her family settle along the Genessee River

1807
HUDSON RIVER

Robert Fulton's steamboat travels up the Hudson River to Albany

1814
LAKE CHAMPLAIN

The American navy defeats the British at the Battle of Plattsburgh

CANADA

Lake Champlain

Rochester

Genesee
River Valley

NEW YORK

Hudson River

New York Harbor

UNITED
STATES

ATLANTIC
OCEAN

1825

**NEW YORK
HARBOR**

**The Erie Canal opens
with the "Wedding of
the Waters"**

1827

ROCHESTER

**Gristmills in "The Flour
City" grind more than
200,000 barrels of flour
a year**

1750   1788   1814   1850   1900   1950

Detail from *Schenectady Harbor, 1814*, painting by L.F. Tantillo, Nassau, N.Y. 1992

THE WESTERN FRONTIER

Focus Activity

READ TO LEARN
Why did people want to settle in Western New York?

VOCABULARY
frontier
Big Tree Treaty
War of 1812
Treaty of Ghent

PEOPLE
Red Jacket
Mary Jemison
Joseph Ellicott
Nathaniel Rochester

PLACES
Utica
Geneseo
Buffalo
Rochester

READ ALOUD

Eliphalet Stark wrote to his brother in 1797 about the place where he lived in what is today Herkimer County. He was proud of how the settlement had grown. "We've got sawmills and gristmills, . . . a chair factory, tailoring establishments, and stores as well stocked as any down the Mohawk [River]." People were living in well-built homes made with boards, nails, and glass. He also explained that "Log cabin country is now out . . . in the Genesee Valley."

THE BIG PICTURE

The Genesee River Valley had been the New York frontier since 1788. A frontier is the edge of a settled area. After the American Revolution, New York owned large areas of land in the northern and western parts of the state. The state wanted to sell the land. As settlers came to the Genesee River, the frontier moved farther west.

The Iroquois Confederacy was angry that all these settlers were moving into this region. But there was no way to stop them. The Confederacy was not as strong as it had once been. Little by little, piece by piece, the Iroquois were forced to sell their land to these newcomers.

THE GENESEE COUNTRY

How did New York sell its land to people? It broke the land into sections of 100 square miles each and sold them to land companies. The companies then sold smaller sections to settlers. By 1791, New York State had sold over 7,800 square miles of land. The land companies built roads and mills to attract settlers.

In 1788, Oliver Phelps and Nathaniel Gorham bought over 3,100 square miles of western land from the Senecas. They wanted to sell parts of this land to new settlers.

The settlers traveled west by following the Mohawk River Valley between the Adirondack Mountains and the Helderberg Hills. Some headed north or south from Utica, but most continued straight west to the Genesee River. Settlers called this land the Genesee Country. Here was some of the best farmland in New York. By 1800, about 15,000 people had settled in the Genesee Country.

Most of the new settlers were from New England. They wanted to own land and be farmers. In the words of New York historian David M. Ellis, New Englanders came "into the Hudson Valley, sweeping up the Mohawk gateway, and spreading out across the fertile lands of central and western New York."

In 1794, a trail used by Native Americans became the Genesee Road. This road ran from Utica to the Genesee River. After 1800, the Genesee Road ran all the way to Lake Erie.

The Granger Collection, N.Y.

After the American Revolution, settlers moved west using old Native American trails.

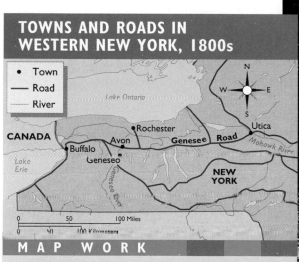

TOWNS AND ROADS IN WESTERN NEW YORK, 1800s

Legend:
- Town
- Road
- River

Lake Ontario
CANADA
Rochester
Avon
Buffalo
Geneseo
Genesee Road
Utica
Mohawk River
Lake Erie
Genesee River
NEW YORK

0   50   100 Miles
0   50   100 Kilometers

MAP WORK

Western New York had very few roads in the 1800s.

1. What towns did the Genesee Road connect?
2. What town shown is not connected by a road?

THE BIG TREE TREATY

The Holland Land Company wanted to buy most of the land west of the Genesee River, as far as Lake Erie. The Senecas owned this land. In 1797, company representatives met with Seneca leaders at the village of Big Tree, now known as Geneseo (je nuh SEE oh).

A Seneca leader named Red Jacket did not want to sell the land. He believed that even if the Senecas kept small areas of land where they could live, that would not be enough. Red Jacket said, "If this should be the case, we could not say we were a free people."

However, the Seneca leaders eventually agreed to sign the Big Tree Treaty. This gave nearly all their land—more than 4,600 square miles—to the company for $100,000.

Red Jacket (above) did not want to sell Seneca land. A statue of Mary Jemison (right) can be found in Letchworth State Park.

Detail from Portrait of Sa-go-ye-wat-ha or Red Jacket by Robert Weir, Collection of The New-York Historical Society

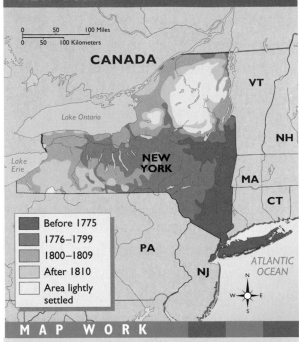

THE SPREAD OF SETTLEMENT IN NEW YORK

Before 1775
1776–1799
1800–1809
After 1810
Area lightly settled

MAP WORK

After the American Revolution, New York settlement spread north and west.

1. What large area was lightly settled in 1810?
2. What 3 areas were settled before 1775?
3. What lake had settlement reached by 1799?

Mary Jemison

Another person who was at the Big Tree Treaty was Mary Jemison. Jemison had been captured by Native American men when she was fourteen, during the French and Indian War. She was adopted by a Seneca family, and grew up as a Seneca.

During the American Revolution, Jemison's Seneca village was destroyed. She and her five children escaped. In the forest they met two African American men who had escaped slavery and lived in a small cabin. She and her family stayed at their cabin through the winter.

This early drawing of Rochester (above) shows Edwin Scrantom's cabin. Nathaniel Rochester (left) mapped out the new town.

The two men left in the spring. The Jemison family stayed on in what was Gardeau Flats. This was a strip of land on the west bank of the Genesee River. Today it is in Letchworth State Park. Jemison built her home, grew crops, and raised cattle.

At the Big Tree meeting, New York gave Jemison the land she had been living on. Jemison lived along the Genesee River until 1831.

Buffalo

Joseph Ellicott, who worked for the Holland Land Company, had also been at the Big Tree meeting. In 1801 he started a settlement near a big creek called Buffalo Creek. He began to plan the city that we now know as Buffalo. Streets were built, and the new town began to take shape. Soon a sawmill, a gristmill, and a post office were built. The first newspaper, the Buffalo *Gazette*, appeared in 1811. By that time more than 400 people lived in town.

Rochester

In 1803, Colonel Nathaniel Rochester and two friends settled along the Genesee River near a series of waterfalls. They built a gristmill, and Colonel Rochester mapped out a new town.

The first family to arrive in the new settlement was the Scrantoms. Edwin, one of the sons, remembered what it was like on the frontier:

It was a wild and deserted place. . . . Not only was it a wilderness, but on both shores of the river, and running back from it a good distance, was a thick jungle in which wild beasts hid and many snakes crawled!

The "wilderness" did not last. As more settlers came, the forests were cut down to make room for the growing village of Rochester. More mills and a post office were built. A bridge was built across the Genesee River that connected roads from Rochester to Buffalo.

163

THE WAR OF 1812

After the American Revolution, Britain went to war with France. The British navy did not have enough sailors in the early 1800s. To get them, British ships stopped American ships and forced many of their sailors to join the British navy. The British also tried to stop our country from trading with France. American traders were losing money.

In June 1812 the United States went to war against Great Britain. This began the War of 1812.

In December 1813, the American army burned several towns in Canada, which was a British colony. The British took revenge. On December 30, 1813, they sent 1,400 soldiers across the Niagara River. The soldiers started toward Buffalo. The people of Buffalo left the town in time. Their settlement, however, was burned to the ground.

American and British ships fought at the Battle of Plattsburgh.

Detail from M'Donough's Victory on Lake Champlain; publisher N. Currier, 1846; The Harry T. Peters Collection, Museum of the City of New York

The Battle of Plattsburgh

In September 1814 the British and the American navies battled on Lake Champlain. When the smoke cleared, the British ships had been destroyed and the Americans had won. This battle convinced the British to sign the Treaty of Ghent. This agreement ended the War of 1812.

WHY IT MATTERS

As our country grew, New York's frontier offered a place for new settlers to buy land, start farms, and build towns. The settlers who came started towns that later became important cities.

✓ Reviewing Facts and Ideas

SUM IT UP

- Land companies bought land on the New York frontier. They then helped start settlements.
- Seneca and other Iroquois had to sell most of their land.
- The Americans and British fought each other in the War of 1812.

THINK ABOUT IT

1. What was the Big Tree Treaty?
2. Where was the New York frontier in 1788?
3. **FOCUS** Why did people want to settle in Western New York?
4. **THINKING SKILL** What *effect* did the Big Tree Treaty have on the Senecas' land?
5. **GEOGRAPHY** Look at the map on page 162. In what time period were the Finger Lakes settled by new settlers?

CITIZENSHIP
MAKING A DIFFERENCE

Sharing Iroquois Ways

BUFFALO, NEW YORK—Joyce Pembleton takes pride in her Native American heritage. She belongs to the Cayuga Indian group and grew up on the Six Nations Indian Reservation in Canada. "Six Nations" is another name for the groups that make up the Iroquois Confederacy. A reservation is land set aside by a government for Native Americans to live on. "As a child," says Joyce Pembleton, "I learned Iroquois stories . . . from the elders, . . . especially my grandfather and great uncle. My brothers played games like lacrosse and snow snake."

Mrs. Pembleton shares her interest in her Iroquois heritage by serving as a special resource teacher at the Native American Magnet School in Buffalo. She began her work there 16 years ago as a volunteer. Mrs. Pembleton and other resource teachers help all the students learn about the Iroquois.

At least half the students at the school belong to one of the Iroquois groups. For these students, the school program provides a link to life on the reservations. Native American students can learn to speak Mohawk or Seneca.

They also learn about celebrations that are being held at the longhouses.

"We call ourselves the Haudenosaunee, or the People of the Longhouse," explains Dr. Lloyd Elm, an Onondaga and principal of the school. "Every reservation has a . . . longhouse where we hold religious ceremonies, dances, marriages, funerals, and council meetings."

Mrs. Pembleton explains, "[In the classroom,] we talk about the history of our people, our dances, games, and medicines. We try to get students to be curious so they will go back to the longhouse and learn some of the ceremonies. Some talk to their parents or grandparents for the first time about what nation and clan they belong to."

"Every group should know what [its] background is. When students see what hardships their people have faced and how they overcame these hardships, it makes them proud."

"We try to get students to be curious . . . "

Joyce Pemblet

165

1750   1807   1842   1900   1950

STEAMBOATS, CANALS, AND RAILROADS

Focus Activity

READ TO LEARN
How did new forms of transportation change New York?

VOCABULARY
canal
lock
toll

PEOPLE
Robert Fulton
De Witt Clinton

PLACES
Erie Canal
Lockport

READ ALOUD

"Fulton's folly" is what some people called Robert Fulton's steamboat. A folly is something foolish. How could a boat move without oars or sails? People thought the steamboat would sink or even explode! On an August morning in 1807, Fulton's steamboat began its first trip up the Hudson. The boat started and then stopped. Then Fulton fixed the problem. The boat moved on. Fulton had built the first successful steamboat.

THE BIG PICTURE

Settlers moving west used horses, mules, or oxen to pull carts filled with their goods. The trip was not easy, and the trails were bumpy and muddy. It was both expensive and difficult for farmers to transport their crops from Western New York to New York City. As New York grew larger, people needed better transportation.

People traveled by boat when they could. However, boats could be very slow. When sailboats traveled up the Hudson River against the current, or flow of water, they needed a strong wind to move quickly. If *someone* could build a ship with an engine, people would not have to depend on a good wind or fight the current.

FULTON'S STEAMBOAT

Robert Fulton was born in 1765 in a small Pennsylvania town. From the time he was a child, Fulton was always curious about how things worked.

Fulton Has Big Plans

When Fulton was 21, he went to Europe to study painting. He tried to earn a living as a painter, but failed. Fulton became interested in how steam engines worked. He returned to America with big plans. He would build a boat with a steam engine. He got right to work. "I now have ship-builders, blacksmiths and carpenters," he wrote, building "my steamboat."

The Steamboat Works

Fulton called his ship *The Steamboat.* Years later people began calling the ship the *Clermont,* which is the name it is known by today. "Clermont" was the name of the home of Fulton's business partner,

Robert Fulton's *The Steamboat* was the first successful steam-driven ship. This color picture of the ship was drawn by an unknown artist about 1830.

Robert Livingston. On August 17, 1807, *The Steamboat* began its first trip on the Hudson River. With smoke puffing from the stacks, *The Steamboat* traveled up the Hudson at 4 1/2 miles per hour. That is about the speed of a person jogging. Yet *The Steamboat* was much faster than the other boats on the river. It passed other ships, Fulton said, "as if they had been at anchor."

A boat with an engine was an incredible sight. One onlooker wrote that "the whole country talked of nothing but the sea monster, belching forth fire and smoke." On the other hand, a passenger said that the boat is "the most pleasant boat I ever went in."

A few years later, steamboats traveled regularly on the Hudson. By 1811, steamboats were also sailing up and down the Mississippi River.

THE ERIE CANAL

Building better boats was one way to make transportation easier. Another way was to change the waterways. **De Witt Clinton** was the mayor of New York City. He wanted the state to build a **canal** that would link the Hudson River with Lake Erie. A canal is a waterway built across land by people. Such a canal would allow boats to travel from New York City all the way to the Great Lakes.

"Clinton's Ditch"

It is a long way from Lake Erie to the Hudson River—about 360 miles. Look at the map below to see the distance the canal would cover. Some people thought it would be impossible to build a canal that long. After all, the land had to be cleared of thousands of huge trees and flattened. Then a channel wide and deep enough for a boat to travel would have to be dug. It would cost at least $7 million to dig the canal. Many people made fun of the idea. They began calling it "Clinton's Ditch."

This did not stop Clinton. He worked hard to convince people that the canal was important to the state. He said that the canal would help businesses and cities grow. The canal, he said, would be "more stupendous, more magnificent, and more beneficial [helpful] than [anything] achieved by the human race [people]."

Building the Canal

On July 1, 1817, De Witt Clinton became the governor of New York. Just three days later, work started on the new canal in Rome, on the Mohawk River. From the beginning, digging the **Erie Canal** was tough. Many problems had to be solved.

This lamp was used to help boats travel on the Erie Canal at night.

Erie Canal Museum, Syracuse, N.Y.

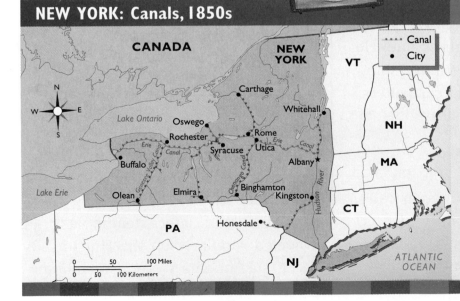

NEW YORK: Canals, 1850s

- - - - Canal
● City

CANADA

NEW YORK

VT

NH

MA

CT

Carthage

Whitehall

Lake Ontario

Oswego

Rochester

Rome

Syracuse

Utica

Albany ★

Buffalo

Lake Erie

Elmira

Binghamton

Olean

Kingston

Honesdale

PA

Hudson River

ATLANTIC OCEAN

NJ

0   50   100 Miles
0   50   100 Kilometers

MAP WORK

In the 1850s, many canals helped the Erie Canal link different parts of New York.

1. What canal connects Utica to Binghamton?
2. What two towns start and end the Erie Canal?
3. What canals would you use to go from Olean to Rome?

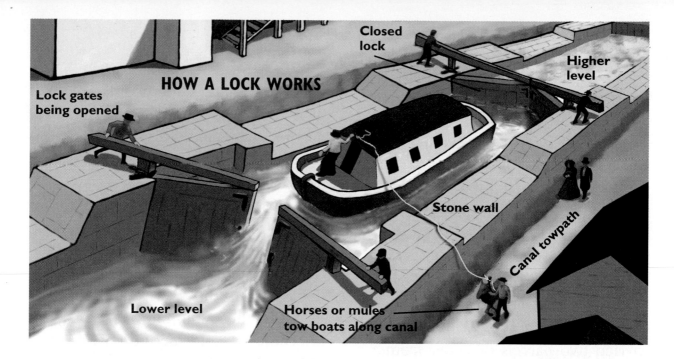

Tree stumps were one problem. At first, workers could only remove about four large trees a day, because the stumps were so hard to take out. To solve this problem, workers invented a giant stump-puller machine. Workers could now remove about 40 trees a day.

Have you ever seen a wheelbarrow? People often use them to carry rocks or dirt. Wheelbarrows were another item invented by people who dug the Erie Canal. First, workers hauled dirt in carts. They would empty the carts using shovels. However, work would go faster if the dirt could be dumped all at once. The wheelbarrow was built to do just that.

Canal Locks

Another problem canal workers faced was the difference in elevation. The land along Lake Erie is 565 feet higher than the land along the Hudson River. The canal, however, had to be level. To solve this problem, the workers built canal locks. A canal lock is a kind of water elevator that moves boats to higher or lower levels. Look at the diagram on this page to see how a canal lock works. In all, workers built 83 locks.

When Jessie Rittenhouse was a little girl, she lived near two locks in the Genessee River Valley. She remembered how much fun it was to take a ride on a boat through the locks.

We could see the boat coming before it gained the lower lock and by taking to our heels [by running] could reach the spot before the gates swung open and the foamy water rushed in. Standing eagerly upon the edge, we would watch the boat rise higher and higher until it reached our level, the signal for us to jump on for our ride to the lock above.

Workers on the Erie Canal invented the wheelbarrow to help them move dirt.

Anthony Mario, Margo Studio/Erie Canal Village

"THE WORK IS FINISHED!"

The Erie Canal was finally finished in the fall of 1825. Now it was time to celebrate. A newspaper in Rochester, *The Telegraph*, wrote, "The work is finished! . . . Let the shouts of triumph be heard from Erie to the Atlantic, and from the Atlantic . . . back to Erie."

A boat named the *Seneca Chief* left Buffalo on October 26, 1825. Governor Clinton was aboard. The boat carried two barrels of water from Lake Erie. People in towns along the way cheered as the boat passed by.

The *Seneca Chief* reached New York Harbor on November 4. Clinton poured the water from Lake Erie into the Atlantic Ocean to represent the new link between the East and the West. This was called the "Wedding of the Waters."

What do you think happened next? The boat returned to Buffalo. At Lake Erie, water from the ocean was poured into the lake.

A Great Success

The Erie Canal was a huge success. In just the first year, 13,000 boats traveled the canal. More than 40,000 settlers traveled west on the canal in that year.

Before the canal, shipping goods over land between Buffalo and New York City took 20 days and cost $100 a ton. The Erie Canal brought the price down to $10 a ton and cut travel time to 8 days.

With the Erie Canal, trade boomed. Eastern merchants sold their iron and trade goods to settlers in the West. Settlers in the West shipped products such as wheat and lumber to cities in the East. New York City quickly became the country's most important port and city.

To pay for the canal, boats traveling on it paid tolls. A toll is a small fee. People who were against the canal in the beginning were now for it. The tolls paid for the cost of building it in just 11 years.

Canal boats were not powered by steam or sail. They were pulled by mules or oxen that walked along a path at the side of the canal.

Bridges along the canal were very low. People could not stand on the boat when it went under a bridge. A worker would warn passengers by yelling, "Low bridge, everybody down." That way, no one would get knocked over.

Many people worked on canal boats. One of the songs they sang is shown on the next page.

Collection of The New-York Historical Society

National Portrait Gallery, Smithsonian Institution/Art Resource, N.Y.

DeWitt Clinton used this barrel to pour Lake Erie water into the Atlantic Ocean.

The Erie Canal

With a steady beat

I've got a mule,_ her name is Sal, Fif-teen miles_ on the E-rie Ca-nal._ She's a

good old work - er and a good old pal. Fif-teen miles_ on the E-rie Ca-nal._ We've

hauled some barg - es in our day, Filled with lum - ber, coal, and hay. And

we know ev-'ry inch of the way. From Al-ban-y_ to_ Buf - fa-lo._

Oh, low bridge, ev-'ry-bod-y down! Low bridge, for we're

com - ing to a town! And you'll al - ways know your neigh-bor, you'll

al-ways know your pal, If you've ev-er nav-i-gat-ed on the E - rie Ca-nal.

THE GROWTH OF TOWNS

All of the goods shipped on the Erie Canal helped towns and cities grow. People poured into New York City to find jobs. Even though 3,000 new houses were built in the city, that was not enough.

In 1825, when the Erie Canal was opened, Buffalo's population was about 2,400. By 1831, Buffalo had more than 10,000 people. In just a short time, Buffalo became the biggest port for grain in the world. In 1841, 1 million barrels of wheat were shipped through Buffalo. So were 67,000 barrels of pork and 300,000 pounds of wool.

The First Boomtown

Rochester is called the first "boomtown" in the country. A boomtown is a town that grows very fast in a short period of time. Rochester's population in 1815 was 331. In 1827, two years after the Erie Canal opened, its population ballooned to almost 8,000.

The increase in population meant there was an increase in building. Warehouses, gristmills, and sawmills sprang up in Rochester. Sawmills in Rochester were so busy they cut enough wood into boards in a year to reach all the way to Mexico!

Utica also grew very quickly. In 1820, Utica was a town of about 3,000 people. Utica was both wealthy and beautiful. In 1835 Ramon de la Sagra, a visitor from Cuba, traveled on the Erie Canal through Utica. This is what he saw:

> We [took] a walk along the . . . streets, which are wider than those in Philadelphia. . . . The houses [are] painted in different clear and quiet colors [with] space for a small garden at one side. . . . The general cleanliness [is] a lovely sight.

By 1850, Utica had become a bustling city of 17,500.

Before the canal was started, there was no town of Lockport. The town started when the canal workers began to build locks there for the new canal. The drop in the canal was so steep at Lockport that there were five locks in a row! Many workers were hired to build the locks. By 1825, more than 1,500 people lived in Lockport.

Detail from *The First Railroad Train* by E.L. Henry. Collection of the Albany Institute of History and Art. Gift of Friends of the Institute

THE FIRST TRAIN

Travel on the Erie Canal was slow between Albany and Schenectady. There were 27 locks in only 24 miles! On August 9, 1831, a steam train began running between Albany and Schenectady to move people faster. The train's engine was called the *De Witt Clinton*. It was named for Governor De Witt Clinton, who built the canal. The train was small compared to today's trains. The *De Witt Clinton* was less than 12 feet long, and it had no brakes.

People realized that trains would be able to carry people and products long distances. They kept on improving trains and building more tracks. By 1842, you could go from Buffalo to Boston by railroad. Eventually, the railroad would take over the work of the canals.

New York's first railroad train, the *De Witt Clinton* (below), is shown in this 1892 painting by E. L. Henry. Lockport (left) had five canal locks in a row.

WHY IT MATTERS

In the early 1800s, three new forms of transportation—the steamboat, canals, and the railroad—helped to increase trade in New York. They also lowered the cost of transportation and convinced many people to move to Western New York. In the next lesson you will read about some other ways in which our state grew in its early years.

✓ Reviewing Facts and Ideas

SUM IT UP

- Robert Fulton built the first successful ship with a steam engine.
- The Erie Canal linked the Great Lakes with the Atlantic Ocean.
- The Erie Canal helped towns and businesses in New York grow.
- The country's first steam passenger train started operation in New York in 1831.

THINK ABOUT IT

1. Why did Robert Fulton want to build a steamboat?

2. Who was De Witt Clinton?

3. **FOCUS** How did new forms of transportation change New York?

4. **THINKING SKILL** Place the following events in the correct *sequence*: the day the Erie Canal opened, the first trip of the *De Witt Clinton*, the first steamboat trip up the Hudson.

5. **WRITE** Suppose you are taking a trip on a steamboat or a canal boat in 1825. Write a letter to your family describing your trip.

The ERIE CANAL

Would you like to take a trip on the Erie Canal? You don't have to go back 175 years in time to do it. The Erie Canal is still in use today. It is part of the New York State Canal System. This system includes smaller canals that link the Erie Canal to Lake Champlain, Lake Ontario, and the Finger Lakes.

The Erie Canal has changed quite a bit from the time it was first built. It has been widened from 40 feet at the top to 75 feet. It is deeper than it was, too. It used to be only 4 feet deep, and now it is 12 feet deep.

Today canal boats usually have motors. The biggest change, though, is how people use the canal. Old towpaths have been made into bicycle paths and parks. People now use the Erie Canal more for having fun than for transporting goods. The Erie Canal is a legacy for everyone to enjoy.

One of the most famous parts of the old Erie Canal is the "Old Flight of Five"—a series of locks built into a rock wall, or cliff, in the town of Lockport.

Erie Canal Museum, Syracuse, N.Y.

Biking on the Canalway Trail is a favorite activity for many New Yorkers. The Canalway Trail runs 524 miles along the entire New York State Canal System.

174

From May to November you can travel the canal by tourboat. The rest of the year the canal is closed because it freezes over.

The canal is a good place to fish. Many different kinds of fish like bass, walleye, and pike are found there.

This painting of early canal days is found in the Canajoharie Library and Art Gallery in Canajoharie. It shows horses pulling a canal boat.

A. Wadsworth Thompson, *Life on the Towpath*, Canajoharie Library and Art Gallery, Canajoharie, N.Y.

STUDYSKILLS

Reading Circle and Line Graphs

VOCABULARY
graph
circle graph
line graph

WHY THE SKILL MATTERS

In Lesson 2, you read many facts about the Erie Canal. Some facts told you what was shipped on the canal. Others told you how much was shipped.

It is hard to remember a lot of different numbers. A graph can help you. Graphs are special diagrams that show information in a clear way. By presenting facts in a picture, they tell you a lot with only a handful of words.

USING CIRCLE GRAPHS

Look at the graph on this page. It is a circle graph. This kind of graph can show you how the parts of something make up the whole. Because each part may look like a slice of pie, a circle graph is also called a pie graph.

Read the title of the graph. The circle shows the types of food products shipped on the Erie Canal. Each "slice" of the graph shows how much of a certain type of food was shipped. You can tell that more flour was shipped than any other

food because this is the largest "slice" of the graph.

USING A LINE GRAPH

Unlike a circle graph, a line graph shows you how a piece of information changes with time.

Look at the line graph on page 177. Start by reading the title. The title tells you that this is a graph of the weight of all the goods shipped on the Erie Canal from 1835 to 1915.

Read the labels at the left side of the graph. These give the weight—the number of tons—of goods carried on the Erie Canal. One ton equals 2,000 pounds, about the weight of a small car. Then read the dates at the bottom. They tell you the years covered by this graph.

Trace the line with your finger. Each dot on the line stands for the number of tons shipped during that year. You can

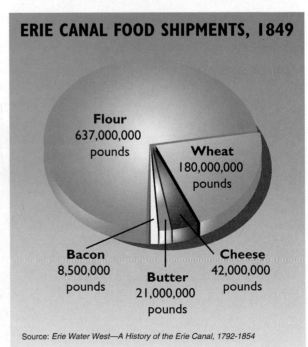

ERIE CANAL FOOD SHIPMENTS, 1849

Flour
637,000,000
pounds

Wheat
180,000,000
pounds

Bacon
8,500,000
pounds

Butter
21,000,000
pounds

Cheese
42,000,000
pounds

Source: *Erie Water West—A History of the Erie Canal, 1792-1854*

see on the graph that the year when the fewest tons were shipped was 1835.

TRYING THE SKILL

Now study the circle graph of the foods shipped on the Erie Canal. Which was shipped in the smallest amount? Use the Helping Yourself box for hints.

Now look at the line graph of tons of goods shipped on the Erie Canal. In what year were the most tons shipped? About how many tons of goods were shipped during that year?

REVIEWING THE SKILL

Use the line graph below to answer the following questions.

1. In what years was there a drop in tons of goods moved on the Erie Canal?
2. Between what years did the number of tons shipped rise most sharply?
3. Which kind of graph would show the change in temperature during the year in New York? Why?
4. How do graphs make it easier for you to understand certain kinds of information?

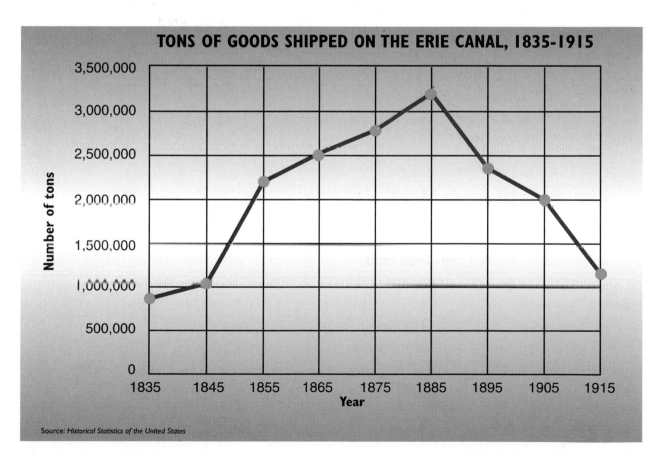

TONS OF GOODS SHIPPED ON THE ERIE CANAL, 1835-1915

Source: *Historical Statistics of the United States*

1750　1800 **1820**　**1857**　1900　1950

ENERGY AND GROWTH

READ ALOUD

"The town had sprung up like a mushroom," said American writer Nathaniel Hawthorne. *He was visiting Rochester in 1832. "The whole street . . . was crowded with pedestrians, horsemen, stage-coaches, . . . light wagons, and heavy ox-teams, all hurrying, trotting, rattling, and rumbling, in a throng [crowd] that passed continually. . . ."*

THE BIG PICTURE

In Lesson 2 you learned how the Erie Canal helped towns such as Rochester grow. Within 30 years, Rochester had become a bustling city. Its flour mills earned Rochester the nickname "The Flour City." In 1827 gristmills in Rochester ground over 200,000 barrels of flour.

Rochester was not alone in growing so quickly. All over the state, the energy and hard work of New Yorkers built up businesses. Artists and writers described New York in their work. People found ways to make city life easier and better. New Yorkers in the early 1800s had great hopes for the future.

NEW YORK INDUSTRIES

You have read how the Erie Canal made goods much easier to transport. For instance, salt made in Syracuse could be carried to other cities on boats. And the wood or coal used to make the salt could be carried to Syracuse. Salt has many uses besides making food taste good. It was used to keep meat and vegetables from spoiling. It was very useful before there were refrigerators. Once the canal was built, Syracuse became the center of New York's salt industry. An industry is all the businesses that make one kind of product or service.

The Glovers of Gloversville

Another industry in early New York was making leather. Leather is made from animal skins that have been treated by tanning. Tanning is a way of scraping and soaking the skins in a mixture of water and tree bark. Shoes, gloves, and many other things were made of leather.

If you wore a pair of gloves in the 1850s, they might have been made in New York. In 1021, factories in Fulton County made 24,000 pairs of gloves. One town was even named after gloves—Gloversville! Fulton County became, and still is, the leather capital of New York.

The Industrial Revolution

By the 1850s, a revolution, or sudden, major change, was well underway. This change was the Industrial Revolution. During the Industrial Revolution, power-driven machines replaced hand tools. Using machines, workers could make goods faster and in greater numbers.

The sewing machine was one product of the Industrial Revolution. Several inventors built sewing machines. The most popular one was built in 1851 by a New Yorker named Isaac Singer. It made sewing clothing much easier and faster. Soon, many factories were using Singer's machine to make clothes. A factory is a place where goods are made in large numbers. Making clothing became one of New York City's main industries—which it still is today.

Fine leather gloves were made by stretching tanned animal skins in factories like this one.

NEW YORK WRITERS AND ARTISTS

Business was not the only thing that changed in the early 1800s. Some New Yorkers directed their energy and hard work toward creating works of art. Many of them chose to write about or to paint the places where they lived or liked to go.

American Books

"Who reads an American book?" That was what many people in Europe said in the early 1800s. They thought that no one in the United States could write good books. The New Yorkers James Fenimore Cooper and Washington Irving would change their minds.

James Fenimore Cooper grew up in Cooperstown, which was founded by his father, William Cooper, in 1790. His first successful book was *The Spy*, which took place in Westchester County during the American Revolution. Cooper's best known books are action-filled stories about life on the New York frontier.

Washington Irving grew up in New York City. When he was young, he loved to read stories and wander outdoors. In a notebook he wrote down what he saw.

Irving visited a small village called Sleepy Hollow in Westchester County.

Collection of the New-York Historical Society

Washington Irving (above) wrote about life in old New York.

In 1820, he completed a book of short stories about life in Sleepy Hollow when it was part of the Dutch Colony. It was called *The Sketch Book*. One of these stories was "Rip Van Winkle." Another was "The Legend of Sleepy Hollow." Have you ever read or heard of this story? It tells about a schoolteacher named Ichabod Crane and a headless horseman.

People in Europe as well as the United States read Irving's books. One reason Irving became so well liked is that he described the people in his stories in colorful detail. Read his description of Ichabod Crane. What image do you have of the schoolteacher from Sleepy Hollow?

MANY VOICES LITERATURE

Excerpt from "The Legend of Sleepy Hollow," written by Washington Irving in 1820.

*He was tall, but **exceedingly lank**, with narrow shoulders, long arms and legs, hands that dangled a mile out of his sleeves, feet that might have served for shovels, and his whole frame most loosely hung together. His head was small, and flat at top, with huge ears, large green glassy eyes.*

exceedingly lank: very skinny

Gift of Martha C. Karolik for the M. and M. Karolik Collection of American Paintings, 1815–1865, Courtesy of the Museum of Fine Arts, Boston

Thomas Cole's painting, *Sunday Morning on the Hudson River,* shows the Hudson in the distance.

The Hudson River School

In the 1820s, several painters turned their attention to New York. Some painted landscapes, or views of the outdoors. One of them was Thomas Cole. Cole loved to hike along the Hudson River. He drew sketches and took notes as he hiked. This is how Cole described a sunrise in the Catskill Mountains:

> *The mists were resting on the vale [valley] of the Hudson like drifted snow. . . . The sun rose from bars of pearly hue: above there were clouds light and warm, and the clear sky was of a cool grayish tint.*

How would descriptions such as this have helped Cole while he painted?

Other artists such as Asher Durand and Frederic Edwin Church noticed Cole's paintings. They, too, celebrated the beauty of our country in their paintings. You can still visit Church's house, Olana, by the river near the town of Hudson. Soon a whole group of artists became known as the Hudson River School. Many of their landscapes showed the Hudson River. They were part of the same "school" because they painted in a similar style. The Hudson River School made New York an important center for art.

Links to ART

Draw Your Own Masterpiece

Do you have a favorite place to go that is outdoors? It could be a park, playground, or your backyard. Carefully observe the trees, buildings, and streets that you see. Get a pad of paper and draw the scene you like the best. Be sure to add details like leaves, street signs, and clouds in your drawing. Now fill in your drawing with crayons, markers, or watercolor paint.

BETTER LIFE IN NEW YORK CITY

After the American Revolution, many immigrants came to the United States. Immigrants are people who come to a new country to live. Most were from Great Britain or Germany. This changed in the 1840s.

In 1845, a plant disease destroyed the potato crop in the country of Ireland. Ireland was then ruled by Great Britain. Many Irish could not afford to buy other kinds of foods that were grown there. That food was grown mostly to sell to the British. The Irish asked the British government for help. However, the British did nothing. More than a million Irish people died. Many people call this terrible event the potato famine, or shortage of food. The Irish call it the Great Hunger.

To escape the famine, many Irish people left Ireland. Between 1846 and 1851, more than 500,000 Irish immigrants arrived in New York City. Many settled in our state and helped build roads, canals, railroads, and businesses.

Water! Water!

With many immigrants coming to New York City, the city grew very fast. It soon became overcrowded and dirty. Water from wells became unsafe for drinking. Sometimes people got very sick from the water.

City leaders had to find a new water supply. They chose the Croton River, about 40 miles north in Westchester County. In 1837, workers started to build the Croton Aqueduct (A kwuh dukt). An aqueduct is a pipe or canal that carries water. First, a dam, or wall, was built across the Croton River to create a lake. Next, workers built a long underground

HOW AN AQUEDUCT WORKS

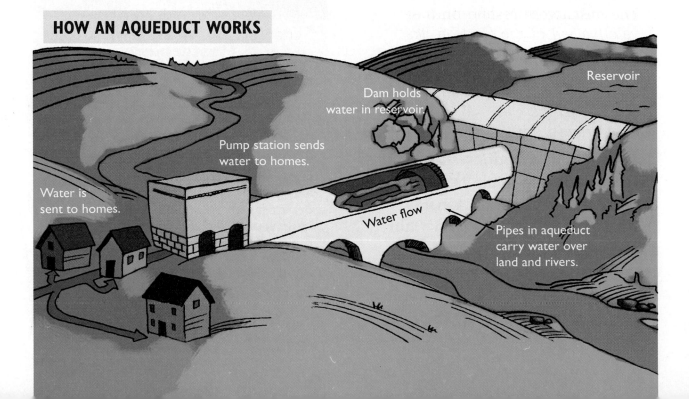

Reservoir

Dam holds water in reservoir.

Pump station sends water to homes.

Water is sent to homes.

Water flow

Pipes in aqueduct carry water over land and rivers.

Today many New Yorkers still have fun in Central Park.

pipeline to bring the water into New York City. Someone wrote that the aqueduct was like a "covered canal" made of "solid stone and brick." Look at the diagram on page 182 to see how an aqueduct works.

Central Park

Overcrowding caused other problems in New York City. Buildings and streets were very close together. In 1851, the city selected a large piece of rocky, swampy land in the middle of Manhattan for a park. Recent immigrants and African Americans who had settled there were forced to move.

The building of Central Park started in 1857. By 1860, over 2 million people ice-skated, walked the paths, or had picnics there. The park was not even open yet! Finally, in 1876 Central Park officially opened.

Today, Central Park has 22 playgrounds, a zoo, and an ice skating rink. You can play checkers, watch a play, or sail model boats. There is fun for everyone!

WHY IT MATTERS

In the 1800s, New York industries grew, and factories were built. People in New York turned their attention to making life better. Writers wrote about New York, and artists painted pictures showing how beautiful New York was. The government built aqueducts and parks. New York was becoming an important center of business and of the arts.

✓ Reviewing Facts and Ideas

SUM IT UP

- Clothing, salt, and leather were important industries in New York.

- Washington Irving, James Fenimore Cooper, and the Hudson River School artists made New York an important art center.

- The building of the Croton Aqueduct and Central Park made life better in New York City.

THINK ABOUT IT

1. What was the Hudson River School?

2. How did the Industrial Revolution change New York industry?

3. **FOCUS** How did life for New Yorkers change in the mid-1800s?

4. **THINKING SKILL** Suppose Central Park had never been built. _Predict_ what would be there instead.

5. **WRITE** Suppose you kept a notebook like Washington Irving did. Write a short description of where you live.

LOCAL CONNECTIONS
SLEEPY HOLLOW:
LEARNING FROM STORIES AND SONGS

The Legend of Sleepy Hollow is a story about Ichabod Crane and life in an early New York village.

The Granger Collection, N.Y.

The students in Mr. Hawn's fourth-grade class in Sleepy Hollow look forward to story time. This is a time when Mr. Hawn reads stories to the class. During story time, the students may also share folklore, stories they know that have been passed down from person to person. Sometimes they even sing songs. The folklore, stories, and songs have one thing in common. They are about the community or region where the students live.

One of the students' favorite stories is *The Legend of Sleepy Hollow*. It tells about local customs and legends. Mr. Hawn asked the class what they learned about Sleepy Hollow from Washington Irving's story.

"I learned that teachers, like Ichabod Crane, weren't paid much money so they had to live with the families of the students they taught," Wendy said. "I'm not sure I would like that very much," she added.

"I like the part where Ichabod Crane is chased by the headless horseman," said Jason. "When Mr. Hawn reads it, he makes it sound really scary."

"Every year, the historical society celebrates Halloween by having the headless horseman wander around the county," said Maureen. "I saw him once, and he *was* scary."

The students all agreed that reading *The Legend of Sleepy Hollow* was a good way to learn about the customs and beliefs of people who lived in earlier times.

Ann said that she liked to hear Mr. Hawn read *Rip Van Winkle*. "I like the descriptions of the mountains and forests. Whenever I hear thunder, I think it might be Henry Hudson's men playing ninepins in the mountains."

"Once during story time, we also looked at the pictures," Abe said. "Mr. Hawn said they were painted by artists who used to live in our area. I liked the paintings because they remind me of the things I see when I take walks in the mountains with my family. We watch the birds, and look at the trees, and listen to the sounds of the water. Sometimes we stop and rest, just like Rip did."

Janet likes to sing. "My favorite song is 'Catskill Valley.' It tells us about the birds, trees blowing in the wind, and the deer jumping."

"Mr. Hawn says the song is about life in the mountains in the early 1900s. Now that there are more people and bigger roads going through the mountains, life isn't as quiet as it used to be," Janet explained.

The students continued sharing their favorite stories and songs. They did more research. Then they made a book that included their favorite stories and songs about their community. They displayed their book in the library for other students to read.

MAKE **Your** LOCAL CONNECTION

What stories, songs, or folk-lore tell about your community or region? Work with other students to find out. How can you share this information with others?

Our History in Story and Song

This booklet of stories and songs (far left) was made by students. The legend tells us that Rip Van Winkle (left) slept for 20 years in the Catskill Mountains.

185

CHAPTER 7 REVIEW

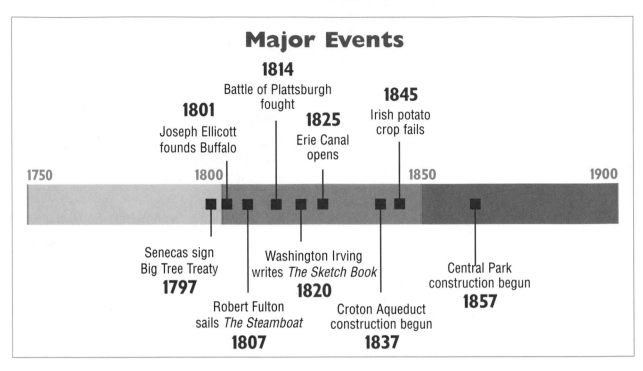

Major Events

1814
Battle of Plattsburgh fought

1801
Joseph Ellicott founds Buffalo

1825
Erie Canal opens

1845
Irish potato crop fails

1750   1800   1850   1900

Senecas sign Big Tree Treaty
1797

Washington Irving writes *The Sketch Book*
1820

Central Park construction begun
1857

Robert Fulton sails *The Steamboat*
1807

Croton Aqueduct construction begun
1837

THINKING ABOUT VOCABULARY

Number a sheet of paper from 1 to 5. Next to each number write the word from the list below that best matches the description.

canal   industry

frontier   landscape

immigrant

1. a waterway built by people
2. all the businesses that make one kind of product
3. person who comes to a new country to live
4. the edge of a settled area
5. a painting showing an outdoor scene

THINKING ABOUT FACTS

1. Name two towns that people started in Western New York after the American Revolution?

2. What British actions helped start the War of 1812?

3. Why did some people call Fulton's steamboat "Fulton's folly"?

4. Why did De Witt Clinton want to build a canal?

5. How did the wheelbarrow help the workers on the canal?

6. What happened to the cost of shipping goods after the Erie Canal was built?

7. How did Issac Singer's sewing machine change the clothing industry?

8. What small village did Washington Irving base some of his stories on?

9. Why did many Irish people immigrate to New York?

10. How did the Croton Aqueduct make life better for people living in New York City?

THINK AND WRITE

WRITING AN INTERVIEW
Suppose you could go back in time to the early 1800s as a newspaper reporter. You are reporting on the plans to build the Erie Canal. Write an interview with De Witt Clinton that tells why he thinks a canal would be good for New York.

WRITING A LETTER
Suppose you live in New York City in the mid-1800s. Write a letter to the mayor explaining why you and your friends need a city park. State what kinds of things you would like to do or see in the park.

WRITING AN EXPLANATION
Write a paragraph that describes the differences in traveling by steamboat, canal, and railroad in the mid-1800s.

APPLYING STUDY SKILLS

1. Describe the difference between a circle graph and a line graph.

2. Look at the circle graph on page 176. What food product was shipped more than any other on the Erie Canal?

3. Look at the line graph on page 177. How many more tons of goods were shipped in 1855 than 1845?

4. What kind of graph would you use to show how many students are in each grade at your school?

5. How do graphs make some information easier to understand?

Summing Up the Chapter

Use the horizontal organization chart below to order information in the chapter. Copy the chart on a sheet of paper. Then write at least three pieces of information under each topic. When you have filled in the outline, use it to write a paragraph that answers the question "How did our state grow in the early 1800s?"

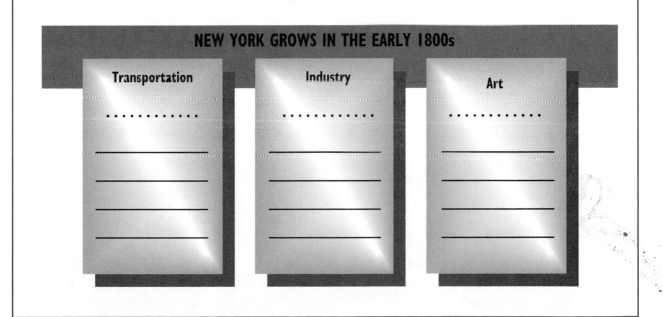

NEW YORK GROWS IN THE EARLY 1800s

Transportation   Industry   Art

CHAPTER 8

In Search of Freedom

THINKING ABOUT HISTORY AND GEOGRAPHY

Chapter 8 begins at a time in our country when women and African Americans struggled to gain their rights as Americans. The story of this struggle continues, telling of a brave journey from slavery in the South to freedom in the North. Finally, the North and the South fight a bloody civil war. Follow these events on the time line below. You will learn much more about them as you read Chapter 8.

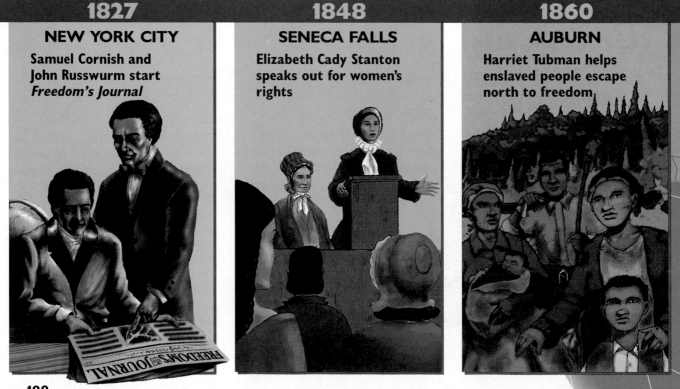

1827
NEW YORK CITY
Samuel Cornish and John Russwurm start *Freedom's Journal*

1848
SENECA FALLS
Elizabeth Cady Stanton speaks out for women's rights

1860
AUBURN
Harriet Tubman helps enslaved people escape north to freedom

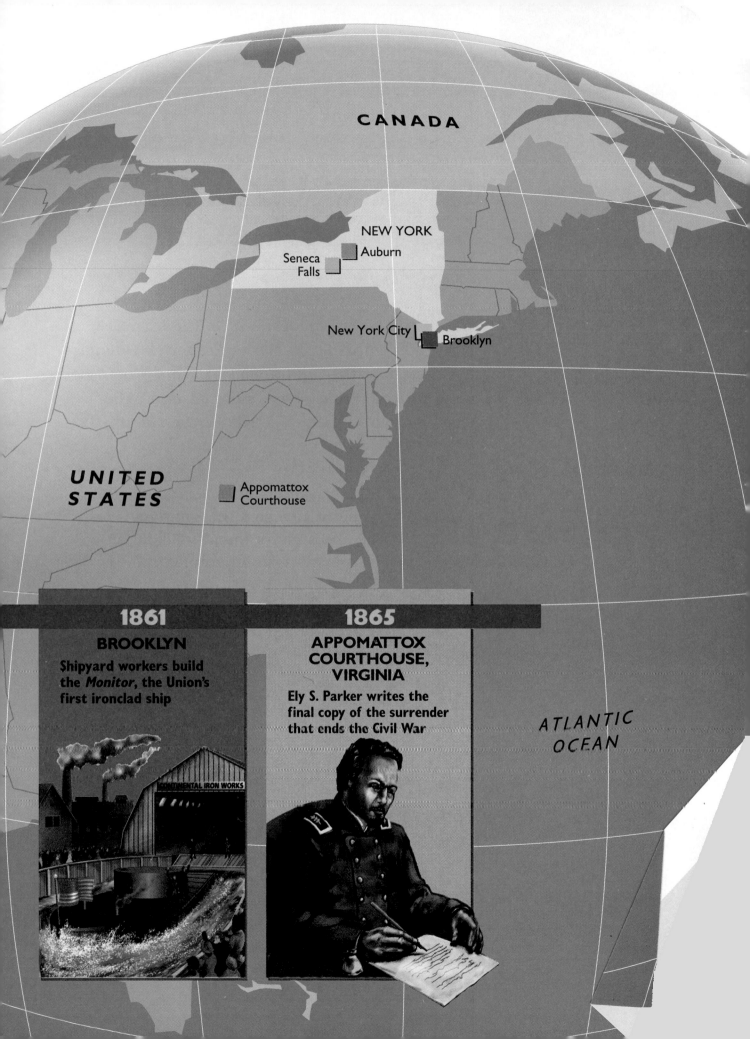

CANADA

NEW YORK

Seneca Falls   Auburn

New York City   Brooklyn

UNITED STATES

Appomattox Courthouse

ATLANTIC OCEAN

1861

BROOKLYN

Shipyard workers build the *Monitor*, the Union's first ironclad ship

1865

APPOMATTOX COURTHOUSE, VIRGINIA

Ely S. Parker writes the final copy of the surrender that ends the Civil War

1800   1825 1827   1869 1875   1900

A CALL FOR CHANGE

READ ALOUD

"I still see before me a life of toil [hard work] and trials [hardships]," wrote Frederick Douglass. He knew that the fight against slavery would be very difficult. "But justice must be done, the truth must be told. . . . I will not be silent."

THE BIG PICTURE

The United States gave many Americans freedom. Yet not everyone was treated the same under the law. In the 1840s, more than 2 million African Americans lived in slavery. As you read in Chapter 4, slavery is the practice of making one person the property of another.

Many New Yorkers in the 1840s and 1850s began to call for reform. Reform means to change things for the better. Frederick Douglass had been born in slavery in Maryland. He escaped and later came to live in Rochester in 1847. He called for an end to slavery.

Women also did not receive fair treatment in the United States. No woman was allowed to vote. Women were not hired for most jobs. They were not allowed to go to most colleges. In the 1840s, women in New York began to demand the same rights and opportunities as men. Reformers in New York worked hard to stop slavery and to gain equal rights for women.

Focus Activity

READ TO LEARN
How did many New Yorkers work for reform in the early 1800s?

VOCABULARY
reform
suffrage
citizen
abolition
Underground Railroad

PEOPLE
Frederick Douglass
Elizabeth Cady Stanton
Susan B. Anthony
William Lloyd Garrison
Samuel Cornish
John Russwurm
Sojourner Truth
Harriet Tubman

PLACES
Seneca Falls

THE STRUGGLE FOR WOMEN'S RIGHTS

Elizabeth Cady Stanton grew up in Johnstown, New York. Later in life, she remembered how hard she worked in school. She hoped "some day to hear my father say: 'Well, a girl is as good as a boy, after all.' But he never said it." This only made Stanton more determined to study. Yet she was not allowed to go to college because she was a girl.

The Convention at Seneca Falls

As an adult, Stanton thought that people should join together to help women get their rights. She helped plan a convention, or meeting, to discuss the rights of all people.

In 1848, the convention started in Seneca Falls, the town where Stanton lived. Over 300 men and women came. Stanton read aloud a statement that borrowed ideas from the Declaration of Independence. Her statement said that "all men and women are created equal."

At the convention, people talked about passing laws that would give women suffrage. Suffrage is the right to vote. They discussed all the rights women should have as United States citizens. A citizen is a person who is born in a country or who has earned the right to become a member of that country by law. One hundred men and women signed a paper that listed these rights.

A Great Team

In 1851 Stanton met Susan B. Anthony in Seneca Falls. Anthony also was working hard for women's rights. They became good friends and worked together as a team for many years. Stanton was a strong public speaker. She made an impression on the people who heard her. Anthony was great at organizing events that got people involved in women's rights. They formed an organization for women's suffrage in 1869. Women finally got the right to vote more than 50 years later, in 1920.

Elizabeth Cady Stanton (top left) and Susan B. Anthony (right) led the fight for women's suffrage. In May 1912, women in New York City (above) marched for the right to vote.

Smithsonian Institution, (74.847)

Smithsonian Institution, (74.847)

THE FIGHT AGAINST SLAVERY

By the 1840s, slavery was splitting the country apart. Most northern states did not allow slavery. The New York State government had passed a law ending slavery in 1827.

The southern states, however, had come to depend on slavery. Cotton was the South's most important crop. Most southerners believed that enslaved people were necessary to work the cotton fields.

In 1833, William Lloyd Garrison formed the American Anti-Slavery Society. This group wanted abolition, an immediate end to slavery.

The J. Paul Getty Museum, Los Angeles, California

This rare photograph shows Frederick Douglass seated to the left of the table at an abolition meeting in Cazenovia.

UNDERGROUND RAILROAD IN NEW YORK

CANADA

NEW YORK

VT

MA

CT

PA

NJ

ATLANTIC OCEAN

Routes

MAP WORK

New York had many Underground Railroad routes.

1. What city would a runaway come from to reach Elmira?

2. What city in Canada is close to Niagara Falls?

African Americans Take a Stand

Free African Americans had built their own communities in northern states. In 1827, African American abolitionists Samuel Cornish and John Russwurm started *Freedom's Journal* in New York City. It was the first African American newspaper. They wrote, "We wish to plead our own cause. Too long have others spoken for us."

Newspapers became an important way for African Americans to speak out against slavery. Frederick Douglass started the *North Star* in Rochester in 1847. Papers also appeared in Troy and Syracuse.

African Americans also made their opinions heard by speaking at abolitionist meetings. One great speaker was Sojourner Truth. She had once been enslaved in New York. Her bold speeches shocked some listeners. Once at a meeting, a man who disagreed with her called out, "I don't care any more for your talk of slavery than for the bite of a flea." Truth answered, "Perhaps not, but the Lord willing, I'll keep you scratching." She was not about to give up.

The Underground Railroad

Harriet Tubman lived in slavery in Dorchester, Maryland. In 1849 Tubman decided to escape from slavery. She later said, "There was one of two things I had a right to, liberty or death; if I could not have one, I would have the other." She packed a few things and sneaked away into the darkness.

Tubman had heard that the Underground Railroad could help her. This was not really a railroad. It was a group of people, white and black, who helped enslaved people escape to freedom. There were "station masters" on the Underground Railroad who hid African Americans and provided them with

food and clothing. Look at the map on page 192 to see some of the routes through New York. Some people followed the Underground Railroad all the way to Canada. Others stayed in New York or other northern states.

Tubman hid in people's houses, barns, or vegetable carts during the day. She walked through woods and swamps at night. After many days, she crossed into Pennsylvania. There slavery was against the law. She was free for the first time in her life. How do you think she felt?

The Granger Collection, N.Y.

Excerpt quoting Harriet Tubman from *Scenes in the Life of Harriet Tubman*, written by Sarah H. Bradford in 1869.

I looked at my hands to see if I was the same person now that I was free. There was such a glory over everything; the sun came like gold through the trees, and over the fields, and I felt like I was in Heaven.

Oberlin College Archives

Harriet Tubman (above) escaped to freedom on the Underground Railroad. Chains (right) were sometimes used to prevent enslaved people from escaping.

The Underground Railroad in New York

One of the major Underground Railroad routes went through the Finger Lakes and Western New York region. The map on this page shows how African Americans could travel all the way to Canada on this route. This is what might have happened to a group of people escaping slavery.

4. Rochester

Frederick Douglass (right) raises money to send them west. Near Niagara Falls they finally cross the bridge to freedom in Ontario, Canada.

The Granger Collection, N.Y.

Lake Ontario

Onondaga Historical Association, Syracuse, N.Y.

3. Auburn/Syracuse

In Auburn they meet Harriet Tubman (below right). She sends them on to Jerome Loguen (above right), stationmaster of Syracuse.

Rochester

Syracuse

2. Etna

Slave catchers are on their trail. They are driven under a wagonload of hay to the Hanford-Todd house. In the kitchen is a secret room (left) where they can hide.

Auburn

Etna

Ithaca

1. Elmira/Ithaca

A group of African Americans escaping from slavery arrive in Elmira. At night they travel to Ithaca and stay at the African Methodist Episcopal Zion Church.

Elmira

New York

Pennsylvania

| 0 | 20 | 40 | 60 Miles |

| 0 | 20 | 40 | 60 | 80 Kilometers |

DARING RESCUES

After Harriet Tubman reached New York, she became a "conductor," or leader, on the Underground Railroad. She made at least 19 dangerous trips back into slave states and led people to freedom. She even rescued her own parents. Slave owners offered a $40,000 reward for her capture. But she was never caught, and she never lost a "passenger."

Tubman made her last trip in 1860. By then about 300 people had followed Tubman to freedom. More than 50,000 African Americans reached freedom on the Underground Railroad.

WHY IT MATTERS

Reformers in New York worked hard to make things better. They acted to secure women's rights and abolish slavery. However, women were still not treated as equals to men, and slavery continued to divide the country.

Links to SCIENCE

Follow That Star

When enslaved people moved north on the Underground Railroad, they usually traveled at night. How did they find their way in the dark? They had no flashlights.

They used the stars. A star called the North Star always points the way north. To find the North Star, they looked for a group of stars called the Big Dipper, or Ursa Major. The two stars on the cup of the Big Dipper point toward the North Star.

The study of stars, planets, and moons is called astronomy. Find the Big Dipper on a star map or in the night sky. Follow the two stars on the cup to find the North Star.

✓ Reviewing Facts and Ideas

SUM IT UP

- Reformers called for more rights for women and for abolition.

- Elizabeth Cady Stanton and Susan B. Anthony were important leaders of the women's rights movement.

- Free African Americans like Frederick Douglass and Sojourner Truth worked to end slavery.

- New York was a major state on the Underground Railroad that helped people escape slavery.

THINK ABOUT IT

1. What did Elizabeth Cady Stanton believe about women's rights?

2. Who was Harriet Tubman?

3. **FOCUS** How did many New Yorkers work for reform in the early 1800s?

4. **THINKING SKILL** What *effect* did the effort to gain abolition have on African Americans in the North?

5. **WRITE** Suppose you are a reporter covering the Seneca Falls Convention. Write a short newspaper story describing the meeting.

NEW YORK IN THE CIVIL WAR

READ TO LEARN
What role did New York play in the Civil War?

VOCABULARY
secede
Confederacy
Union
Civil War
Emancipation
 Proclamation
draft

PEOPLE
Abraham Lincoln
Elizabeth Blackwell
Ulysses S. Grant
Ely S. Parker

READ ALOUD

Caroline Richards of Canandaigua wrote in her diary, "The whole United States has been like one great household for many years." In 1861, the household was dividing in two. People "are taking sides, some for the North, some for the South," she wrote. "There has been a storm in the air for a long time."

THE BIG PICTURE

Caroline Richards remembered the day Abraham Lincoln of Illinois became President in 1860. His election thickened the storm clouds that hung over the country. Lincoln did not support abolition. However, he did not want new states to allow slavery. Southerners worried that Lincoln might try to end slavery in the South as well.

Eleven southern states decided to secede, or withdraw, from the United States in 1861. They formed a new country called the Confederate States of America, or the Confederacy. The states that did not secede were called the Union. You can see on the map on page 197 which states formed the Confederacy and which were part of the Union.

On April 12, 1861, the Confederate army attacked Fort Sumter. This Union fort is in South Carolina. This battle started the Civil War. A civil war is a war fought between people of the same country. The bloodiest conflict in American history would rage on for four terrible years.

THE WAR BEGINS

"The storm has broken upon us," wrote Caroline Richards when she heard the news of Fort Sumter. People eagerly bought newspapers to read about the fighting.

Soldiers Sign Up

President Lincoln was determined to keep the United States together. He called for 75,000 volunteers to join the Union army. Colonel Elmer Ellsworth from Mechanicville formed his own group of volunteers. "Many of the young men are going from Canandaigua and all the neighboring towns. It seems very patriotic and grand," wrote Richards. New Yorkers were the first soldiers to arrive in Washington, D.C.

The Hardships of War

The Union learned quickly that the war would be long and hard. Ellsworth became the first Northern officer to die in the Civil War. The first major battle of the war was at Bull Run, Virginia, on July 21, 1861. It was a serious Union defeat.

Union soldiers also faced long hours of marching and camp duties. They dealt with bad weather, bad food, and not enough clothing and blankets. In 1863, Hermon Clarke wrote to his family near Waterville, "I sleep in the open air in the mud and rain and sometimes don't have a dry thing on in three days." He ate dried meat and hard biscuits. But "my health is good [and I] never felt so well in my life."

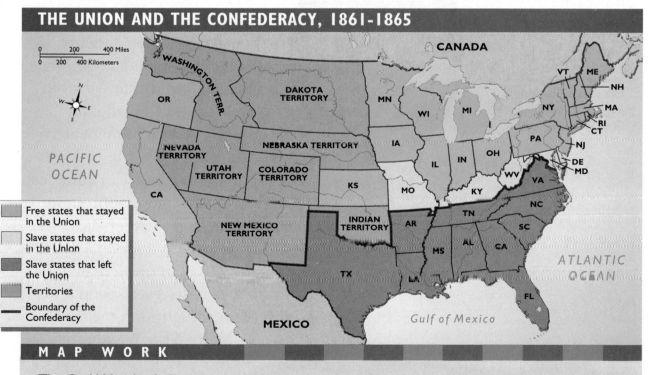

THE UNION AND THE CONFEDERACY, 1861–1865

Free states that stayed in the Union
Slave states that stayed in the Union
Slave states that left the Union
Territories
Boundary of the Confederacy

MAP WORK

The Civil War divided our country.

1. How many Confederate states were there? How many Union states?

2. Which two Union states did not touch the other states?

SUPPORT FOR THE UNION

Everyone in New York helped out in the war effort. Farmers raised horses, cattle, and crops for the troops. Factories in Watervliet, Ilion, Troy, and Albany made guns, uniforms, and wagons.

New York women were an important part of the war effort. Mary Walker was a Union doctor who worked in tent hospitals close to the fighting. Elizabeth Blackwell graduated from Geneva Medical College. She was the first woman doctor in America. Blackwell and her sister, Emily, started a school in New York City to train nurses for the war.

Do you remember Harriet Tubman? During the war she became a Union spy. She also led a raid on

Radcliffe College

Elizabeth Blackwell (right) was America's first woman doctor.

STATES WITH THE MOST SOLDIERS IN THE UNION ARMY	
STATE	SOLDIERS
New York	448,850
Pennsylvania	337,936
Ohio	313,180
Illinois	259,092
Indiana	196,363
Massachusetts	146,730

a Confederate fort in South Carolina. The hard work of these New Yorkers helped the Union win the war.

Iron Ships

New York provided the Union with a new kind of weapon. In 1862, the Continental Iron Works in Brooklyn built an iron-covered ship. A steam engine powered this ship. It was called the *Monitor*. On March 8, the Monitor fought a similar Confederate "ironclad" called the *Merrimac* in Chesapeake Bay. For two hours they pounded each other with cannonballs. Yet neither was badly damaged. This was the first time iron ships fought in a war. It forever changed the way ships were built.

More Soldiers!

President Lincoln announced the Emancipation Proclamation on January 1, 1863. This proclamation, or statement, said that enslaved people in the Confederacy were free. African Americans were allowed to join the Union army. Over 180,000 African American soldiers joined. Some fought under a banner that said "Rather die a free man than live to be a slave!"

President Lincoln also created a draft, or a plan to select people to be forced to serve in the military. Many New Yorkers did not like the draft. They believed New York had given its share of volunteers.

Courtesy Broome County Historical Society

In July 1863, people marched in the streets of New York City to protest the draft. The marchers began to fight with police. After four days of violence, many people were hurt.

The War Ends

General **Ulysses S. Grant** took over the Union Army in 1864. Under his strong leadership, Union soldiers began to win the war. On April 9, 1865, the Confederacy surrendered, or gave up, to the Union.

Present at the surrender was **Ely S. Parker**. He was a Union officer and a Seneca chief. Parker made corrections to the poorly written terms of surrender. He had a neat copy ready for Union and Confederate generals to sign.

In New York, people were overjoyed that the war had ended. Caroline Richards wrote, "The bells are ringing, boys and girls, men and women are running through the streets wild with excitement; the flags are all flying."

WHY IT MATTERS

New York was important to the Union winning the Civil War. Even though the war was long and terrible, it ended slavery in America. The North and the South became one country again.

✓ Reviewing Facts and Ideas

SUM IT UP

- Thousands of New Yorkers volunteered to fight for the Union.

- The hard work of many men and women in New York helped the Union win the war.

- The Civil War led to the end of slavery in the United States.

THINK ABOUT IT

1. Why did the southern states leave the Union?

2. Why did New Yorkers protest the draft?

3. **FOCUS** What role did New York play in the Civil War?

4. **THINKING SKILL** *Predict* what plans the United States Navy had for building their ships after the battle between the *Monitor* and the *Merrimac*.

5. **GEOGRAPHY** Look at the map on page 197. Why do you think there were no major battles in California and Oregon?

THINKING SKILLS

Making Conclusions

VOCABULARY
conclusion

WHY THE SKILL MATTERS

In Lesson 1 you read about reformers, people who wanted to change the way things were in the United States. Many of these people worked together to solve common problems. You might conclude that the reformers made life better for Americans.

When you make a **conclusion**, you put together several pieces of information and decide what they mean. A conclusion does not repeat specific facts. Instead it adds up these facts and tells how they are connected.

USING THE SKILL

In the last lesson you studied why some people wanted to work for reform in the United States. Read each of the following statements.

• Some women wanted to have the same rights as men.

• Many northern states, like New York, passed laws ending slavery.

• Abolitionists spoke out to end slavery everywhere in the country.

FREEDOM'S JOURNAL.

"RIGHTEOUSNESS EXALTETH A NATION."

BY JNO. B. RUSSWURM.   NEW-YORK, FRIDAY, MARCH 14, 1828.   VOL. I.—NO.

Schamburg Center for Research in Black Culture, The New York Public Library

African American abolitionists Samuel Cornish (left) and John Russwurm (right) started the first African American newspaper, *Freedom's Journal*, in New York City in 1827.

First ask yourself, "What do all of these statements have in common?" All of these statements have the common theme that many Americans wanted to change things for the better in the country. Now state this common theme in your own words. A conclusion you might make is "Many Americans wanted reform." This conclusion connects all three statements. It finds a common idea behind the statements and says it in a sentence.

TRYING THE SKILL

You have practiced drawing a conclusion about the demands for change in America in the early 1800s. Now read the following statements about the United States during the mid-1800s, as the Civil War began. Then make a conclusion from the statements. Use the Helping Yourself box for hints.

- President Lincoln did not want slavery to spread to new states.

- Northern abolitionists continued to help enslaved people escape to freedom.

- People in the South were afraid Lincoln would end slavery altogether.

- The South seceded from the Union.

HELPING Yourself

- When you make a **conclusion** you "add up" several facts or statements to see how they are connected.

- Skim through the information for a common idea.

- State this meaning in your own words.

What common theme or meaning did you find in all four statements? How do they "add up" to a conclusion? What conclusion can you make about the United States in the mid-1800s?

REVIEWING THE SKILL

1. How did you reach your conclusion?

2. What did the four statements suggest about the United States in the mid-1800s? How do you know?

3. Did the people of the mid-1800s come to the same conclusion that you did?

4. How might making conclusions help you to learn about history?

Seneca Chief Ely S. Parker (far right) was a staff officer for General Ulysses S. Grant (left center, wearing hat). Parker helped write the surrender terms that ended the Civil War.

LOCAL CONNECTIONS
PEEKSKILL:
LEARNING FROM MONUMENTS AND SCULPTURES

The students in Mrs. Norman's class in Peekskill were studying the Civil War. "We have a piece of Civil War history right here in our own city. Today, we are taking a walk to look at it," she told the class.

When they reached Monument Park, the class stopped in front of a large stone statue.

"This is the Soldiers and Sailors Monument," said Sharma.

"Yes, and here to greet us is Mrs. Barbara Zimmer, a librarian who works at The Field Library. She will tell us about the monument."

"The first thing to do is to look carefully at the monument. Who wants to read the inscription, or writing, here on the side?"

Casey volunteered. "To the memory of the soldiers and sailors from the town of Cortlandt who served in the Civil War 1861-1865," he read proudly. "Cortlandt is right next to Peekskill."

Mrs. Zimmer then explained that when President Lincoln called for volunteers to serve in the Civil War, about 690 men from the Peekskill area went. They fought at battles such as Gettysburg, Vicksburg, and Antietam (an TEE tum). Some died fighting in the war.

"This monument," she said, "is one way people in the present and future can remember the sacrifice the soldiers and sailors made to preserve the Union."

Mrs. Zimmer told the students that the monument is 55 feet high from the base to the top of the soldier's flag staff. It is made from granite that came from Vermont.

"How many carved statues are on the monument?" Mrs. Zimmer asked.

"Four. But they are all different," said Jose.

This monument honoring soldiers and sailors who served in the Civil War in the Peekskill area.

"That's right, Jose. Each of the statues represents a different branch of the military. The flag bearer at the top represents the foot soldiers in the Infantry. The statue in the front of the monument represents an officer in the U.S. Cavalry, those who fought on horseback. Another statue represents the soldiers who shot the cannons in the Artillery. The fourth statue represents the sailors who served in the Navy."

"After the Civil War, it took almost 50 years to raise the money to build the monument. It was finally dedicated on Labor Day in 1916," Mrs. Zimmer added.

Looking at the monument and reading the inscription gave the students a better understanding of the sacrifices made by people who serve their country. The students also realized that monuments and statues can tell a lot about the history of their community. When they returned to school, they made their own models of the monument that they could display.

MAKE *your* LOCAL CONNECTION

What monuments or sculptures are located in your community? How can you find out about their history? Make your own monument or sculpture to honor a person or an event in your community. Work with other students to make displays of your work.

▌Students built clay models (below)
▌of the monument. The Soldiers
▌and Sailors Monument (right) has
▌an inscription on one side.

IN THE MEMORY
THE SOLDIERS AND SAILORS FROM
THE TOWN OF CORTLANDT
WHO SERVED IN THE CIVIL WAR
1861 — 1865

CHAPTER 8 REVIEW

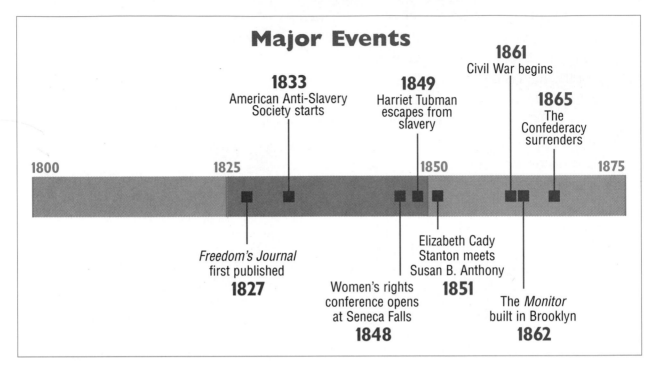

Major Events

1861
Civil War begins

1833
American Anti-Slavery
Society starts

1849
Harriet Tubman
escapes from
slavery

1865
The
Confederacy
surrenders

1800   1825   1850   1875

Freedom's Journal
first published
1827

Women's rights
conference opens
at Seneca Falls
1848

Elizabeth Cady
Stanton meets
Susan B. Anthony
1851

The *Monitor*
built in Brooklyn
1862

THINKING ABOUT VOCABULARY

Number a sheet of paper from 1 to 10. Next to each number write the term from the list that best fits the description.

abolition   reform

Civil War   secede

Confederacy   suffrage·

draft   Underground

Emancipation   Railroad

  Proclamation   Union

1. The right to vote

2. An end to slavery

3. To change something for the better

4. The war fought between the northern and southern states

5. To withdraw from a country

6. The states that seceded from the United States

7. A group of people who helped enslaved people escape to freedom

8. A plan to select people to serve in the military

9. The states that remained in the United States during the Civil War

10. A statement that said all enslaved people in the Confederacy were free

THINKING ABOUT FACTS

1. What battle started the Civil War?

2. What was the first African American newspaper in our country?

3. How did Harriet Tubman escape to freedom?

4. What were some ways that New Yorkers supported the Union?

5. What rights did the reformers who met at Seneca Falls want?

THINK AND WRITE

WRITING AN OPINION

Think about something in your community that you would like to see changed for the better. Write an opinion that explains why you think it is a problem and how you would go about changing it.

WRITING A DIARY

Suppose you are traveling on or helping people along the Underground Railroad. Write several diary entries that describe your activities.

WRITING A LETTER

Suppose you are a Union soldier. Write a letter to your family telling them the Civil War is over and you are coming home.

APPLYING THINKING SKILLS

MAKING CONCLUSIONS

1. What is meant by making conclusions?

2. What steps should you follow when making a conclusion?

3. Read the section under "The Struggle for Women's Rights" on page 191. What conclusion could you make about women's suffrage?

4. Read the section under "Support for the Union" on page 198. What conclusion could you make about New York's role in the Civil War?

5. Why is it important to make conclusions about what you read?

Summing Up the Chapter

Use the following cause-and-effect chart to organize information from the chapter. Fill in the blank spaces with causes or effects. When you have completed the chart, use it to write a paragraph titled "What caused changes in New York before and after the Civil War?"

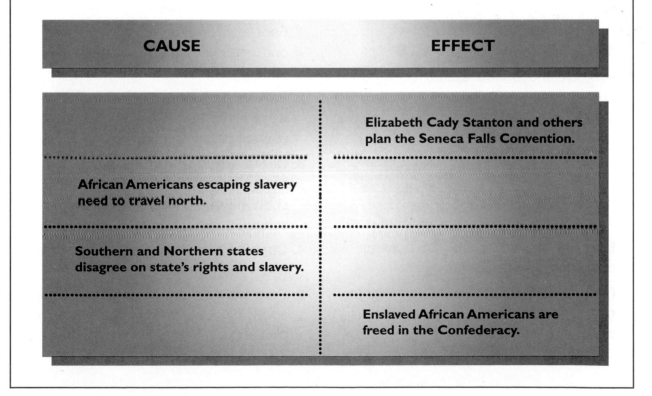

CAUSE	EFFECT
	Elizabeth Cady Stanton and others plan the Seneca Falls Convention.
African Americans escaping slavery need to travel north.	
Southern and Northern states disagree on state's rights and slavery.	
	Enslaved African Americans are freed in the Confederacy.

UNIT 3 REVIEW

THINKING ABOUT VOCABULARY

Number a sheet of paper from 1 to 5. Beside each number write the word from the list below that best completes the sentence.

bank
constitution
immigrant
industry
lock

1. An _____ is all the businesses that make one kind of product or service.

2. A _____ is a plan for a government.

3. An _____ is a person who moves to a new country to live.

4. _____ is a business that helps people save and borrow money.

5. A _____ is a water elevator that moves boats to higher or lower levels.

THINKING ABOUT FACTS

1. How did the United States Constitution become law?

2. Where are stocks traded on Wall Street?

3. Who founded Rochester?

4. Why did the United States and Great Britain go to war in 1812?

5. Why were locks built on the Erie Canal?

6. How did many workers' jobs change during the Industrial Revolution?

7. From what did Elizabeth Cady Stanton borrow ideas for her Seneca Falls speech?

8. Who was Sojourner Truth?

9. What was the Underground Railroad?

10. Why was the *Monitor* different from other ships in the Union navy?

THINK AND WRITE

WRITING AN INTERVIEW
Suppose that you were able to interview Harriet Tubman. Write three questions you would ask her. Then write the answers she might give.

WRITING A COMPARISON
Write a paragraph comparing forms of transportation used during the 1800s with forms used today.

WRITING AN EXPLANATION
Explain how the Erie Canal helped New York grow.

BUILDING SKILLS

1. **Fact and opinion** Find one fact and one opinion in Unit 3. Explain your choices.

2. **Fact and opinion** What are some word clues that tell you the writer is expressing an opinion?

3. **Circle and line graphs** Would you use a line graph or a circle graph to show how you spend your time after school?

4. **Conclusions** What steps should you follow when making a conclusion?

5. **Conclusions** In Chapter 8, you read about the Civil War. What is one conclusion you can draw from this event?

YESTERDAY, TODAY &
TOMORROW

In this unit you have read about the expansion and settlement of New York. Only 200 years ago, Europeans had settled only a few areas of New York. Today, New York is one of the most populated states in the country. How do you think New York will change in the future?

READING ON YOUR OWN

These are some of the books you could find at the library to help you learn more.

THE AMAZING, IMPOSSIBLE ERIE CANAL
by Cheryl Harness
This interesting story tells how the Erie Canal was built, from start to finish.

CIVIL WAR
by Martin W. Sandler
The people, places, and events of the war are described with text, photographs, and quotations.

HARRIET TUBMAN AND THE FIGHT AGAINST SLAVERY
by Bree Burns
This biography describes the life of a brave woman who helped hundreds of people escape to freedom.

UNIT PROJECT

Make a Canal Game

1. As a group, research how people traveled on the Erie Canal in the 1800s.
2. Make a game that allows players to travel the canal's route. Each group will choose one of the following four tasks:
   - On a large piece of cardboard, draw a map that shows the route of the Erie Canal. Identify major cities along the way. Then mark spaces along the route.
   - On "chance" cards, write instructions that help or slow travel. For example, "Boat leaks. Stop for repairs. Lose one turn."
   - Make the game pieces.
   - Write a set of rules for the game.
3. Form teams and play your game.

FIRST
ELECTRIC
POWER
STATION IN
NEW YORK
CITY (RIGHT)

COMPOSER
DUKE
ELLINGTON
(ABOVE)
IMMIGRANTS
IN
MANHATTAN
(RIGHT)

Lewis W. Hine, Courtesy of George Eastman House

Maurice
CHICAGO

ALBANY COUNTY
FAMILY IN 1937 (LEFT)
STOCK MARKET
TICKERTAPE MACHINE
(RIGHT)

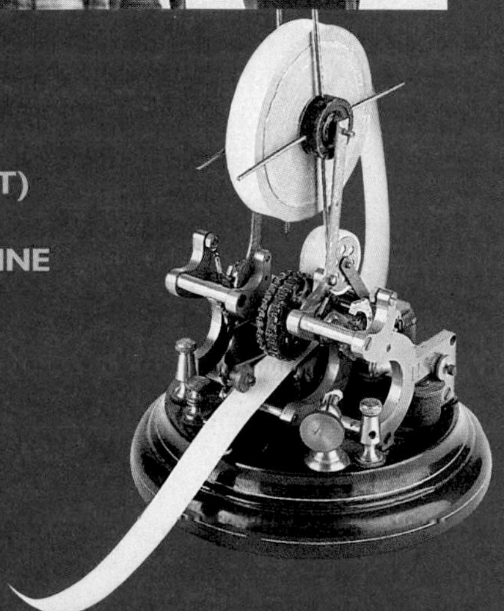

Building the Empire State

"Take just one star."

from a poem by Langston Hughes
See page 244.

WHY DOES IT MATTER?

New York was growing fast. People from all over the world were streaming into New York hoping for a better life. They settled down in tall buildings in the cities and the forests of the countryside. They planted, invented, and built New York into a great state—the Empire State!

THE EMPIRE STATE BUILDING (FAR RIGHT) RAILROAD ENGINE WHEELS (RIGHT)

Charles Sheeler, *Rolling Power*, Smith College Museum of Art, Drayton, Hillyer Fund

209

Adventures with
NATIONAL
GEOGRAPHIC
with

A Wonderful Waterfall

You're going to get soaked. Even the best rainwear can't repel 700,000 gallons of water per second. That's what spills over Niagara Falls—a place where water from four Great Lakes falls over a cliff.

Daredevils sealed inside barrels once plunged over the falls for fun and glory. You can't do that today, but you can hike to observation areas and see rainbows in the silvery mist. Then take a boat ride along the base of the falls, and you'll shake in the roar of Niagara—an Indian word meaning "thunder of waters." Behind the falls you can explore a dripping cave created by the scouring force of the water. Niagara Falls—it's wet, it's wild, it's one of the wonders of New York.

GEO JOURNAL

In your Geo Journal, describe what you would like to see, smell, feel, hear, and taste on a visit to Niagara Falls.

211

CHAPTER 9

New York, A National Leader

THINKING ABOUT GEOGRAPHY AND ECONOMICS

The story of Chapter 9 begins after the Civil War, when railroads grew rapidly and helped New York industries grow. Inventions like the light bulb lit up the state and changed the way people lived. Follow the story as you read the time line. You will learn much more about these events as you read Chapter 9.

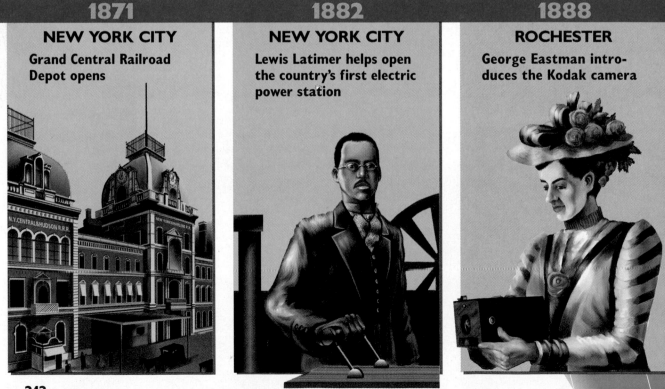

1871
NEW YORK CITY

Grand Central Railroad Depot opens

1882
NEW YORK CITY

Lewis Latimer helps open the country's first electric power station

1888
ROCHESTER

George Eastman introduces the Kodak camera

CANADA

Adirondack Mountains

Rochester

NEW YORK

New York City

Ellis Island

UNITED STATES

ATLANTIC OCEAN

1892

ELLIS ISLAND

Immigration station opens

1894

ADIRONDACK MOUNTAINS

New York passes law to keep Adirondacks "forever wild"

1860　　　　1893　1900　　　1920　　　1940

The Granger Collection, N.Y.

BIG BUSINESS AND BOLD IDEAS

READ ALOUD

On a beautiful May morning in 1893, the New York Central train known as the Empire State Express started out of the Batavia railroad station. On a straight stretch of track west of Batavia, the train reached a record speed of over 100 miles an hour. It was the fastest machine on Earth.

THE BIG PICTURE

After the Civil War, many industries in New York grew very fast. New railroads spread across the state. New inventions made people's lives easier. New businesses brought new products to the public. Everything seemed to be becoming bigger, better, or faster.

Most of these businesses and the factories that made their goods were located in cities. As more and more factories in New York were built, more New Yorkers moved to cities to work in them. Until this time, most people in New York lived in rural areas, or the countryside. They were farmers or they worked for small businesses in towns. By the late 1800s, however, most New Yorkers were urban. That means they lived in cities. Most people worked in businesses owned by others. Cities like Buffalo grew to a huge size. People's lives changed in many ways during this time.

Focus Activity

READ TO LEARN
What industries helped make New York a center for business?

VOCABULARY
rural
urban
labor union
strike

PEOPLE
Cornelius Vanderbilt
Lewis Latimer
George Eastman
J. P. Morgan
Hetty Green
Charles Loring Brace
Samuel Gompers
Theodore Roosevelt

PLACES
Grand Central Terminal

214

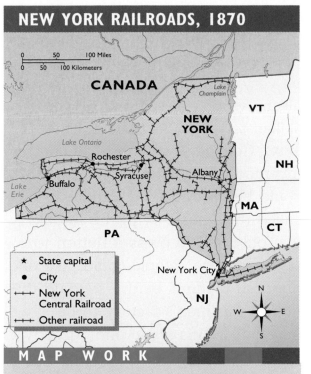

NEW YORK RAILROADS, 1870

CANADA

Lake Champlain

VT

NEW YORK

Lake Ontario

Rochester

NH

Syracuse

Albany

Buffalo

Lake Erie

MA

CT

PA

New York City

★ State capital
● City
╅ New York Central Railroad
╅ Other railroad

NJ

N W E S

MAP WORK

By 1870, railroads connected all major cities in the state.

1. From looking at the map, why do you think Vanderbilt's railroad was called the New York Central?

2. Why were there so few railroads in northern New York?

THE GROWTH OF RAILROADS

One reason New York became a center of business was its good railroad system. The first railroad in New York, which you have read about, had rickety trains that broke down often. Railroad companies kept making changes, and the trains became better.

Trains had advantages over steamships and canalboats. Trains could operate in the winter time. In many places, boats could not because the canals and rivers would freeze. Trains could also link many places without waterways.

The New York Central

By the time the Civil War had ended, most people were shipping products on railroads instead of canals. Some people earned millions of dollars in the railroad industry. One of those people was New Yorker **Cornelius Vanderbilt**.

In the 1860s, Vanderbilt bought two railroads that connected New York City and Albany. He then bought another that connected Albany and Buffalo. Vanderbilt combined them all and created what became known as the New York Central Railroad. Soon Vanderbilt's railroad reached all the way to Chicago, Illinois and St. Louis, Missouri.

In 1871, Vanderbilt built a large train depot (DEE poh) or station in New York City. It was rebuilt in 1913 and called the **Grand Central Terminal**. It was—and still is—"grand" in many ways. It became the largest railroad terminal in the world. It has 123 tracks.

On the outside, toward the top of the building, is a clock that is 13 feet high. Underneath the clock is a bronze statue of Vanderbilt. Each day, more than 140,000 people move through Grand Central on their way to and from work.

From the Collections of Henry Ford Museum & Greenfield Village

Hand lamps (above) were used to signal trains on the New York Central Railroad.

INVENTIONS AND BIG BUSINESS

Railroads were able to grow into a big business because people kept on inventing ways to make them better. These inventions included better brakes and better tracks.

In the 1800s, thousands of Americans tried their hand at inventing new products. Some inventions from New York changed the world. One of them was the electric light bulb. Thomas Edison, who lived in New Jersey, had worked hard to invent the light bulb. In 1882, Edison built the country's first electric power station on Pearl Street in Manhattan. It sent electricity over wires to buildings and was the start of the electric system we have today. At the turn of a switch, more than 40 buildings were lit up.

In 1882 Lewis Latimer improved Edison's light bulb by inventing a way to make it last longer. Latimer soon went to work for Edison in New York City. Latimer had good advice for those who want to succeed. "Think of your future and plan for it the best you can. But now and then ask yourself, 'What can I do today?'"

George Eastman

Think of how often you look at photographs. Photography used to be very complicated. You had to do all the work yourself and be very skilled to work the camera. Then in 1888, George Eastman of Rochester invented a new kind of film that could be used in a new camera called the Kodak. With the Kodak you only had to press a button to take a picture. People could take one hundred pictures before sending the film to Eastman's factory to be developed. This made photography much easier. Look at the Infographic on page 217. It shows some other important inventions from New York.

Courtesy of George Eastman House

George Eastman (above) is holding a Kodak camera. This picture was also made with a Kodak. The electric light (left) was improved by Lewis Latimer.

Infographic

Made in New York

Inventors often look for ways to do things faster or easier. They come up with solutions to problems. New York inventors made products that changed the lives of many people.

The Granger Collection, N.Y.

ISAAC SINGER improved the sewing machine, making it easier to use. He opened a sewing machine company in New York City in 1851.

Collection of The Corning Museum of Glass, Corning, N.Y., Gift of Jerry E. Wright

AMORY HOUGHTON (HOH tun) opened a glass-making factory in Corning in 1868. Houghton's company invented Pyrex dishware that would not break when heated.

In 1869, **JOHN HYATT** from Albany invented a plastic called celluloid. It was used to make many things, including piano keys and toys.

The Granger Collection, N.Y.

In 1874, **E. REMINGTON AND SONS** from Illon was the first company to make typewriters.

GEORGE EASTMAN of Rochester invented a lightweight and easy-to-use camera called the Kodak in 1888.

WILLIS CARRIER, from Buffalo, invented the air conditioner in 1902.

NEW BUSINESSES

Many of these new inventions were the start of new businesses. Some people, like banker **J. P. Morgan**, made millions of dollars by lending money to big companies and by buying and selling stocks. Others, like **Hetty Green**, made their fortune by buying and selling stocks and land. Green was one of only a few women who ran their own business at this time.

Business and Labor

All these new industries offered people jobs. Thousands of people worked in huge factories or offices. However, most companies wanted to save money. Many workers earned less than $10 per week. They worked in rooms that were overcrowded and poorly-lit. Fire was a great disaster. Factories were also dangerous if the machines weren't in good condition.

Child Labor

Since families did not earn much money, even children your age had to work. The workday was sometimes 12 hours long or more. Imagine starting work at about the time you wake up for school and not going home until after suppertime!

Reformers like **Charles Loring Brace** were against child labor. The children, he said, knew "nothing but hardship [difficulty]." To end child labor, Brace started the Children's Aid Society in New York City in 1853. By the early 1900s, the Children's Aid

Samuel Gompers formed one of the first **labor unions**.

Society had helped make child labor against the law.

Labor Unions

Many workers thought the companies were not fair. Some believed the best way to get fair treatment was to form a **labor union**. Labor means "work" or "workers." A labor union is a group of workers who push for better conditions.

Samuel Gompers, a cigar maker from New York City, helped form one of the first labor unions in 1873. Gompers and other cigar makers joined together to demand better pay and shorter working days.

Sometimes workers would go on **strike**. When workers strike, they stop working and say they will not start again until they get what they want. Sometimes a strike worked, and sometimes it did not. However, workers found that they could get more of what they asked for when they joined together.

Theodore Roosevelt agreed that businesses were not always fair to workers. Roosevelt was governor of New York from 1899 to 1900. He supported laws to protect workers from dangerous conditions. Later, as President of the United States, he continued to support laws about big business.

WHY IT MATTERS

Many of the inventions of the late 1800s still shape our lives today. Can you imagine not having electricity in your home? The growth of huge factories caused urban areas to grow quickly. Changes in the way people worked also led to the forming of labor unions. These unions helped convince our government to make laws for better working conditions. These laws still protect workers today.

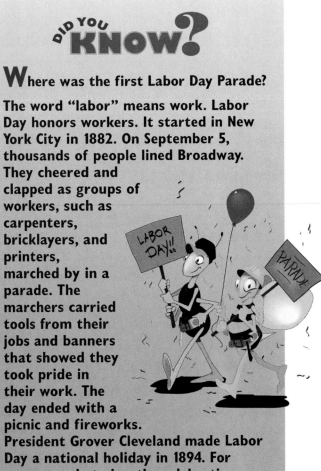

DID YOU KNOW?

Where was the first Labor Day Parade?

The word "labor" means work. Labor Day honors workers. It started in New York City in 1882. On September 5, thousands of people lined Broadway. They cheered and clapped as groups of workers, such as carpenters, bricklayers, and printers, marched by in a parade. The marchers carried tools from their jobs and banners that showed they took pride in their work. The day ended with a picnic and fireworks. President Grover Cleveland made Labor Day a national holiday in 1894. For many people today, the celebration marks the end of summer.

✓✓ Reviewing Facts and Ideas

SUM IT UP

- After the Civil War, railroads became the main form of transportation in New York and across the country.
- New inventions helped start new industries in the state.
- Labor unions and reformers tried to make working conditions in factories better.

THINK ABOUT IT

1. Why might people choose to travel on the railroad rather than the Erie Canal?
2. Why would workers strike?
3. **FOCUS** What industries helped make New York a center of business?
4. **THINKING SKILL** How did new inventions *cause* new industries to form?
5. **WRITE** Write a description of an invention you would like to make.

STUDYSKILLS

Using Reference Sources

VOCABULARY

reference source   encyclopedia

dictionary   CD-ROM

guide word

WHY THE SKILL MATTERS

In the last lesson you read about George Eastman, J. P. Morgan, the New York Central Railroad, and labor unions. Your teacher might ask you to write a report on one of these topics. Suppose you chose to write your report on the forming of the New York Central Railroad. Although you learned about this event in the last lesson, you would need more information for your report.

You could find the information you need in reference sources. These are books and other sources that contain facts about many different subjects. They can be found in a special part of the library called the reference section.

USING A DICTIONARY

Before you start your report, you might want to know the exact meaning of the word *depot*. To find out, you would look in a dictionary. A dictionary gives the meanings of words. It shows how to pronounce and spell each word. Sometimes a dictionary will also explain where a word came from, or use it in a sentence.

The words in a dictionary are arranged in alphabetical order. To find your word faster, you can refer to the guide words. These appear at the top of each page of the dictionary. Guide words tell you the first and last words that are defined on that page.

Look at the guide words on the sample dictionary page. According to them, what is the first word to be defined on the page? Would the word *dentist* appear on the page? Now find the word *depot*. What does this word mean?

USING AN ENCYCLOPEDIA OR CD-ROM

Another useful reference book is the encyclopedia. This book or set of books gives information about people, places, things, and events. Like a dictionary, an encyclopedia is arranged in alphabetical order. Most encyclopedias also use guide words.

Let's say you want to learn more about the history of railroads. You would look in the encyclopedia volume, or book, with an *R* on the spine. Which volume would you look in to learn about the history of the camera?

A newer kind of reference source is the CD-ROM. This is a compact disc that you "read" with the aid of a computer. Like an encyclopedia, a CD-ROM contains facts about many subjects. It also may include sounds, music, and even short movies! Your teacher or librarian will help you use this type of reference source.

TRYING THE SKILL

You have practiced using reference sources. Now suppose that you want to write a report on George Eastman. Which reference sources would you use? How would you find the information you need? Use the Helping Yourself box before you begin your report.

REVIEWING THE SKILL

1. What is a reference source?

2. Which reference source would you use to find the word *invention*?

3. Some encyclopedias have guide words on their spines instead of letters. Suppose you had a volume covering everything from *gunpowder* to *house*. Would this volume contain an article about the Great Lakes?

4. When are reference sources useful?

---

dependable / depressant

needed or wanted: *While he was a student he depended on his parents for support.* **3.** to be influenced or determined: *Whether she takes the job depends on what the salary is.* ▲ usually followed by *on*.

de·pen·da·ble (di pen′də bəl) *adj.* able to be depended on; reliable: *a dependable worker who is always on time.* —**de·pen′da·bil′i·ty,** *n.* —**de·pen′da·bly,** *adv.*

de·pen·dence (di pen′dəns) *n.* **1.** the state of relying on another for what is needed or wanted: *the dependence of a baby on its parents.* **2.** the state of being influenced or determined by something else: *the dependence of crops on rain.* **3.** trust; reliance. **4.** a physical or psychological need for a drug not taken for medicinal purposes, resulting from prolonged use of the drug. Also, **dependency.**

de·pen·den·cy (di pen′dən sē) *n., pl.* **de·pen·den·cies. 1.** a country or territory that is governed by another country but is not part of the governing country: *Puerto Rico is a dependency of the United States.* **2.** another word for **dependence.**

de·pen·dent (di pen′dənt) *adj.* **1.** relying on another for what is needed or wanted: *I am dependent on you for help with this project.* **2.** influenced or determined by something: *Our plans for the picnic are dependent on the weather.* —*n.* a person who depends on another for support or help. —**de·pen′dent·ly,** *adv.*

dependent clause, a clause that functions as a noun, adjective, or adverb within a sentence and cannot stand alone. In the sentence *After we had played tennis for an hour, we decided to go for a swim,* the clause *After we*

from a throne or other high office: *The rebels deposed the monarch.* **2.** *Law.* to declare under oath, especially in a written statement.

de·pos·it (di poz′it) *v.t.* **1.** to put (money or valuables) in a bank or other place for safekeeping: *She deposited five dollars in her savings account.* **2.** to set or lay down; place: *He deposited the groceries on the table. The river deposited silt at its mouth.* **3.** to put in; insert: *Deposit a coin in the slot.* —*n.* **1.** something put in a place for safekeeping, especially money in a bank. **2.** something given as part payment or security: *They put a deposit of $150 on a new car.* **3.** something that has settled: *a deposit of dust on the window sill.* **4.** a natural layer, as of a mineral: *a large deposit of iron ore.*

dep·o·si·tion (dep′ə zish′ən) *n.* **1.** removal from a throne or other high office. **2.** a sworn statement given by a witness out of court, intended to be used as testimony in court. **3.** the act or process of laying down: *The delta at the mouth of the river was formed by the deposition of silt.* **4.** something deposited; deposit.

de·pos·i·tor (di poz′i tər) *n.* a person who makes a deposit, especially a person who deposits money in a bank.

de·pos·i·to·ry (di poz′i tôr′ē) *n., pl.* **de·pos·i·to·ries.** a place where something is deposited for safekeeping.

de·pot (*def. 1* dē′pō; *def. 2* dep′ō; *def. 3* dep′ō, dē′pō) *n.* **1.** a railroad station or bus terminal. **2.** a place where military supplies and equipment are stored. **3.** a storage place; storehouse; warehouse.

D

DREAMS OF A BETTER LIFE

Focus Activity

READ TO LEARN
What was life like for immigrants coming to New York?

VOCABULARY
tenement
sweatshop

PEOPLE
Lillian Wald
Jacob Riis

PLACES
Ellis Island

READ ALOUD

Benjamin Erdberg came to New York from Russia in 1905. "Everybody's dream in the old country was to go to America," he said. "We heard people were free and we heard about better living. . . . I figured, I have a trade [skills], I have a chance more or less to see the world. I was young."

THE BIG PICTURE

You have already read about many immigrants to New York. The Dutch, British, Germans, and Irish were among the immigrants who came here. From 1880 to 1920, over 17 million new immigrants came to New York from all over the world. Benjamin Erdberg was one of thousands of Jews who came from Russia and Eastern Europe. Jewish people in these places had no political freedom. Great numbers of people came also from Italy and Greece. Others came from Norway, Sweden, Japan, China, Mexico, and Canada.

Most immigrants arrived by boat in New York Harbor in those years. Many moved on to settle upstate, or in other parts of the country. Millions of immigrants stayed where they landed, in New York City. Large immigrant neighborhoods formed in Lower Manhattan. There you could hear Italian, Polish, Czech, Greek, or other languages in the shouts of street sellers and the hubbub of open markets.

ELLIS ISLAND

The first stop for many new immigrants to America was Ellis Island. This rocky island lay one mile off the coast in New York Harbor. Buildings were built on this island in 1892 to handle the flood of new immigrants. The first immigrant to arrive was Annie Moore, a fifteen-year-old girl who came from Ireland to join her parents.

Sometimes 5,000 people a day walked through the doors. Long lines of people waited to be examined by doctors to make sure they were healthy enough to work. Some were sent back home. Most went on to an immigration officer. "Where are you from?" the officer would ask. "What kind of work can you do? Can you read and write?"

Ellis Island was a frightening experience for many. Rahel Mittelstein remembered the day her family arrived in the United States:

Every immigrant who was sent to the Island spent at least the first day in tears. We cried because of fear and disappointment. We had come a long way: we had sold everything we had and spent every cent, and now we were afraid of being sent back.

Most immigrants, however, were led down a hallway to a door that said "PUSH TO NEW YORK." Beyond that door was a ferry to New York City.

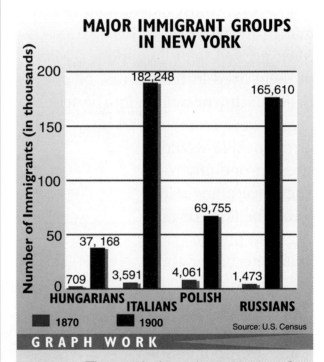

MAJOR IMMIGRANT GROUPS IN NEW YORK

Number of Immigrants (in thousands)

Hungarians: 1870: 709; 1900: 37,168
Italians: 1870: 3,591; 1900: 182,248
Polish: 1870: 4,061; 1900: 69,755
Russians: 1870: 1,473; 1900: 165,610

■ 1870 ■ 1900

Source: U.S. Census

GRAPH WORK

This graph shows how the size of immigrant groups in New York changed.

1. Which group was the largest in 1870

2. Which group was the largest in 1900?

3. Predict what happened to the size of other immigrant groups in New York from 1870 to 1900.

The Collection of Walter and Naomi Rosenbloom

This photograph by Lewis Hine shows the Lower East Side of Manhattan where there were large immigrant neighborhoods.

NEW LIFE IN A NEW LAND

For most immigrants New York City was a strange and fantastic place. "The city dazzled us. We had never seen such buildings, such people, such activity," said one young immigrant from Slovenia, in Eastern Europe. "Maybe the stories were true. Maybe everything was possible in America."

However, most immigrants faced many difficult years of hard work. Most arrived with little money. Many of them lived in tenements, or poorly built apartment buildings. The tenements were cramped and dirty. Five or six people would sleep in one tiny room. There were few windows for light or air.

Some people tried to make life better for these newcomers. In 1895, nurse Lillian Wald began to visit the homes of poor immigrant families and provide basic health care. By 1913, under Wald's leadership, over 90 nurses worked in poor neighborhoods.

A newspaper reporter named Jacob Riis (REES) wrote about the tenements in immigrant neighborhoods and took photographs of them. Riis himself came from Denmark, a country in Europe. Why do you think Riis wanted to write about these places?

Excerpt from *How the Other Half Lives*, written by Jacob Riis in 1890.

In a miserable tenement in Cherry Street . . . the man, his wife, and three children [were] shivering [from] winds of winter. . . . The room was almost barren of furniture; the parents slept on the floor, the elder children in boxes, and the baby was swung in an old shawl attached to the rafters by cords.

barren: empty

Jacob A. Riis, Museum of the City of New York

Jacob Riis took this photograph of an Italian immigrant and her baby in a tenement in New York City.

Sweatshops

Immigrants did all sorts of jobs to support themselves. Many went to work in the "needle trades," making clothing. Most worked in sweatshops. These were places where workers were paid poor wages and worked in unhealthy conditions. Sweatshops were often the cramped homes of their owners.

Lewis Hine photographed this poorly lit clothing factory in New York City.

The Collection of Walter and Naomi Rosenbloom

Immigrants Form Communities

Immigrants settled all over New York. Italians, Poles, Ukrainians, and Syrians moved to Utica to work in the clothing and shoe factories. A Chinese immigrant community formed in Albany in the area around Hudson Avenue and Green Street.

A Polish neighborhood in Buffalo called "Polonia" formed in the area of Broadway and Fillmore Avenue. Sicilians lived in an area called "Little Italy" on Buffalo's lower west side. The immigrants in these neighborhoods kept some of their old ways of life while learning new American ways. The Italians in Buffalo published a newspaper called *Il Corriere Italiano* (*The Italian Courier*). Shops sold Italian pasta or kielbasa [keel BAH sah], a Polish sausage. The Broadway Market, opened in 1888, is a copy of a market in Krakow, Poland.

WHY IT MATTERS

America was not always the dream that immigrants had imagined. Some struggled their whole lives. Yet they were determined to make a life for themselves here. As one young immigrant from Albania said, "My father never lost hope. 'We're in America,' he'd say. 'We'll work hard and things will get better.' And he was right."

Reviewing Facts and Ideas

SUM IT UP

- A huge wave of immigrants came to the United States between 1880 and 1920.
- New immigrants often were very poor and lived in tenements.
- Immigrants formed communities all over New York.

THINK ABOUT IT

1. What happened at Ellis Island?
2. Why did immigrants move to cities such as Utica in the early 1900s?
3. **FOCUS** What was life like for an immigrant in New York in the early 1900s?
4. **THINKING SKILL** Make a *conclusion* about why immigrants come to the United States.
5. **GEOGRAPHY** Think of reasons why New York City was an important center of immigration.

1860 1865 1898 1920 1940

CHANGING LANDSCAPES

READ ALOUD

In 1886, New Yorker Theodore Roosevelt ran for mayor of New York City. In a speech, he said, "Like all Americans, I like big things: big prairies, big forests, and mountains, big wheat fields, railroads—herds of cattle, too—big factories, steamboats, and everything else."

THE BIG PICTURE

Theodore Roosevelt's speech said a lot about what was going on in New York. By the late 1800s, New York's geography was changing rapidly. If Peter Stuyvesant had come back to visit New York in the 1880s, he would have hardly recognized it. He would have been amazed by almost everything he saw. Farms and villages had spread across all of the state. Small villages had become lively towns. Small towns had grown into busy cities. Just about everything had grown bigger.

The growing population and businesses caused changes throughout the state. Great parks were set up. Giant bridges like the Brooklyn Bridge were built. Even the capital in Albany changed greatly. How? You guessed it! It got bigger.

Focus Activity

READ TO LEARN
How did New York change before 1900?

VOCABULARY
suspension bridge
hydroelectric power

PEOPLE
Theodore Roosevelt
Frederic-Auguste Bartholdi
John Roebling
Emily Roebling
Nikola Tesla
George Westinghouse

THE STATUE OF LIBERTY

The story of the Statue of Liberty begins in 1865, when some people in France talked about giving the people of America a gift of friendship. A young French artist named **Frederic-Auguste Bartholdi** (bahr TAHL dee) drew designs for a statue he called Liberty. He wanted to build the statue to celebrate the 100th birthday of the Declaration of Independence. He traveled to America to ask for help. People from France and America joined together. People in France would pay for the statue. People in America would pay for the platform, or base, on which the statue would stand.

The statue would be built in France. It was made of thin sheets of copper, because copper is light in weight. Workers needed about 100 tons of copper sheeting to make the statue.

At a height of 151 feet, the statue would be the tallest ever built! It would be as high as a 50-story building. It was so big that it had to be built in pieces. Workers put the statue together to make sure the pieces fit right. Then they took it apart and shipped it to America.

In America, raising money for the platform was not going well. A New York City newspaper called the *World* asked people to give money. The newspaper itself gave $100,000. Schoolchildren sent in their pennies. Soon, enough money was saved. The platform could now be built.

On October 28, 1886, the Statue of Liberty was presented to the people of the United States. It became a symbol of freedom to people all over the world. Elizabeth Phillips, an immigrant from Ireland, recalled what it was like when she sailed to America. She said, "The first time I saw the Statue of Liberty all the people were rushing to the side of the boat. 'Look at her, look at her.'" They knew that the statue meant a new life in a new land.

Edward Moran, Museum of the City of New York

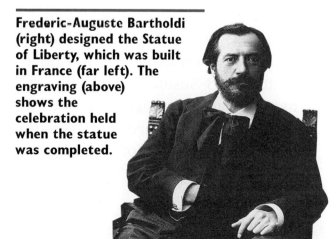

Frederic-Auguste Bartholdi (right) designed the Statue of Liberty, which was built in France (far left). The engraving (above) shows the celebration held when the statue was completed.

BUILDING FOR THE FUTURE

As New York grew in population, life for New Yorkers became more complex. Many new things had to be built to keep pace with the changes in New York life.

The State Capitol

In 1865, New York's government had grown too large for the old state capitol building. New York leaders decided to build a new one.

Work started in July 1869. Horses clopped down the streets of Albany pulling wagons piled high with blocks of stone. Hundreds of workers—especially Irish and Scottish immigrants—put in long hours to cut the stone and build the walls.

It took a long time to finish building the new capitol—about 30 years! It was only supposed to cost $4 million. By the time it was finished, in 1898, it had cost $25 million.

The New York capitol is like no other state capitol building. From the outside, it looks like a white stone palace with four corner towers. Inside, wide staircases lead to beautiful rooms where the representatives meet. Carved on the sides and above the staircases are the faces of famous Americans. Among them are Abraham Lincoln, Robert Fulton, and Susan B. Anthony. Visitors will also see faces that are not so famous. These are the faces the stonecutters carved of themselves and their families!

Workers (right) on the Brooklyn Bridge (below right) had very dangerous jobs. Carvings in the state capitol (below, bottom) include this one of Lincoln.

The Brooklyn Bridge

In the 1860s, people traveled in boats across the East River to go between the separate cities of Brooklyn and New York City. In warm months, the trip was easy. But the winter brought cold temperatures and icy winds. When the river froze, no one could get across. A

large boats pass under it. The kind of bridge Roebling planned is called a suspension bridge. A suspension bridge hangs, or is suspended, over the water. The towers that help hold up the bridge are at either end, not in the middle.

Roebling was hurt in an accident on the job and died in 1869. His son, Washington Roebling, became the head of the project. Then Washington was hurt while helping to build one of the towers. He had to stay at home. Now Emily Roebling, Washington's wife, took over many important duties. Washington would watch the construction with a telescope from his bedroom window. He would give Emily instructions to give to workers at the building site.

The bridge opened on May 24, 1883. Author Judith St. George calls it "the most photographed, painted, written about and perhaps the best loved man-made structure in America." It reached 1,595 feet from tower to tower. It was the longest bridge in the world. New Yorkers made the day a holiday. Children stayed home from school. More than 150,000 people came to celebrate the opening. That evening the bridge was lit with electric lights. The New York *Sun* newspaper reported, "One by one the series of electric lights on the bridge leaped [lit] up until the chain was made from Brooklyn to New York." Later, 14 tons of fireworks lit the sky.

bridge between Manhattan and Brooklyn would solve the problem.

A bridge builder named John Roebling (ROHB ling) prepared plans for a bridge in 1867. The bridge had to be high enough to let

New Yorkers can enjoy the natural beauty of the Adirondacks

THE POWER OF NATURE

The Adirondack region had not changed much since colonial times. The rugged mountains and cold winters made settlement there difficult. In the mid-1800s people in New York discovered that the Adirondacks were a great place for vacations. They went there to camp, fish, and hunt. Some animals, like the wolf, were hunted so much that almost none were left. Logging companies found that the Adirondacks were a good place to get timber. They began cutting down whole forests.

Logging caused problems in the environment. Where the land was cleared, rain washed away the good soil. Many animals had no place to live because the forests had been cut down. Fire was a constant danger because tree stumps, branches, and dead leaves were left where trees once stood. Something had to be done.

Forever Wild

In 1894, the state constitution was being rewritten. Representatives added a law to make the Adirondacks a protected park. The law says that the Adirondacks "shall be forever kept as wild forest lands." They were to be "forever wild."

Today, the Adirondacks are still a vacation spot, but people are much more careful about how they use the land. Everyone can enjoy the natural beauty of the mountains.

Niagara Power

On December 14, 1881, the *Niagara Gazette* announced that Jacob Schoellkopf (SHOHL kahpf) had built a station to make hydroelectric power. Hydroelectric power is electricity made from flowing water in rivers. The diagram below shows how hydroelectric power is made. Schoellkopf built his station at one of the best spots in North America for hydroelectric power—Niagara Falls.

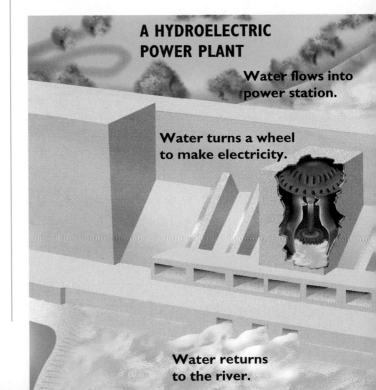

A HYDROELECTRIC POWER PLANT

Water flows into power station.

Water turns a wheel to make electricity.

Water returns to the river.

Not long after, the town of Niagara was lit with electric lights. Buffalo also wanted electric power. The problem was the electric company did not know how to send power over 20 miles away to Buffalo. The person who could solve the problem would receive a prize of $100,000.

Inventors Nikola Tesla and George Westinghouse solved the problem. Tesla had recently immigrated to New York from Croatia (kroh AY sha). With Westinghouse's support, Tesla worked out a way to send electric power over long distances over wires. "The power of the Falls will be transmitted to Buffalo as surely as the sun will shine," he said. At the stroke of midnight on November 16, 1896, a switch was pulled at the Niagara Falls Power Company's Power House No. 1. Electricity flowed through 20 miles of wire to light a small lamp in Buffalo.

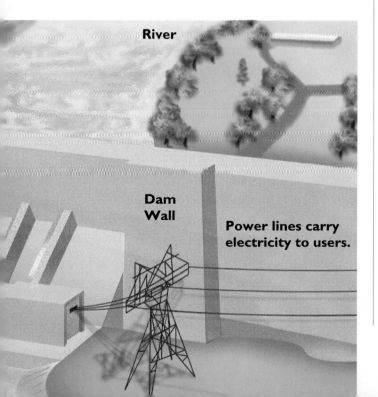

River

Dam Wall

Power lines carry electricity to users.

Electricity changed the lives of everyone in the Niagara region. Buffalo became one of the first large cities to use electric street lights.

WHY IT MATTERS

The growth of New York prepared it for its entry into the next century. From the Brooklyn Bridge to the Adirondacks, New York was becoming a modern state.

Reviewing Facts and Ideas

SUM IT UP

- The Brooklyn Bridge made it easier for people to travel between Brooklyn and New York City.
- France gave the United States the Statue of Liberty as a gift of friendship.
- New York built an expensive new state capitol building.
- Electricity changed the way people in the Niagara region lived.
- In 1894, New York passed a law to protect the Adirondacks.

THINK ABOUT IT

1. Why did New York build a new capitol building?

2. Why was Niagara Falls a good place for hydroelectric power?

3. FOCUS How did New York change before 1900?

4. THINKING SKILL Describe the _effect_ of the opening of the Brooklyn Bridge.

5. GEOGRAPHY Why does cutting down a forest make it hard for some animals to live?

CITIZENSHIP
VIEWPOINTS

Hiking and rock climbing are ways to enjoy the wilderness areas of the Adirondacks.

HOW SHOULD WE USE THE LAND OF THE ADIRONDACKS?

The Adirondack Park covers one-fifth of New York State's land. It contains six million acres. That is as big as the state of Vermont! Some of Adirondack Park is public land—land owned by the government. Over half the parkland is privately owned. Its owners include more than 100,000 people who live in the park all year. About 200,000 other people own land on which they have summer homes. Other private owners include lumber companies and people who run hotels, restaurants, and tourist spots.

Since 1895 some of the public land has been protected as "forever wild" by the state constitution. In other wilderness areas no cars, dirt bikes, or other vehicles are allowed.

Some people, like Barbara Sweet, think that more of the private lands should be developed to start businesses. This would give people jobs. Peter Bauer is among those who want to keep the park as it is or turn more of the private land into public land. Michael Martin thinks that more care is needed to protect water quality in the Adirondacks. Consider three viewpoints on this issue. Then answer the questions that follow.

Three DIFFERENT Viewpoints

1 PETER BAUER
Director of an environmental organization, North Creek
Excerpt from Interview, 1996

The future . . . health of the park depends both on our resource-based economy, which harvests trees on private land to make paper, lumber, and furniture, and on the tourist industry. People up and down the East Coast come to the Adirondacks for outdoor recreation and wilderness experiences that are disappearing in many other places. We have a success story of people living with nature without destroying it.

". . . a success story of people living with nature . . ."

2 MICHAEL MARTIN
Scientist, Paul Smith's
Excerpt from Interview, 1996

More care has to be taken where development takes place. . . . Lakes are threatened by the building of roads and homes. We need to know more about the effects of development on water quality. . . . We have to develop in ways that do not harm the water quality of our lakes.

"more care has to be taken . . ."

3 BARBARA SWEET
Town council member, Newcomb
Excerpt from Interview, 1996

We need to be thinking about the future of the communities of the park, not just about its natural resources. We need more, better-paying, year-round jobs so that young people who grow up here can stay here when they have finished with school. Over half the land in the park is already . . . protected, but there are many places . . . where small businesses could be started.

"We need more, better-paying, year-round jobs . . ."

BUILDING CITIZENSHIP

THINKING ABOUT VIEWPOINTS

1. What is the viewpoint of each person? What issue in the park most concerns each person?
2. How are some of the viewpoints alike? How are they different?
3. What other viewpoints might people have on this issue?

SHARING VIEWPOINTS

Discuss what you agree with or disagree with about these and other viewpoints. Then as a class, write three statements about land use in the Adirondack Park that all of you can agree with.

LOCAL CONNECTIONS
ROCHESTER:
LEARNING FROM PICTURES

"Today we are going to 'read' pictures," Mrs. Moser announced to her fourth-grade class in Rochester.

"What do you think these children are doing?" she asked.

"It looks like they are delivering newspapers," said Joyce, "but they really look different."

"One picture was taken in 1860. The other was taken recently," Mrs. Moser explained. "What do these pictures tell us about the clothes these children wore and the way they delivered their papers?"

"The newspaper boy is wearing a long coat. The newspaper girl is wearing tennis shoes and a baseball cap," said Brian.

"The girl is on a bike. She is carrying her papers in a bag," said Courtney. "The boy is standing, and he is carrying his papers in a strap."

"Why does he carry a lantern?" asked Ron.

"He may be out selling papers late at night or early in the morning when it is still dark, so he uses the lantern for light," Aaron said.

The teacher then asked the students to look at the photographs taken at the corner of East Avenue and Stillson Street. "One photograph was taken during World War II. The other photo was taken recently," she explained.

Mrs. Moser asked the students to read the signs by the lamp post in the picture taken during the war.

"No parking—reserved for U.S. Army cars. Enlist in the WAVES," Marty read. "What are WAVES?"

"WAVES was the name given to the women who served in the Naval Reserve," Mrs. Moser explained. "The signs and the banners with red crosses are also a reminder of the war."

"The other picture looks just like East Avenue and Stillson Street today," Dennis said. "Now the signs say, 'No Parking Anytime' and 'One Way.'"

Rochester Public Library

Rochester newspaper carriers in 1860 and today.

234

"The fire hydrant is still there," said Sandy, "but the sidewalk now has a curb cut for wheelchairs."

The students also looked at photographs of an early fire fighter and fire fighters today. They looked for more photos in old magazines and newspapers. They decided that photographs were a good way to learn about the history of their community. So they made a display on the bulletin board as a way of sharing their information with others.

▌ The students in Mrs.
▌ Moser's class made this
▌ bulletin-board display of
▌ historic and modern
▌ pictures of Rochester.

MAKE your LOCAL CONNECTION

Where can you find old photographs of your community? What do these photographs tell you about life in your community? Work with other students to collect photos. Then make a display for others to see.

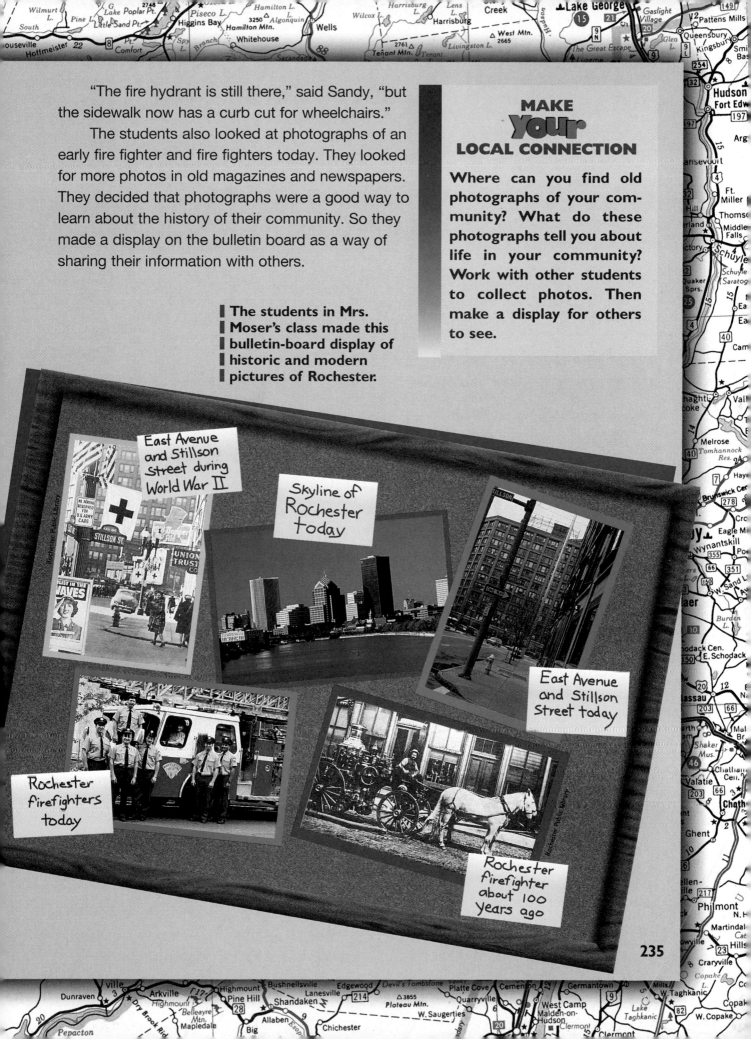

East Avenue and Stillson Street during World War II

Skyline of Rochester today

East Avenue and Stillson Street today

Rochester firefighters today

Rochester firefighter about 100 years ago

CHAPTER 9 REVIEW

Major Events

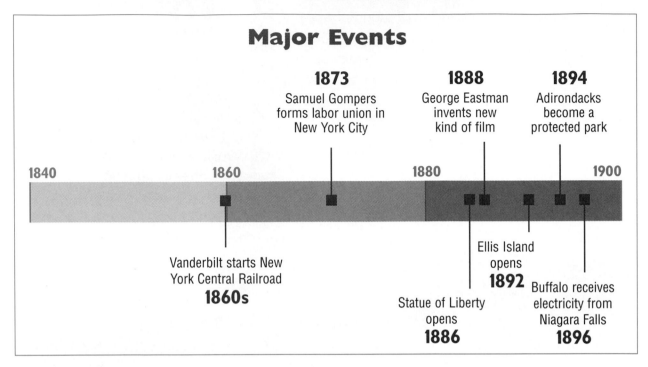

1873
Samuel Gompers forms labor union in New York City

1888
George Eastman invents new kind of film

1894
Adirondacks become a protected park

1840   1860   1880   1900

Vanderbilt starts New York Central Railroad
1860s

Ellis Island opens
1892

Statue of Liberty opens
1886

Buffalo receives electricity from Niagara Falls
1896

THINKING ABOUT VOCABULARY

Number a sheet of paper from 1 to 5. Next to each number write the letter of the definition that best matches the word or phrase.

1. rural
   a. of a park
   b. of the countryside
   c. of a neighborhood in a city

2. labor union
   a. all the people working in a factory
   b. a company
   c. a group of workers who work for better conditions

3. tenement
   a. a poorly built apartment building
   b. an elegant home in a city
   c. a small house in the countryside

4. suspension bridge
   a. a short stone bridge
   b. a bridge made of stone and steel
   c. a large bridge that hangs from cables

5. strike
   a. workers refusing to work in order to demand changes
   b. people working without any rest
   c. workers suffering from dirty, dangerous conditions

THINKING ABOUT FACTS

1. What advantages do trains have over steamships and canalboats?
2. What did Lewis Lattimer improve?
3. How did George Eastman's invention change photography?
4. Why did immigrants come to the United States?
5. Who was Emily Roebling?

236

THINK AND WRITE

WRITING A LETTER

Suppose you arrived in the United States from another country in 1910. Write a letter to your family describing the United States.

WRITING AN EXPLANATION

Write a paragraph explaining how an invention has changed your life.

WRITING A TRAVEL BROCHURE

Write a travel brochure encouraging people to visit the State Capitol building in Albany.

APPLYING STUDY SKILLS

REFERENCE SOURCES

1. What is a reference source?
2. Which reference source would you use to find an article about the Brooklyn Bridge?
3. What kind of information can you find in a dictionary? How is a dictionary different from an encyclopedia?
4. When you look for a word in the dictionary, what should you look for at the top of each page?
5. How might reference books be helpful when you are studying history?

Summing Up the Chapter

Use the following time line to organize information from the chapter. Copy the time line on a piece of paper. Then add events that took place in the years given on the time line. When you have filled in the time line, use the information to write an answer to the question "How did New York develop?"

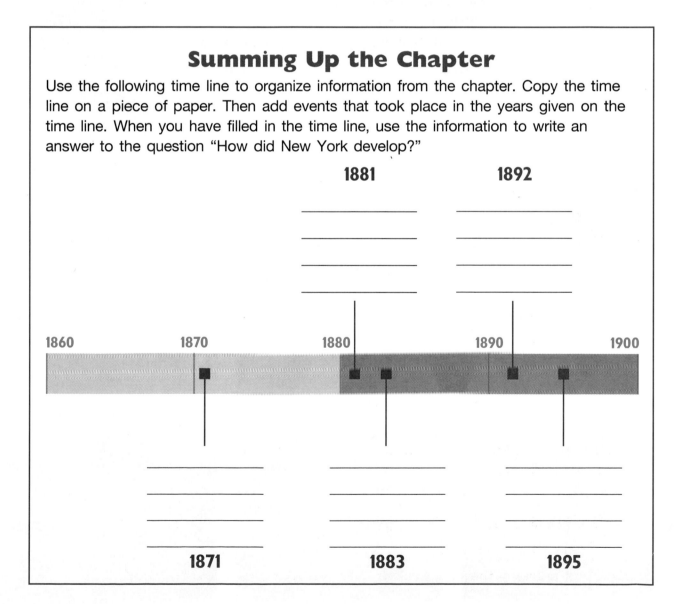

CHAPTER 10

A New Century

THINKING ABOUT HISTORY AND ECONOMICS

The 1900s brought both good times and hard times to New York. People came to New York to find jobs and start new lives. The people of New York fought in two world wars in Europe. At home they worked hard to get the right to vote and the right to be treated fairly. In Chapter 10, you will read about all of these events in our state's history and more.

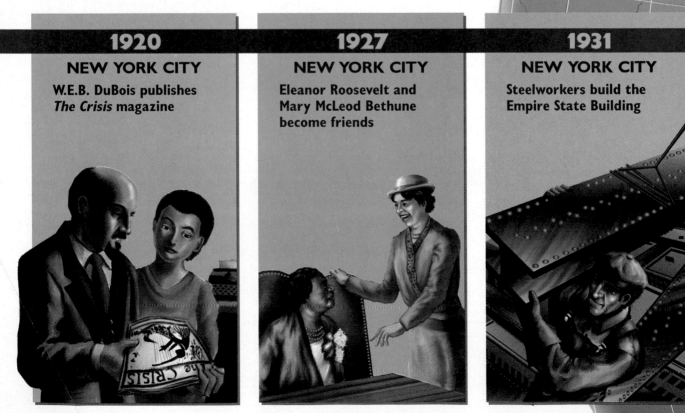

1920
NEW YORK CITY
W.E.B. DuBois publishes *The Crisis* magazine

1927
NEW YORK CITY
Eleanor Roosevelt and Mary McLeod Bethune become friends

1931
NEW YORK CITY
Steelworkers build the Empire State Building

CANADA

Buffalo

Lowell

NEW YORK

New York City

UNITED
STATES

ATLANTIC
OCEAN

1943

BUFFALO

Women work in factories during World War II

1954

LOWELL

First section of New York State Thruway opens

239

1890　1900　　　　　1930　　1950　　1970

Buffalo and Erie County Historical Society

NEW YORK IN THE EARLY 1900s

Focus Activity

READ TO LEARN
What happened in New York during the early 1900s?

VOCABULARY
Allies
Central Powers
neutral
amendment
Great Migration
Harlem Renaissance
subway
skyscraper

PEOPLE
Carrie Chapman Catt
Harriot Stanton Blatch
W.E.B. Du Bois
Duke Ellington
Langston Hughes

PLACES
Empire State Building

READ ALOUD

On April 2, 1917, President Woodrow Wilson told Americans to prepare for war. "It is a fearful thing to lead this great peaceful people into war," he said. "But [doing] the right [thing] is more precious than peace, and we shall fight for the things which we have always carried nearest our hearts."

THE BIG PICTURE

World War I had started in Europe in 1914. It was a war between two groups of countries. On one side were Great Britain, Russia, France, and Italy. These countries were called the Allies. On the other side were Germany, Austria-Hungary, and Turkey. This side was called the Central Powers.

At first, most Americans wanted to remain neutral. Neutral means not taking sides. Then Germany's submarines began attacking ships with American citizens on board. This made Americans angry. Four days after President Wilson's speech, the United States entered the war on the side of the Allies.

World War I certainly changed things in New York. Business and industry boomed as factories began making products to supply Allied troops. Workers were needed to replace the men who had become soldiers. Women took many of these jobs. So did African Americans who left the South and began to make a new life in the North.

240

A CHANGING WORLD

The war was already three years old when the United States joined the fight. The large numbers of American troops would turn the war in favor of the Allies. About 600,000 New Yorkers served during the war. That was more than any other state. About 5,000 New York women served as nurses.

On the home front, New York factories made military equipment, ammunition, and uniforms. The Brooklyn Navy Yard built battle-ships. Pilots trained at two large airfields on Long Island. Families in New York cut down on the foods they bought so that soldiers would have enough.

In the fall of 1918, the war ended. The Allies won. The countries in Europe suffered greatly because the war was fought on their land. The United States was now the strongest country in the world.

Women Get the Right to Vote

One result of World War I is that women in the United States finally got the right to vote. In Chapter 8 you read about women organizing to demand equal rights. In the 1900s new leaders stepped forward to continue the fight. Many were from New York, including Carrie Chapman Catt and Harriot Stanton Blatch. Blatch was the daughter of Elizabeth Cady Stanton.

In 1910, Blatch organized the first big suffrage parade. It took

The first suffrage parade in New York City was organized by Harriot Stanton Blatch.

place in New York City. Marchers carried banners and wore yellow "Votes for Women" sashes. The march grew larger every year after that.

In 1915, Catt led the National American Woman Suffrage Association. She insisted that women work just as hard for the war effort as for suffrage. Women worked in factories, raised food and money, and made clothing and bandages. Their work finally helped convince male voters that women should be allowed to vote. An amendment, or change, was made to the Constitution that gave women the right to vote. The Nineteenth Amendment became law in 1920.

THE HARLEM RENAISSANCE

When America joined the fight in World War I, New York had many jobs. There were not enough people to fill them. Thousands of African Americans moved, or migrated, from their homes in the South to take these jobs. So many people migrated to the northern states that their move is called the **Great Migration**.

Harlem

By 1920, Harlem was home to the largest African American community in the United States. It was also home to artists of all kinds. Painters, sculptors, writers, poets, dancers, and musicians lived in Harlem. Together, their artistic efforts became known as the **Harlem Renaissance** (RE nuh sahns). Renaissance refers to a time when important works of art and learning are being created.

W.E.B. Du Bois (doo BOYZ) was one of the first to encourage the Harlem Renaissance. He helped start a magazine called *The Crisis* (KRI sihs). It published works by African American writers. In 1920 DuBois said that it was time for a "renaissance" in African American art. "Only we can tell the tale and sing the song from the heart."

During the 1920s, jazz music became very popular. Jazz is rooted in African American culture. **Duke Ellington** wrote some of the

best known jazz songs. One of them is on the next page. What do you think Ellington meant by "that swing"? Today Ellington is considered one of America's greatest composers.

Langston Hughes

Perhaps the most famous writer of the Harlem Renaissance was **Langston Hughes** (HYOOZ). He wrote plays and stories and books for children. However, he is best known for writing poems. Read his poem "Stars" below.

O, sweep of stars over Harlem streets,
O, little breath of oblivion [nothingness] that is night.
A city building
To a mother's song.
A city dreaming
To a lullaby.
Reach up your hand, dark boy, and take a star.
Out of the little breath of oblivion
That is night,
Take just
One star.

Harlem sculptor Augusta Savage made the sculpture *Gamin* (above). Langston Hughes (left) was a writer of the Harlem Renaissance.

DOWN AND UP IN NEW YORK

In the early 1900s, New York City had almost 4 million people. It had new bridges and new businesses. Manhattan was very crowded. There was not much land to spread out on. The streets were filled with horses, carriages, and trolleys. Traveling around the city was slow. As the population and businesses grew, New Yorkers had to look beneath the ground and up toward the sky to solve their "space" problems.

NEW YORK SKYSCRAPERS	
BUILDING AND CITY	**HOW BIG**
Guaranty Building Buffalo (1896)	13 stories 152 feet
Flatiron Building New York City (1903)	20 stories 286 feet
Woolworth Building New York City (1913)	60 stories 792 feet
Chrysler Building New York City (1930)	77 stories 1,046 feet
Empire State Building New York City (1931)	102 stories 1,250 feet
World Trade Center New York City (1976)	110 stories 1,350 feet

CHART WORK

This chart shows New York's most famous **skyscrapers**.

1. How tall is New York's tallest building?

Traveling Underground

How did New Yorkers solve the problem of crowded streets and slow traffic? The **subway** was the answer. The subway is a network of trains that run through tunnels under the streets. Some tracks were built above the street. Building began in 1900. The workers sometimes had to blast through solid rock.

On October 27, 1904, the first subway in New York began its first trip up and down Manhattan. People crowded into the entrance ways to take a look. Harry Lake was just nine years old when the subway opened. He remembered, "How new and clean it was and how fast the trains ran. Everything even smelled new."

The subway was a success. In the first year it was open, 106 million people rode the subway. Subway trains still serve millions of New Yorkers.

Scraping the Sky

When you picture New York City in your mind, what do you think of? Many people think of the city's skyline of tall buildings, or **skyscrapers**.

Skyscrapers have many stories. Is it tiring to walk up all those stairs? Thanks to Elisha Graves Otis, you don't have to. While building a factory in Yonkers in 1854, Otis invented a device that made elevators safe.

Otis's invention came in handy in the 1880s. That is when builders figured out a way to construct buildings using a steel "skeleton." The skeleton, or framework, made the building very strong without making it weigh too much. For the first time, buildings 10 stories or more became possible.

The Flatiron Building (far left) was one of New York City's first skyscrapers. Workers (above) place the last bolt on the Empire State Building. The Chrysler Building is in the center of the photo.

The first skyscraper in New York was the Guaranty (GA ran tee) Building in Buffalo. Built in 1896, it is 13 stories high. Soon skyscrapers began to rise in the skies of Manhattan.

The most famous skyscraper in New York is the Empire State Building. Construction began in 1930. The *New York Times* said it was "a chase up into the sky." Workers climbed high into the air. They put together steel beams that made the frame for the skyscraper. Then they added floors, walls, and other parts.

When the Empire State Building opened on May 16, 1931, it stood 1,250 feet high—at that time the tallest building in the world.

WHY IT MATTERS

The early 1900s was a time of great change. Americans helped win what was called the "war to end all wars." The United States had become the most powerful country in the world. Life was better than it had been for most New Yorkers, including women and African Americans. In Lesson 2 you will read about how life changed in the 1930s.

✓✓ Reviewing Facts and Ideas

SUM IT UP

- The United States became the most powerful country in the world after World War I.

- After years of struggle, women got the right to vote.

- During the Harlem Renaissance, many African Americans expressed their ideas and feelings through art.

- People in New York solved problems of too much traffic and too little land by building subways and skyscrapers.

THINK ABOUT IT

1. Give two ways that New Yorkers helped win World War I.

2. Who were Carrie Chapman Catt and Harriot Stanton Blatch?

3. **FOCUS** What happened in New York during the early 1900s?

4. **THINKING SKILL** Identify a *cause* and *effect* that you read about in this lesson.

5. **WRITE** Write a poem or a description about a building in your community.

Photography

There is an old saying that "a picture is worth a thousand words." This means that you can tell just as much by looking at one picture as you can by reading a description a thousand words long! Some photographs are worth many thousands of words. Like some paintings, these photographs are works of art. They tell us about the past or the present. They can amaze us with beauty.

Many of the country's most famous early photographers lived and worked in New York. Lewis Hine photographed immigrants to New York in the early 1900s. Through his pictures, he showed what life was like for these newcomers.

Like Hine, James VanDerZee also showed what life was like in New York. Many of his photographs show life in Harlem in the 1920s and 1930s.

Berenice Abbott focused her camera on the buildings and streets of New York City. In the 1930s she photographed the city as it changed and grew.

These photographers let us see and feel how things looked in the past. Their photographs are a legacy we learn from today.

The Collection of Walter and Naomi Rosenblum

Lewis Hine photographed this young Jewish woman (above) at Ellis Island and an Irish family (right) in a New York City tenement.

Berenice Abbott showed the Blossom Restaurant (below) on the Bowery, a street in New York City. Her photograph of ironwork at 60 Wall Tower looks northeast across Manhattan (right).

James VanDerZee made these portraits of a bookkeeper (left) and World War I soldiers (below).

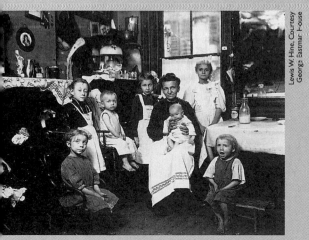

1890   1910   1929   1945 1950   1970

Focus Activity

READ TO LEARN
How were New Yorkers affected by the Great Depression and World War II?

VOCABULARY
Great Depression
New Deal
ration
Allies
Axis Powers

PEOPLE
Franklin Delano Roosevelt
Eleanor Roosevelt
Mary McCleod Bethune
John D. Rockefeller, Jr.

THE GREAT DEPRESSION AND WORLD WAR II

READ ALOUD

In 1929, a photographer named Gordon Parks was 16 years old. He was working his way through high school. On October 24, the stock market "crashed." The prices of stocks fell sharply. Parks wrote, "I couldn't imagine such . . . disaster touching my small world; it surely concerned only the rich. But by the first week of November I too knew differently; along with millions of others across the nation, I was without a job."

THE BIG PICTURE

After World War I, many people put their money in the stock market. Some people borrowed money from banks to buy stocks, too. The prices of stocks climbed sky high. Then, in the fall of 1929, the prices started to drop. People tried to sell their stocks before the prices fell even more. The problem was that almost no one wanted to buy them. As a result, the prices of stocks came crashing down.

Many people lost all their money. Those who had borrowed money could not repay the banks. Each day dozens of banks closed down. So did businesses. Millions of people lost their jobs. This was the start of a time in the United States called the Great Depression—a time when businesses failed and many people had no jobs.

NEW YORK IN HARD TIMES

The Great Depression hit hard in our state. People lost their savings when banks closed. Factory workers in cities like New York City, Buffalo, and Rochester lost their jobs. Families in places like Clinton County lost their farms.

Franklin Delano Roosevelt, often known as FDR, had been elected governor of New York in 1928. After visiting "practically every part of the state," FDR noted that "the depression exists not only in a few of the larger cities but extends to all the smaller cities and even to the villages and rural districts." Many people were left homeless or had to live in rundown shacks. When people looked for jobs, they often found locked factories with the sign: "No Help Wanted."

Help for New York

Governor Roosevelt set up programs to help New Yorkers who were out of work. The state government provided money to build roads, bridges, and other projects. By 1932, about 75,000 New Yorkers had been hired to work on public projects such as roads, bridges, and reservoirs. In Albany, workers built the Alcove and Basic Reservoirs to bring more drinking water to the people in the city.

Often farmers did not have enough money to pay their taxes. If they did not pay them, they would lose their farms. Roosevelt helped to lower the amount of state taxes that farmers had to pay. Roosevelt also made sure that schools in these communities got help from the state government to keep running.

Since Governor Roosevelt was helping people in New York, many people thought he could help all the states. They thought he should run for President.

Some people out of work in New York City were homeless (right) and many stood in long lines for free bread (above).

FDR AS PRESIDENT

In 1932, FDR was elected President. He was not the first Roosevelt to be President. In Chapter 9, you read about President Theodore Roosevelt. Franklin and Theodore were cousins.

The New Deal

When FDR agreed to run for President, he said these words: "I pledge [promise] you, I pledge myself, to a new deal for the American people." When he became President, his programs to fight the Depression were called the New Deal.

Some of Roosevelt's programs lent money to banks and businesses to keep them open. Other programs, like the ones in New York, let people earn money by working at government jobs. Two of the best-known programs were the Civilian Conservation Corps (CCC) and the Works Progress Administration (WPA).

The CCC planted trees in the Adirondacks. In the summer, fires were often a great danger there. When a fire would break out, CCC workers helped to fight it.

The CCC was run like the Army. Workers lived in barracks. Their rent and food were paid for, so the workers sent most of the money home to help their families.

WPA workers built bridges, parks, and airports. One airport they built was La Guardia Airport in Queens. They paved roads and fixed up schools. Many miles of road were paved in Albany. In New York City, 255 playgrounds were built.

Some WPA workers taught classes and made clothing. There were projects for artists and writers. Actors and musicians entertained at schools. Photographers recorded on film how people lived during the Great Depression. Some painters made murals, or large wall paintings, for public buildings. The post office in Amsterdam has a mural that was painted during the Great Depression.

A Tompkins County farm wife (right) was one of many New Yorkers helped by the New Deal. Franklin and Eleanor Roosevelt (center) make speeches broadcast on radio. American troops (far right) fight in Italy in World War II.

The First Lady

As the wife of FDR, Eleanor Roosevelt went from being the First Lady of New York State to the First Lady of the United States. Eleanor Roosevelt cared about people of all races and religion. She believed that people should be treated equally and fairly. When she lived in New York, she had become friends with the African American leader Mary McLeod Bethune (mi KLOWD be THOON). They met in 1927 at a meeting of the National Council of Women at the Roosevelt home. Bethune talked with Eleanor Roosevelt about the unfair treatment and lack of opportunities that African Americans faced. Mrs. Roosevelt spoke out. She said, "The day of working together has come, and we must learn to work together, all of us, regardless of race or creed or color." *Creed* means someone's beliefs. Until she died in 1962, Eleanor Roosevelt worked hard for the rights of all Americans.

World War II

Slowly, the United States economy improved after 1932. However, the Great Depression did not really end until World War II began in 1939.

The war was fought in Europe, Asia, and Africa. On one side were countries known as the Allies: Great Britain, France, the United States, and the Soviet Union. On the other side were the Axis Powers: Germany, Italy, and Japan. The war began when Germany invaded Poland and other countries. The Allies stepped in to stop the Germans.

At first, factories in the United States made supplies for the Allied countries. As the factories grew larger, more workers were needed. Many who lost their jobs in the Great Depression were working again. When Japan bombed Pearl Harbor, Hawaii, on December 7, 1941, the United States entered the war. About 1,700,000 people from New York fought in the war.

THE HOME FRONT

New York played an important role in the war effort. Industries were busy making war goods for the United States government. Factories in Rochester built telescopes and telephone switchboards. In the Buffalo-Niagara area one aircraft company built about 10,300 airplanes. In Bethpage another company built more than 17,000 fighter planes. That was more than any other factory in the country made.

The war effort needed a lot of resources. The government asked people all over the country to **ration** (RA shun), or use less of, things like rubber, metal, and food.

People drove their cars as little as possible, saving gas and tires for the war. They also collected scrap metal, newspapers, rags, and even grease. These materials were recycled and made into war products.

New York's farms were growing lots of food. Much of it was being sent overseas. People who weren't farmers were encouraged to grow some of their own food. Many planted "victory gardens" to help the United States win the war.

Josephine Case remembers what it was like in Hamilton during the war years. What do you think it was like growing up then?

Women such as this Buffalo steel worker (right) and these Bethpage airplane builders (far right) were an important part of the war effort.

Excerpt from "The Home Front in Upstate New York," *Yorker Magazine,* **Summer 1995 by Josephine E. Case**

*Gasoline was rationed; like food, it was needed by the men and women who were fighting the war. And no new cars were made, only tanks and jeeps, so we didn't go on long car (or bus or plane) trips. If we traveled at all, it was by train, and the trains were filled with men in Army or Navy uniform. Mostly we stayed home, walked or bicycled to school, put on **dramatic productions**, sledded in winter, and played softball on summer evenings.*

dramatic productions: plays

Cradle of Aviation Museum

KEEPING THE PEACE

On September 2, 1945, newspapers and radios blared the news, "The war is over!" People ran into the streets laughing and cheering. Now Americans turned their attention to keeping the peace.

In the spring of 1945, before the war was over, representatives from 50 countries met in San Francisco. They laid out the plans for an organization to keep peace throughout the world. The organization was the United Nations, or UN.

New York City was chosen for the UN's headquarters. Wealthy New York businessman John D. Rockefeller, Jr., gave the UN $8.5 million to buy land for its buildings. The United Nations still works to keep world peace. Today, 185

The United Nations buildings (above) display the flags of all the member countries.

countries send representatives to the UN. It brings all the world to New York!

WHY IT MATTERS

The Great Depression was a very hard time for many New Yorkers. Ideas that FDR first acted on in New York continued to lead the way in the effort to win World War II and keep the peace afterward.

✔ Reviewing Facts and Ideas

SUM IT UP

- During the Great Depression, many businesses closed down, and many people lost their jobs.

- Both New York and the national government set up programs to put people back to work.

- New York's industry helped to win World War II.

- The United Nations was started to keep peace between countries.

THINK ABOUT IT

1. What were the CCC and WPA?

2. Name two things New Yorkers did or produced for the war effort.

3. **FOCUS** How were New Yorkers affected by the Great Depression and World War II?

4. **THINKING SKILL** Place these events in *sequence*: World War II, the start of the UN, the Great Depression, the stock market crash.

5. **WRITE** Suppose you had been a reporter during the Great Depression. Write a paragraph describing what life might have been like.

1890   1910   1930 1946   1978

NEW WAYS OF LIVING

Focus Activity

READ TO LEARN
What changes took place in New York after World War II?

VOCABULARY
suburb
commute
interstate highway
discrimination
civil rights
pollution

PEOPLE
Nelson Rockefeller
Thurgood Marshall
Shirley Chisholm
Herman Badillo
Betty Friedan

PLACE
Levittown
Love Canal

READ ALOUD

Nelson Rockefeller was elected governor of New York in 1958. In a speech that year he talked about how he would govern the state. "Government must be given a new energy" to solve many new problems, he said. Only with courage and good ideas would government "match the aspirations [hopes] of the sixteen million people of this great state."

THE BIG PICTURE

The end of World War II brought many changes to life in the United States. In 1946, soldiers returning from the war were eager to settle down and start families. Many of these new families moved to the suburbs. Suburbs are communities outside of, but close to, a larger city. There was a big demand for new houses and roads. Businesses needed to supply more jobs for a rapidly-growing population.

After World War II, African Americans continued their struggle for equal rights. Women also wanted more rights as they looked for work outside their homes. Many people were concerned about the wasteful use of resources and damage to the environment.

New York leaders would need a lot of courage and good ideas to deal with these changes. People must have believed Nelson Rockefeller had them. They elected him governor four times.

Highways like the New York State Thruway (left) allowed workers to commute to work. Suburbs like Levittown (above) grew quickly in the 1940s and 1950s.

FROM CITY TO SUBURB

In the 1950s, many people wanted to raise their families in the suburbs. They wanted quiet neighborhoods for their children to play in. They wanted shopping centers and schools nearby.

Many older suburbs had large houses for wealthy families. In 1946, however, the building firm of Levitt and Sons bought farmland on Long Island. Their plot was only 25 miles from Manhattan. They built hundreds of houses. Because the houses were alike, they could be built quickly and cheaply. Levitt and Sons sold them for less than $10,000 each.

People flocked to the new suburb called Levittown. Over 1,400 homes were sold on one day in March 1949, after some families had stood in line for four days. Levittown grew to over 17,000 homes and more than 80,000 people. The well-planned methods used by the Levitts were followed by builders in suburbs across the country.

Highways Span New York

Suburbs meant that people no longer needed to live close to where they worked. Instead they could commute, or travel back and forth, to work each day. Many commuters took trains. Others drove from suburbs to cities everyday. With so many cars on the road, the need for new highways was great.

A major highway called the New York State Thruway opened in 1954. The first completed section ran between Lowell and Rochester. The map on page 258 shows where the Thruway runs.

In 1956, our country's government passed a law that provided money for road building. With this law, the interstate highway system was set up. An interstate highway is a road that connects two or more states with at least two lanes of traffic in either direction. The Thruway became part of that system. It linked New York with Massachusetts, New Jersey, and Pennsylvania.

FAIR TREATMENT FOR EVERYONE

Suburbs and interstate highways improved life for many New Yorkers. But other problems were harder to solve. Some people still faced **discrimination**. Discrimination is an unfair difference in the way people are treated. For example, many African Americans and Puerto Ricans were paid less than other workers. Some were not hired for jobs they were well qualified for. Many were not able to go to good schools.

The National Association for the Advancement of Colored People, or NAACP, was formed in New York City in 1909 to work for **civil rights**. Civil rights are the rights of all people to be treated equally under the law. In the 1950s NAACP leaders such as New Yorker **Thurgood Marshall** fought against discrimination in schools. Marshall later became a judge.

Puerto Ricans also believed in the importance of education. In 1961, an organization called Aspira formed to help Puerto Ricans prepare for college.

African Americans and Puerto Ricans also became more involved in government. In 1968, New York City's **Shirley Chisholm** was the first African American woman to be elected to the United States House of Representatives. **Herman Badillo** (bah DEE yo) was the first Puerto Rican

member of the House in 1971. Chisholm and Badillo both worked to pass laws to end discrimination.

Concerns of Women

Women gained the right to vote in 1920. Yet in some ways they were still not treated as the equals of men. In 1966 **Betty Friedan**, who lived in Queens, helped start the National Organization for Women, or NOW. This organization worked to end job discrimination against women. It also tried to change peoples' attitudes about what contributions women could make to society.

Shirley Chisholm (above), Betty Friedan (top left), Thurgood Marshall (middle left), and Herman Badillo (left) are New Yorkers who worked for fair treatment for everyone.

LOVE CANAL

The growth of cities and suburbs had created serious problems in our environment. In 1978 people living at Love Canal, near Niagara Falls, were getting sick. They discovered that their homes were built over an old canal that had been filled with chemical wastes. The sickness caused by these chemicals forced everyone to leave the community. The wastes had to be cleaned up. It took 10 years before it was safe to move back into the area.

Love Canal became a symbol of the dangers of pollution. Pollution is what makes our air, water, or soil dirty.

Time to Clean Up

Too many cars and trucks pollute the air we breathe. Chemicals pollute the water we drink. The garbage we make pollutes the land. Americans throw out about 160 million tons of paper, glass jars, plastic containers, and bags of yard waste each year.

New Yorkers are learning to work together to solve environmental problems. Cleanups of Love Canal and the Hudson River, which you read about in Chapter 2, show that hard work can make a difference. There is still more to do. There is still more to learn about the careful use of our natural resources.

WHY IT MATTERS

After World War II, large suburbs and automobiles had a major effect on many people's lives. At the same time, there were many demands for reform. African Americans and women asked for equal rights. Problems in the environment affected everyone. These concerns are still important today. New Yorkers are still working hard to make life better.

✓ Reviewing Facts and Ideas

SUM IT UP

- After World War II, many people moved from cities to suburbs.
- African American groups, women's groups, and others organized to demand equal rights.
- The problem at Love Canal made many New Yorkers concerned about the environment.

THINK ABOUT IT

1. Why did people want to live in the suburbs?

2. What was one form of discrimination that the NAACP fought against in the 1950s?

3. **FOCUS** What changes took place in New York after World War II?

4. **THINKING SKILL** *Classify* different kinds of pollution mentioned in this lesson.

5. **GEOGRAPHY** How did people moving to the suburbs affect transportation in New York?

GEOGRAPHY SKILLS

Using Map Scales

VOCABULARY
scale

WHY THE SKILL MATTERS

Suppose your new job requires you to travel to many cities in New York. How can you find out how far apart these cities are? Scale on a map can tell you the answer. Scale is the relationship between the distance shown on a map and the real distance on Earth. A map has a scale because it is not as large as the area it shows.

Look at the map of New York and the East on this page. It is marked Map A. Then look at the map of New York on the facing page. It is marked Map B. The two maps are drawn to different scales.

Why are the two maps here drawn to different scales? Some maps need to include many details. To show many details, a map cannot include a very large area. A very detailed map that shows every street, tree and building might cover an area of only a few blocks. If less detail is necessary, a map can show a much larger area.

USING THE SKILL

Look again at Map A on this page. Find the map scale. The top line shows how many miles on Earth are shown by one inch on the map. One inch stands for 200 miles. The bottom line shows

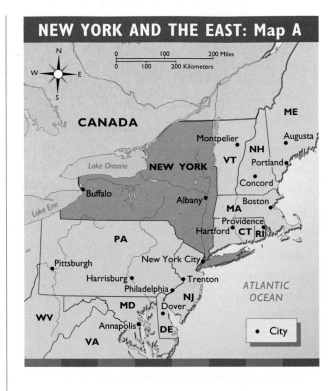

NEW YORK AND THE EAST: Map A

how many kilometers on Earth are shown by one and one-half centimeters.

Suppose you wanted to measure the distance from Buffalo to New York City. You might make a guess by looking at the map scale. However, you could make a more accurate measurement by using a scale strip.

Use the scale on Map A to make a scale strip. Place a piece of paper below the scale and mark the distances. Your scale strip should look like this:

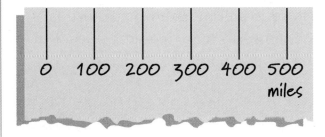

Place the edge of the scale strip between the symbols for the two New York cities. Make sure the zero is directly below Buffalo. Then read the numbers beneath New York City. You can see that the distance between the cities is about 300 miles. How far is Albany from Augusta, Maine? What is the distance in inches on the map?

TRYING THE SKILL

Now look at Map B on this page. This map shows some of the same area of land as the first one. As you can see, however, the maps are different sizes. If you compare the two map scales, you will see that they are different. On which map does one inch stand for a greater distance? Which map shows greater detail?   Use the Helping Yourself box for hints.

Make a scale strip for Map B. Using your scale strip, measure the distance between Watertown and Malone. What is the distance in miles? What is the distance in kilometers?

HELPING Yourself

- **Different scales allow maps to show either more detail or a greater area.**
- **Study the scale on the map.**
- **You can make a scale strip to find out the exact distance between points on a map.**

REVIEWING THE SKILL

1. What information does a map scale give us about a map?

2. How does using a scale strip help to make accurate measurements?

3. Which map would you use to find the distance between Malone and Utica? What is the distance between the two cities in miles? What is the distance in miles between Rochester and Rivehead?

4. What information is shown on Map A that is not shown on Map B?

5. When might it be helpful to use maps drawn to different scales?

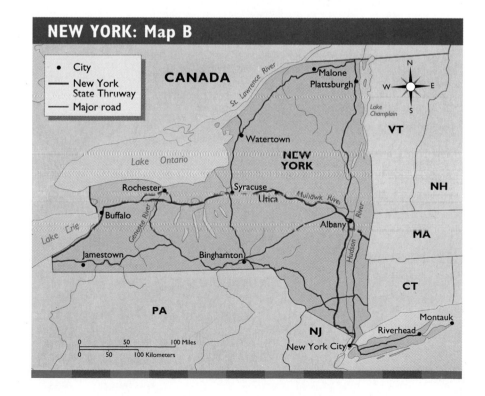

NEW YORK: Map B

- City
— New York State Thruway
— Major road

CANADA

St. Lawrence River
Malone
Plattsburgh
Lake Champlain
VT
Watertown
Lake Ontario
NEW YORK
Rochester
Syracuse
Utica
Mohawk River
Buffalo
Genesee River
Albany
Hudson River
NH
MA
Lake Erie
Jamestown
Binghamton
CT
Montauk
PA
Riverhead
NJ
New York City

0   50   100 Miles
0   50   100 Kilometers

259

LOCAL CONNECTIONS
THE BRONX:
LEARNING FROM INTERVIEWS

Students in Mr. Plagata's fourth-grade class in the Bronx were studying World War II.

"What did people in the Bronx do during the war?" asked Larry.

"That's an excellent question, Larry. Class, how can we find out about our community during the war?" Mr. Plagata asked.

"We could talk to someone who lived during the war," Susan said. "Sometimes my grandparents talk about things they did during the war."

Mr. Plagata explained that asking people questions to get information is called an interview. "I'll invite a friend of my family, Mrs. Beatrice Johnson, to visit our class and tell us about life during the war. To prepare for the interview, we'll make a list of the questions we want to ask her."

People could not get enough gasoline to run their cars during the war. They walked to shops and to visit others.

The next day Mrs. Johnson visited the class. She began her answers by saying, "I was 21 years old when the war began. I was a teacher in an elementary school here in the Bronx. My students were about your age."

She then explained that when war was declared, goods like gasoline, rubber, sugar, butter, and meat were rationed. Citizens at home could buy only small amounts over certain periods of time so the products could be used for the troops.

"People had to stop using their cars because the Army needed the gasoline. They walked or rode buses and trains. Bicycles were also rationed because the metal was needed. I was allowed to buy one so that I could get to work."

260

"Did kids our age help win the war?" Alex asked.

Mrs. Johnson told the class that people recycled everything that could be used for the war. Children collected scrap metals. They even saved balls of string and aluminum foil. These things were shipped to factories and used to make planes, trucks, and tanks. Fat and bacon drippings were saved because the grease could be used in making ammunition.

Mrs. Johnson also said that children helped by growing food in victory gardens. "If we raised our own food at home, there would be more food to send to the troops," she added.

"Were you afraid?" asked Clair.

"Sometimes. We were afraid of being attacked by enemy airplanes. So we held air raid drills. When the sirens blew, we turned off the lights and pulled down black shades that covered our windows. Citizens also took turns watching for enemy airplanes," she explained. "Americans gladly volunteered for any activity if it would help us win the war."

When she had answered all their questions, the students thanked Mrs. Johnson for sharing her experiences with them. Then they wrote a report on the interview that they could share with others.

MAKE your LOCAL CONNECTION

What was life like for people who lived in your community during an event in the past? Interview an older adult about an important time in the history of your community. Write a report on your interview. Then put the interviews in a booklet and display the book in the library for other students to read.

Asking people questions about their experiences is an interesting way to learn about historical events.

261

CHAPTER 10 REVIEW

Major Events

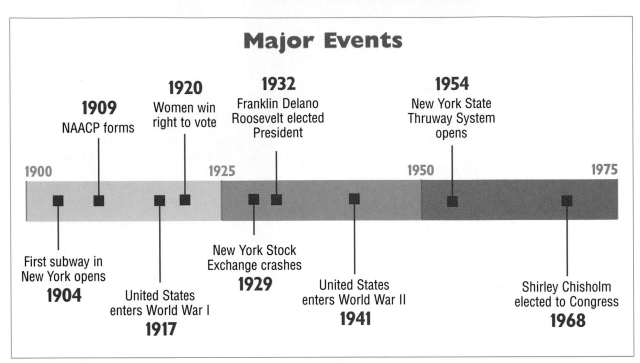

1909
NAACP forms

1920
Women win right to vote

1932
Franklin Delano Roosevelt elected President

1954
New York State Thruway System opens

1900   1925   1950   1975

First subway in New York opens
1904

United States enters World War I
1917

New York Stock Exchange crashes
1929

United States enters World War II
1941

Shirley Chisholm elected to Congress
1968

THINKING ABOUT VOCABULARY

Number a sheet of paper from 1 to 10. Beside each number write the word from the list below that best completes the sentence.

amendment	neutral
civil rights	pollution
commute	ration
discrimination	suburb
Great Depression	subway

1. The _____ was a time when businesses failed and many people lost their jobs.

2. _____ is something, such as a chemical, that makes air, water, or soil dirty.

3. An _____ is a change to the Constitution.

4. Many people live in a _____, outside of a city.

5. The rights of people to be treated equally under the law are _____.

6. _____ is an unfair difference in the treatment of people.

7. During World War II, people had to _____ things like rubber, metal, and food.

8. A _____ is a network of trains that run through tunnels underground.

9. People who _____ travel back and forth to work.

10. To be _____ is to not take sides.

THINKING ABOUT FACTS

1. What was the Harlem Renaissance?
2. What happened after the 1929 stock market crash?
3. Why were food, rubber, and metal rationed during World War II?
4. What helped people commute to work from suburbs faster?
5. Who was Thurgood Marshall?

THINK AND WRITE

WRITING AN INTERVIEW

Suppose you are a newspaper reporter preparing an interview with Eleanor Roosevelt. Write three questions you would like to ask her.

WRITING AN ART REVIEW

Write a review of a favorite work of art. Describe it and say why you like it.

WRITING A JOURNAL ENTRY

Suppose you worked for the CCC or the WPA during the New Deal. Write a journal entry describing what you did today.

APPLYING GEOGRAPHY SKILLS

USING MAP SCALES

Refer to the map on page 258 to answer the following questions.

1. How does a scale strip help to measure distances accurately?
2. What is the distance between Buffalo and New York City?
3. Approximately how many miles is it from Albany to Pittsburgh, Pennsylvania?
4. Which cities are closer to each other, Albany and Trenton, New Jersey, or Buffalo and Harrisburg, Pennsylvania?
5. Why is it useful to have maps drawn at different scales?

Summing Up the Chapter

Use the following cause-and-effect chart to organize information from the chapter. Copy the chart on a piece of paper. Then write at least two effects of each cause. When you have completed the chart, use it to write a paragraph titled "What impact did events of the first half of the 1900s have on New York?

CAUSE	EFFECT
The New York Stock Exchange crashes	
	Roosevelt's New Deal helps millions of people
The war effort needed a lot of resources.	
	Transportation becomes easier in New York.

UNIT 4 REVIEW

THINKING ABOUT VOCABULARY

Number a sheet of paper from 1 to 10. Next to each number write the word or term from the list that best matches the description.

amendment
civil rights
hydroelectric power
labor union
neutral
pollution
ration
suburb
sweatshop
tenement

1. A group of workers who push for better working conditions
2. Not taking sides
3. A change to the constitution
4. A poorly built apartment building
5. To use less of something
6. A substance that makes air, water, or soil dirty
7. Electricity made from flowing water
8. A factory where workers are paid low wages and work in unhealthy conditions
9. The rights of all people to be treated equally under the law
10. A community outside of, but close to, a larger city

THINK AND WRITE

WRITING A SONG LYRIC
Write the words to a song about your neighborhood.

WRITING AN EXPLANATION
Write a paragraph that explains the different kinds of reference books you might use at your school library.

WRITING A REPORT
Think of an invention you would like to learn more about. Do some research in the library and write a short report about the invention you chose.

BUILDING SKILLS

1. **Map scales** Why might you want to have the same area mapped at different scales?

2. **Map scales** Look at the maps on pages 258 and 259. Find three details shown on Map B that are not on Map A.

3. **Map scales** If you were planning to travel by car in New York, would you take Map A or Map B? Explain your answer.

4. **Reference books** Which reference book would you use to find the meaning of the word *tenement*?

5. **Reference books** How are reference books different from other books?

YESTERDAY, TODAY &
TOMORROW

The Statue of Liberty, Ellis Island, and the home of George Eastman are New York historical sites. They have been preserved so everyone can enjoy them. What do you think is the purpose of preserving historical sites? Do you think New York should continue to do so in the future? Why or why not?

READING ON YOUR OWN

These are some of the books you could find at the library to help you learn more.

COMING TO AMERICA: THE STORY OF IMMIGRATION
by Betsy Maestro
This beautifully illustrated book tells the story of immigration to the United States.

THE BIG BOOK OF REAL SKYSCRAPERS
by Gina Ingoglia
Read how skyscrapers are built, step by step. This book includes descriptions of many New York skyscrapers.

FARMER BOY
by Laura Ingalls Wilder
This book tells the story of a young boy growing up on a farm in northern New York.

UNIT PROJECT

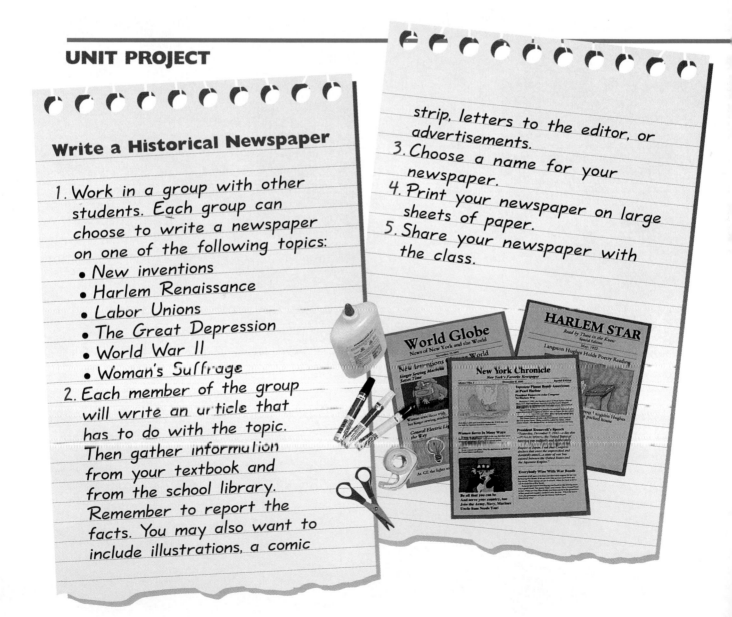

Write a Historical Newspaper

1. Work in a group with other students. Each group can choose to write a newspaper on one of the following topics:
   - New inventions
   - Harlem Renaissance
   - Labor Unions
   - The Great Depression
   - World War II
   - Woman's Suffrage
2. Each member of the group will write an article that has to do with the topic. Then gather information from your textbook and from the school library. Remember to report the facts. You may also want to include illustrations, a comic strip, letters to the editor, or advertisements.
3. Choose a name for your newspaper.
4. Print your newspaper on large sheets of paper.
5. Share your newspaper with the class.

GRAPE GROWING IN
WALKER VALLEY IN THE
CATSKILLS (LEFT)
NEW YORK CHEESES
(BELOW)
FREE CONCERT IN
CENTRAL PARK IN NEW
YORK CITY (RIGHT)

THE ROCHESTER
SKYLINE (ABOVE)
BOLDT CASTLE IN
THE THOUSAND
ISLANDS (LEFT)
NEW YORKERS AT
WORK (RIGHT)

New York Today

"New York has everything."

from Damir Lecek
See page 317.

WHY DOES IT MATTER

What is life like in New York today? What kinds of work do New Yorkers do? Do they work on farms, in factories, or in offices? Who makes laws in New York, and what do New York's citizens do to help the state? Who are New Yorkers, and what do we do to have fun? How do we celebrate our state?

THE EMPIRE STATE PLAZA IN ALBANY (FAR RIGHT) WORKING WITH HIGH TECHNOLOGY (RIGHT)

Adventures
with
NATIONAL GEOGRAPHIC

MetLife

City Sights

Go on! Bite the Big Apple! No matter how you slice it, New York City is big enough to go around. Start your day with a visit to the big green lady in the harbor—the Statue of Liberty. Climb the staircase to her crown for an awesome view. Next, travel to the Stock Exchange in Manhattan to see how fortunes are made (and lost) in a day. Then it's off to Central Park for a swinging time! Besides playgrounds, there are lots of scenic paths to stroll beneath the trees. In winter, you can even strap on a pair of skates and glide on the ice beneath the towering skyscrapers at Rockefeller Center. It's a great way to end your adventure in New York City— the Big Apple.

GEO JOURNAL

In your Geo Journal, list the sights that you'd like to see on a day trip to New York City.

CHAPTER 11

Working in New York

THINKING ABOUT
ECONOMICS AND GEOGRAPHY

People in New York work at many different jobs. They work in businesses and industries that produce all kinds of goods and services. These goods and services help make our lives better. As you read the chapter, you will learn more about businesses and industries in New York.

CANADA

Lake Ontario

Buffalo

NEW YORK

Odessa

Troy

Lake Erie

New York City

UNITED
STATES

ATLANTIC
OCEAN

Odessa

Valerie Hoffman helps her family to raise dairy cattle by hand-feeding the calves.

Buffalo

Ships carrying goods dock at New York's major port on Lake Erie.

Troy

Ball bearings for automobiles are one of the products manufactured in Troy.

New York City

Stock brokers buy and sell stocks on the New York Stock Exchange.

271

FARMING IN NEW YORK

READ ALOUD

Jeremy Hoffman is 14 years old. He and his family live on a large dairy farm in Odessa. Each year Jeremy shows his cows at the New York State Fair in Syracuse. He says, "The things I like about showing cows is that I get to meet lots of people that enjoy the same things I do. I also get to spend time with my animals. I make them look good, and explain farming to the people that come through the barns."

THE BIG PICTURE

The Hoffmans are one of thousands of families in New York who raise animals and crops to feed you and your family. Farming is very important in New York. Much of the land in our state is covered with rich soil and low, rolling hills that make it ideal for farming. In fact, over one quarter of New York's land is used for agriculture (AG rih kul chur). Agriculture is the business of growing crops and raising animals. The sale of crops and cattle is important to the state's economy. Around 70,000 New Yorkers make their living on farms. You can find food from New York farms on dinner tables all over the country.

Focus Activity

READ TO LEARN
What foods come from New York farms?

VOCABULARY
agriculture
livestock

GROWN IN NEW YORK

If you have corn for dinner tonight, you may be eating a vegetable grown in New York. Farmers in Western New York grow millions of bushels of corn a year. Besides corn, New York farmers grow potatoes, carrots, onions, snap beans, and cabbage.

Fruits grown in New York include strawberries, blueberries, and pears. Tons of grapes are grown near Lake Erie and in the Finger Lakes region. In fact, New York is the third largest grower of grapes in the United States.

You just read that the Hoffmans have a dairy farm. They raise cows to produce milk, butter, cheese, and other milk products. So do many of their neighbors. Other farmers raise livestock, or farm animals, for meat.

For example, many farmers in the St. Lawrence Valley raise beef cattle. Farmers in New York also raise chickens and turkeys.

No Bad Apples Here

What is your favorite kind of apple? It may have been grown right here in our state. New York is the second largest apple-growing state in the country. Over 25 million bushels of apples are grown in New York every year.

The chart below shows that some of the apples grown in New York are sold fresh in stores, and the rest are used to make products like juice, sauce, and pie filling.

Some kinds of apples grown in New York include MacIntosh, Red Delicious, and Empire. How do you think Empire apples got their name? Think about New York's nickname.

APPLES FROM SEED TO STORE

1. Seeds sprout from the ground.
2. Trees grow.
3. Apples are hand picked.
4. Apples are washed and sorted.
5. Apples are packed in bags.
6. Apples are shipped to stores or sent to make applesauce and juice.

LIFE ON THE HOFFMAN FARM

The Hoffman family works every day of the year. Jeremy feeds the cows and helps his father repair the farm machines. Valerie, Jeremy's older sister, feeds all the calves.

Ron Hoffman, Jeremy's father, runs the farm. His family has owned the farm since 1905. Mr. Hoffman takes care of all the cows and plants the crops. The Hoffmans grow hay, alfalfa, and oats to feed their cows. Mr. Hoffman likes what he does because "it is interesting and there is always something to do."

Carmella Hoffman, Jeremy's mother, helps with the milking each morning. She also pays the bills. She uses a computer program to keep track of how much money the farm makes and spends.

From Cow to Supermarket

The cows are milked twice a day. Mr. Hoffman's great-grandfather milked the cows by hand. Now farmers use machines to do this. About six cows can be milked at the same time. A computer system runs the milking machines. It tells the machines when to stop milking. The milk is pumped into a large cooled tank, where it is stored.

Every other day a truck comes and takes the stored milk to a milk plant. There it is put in jugs or cartons or made into cheese or butter. Then it is sent to the supermarket.

Carmella Hoffman keeps track of farm spending on a computer. Ron Hoffman milks the cows.

The Four Seasons

Each new season means different jobs must be done on the farm. Winter begins after the corn is harvested. Then it is time to repair the equipment and barns. The equipment must be in working order for the spring.

"Spring is the time of high energy," Mrs. Hoffman says. The fields have to be plowed and planted. Mr. Hoffman's great-grandfather used horse-drawn plows. Today many farmers pull their plows as they sit in air-conditioned tractors and listen to a radio or their favorite CDs. Besides raising food for the livestock, the Hoffmans plant vegetables for themselves.

In summer the hay is cut and then stored in the barns. This is also the time when Jeremy and Valerie show their cows at the Chemung County fair.

In the fall the corn is harvested, and the cows are put in the main barn. This must be done before the first snowfall.

All the work the Hoffmans do on the farm is important. You just might pour the milk from their cows on your breakfast cereal tomorrow!

WHY IT MATTERS

Farmers in New York grow many fruits and vegetables. They also raise animals for their milk, eggs, and meat. They provide food for people all over the world.

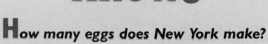

How many eggs does New York make?

New York chickens lay about 2 billion eggs a year. That's more than 100 eggs for every person in our state! With that many eggs you could make an omelet taller than the Empire State Building!

Reviewing Facts and Ideas

SUM IT UP

- The business of growing crops and raising animals is called agriculture.

- One quarter of the land in New York is used for agriculture.

- Apples, grapes, potatoes, cabbage, and dairy products are among New York's most important agricultural products.

- Farmers now use computers and other machines on the farm.

THINK ABOUT IT

1. What is agriculture?

2. Name two kinds of machines a farmer might use.

3. **FOCUS** What foods come from New York farms?

4. **THINKING SKILL** *Predict* how life would be different if farmers did not grow our food.

5. **WRITE** Suppose you live on a dairy farm. Describe what your day is like.

MADE IN NEW YORK

Focus Activity

READ TO LEARN
How is manufacturing an important part of New York's economy?

VOCABULARY
manufacturing
consumer
profit
import
export
publishing
technology
high technology

PLACES
Corning
Rochester
Syracuse

READ ALOUD

*New York State's motto is "Excelsior"
(ek SEL see or), which means "Ever Upward."
The state lives up to this motto by building new
businesses and creating new jobs for the people
of New York.*

THE BIG PICTURE

You read in the last lesson about New York's agriculture. What do farmers like the Hoffmans need besides animals and land? They use farm machines to plow the soil and harvest crops. They use trucks to transport animals. They need tools to repair those machines. They use chemicals to help plants to grow and to kill harmful insects. They use computers to run their businesses.

Where do all these things come from? They are products of manufacturing. Manufacturing means making goods in factories. New York has thousands of factories. They manufacture all kinds of useful goods—from farm machines to the shoes on your feet.

Manufacturing provides people with jobs and with goods to buy in stores. It is very important to New York's economy. With 18 million people, New York has one of the largest economies of any state.

276

BUSINESS IN NEW YORK

As you learned in Chapter 6, business in New York is based on the free enterprise system. Business people decide what to produce. Consumers decide if they want the product. Consumers are people who buy goods—like you.

Many people start up businesses to make a product that consumers need. Renee Allen Mancino is the owner of Carrot Top Pastries in New York City. Her mother and grandmother taught her how to bake. Renee started cooking as a way to earn money. She began selling carrot cakes to families in the late 1970s. In 1980 she was selling cakes from the back of a truck on Wall Street. Today, Renee owns two cafes and one large bakery. Her carrot cakes are now sold to

Renee Mancino's baking business is part of the free enterprise system.

New York City's best restaurants. Many businesses start small, like Renee's, and then grow larger as they become more successful.

The money a business has left after it pays its workers and its bills is called a profit. Profits can be used to expand the business, buy better equipment, or start other businesses.

New York Trade

New York is a world center for the trade of goods. Goods bought from another country are called imports. Goods sold to another country are called exports.

New York's ports are an important reason why the state is a leader in trade. New York has two coasts, one along the Atlantic Ocean and the other along Lake Erie. Hundreds of ships dock at ports to load and unload goods each day.

NEW YORK PRODUCTS

1. New York City ——→ Publishing

2. Buffalo ——→ Auto parts

3. Olean ——→ Ceramic tile

4. Troy ——→ Sporting goods

5. Schenectady ——→ Electric machinery

6. Keeseville ——→ Furniture

CHART WORK

Consumers use many different New York products.
1. Name three New York products.
2. What products do you use or own that come from New York?

MANUFACTURING IN NEW YORK

Most large manufacturers are located in cities. That is because factories need many workers who live nearby. One of New York City's main manufacturing industries is making clothing. Another is **publishing**, or the writing and printing of books, newspapers, and magazines. There are four major newspapers in New York City which together sell more than 1 million copies each day.

Buffalo is an important manufacturing city. Factories in Buffalo make iron and steel parts for automobiles and airplanes. The city's chemical factories make medicines and other chemical products. Other manufacturers make flour and animal feed from the grain grown in New York and other states.

Cameras and office machines are made in Rochester. Syracuse factories make air conditioners and auto parts. **Corning** is a leader in the glass industry. About 60,000 different glass products, from cookware to computer screens, are made in Corning. In fact, every American astronaut has looked out into space through a special window made by Corning.

High Technology

Manufacturing glass is an example of the way **technology** is used by industry. Technology is the use of skills, tools, and ideas to meet peoples' needs. Computers and

New Yorkers in Troy (above) manufacture small metal parts for cars. Other workers in New York (right) often use high technology to do their jobs.

other electronics are examples of **high technology**. High technology is the use of advanced scientific ideas and tools.

IBM is one of the largest makers of computers in the world. Its headquarters are in Armonk. IBM helped make New York a leader in manufacturing high-technology products.

Computers, electronic mail, the Internet, fax machines, and other high-technology products have changed the way people work. For example, people can now work at home and communicate with the business they work for by computer.

Elizabeth Booth works for The Wooden Spoon, a company that sells kitchen products. The business is based in Connecticut, but Booth works from an office in Fredonia, New York. She says that "my

computer and fax machine make it possible for me to travel 500 miles a day without ever leaving home."

Changes in Trade

From the 1860s, New York was a leader in manufacturing. However, in the 1980s and early 1990s, manufacturing slowed down. Buffalo's largest business, a steel company, closed its factory in 1983. Many other cities had factories close. Some businesses moved to southern states or to other countries where costs such as taxes are lower.

New York has begun to adjust to these changes. Smaller businesses have increased their trade with foreign countries. In addition, new businesses have been started that do not manufacture goods. You will learn more about these industries in the next lesson.

WHY IT MATTERS

Manufacturing is an important part of New York's economy. New York produces more manufactured goods than any other state except California. Companies in New York produce large amounts of photographic equipment, computers, glassware, steel parts, books, and magazines.

New York continues to grow because of new technology. High-technology products like computers have made many jobs easier to do.

✓ Reviewing Facts and Ideas

SUM IT UP

- Manufacturing is the making of goods in factories.
- New York's economy is based on the free enterprise system.
- New York's industry is mainly in cities like Buffalo, New York, Rochester, and Syracuse.
- High-technology products like computers make it easier to do many types of jobs.

THINK ABOUT IT

1. Identify three goods that are made in New York.

2. What is the free enterprise system?

3. **FOCUS** How is manufacturing an important part of New York's economy?

4. **THINKING SKILL** What *effect* do computers have on industry?

5. **GEOGRAPHY** Look at the map on page R14. Name at least five bodies of water that Buffalo's harbor connects.

NEW YORK SERVICES

Focus Activity

READ TO LEARN
How do service industries affect your life?

VOCABULARY
services
broadcasting
communications
financial services
insurance
tourism

READ ALOUD

Lois Johnson is the principal of an Early Child-hood Center in Buffalo. She has been a principal there for three years. "I love my job as principal. It is very hard work. Most of all, I love my school and all of the children and parents I see everyday. It gives me the greatest joy to know that teachers enjoy coming to work, parents enjoy visiting, and children enjoy learning."

BIG PICTURE

Lois Johnson helps children to learn. There are 650 children at her school. The Early Childhood Center teaches them from preschool through second grade. Teaching is an example of a service industry. Services are jobs that help people. Doctors, teachers, dentists, and waiters are all service workers. So are government workers, barbers, and people who work in stores. They help make our lives better. Industries that provide services are the largest part of our state's economy. In fact, over 5 million New Yorkers work at service jobs. Every year New Yorkers provide services worth more than 200 million dollars. Do people in your family have service jobs? What do they do?

HOW TV NEWS GETS TO YOU

2 The signal is sent to satellites in space.

3 Satellites beam signals to TV stations.

4 An antenna picks up signal and sends it to your TV.

1 Television programs are filmed.

AT YOUR SERVICE

Service industries do not make goods. Instead, they help people in many ways. Grocery stores, hospitals, and trucking are examples of service industries. The government also provides services. Building public parks to play in is an example of how the government provides a service.

Broadcasting and Communications

Before televisions, telephones, and radios were invented, it took people a long time to get news. Today, people hear about what is happening in the world using the broadcasting and communications industry. Broadcasting (BRAWD kast ing) means to send

Cellular telephones are one form of communications in New York.

news and information through television and radio. Communications (kuh myoo nih KAY shenz) is the exchange of sights, sounds, ideas, and other information, often using technology. Communications include telephones and electronic mail, as well as radio and television,

New York City is the broadcasting and communications center of the country. The four major television networks in our country are based there. They provide people with news, information, and our favorite television shows. Radio stations are found in cities and towns all across New York. They provide people with news, weather reports, and music every day. The broadcasting and communications industry helps people get information they need.

DID YOU KNOW?

Where did the first TV news broadcast take place?

In Schenectady, on August 22, 1928, the television station WGY broadcast a story about the United States presidential race between Herbert Hoover and Alfred E. Smith. Television news was a new way for people to see and hear important information about our state, country, and world.

Infographic

New York's Economy

From applesauce to zoos, New Yorkers produce many kinds of goods and provide many services. All these goods and services help to keep New York's economy healthy.

Cheese Please!

New York has a large dairy industry. It leads the country in cottage cheese production. More than 120 million pounds are made in New York each year.

Take a Trip

Millions of people visit New York each year. This makes tourism one of the biggest industries in our state. Visitors spend more than a billion dollars in New York each year!

Strike a Pose!

New York City is the fashion center of the world. Clothes are made in the garment district. Some of the world's top designers show their clothes at fashion shows in New York City every season.

Add It Up

International Business Machines, or IBM began as a small company in Endicott in 1890. It made punch cards that helped to count our country's population. Today, IBM makes computers. It is the fourth largest company in the United States.

Get Smart

Established in 1948, the State University of New York, or SUNY, is the largest university system in the country. It has 64 colleges, universities, and agricultural schools across the state. More than 300,000 students go to SUNY schools each year.

TOURISM

New York is a big state with many things to see and do. People come from everywhere to visit New York. They often go to places like Niagara Falls, Adirondack Park, or the Statue of Liberty. These are all part of the tourism industry. Tourism provides services such as hotels, tour-bus rides, or attractions to tourists, people who travel for fun. It is one of the largest service industries in the state. When tourists visit and spend money at parks, zoos, and museums, they help the economy grow.

Boating on the Hudson River is one of the forms of tourism in New York.

FINANCIAL SERVICES

You probably don't spend too much time thinking about money. But your parents, teachers, and other adults do. They often use financial services. These industries are involved with managing money. The main financial industries in New York are banking, insurance, and trading stocks. New York provides financial services for the entire country.

Banking

People and businesses use banks to keep and save their money. People and businesses can also borrow money from banks to open a bookstore or buy a house. Jessica Stein Diamond works for M & T Bank in Buffalo. She says the thing she likes best about working for a bank is "all the ways banks help people in the community. They make it easier for people to save money for college and to buy their first homes."

You will find banks in every town across the state. In fact, five of the six largest banks in the country are located here. More than 200,000 people in our state work for banks.

Insurance

If you have a bike, it is a good idea to have a bike lock. A lock protects your bike from being lost or stolen. Insurance is like a bike lock. It is an agreement people make to protect things like their house, health, or cars. The customer pays a sum of money to an insurance company. In return, if a tree falls on their house and breaks a window, home insurance helps pay for the damage. Sometimes people get sick and have to go to the doctor. Health insurance pays some of the doctor bills. There are insurance companies all over the state. Just like banks, about 200,000 people work for insurance companies in New York.

Stocks

Do you remember reading about the stock exchange in Chapter 6? Today the New York Stock Exchange is a huge room where people buy and sell shares of companies. It is still located on Wall Street. More than 4,500 people work at the Exchange selling more than 400 million shares of stock each day.

Two other stock exchanges are located nearby. They sell stocks for businesses not on the New York Stock Exchange. Business people all over the world keep their eyes on what happens on Wall Street.

THE ARTS IN NEW YORK

New York is famous for its arts. Artists provide a service when they create things for everyone to enjoy. Many writers, painters, musicians, dancers, and actors live in New York.

There are many ways to see and hear art in New York. Most cities and towns in New York have theaters, museums, concert halls, and libraries. You can go and watch a play, look at paintings, listen to a concert, or read a book.

Sherry Robbins, a poet who grew up in Washingtonville, says "the best part about being an artist is touching the lives of other people, especially kids. It's the best feeling to see a kid take an interest in art."

The arts can be fun for everyone. They are also good for New York's economy. Millions of people go to New York arts programs each year.

Concerts of the New York Philharmonic orchestra (below) are some of the many forms of the arts in our state. Poet Sherry Robbins (left) helps children to write in Buffalo.

WHY IT MATTERS

New York State has many service industries such as banking, tourism, and the arts. The state government also provides people with services like building roads and keeping our state parks clean and safe. As factories continue to move out of our state and our country, fewer New Yorkers work in manufacturing. That means that services play a more important role in our economy every year.

✓ Reviewing Facts and Ideas

SUM IT UP

- Service jobs help people rather than make things.
- Over 5 million New Yorkers are employed in services.
- Banking, insurance, tourism, and the arts are large service industries in New York State.

THINK ABOUT IT

1. What are some service industries in our state?

2. What is communications?

3. **FOCUS** How do service industries affect your life?

4. **THINKING SKILL** _Compare_ and _contrast_ how people communicated with each other before and after modern broadcasting and communications.

5. **WRITE** Write a paragraph explaining the kind of job you would most like to have. Why do you want that job? Is it a manufacturing job or a service job? How can you tell?

GEOGRAPHYSKILLS

Reading Time Zone Maps

VOCABULARY
time zone

WHY THE SKILL MATTERS

Many people today are able to do business over long distances with the help of computers, telephones, fax machines, and plane travel. Suppose a business person in Albany wants to talk to someone in Denver, Colorado. She would need to know what time it is in Denver before calling. If it is 9:00 A.M. in Albany, it's only 7:00 A.M. in Denver.

USING THE SKILL

Until the late 1800s towns across the country set their own time by the location of the sun in the sky. For example, it would be noon in Albany when the sun was directly overhead. However, a person traveling across the country by train would have no way of knowing what time it was in each town along the way. It was also hard for people who set train schedules to know when trains from different cities would arrive.

Time zones were set up to solve this problem. The world was divided into 24 different time zones—one for each hour in a day. Every town and city in the same time zone would use the same time. Starting from the prime meridian the time zones were laid out at every 15 degrees of longitude.

As you can see from the map key on page 287, the United States lies in six time zones. The map shows that the borders of the time zones no longer follow exact longitude lines. In many places they shift to follow the borders of states.

The time zone map will help you figure out what time it is in different parts of the United States. The time in any zone east of you is always later than it is in your time zone. As you move to the east, add one hour to the time for each time zone that you cross. The time in any zone west of you is always earlier than it is in your zone. As you move west, subtract one hour for each time zone that you cross.

Suppose it is 7:00 P.M. in Binghamton. What time is it in Seattle, Washington? To figure this out, count the number of time zones to the west of Binghamton until you reach Seattle. How many time zones are there? Now subtract one hour for each time zone going west. Binghamton and Seattle are three time zones apart. When it is 7:00 P.M. in Albany, it is 4:00 P.M. in Seattle.

If it is 9:00 A.M. in Seattle, what time will it be in Binghamton? Binghamton is three time zones east of Seattle, so the answer is 12:00 P.M.

TRYING THE SKILL

Using the time zone map and the Helping Yourself box, figure out the following time zone problems.

Suppose a person lives in Chicago and has a friend living in Orlando, Florida. How many time zones apart are they? Is Orlando east or west of Chicago?

What is the name of the time zone to the west of Phoenix? What time zone is to the east?

If the President plans to broadcast a live speech from Washington, D.C. at 5:00 P.M., what time will people hear the broadcast in Los Angeles, California? What time would people hear it in Dallas, Texas? How did you figure out the broadcast times?

Suppose your family is on vacation in Honolulu, Hawaii, and wants to call friends in New York City. It is 9:00 P.M. in Honolulu. What time is it in New York? Is it too late to make the call?

HELPING Yourself

- **A time zone is one of 24 divisions of Earth used to measure standard time.**
- **Find your starting point on the map.**
- **Add an hour for each time zone east of you. Subtract an hour for each time zone west of you.**

REVIEWING THE SKILL

1. What is a time zone?

2. What time zone do you live in?

3. When people in San Francisco, California, are waking up at 7:00 A.M., what time is it in your town? In Anchorage, Alaska? How do you know?

4. If you leave at 4:00 P.M. to take an hour-long plane trip from Columbus, Ohio to Chicago, Illinois, what time will it be when you arrive in Chicago?

5. Why might knowing how to read time zone maps be an important skill to have when doing business with people across the United States?

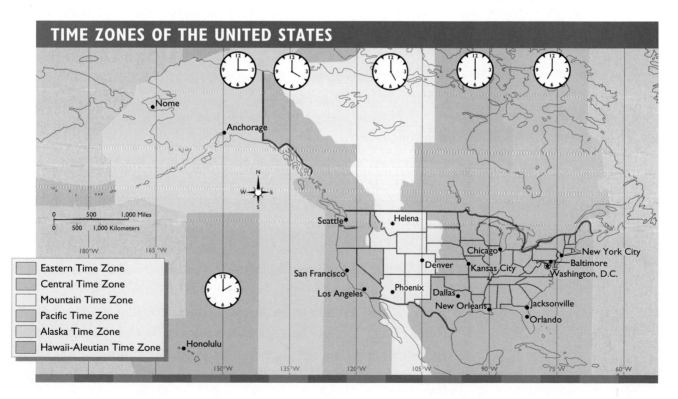

TIME ZONES OF THE UNITED STATES

Eastern Time Zone
Central Time Zone
Mountain Time Zone
Pacific Time Zone
Alaska Time Zone
Hawaii-Aleutian Time Zone

287

LOCAL CONNECTIONS
WATERTOWN:
LEARNING FROM WRITING LETTERS

Harold T. Wiley School
1351 Washington Street
Watertown, New York 13601
April 15, 1997

Mr. Mark Keaton, Vice President
Champion International Corporation
400 Anderson Avenue
Deferiet, New York 13628

Dear Mr. Keaton:
Our class is learning about the jobs people in our community do.

Please send us information about your company and how you make paper.

Thank you very much.

Sincerely,
Margaret Savas

Computers are used at a paper factory in Deferiet.

"Mrs. Bentley, when I grow up, how will I know what kind of job I want to do?" asked Ricardo.

"That's a good question, Ricardo," said Mrs. Bentley, his fourth-grade teacher in Watertown.

Mrs. Bentley asked the class how they could find out about jobs in their community.

"We've been learning how to write letters. We could write to businesses and ask them what kinds of jobs their workers do," Shawna suggested.

The students agreed that writing letters was a good way to get information. First, they wrote a letter to the Greater Watertown Chamber of Commerce. They asked for information about some of the businesses in their area.

In a few days, a large packet from the Chamber arrived. It included a directory, or book, of all the businesses in Jefferson County. The directory had information about the goods or services the businesses provided, the number of workers they had, their addresses, and the names of their presidents.

The students discovered that some businesses made food, paper, wood products, and chemicals. One company printed magazines. They also read about service businesses such as laboratories and hospitals.

The directory helped the students decide where they wanted to write to get information about jobs people do.

"I want to write a letter to the Champion International Corporation," said Margaret. "It makes paper and has 610 workers. My father works there. "

"My mother makes air fresheners for cars at the Car-Freshner Corporation. I want to know where the idea to start this business came from," said Winata.

Susan wrote to the area's largest employer, Fort Drum, which has more than 27,000 soldiers and other workers. She asked what kind of jobs the U.S. Army offers.

Rana wanted to learn more about surveying, or measuring land. She wrote a letter to LaFave, White & McGiven, a surveying company.

After the students received answers to their letters, they wrote reports. These reports included charts and graphs that showed what they had learned about the companies. The students also made a directory of businesses in their community. They displayed their directory in the library for other students to see.

MAKE **Your** LOCAL CONNECTION

What businesses are located in your community? What industries are important? What kinds of jobs do people do? Write letters to find out. Then work with other students to write a report your findings.

The Number of Workers at Companies in Our Community

Businesses in Our Community

Surveyors (top left) measure land when building new roads. Soldiers at Fort Drum (above) learn about artillery. Students made a report and directory (left) about businesses in Watertown.

289

CHAPTER 11 REVIEW

THINKING ABOUT VOCABULARY

Number a sheet of paper from 1 to 10. Beside each number, write the word from the list below that best matches the description.

agriculture
communications
export
financial service
insurance
livestock
manufacturing
publishing
service
technology

1. The writing and printing of books, newspapers, and magazines
2. The making of goods in factories
3. The business of growing crops and raising animals
4. A job that helps people
5. All the businesses involved with managing money
6. An agreement people make to protect themselves from losing money
7. Goods sold to other countries
8. The exchange of sights, sounds, ideas, and other information
9. Animals raised on farms
10. The use of skills, tools, and ideas to meet people's needs

THINKING ABOUT FACTS

1. Name three crops grown in New York.
2. What products are made in Buffalo?
3. What new technology has changed the way people work?
4. Name two different service industries in our state.
5. What are two different ways to broadcast news and information?
6. How are service jobs different from other jobs?
7. Who are consumers?
8. How can profits be used?
9. How has New York adjusted to changes in trade?
10. What are financial services?

THINK AND WRITE

WRITING AN EXPLANATION
Write a paragraph explaining why service industries are important to us in New York.

WRITING A DIARY
Imagine you are a dairy farmer. Write a diary entry explaining what you did today.

WRITING AN ADVERTISEMENT
Imagine you have set up your own manufacturing business. Write and illustrate a newspaper advertisement that explains what products you make.

APPLYING GEOGRAPHY SKILLS

Look at the map on page 287.

READING TIME ZONE MAPS

1. Into how many time zones is Earth divided?

2. How many time zones are there across the United States including Alaska and Hawaii?

3. Is the time in a zone east of you later or earlier that the time in your zone?

4. If you are in Syracuse at 8:00 P.M. and need to telephone a friend in Denver, what time is it in Denver?

5. Why is it useful to be able to read a time zone map?

Summing Up The Chapter

Use the following word map to organize information from the chapter. Copy the chart on a sheet of paper. Then write at least three pieces of information under each topic. When you have filled in the chart, use it to write a paragraph that answers the question "What goods and services do New Yorkers contribute to the world?"

NEW YORK'S GOODS AND SERVICES

Agriculture

Manufacturing

Services

CHAPTER 12

New York's Government

THINKING ABOUT GEOGRAPHY AND CITIZENSHIP

Have you ever wondered how you could help make changes in your community? Have you ever thought about ways you would like to help our state? Do you understand your responsibilities as an American? This chapter answers these questions and explains how you can become a good citizen.

CANADA

NEW YORK

Albany

UNITED STATES

ATLANTIC OCEAN

OUR LOCAL GOVERNMENT

Focus Activity

READ TO LEARN
What is the role of local governments in our communities?

VOCABULARY
government
municipal government
elect
city council
mayor
city manager
county
sheriff

READ ALOUD

Rosie Hoag is the mayor of Salamanca, New York. When she decided to run for office, she said, "I was born in Salamanca and have spent my whole life here. I decided to run for the mayor's office because I wanted to change things. If everyone works together it can be something different, something better."

THE BIG PICTURE

Rosie Hoag is enjoying one of the rights of citizens in the United States—the right to take part in government. As you read in Chapter 5, government is the laws and people that rule a country, state, or town.

The government has responsibilities, or duties. As mayor, Rosie Hoag works with the Salamanca city council to pass laws that make life in Salamanca better. Passing laws is one of government's responsibilities. Making sure the laws are carried out is another of government's responsibilities.

What are some other responsibilities of government? In this lesson you will read about the ways in which our city, county, and other local governments affect our lives.

GOVERNMENT IN YOUR COMMUNITY

People make many decisions for themselves. For example, you may like to go to your local playground. But what happens if your playground needs new equipment? This would cost a lot of money and would affect many people. A decision like this would be made by your local government. That is what governments do. They make decisions that affect your community.

The community where you live has a municipal (myoo NIS uh pul) government that provides services. A municipal government is the government of a village, town, county, or city. Some of the people who work in a municipal government are officials elected by the citizens. To elect means to

choose by voting. Other government workers are hired by elected officials.

Municipal governments take care of the streets and sidewalks where you live. They also run libraries, parks, and local police departments. If there is a fire, a municipal fire department puts it out.

Look at the photographs on this page. They show some of the services that municipal governments provide.

Some of the services provided by local government are street repair (top), libraries (above), police (left), and firefighting (far left).

295

MUNICIPAL GOVERNMENT

Like the city of Salamanca, most municipalities are governed by a **city council** and a **mayor**. The city council is a group of people who make laws for and help run a city or town. The city council is elected by the people who live in the city. The mayor is the head of the municipal government. In some cities, the mayor is elected. In other cities the city council chooses the mayor.

Mayors and city council members often do not work for the government full-time. They have other jobs. You can see from the chart on this page that some cities also have a **city manager**. In cities such as Watertown and Elmira, the mayor and city council hire a full-time city manager to run the city's daily business.

New York City's Government

New York City is the largest city in the United States. Because of its size, it is governed somewhat differently from other cities. You learned in Chapter 9 that New York City is made up of five boroughs (BU roz). Each borough elects a borough president. Borough presidents help run their boroughs.

New York City is governed by a mayor and a city council. They make laws for people in all five boroughs. People from the five boroughs elect the mayor and the council members.

Other government groups help the city government take care of the city. For example, the Port Authority of New York and New Jersey runs New York Harbor and the World Trade Center. It also controls the city's bus stations and larger airports. The Port Authority helps keep travelers safe.

County Government

County government is another kind of local government. A county is one of the areas into which a state is divided. Cities, towns and countryside make up a county. There are 62 counties in New York State. Look at the county map on page R15 and find the county in which you live.

In Chautauqua County, the government takes care of roads and public parks. Other counties manage museums, libraries, and community colleges. Counties have a court system, a police force, and a **sheriff**. A sheriff is the person in charge of making sure the laws are obeyed in the county.

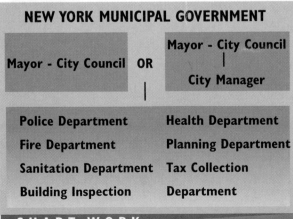

NEW YORK MUNICIPAL GOVERNMENT

Mayor - City Council	OR	Mayor - City Council
		City Manager

Police Department	Health Department
Fire Department	Planning Department
Sanitation Department	Tax Collection
Building Inspection	Department

CHART WORK

There are many departments in city government.
1. Why do we need a health department?
2. What does the fire department do?

Special Districts

New York has special districts, or government areas, that are formed for special reasons. One kind of special district is the school district. All the schools in a school district are governed by a group of officials called a board of education. The members of the board decide how to spend the district's money and make other decisions about the schools in their district.

WHY IT MATTERS

Local government makes decisions that affect the health, safety, and education in our local communities. Local government also works with state government to solve problems. In the next lesson, you will learn about the government of New York State.

School districts are a type of special district in New York.

✓ Reviewing Facts and Ideas

SUM IT UP

- Local governments make decisions that affect your community.

- Municipal governments are often run by a mayor and a city council.

- New York City has five borough presidents who help the mayor govern the city.

- County governments are responsible for doing jobs like repairing county roads.

THINK ABOUT IT

1. What are two tasks that a municipal government does?

2. What is a special district?

3. FOCUS What is the role of local governments in our communities?

4. THINKING SKILL *Compare* and *contrast* the government of New York City with that of Salamanca.

5. WRITE Write to the mayor of your town or city to find out more about what he or she does.

OUR STATE GOVERNMENT

Focus Activity

READ TO LEARN
What are the jobs of the three branches of state government?

VOCABULARY
checks and balances
budget
executive branch
veto
legislative branch
State Senate
State Assembly
bill
judicial branch

PLACES
Albany

READ ALOUD

Students in Niagara and Erie counties voted on Election Day in November 1996. They took part in "Kids Voting New York." They voted for President as well as for people running for local office. Their votes did not count in the election, but they learned what it was like to vote.

Johanna Rodriguez is an 8-year-old who went with her mother and brother to vote. She said, "I think it's kind of cool that they let kids vote too."

THE BIG PICTURE

In order to vote, the students who took part in "Kids Voting New York" learned about some of the people who run our state's government. The jobs these people do are described in the New York State Constitution. The state constitution outlines how our state government works. The constitution explains that the state government is made up of three branches, or parts. Each branch has different jobs and different powers. The reason there are three branches is so that no one group will have too much power. This idea of limiting each branch's power is called checks and balances.

MAKING NEW YORK WORK

Have you ever visited **Albany**, our state capital? That is where the representatives of state government meet. The state government provides services to all the people in New York. For example, the state government hires workers to take care of state highways. The government also has laws to keep New York's air and water clean.

The money to pay for government workers and programs comes from taxes that New York citizens pay. The government makes a plan for using this tax money. This plan is called a **budget** (BUJ it). Look at the chart on this page. It shows how the money in our state is spent.

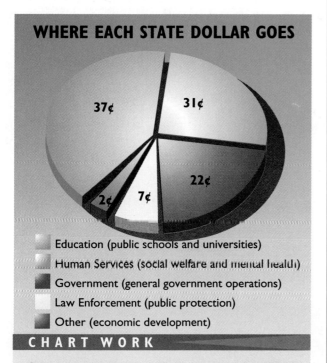

WHERE EACH STATE DOLLAR GOES

37¢ 31¢ 22¢ 7¢ 2¢

- Education (public schools and universities)
- Human Services (social welfare and mental health)
- Government (general government operations)
- Law Enforcement (public protection)
- Other (economic development)

CHART WORK

Our state leaders create a budget to plan how to spend state money.

1. What does our state spend the most on?
2. How much is spent on law enforcement?

The Executive Branch

The branch of state government that plans the budget is the **executive** (eg ZEK yoo tiv) **branch**. The executive branch carries out New York's laws.

The executive branch has many departments. For example, the Department of Transportation makes sure that traffic flows safely on state roads. The Department of Education makes sure that New York students get a good education.

The head of the executive branch is the governor, who is elected every four years. The governor chooses many of the people who will help run the state. He or she has the power to **veto**, or say no, to an idea for a law.

What do you think it would be like to be governor of New York? Mario Cuomo was governor from 1983 to 1994. He said that in just his first seven days of being a governor, he had "given two major speeches, met personally with record [very large] numbers of visitors and legislators [lawmakers], . . . appointed a Court of Appeals judge, . . . and begun the hard process of preparing the budget."

Sometimes the governor makes proclamations, or official statements. On July 1, 1980, Governor Hugh Carey signed a proclamation that made the song "I Love New York" the state song. You can find the words and music to this song on the next page.

I Love New York

Words and music by Steve Karmen

Disco beat
Chorus

I____ Love New York.____ I____ Love New York.____

There is-n't an-oth - er like it no mat-ter where you go,

and no-bod-y can com - pare it, it's win and place and show, you know.

New York is spe - cial, you know. New York is diff - 'rent 'cause there's

no place else on earth quite like New York.____ And that's why

I____ Love New York.____ I____ Love New York.____

THE LEGISLATURE

The **legislative** (LEJ is lay tiv) **branch** makes the laws. This branch has two parts—the **State Senate** and the **State Assembly**. The Senate has 61 members, and the Assembly has 150. Senators and Assembly members are elected by voters. They serve for two years.

Anyone can suggest an idea for a law. The governor can, citizens can, and members of the legislature can. However, only the legislature can turn that idea into a law.

From Bill to Law

A written idea for a law is called a **bill**. How does a bill become a law? Look at the chart below. Then follow the story of how a bill about bike helmets became a law.

In 1993, Senator Norman Levy from Long Island decided that children under 14 should be required to wear a helmet when riding a bike. Helmets help prevent head injuries. Senator Levy wrote down his idea. Then he proposed his bill to the Senate. The bill became known as Senate Bill 69-C. Members of the Senate discussed the bill. Then they voted for it.

Next, Assembly member Aurelia Greene from the Bronx proposed the bill to the Assembly. The members of the Assembly discussed the bill. They too voted for it.

Now only one more step remained. Governor Mario Cuomo had to approve the bill. As part of the system of checks and balances, the governor can veto the bill. In this case, Governor Cuomo liked the bill and signed it. On July 21, 1993, Senate Bill 69-C became a New York law.

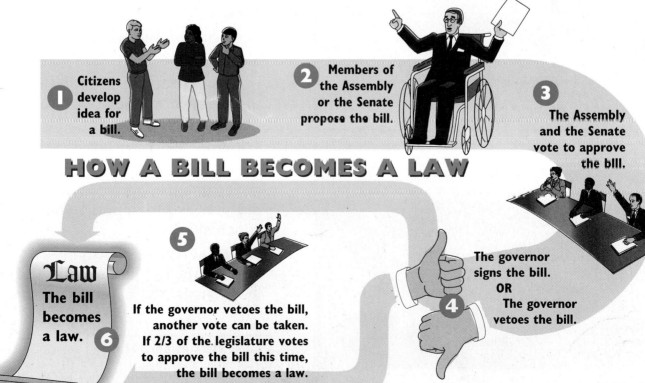

HOW A BILL BECOMES A LAW

1 Citizens develop idea for a bill.

2 Members of the Assembly or the Senate propose the bill.

3 The Assembly and the Senate vote to approve the bill.

4 The governor signs the bill. OR The governor vetoes the bill.

5 If the governor vetoes the bill, another vote can be taken. If 2/3 of the legislature votes to approve the bill this time, the bill becomes a law.

6 Law The bill becomes a law.

THE JUDICIAL BRANCH

All the courts in our state are part of the judicial (joo DI shul) branch. This branch decides whether someone has broken the law. The highest, or most powerful, court in New York is the Court of Appeals. This court hears cases from lower courts and makes decisions about the laws themselves. The Court of Appeals is made up of seven judges. Each judge serves for 14 years.

How judges are chosen is another example of checks and balances. The governor picks the people to be judges. However, the Senate must approve of the governor's choice. If the Senate does not approve, the governor must choose again.

WHY IT MATTERS

A government works well when its citizens take an interest in what is happening. There are many ways to take part in government. It's up to all our citizens to make New York the special place described in the song on page 300.

✓✓ Reviewing Facts and Ideas

SUM IT UP

- The governor is head of New York's executive branch, which makes sure laws are carried out.
- The legislature of New York makes the laws of the state. The legislature is made up of the Senate and the Assembly.
- The state courts make up the judicial branch. They make sure that the laws are obeyed.

THINK ABOUT IT

1. Name two jobs the governor does.

2. How does a bill become a law in our state?

3. **FOCUS** What are the jobs of the three branches of state government?

4. **THINKING SKILL** Make a _conclusion_ about how our state government works. What facts did you use to support your conclusion?

5. **GEOGRAPHY** Find Albany on a map. Figure out how far away from the capital you live.

A judge (left) is part of New York's judicial branch.

CITIZENSHIP
MAKING A DIFFERENCE

The Penny Harvest

NEW YORK CITY, NEW YORK— When Nora Gross was four years old, she saw a homeless man sitting on the street. Nora asked her father, Teddy Gross, if they could take the man home with them. Her father said no, but he began thinking about how they might help the homeless.

A few days later, Mr. Gross overheard a conversation that gave him an idea. Nora's baby-sitter was complaining about the pennies in her penny jar. "Oh, these old pennies, they are of no use to me," she said.

The Gross family had a penny jar too, and Nora's dad knew many families whose pennies had piled up. Nora's dad thought these pennies might be used to help needy New Yorkers.

That's how the Penny Harvest started. Students from Nora's school "harvested" pennies from home and brought them to school. They also collected coins from neighbors. They used the money to help New Yorkers in need of food, clothing, or shelter.

The idea caught on quickly. Many schools in New York City joined in. With the help of businesses and friends in New York City, Teddy Gross formed an organization called Common Cents.

Since 1991, when Nora's school had the first Penny Harvest, Common Cents has collected over 50 million pennies. That's half a million dollars! Teddy Gross says, "We turn pennies into dollars and dollars into deeds [actions]."

Students at each school decide how the money they have collected will be spent. Students at P.S. 62 in the Bronx gave coats, boots, and other warm clothing to 50 children living in homeless shelters in their neighborhood. Children at I.S. 59 in Queens held a Thanksgiving dinner for 200 homeless people.

Nora is now ten years old. "Even if I can't change the whole world," she says, "I can change a little part of it. And if everybody does a little, who knows— maybe we will change the world."

"If everybody does a little . . . maybe we will change the world."

Nora Gross

STUDYSKILLS

Reading Newspapers

VOCABULARY
news article
feature article
editorial
headline
byline
dateline

WHY THE SKILL MATTERS

You just read about how New York's government works. What if you wanted to follow current events in the government? A good way to do this would be to read a newspaper.

Reading a newspaper is often the best way to get information about what is happening today. Many newspapers cover events from all over our country and around the world. Some focus on events from a state, city, or town. Use the Helping Yourself box to guide you in reading newspapers.

USING A NEWSPAPER

When you read a newspaper, it is useful to know the different parts. The front section of a paper is made up mostly of **news articles**. These are news stories based on facts about recent events. However, you may sometimes find the writer's opinion in a news article.

Another kind of newspaper article is a **feature article**. A feature article takes a detailed look at a certain person, subject, or event.

Newspapers also include sports articles, cartoons, letters to the editor, and **editorials**. In an editorial, the editors—the people who run the paper—share their ideas about an issue. Unlike a news article, an editorial gives opinions, rather than facts.

USING A NEWS ARTICLE

A news article usually begins with a **headline**—a title printed in large letters at the top of the story. The headline gives the main idea of the story.

Look at the news article on the facing page. As you see, the headline is "New Yorkers Change Village Name."

In addition, news articles often have a **byline**. The byline tells the reader who wrote the story. The author of that story is Alice McMullen.

Finally, many news articles include a **dateline**. This tells when and where the story was written. As you can see, the dateline in the story tells that it was written in Sleepy Hollow on December 11.

A good news article should answer five questions: (1) *Who* was involved in the story? (2) *What* took place? (3) *When* did the event happen? (4) *Where* did it happen? (5) *Why* did it happen?

Read the article on page 305. Does it answer the five questions? The answer to the first question, for example, might be "the people of Sleepy Hollow."

Can you explain *what* happened in your own words?

TRYING THE SKILL

You just read a news article about a New York village that changed its name. Why do you think that reading a newspaper is a good way to learn about such an event? Can you think of any other sources for this kind of information?

Now suppose that your class is curious about a different topic: the construction of a new state highway. An article in the newspaper is called "Highway Opening Delayed." Is this a news article or a feature article? Why do you think so?

Another is called "New Highway Is a Step in the Right Direction." What kind of article is this? Why do you think so?

REVIEWING THE SKILL

1. Name three different kinds of articles that appear in newspapers.

2. How can you tell that the article below is a news article instead of an editorial?

3. Why is it important for some news articles to have a dateline?

4. How would a newspaper help you learn about our state?

New Yorkers Change Village Name
By Alice McMullen

SLEEPY HOLLOW, December 11—It's official. North Tarrytown no longer exists. Voters decided on Tuesday to change the name of North Tarrytown to Sleepy Hollow, the place made famous in Washington Irving's classic story, *The Legend of Sleepy Hollow.*

Since a large automobile manufacturer closed its factory last summer, the 8,000 residents of this scenic Hudson River village have been looking for ways to boost the local economy. It is hoped that the name change will bring tourists to the village.

Maria Santiago, who moved to the area two years ago, is excited about the name change. She said

"most people have read about Sleepy Hollow. I believe that they will want to come to see where Irving's stories took place. They can have lunch, go shopping, and try to guess where Ichabod Crane took his famous last ride."

Not everyone, however, was happy about the change. William Clements, a life-long resident, said that "the only thing a new village name means is that we have to spend our tax dollars on changing the village signs. What we need is a large business to come here, not tourists."

Villagers celebrated the name change with the ringing of a 311-year-old bell at the Old Dutch Church. Now residents will have to wait and see if the name of Sleepy Hollow will bring in the tourists and their spending money.

305

OUR NATIONAL GOVERNMENT

Focus Activity

READ TO LEARN
What are the parts of our national government?

VOCABULARY
democratic republic
Congress
Senate
House of Representatives
Supreme Court

PEOPLE
Thurgood Marshall
Ruth Bader Ginsburg

PLACES
Washington, D.C.

READ ALOUD

In 1863, President Abraham Lincoln described our country. He said that the United States had a "government of the people, by the people, for the people." These words are as true today as they were more than 130 years ago.

BIG PICTURE

What exactly do Lincoln's words mean? A government of the people means that the citizens of the United States have a say in how the country is run. They can make suggestions about the laws our country should have. They can help decide what jobs the government should do.

A government *by* the people means that voters elect representatives to run the government and make decisions for them. This type of government is called a democratic republic. The representatives pass and carry out laws.

A government *for* the people means that the government works for the good of the people in the country. The job of the government is to keep people safe and free.

WHAT DOES THE GOVERNMENT DO?

Our country's government is called the national or federal government It provides services to people all across the country. When you buy something in a store, you are using money that is made by the government. Only the national government can make money. If you listen to the weather, you might hear a report from the National Weather Service. It is also run by the government.

The national government helps states after floods, hurricanes, earthquakes, and tornadoes. One of the government's more important duties is to provide armed forces—the army, navy, air force, and marines. They protect the United States and its allies during times of trouble.

A Free People

Every American has the right to say what he or she believes about our country. We all have the right to practice our own religion and to be treated fairly under the law. As Americans, wc also have the right to elect our leaders.

Along with these rights, we also have responsibilities. Besides having the *right* to vote, we have the *responsibility* to vote. A democratic republic needs its citizens to make choices by voting.

Another responsibility is to pay taxes. You just read about some of the services the government provides. These services cost money. We pay for them with our taxes. Without taxes the government could not provide the services that we need.

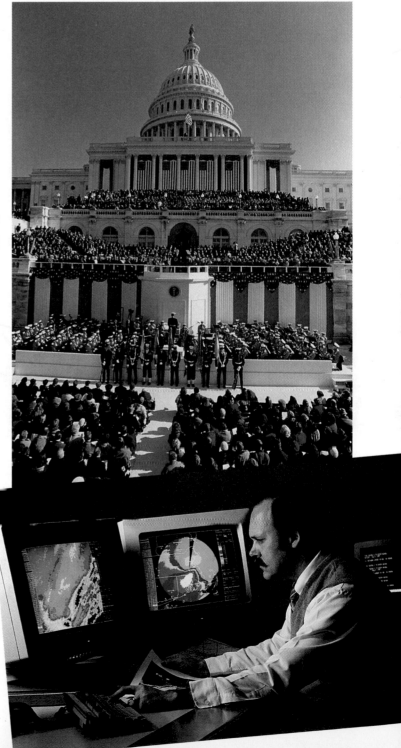

The United States capitol (above) is where Congress meets. Weather radar for the National Weather Service warns of severe weather.

THE GOVERNMENT IN WASHINGTON

As you read in Chapter 6, the Constitution of the United States outlines the plan of government for our country. If you visit Washington, D.C., you can see the Constitution "in action." Washington, D.C., is the capital of the United States. The national government meets there. Like New York State, the national government has three branches. They are shown in the chart below.

The President

Every four years, people in the United States elect the President. The President is the head of the executive branch. The President makes sure that laws passed by Congress are carried out. What other jobs does the President have?

Congress

Congress is the legislative branch of the national government. It makes laws for the whole country. The American people elect the members of Congress.

Congress has two parts, the Senate and the House of Representatives. Voters in each state elect two senators.

The number of representatives a state has depends on how many people live there. Because New York State has a large population, it has a large number of representatives. In the last election New Yorkers elected 31 members to the House.

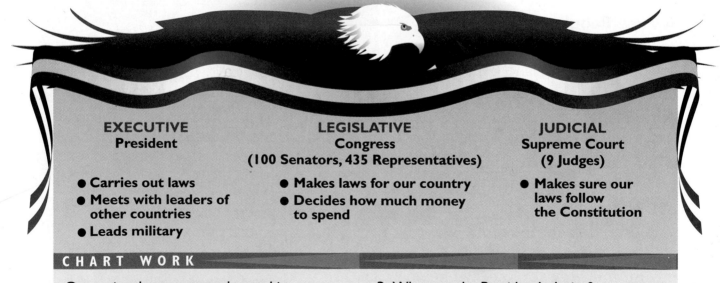

NATIONAL GOVERNMENT: Three Branches

EXECUTIVE President	LEGISLATIVE Congress (100 Senators, 435 Representatives)	JUDICIAL Supreme Court (9 Judges)
• Carries out laws • Meets with leaders of other countries • Leads military	• Makes laws for our country • Decides how much money to spend	• Makes sure our laws follow the Constitution

CHART WORK

Our national government, located in Washington, D.C., has three branches.

1. How many senators does Congress have? How many representatives?
2. Which branch does the President head?
3. What are the President's duties?
4. Who are the highest officials of the judicial branch of our government?

Ruth Bader Ginsburg is a judge on the United States Supreme Court

The Courts

The courts are the third branch of the national government. The United States Supreme Court is the highest court. Justices on the Supreme Court are not elected. Instead, the President chooses them. They must also be approved by the Senate. The Supreme Court judges serve for life.

Fifteen judges from New York have served on the Supreme Court. They include John Jay. Jay was the first Chief Justice, or head of the court. Thurgood Marshall served on the Court from 1967 to 1991. Marshall was the first African American to serve on the Court. Ruth Bader Ginsburg of Brooklyn was appointed by President Clinton in 1993. She is the second woman to sit on the Supreme Court.

New York's senators are Daniel P. Moynihan and Charles E. Schumer.

WHY IT MATTERS

As Americans, we must understand how government works in order to make good decisions as citizens. When you turn 18, you will be able to vote in national, state, and local elections. You may even decide to run for office one day!

✓ Reviewing Facts and Ideas

SUM IT UP

- The United States government makes laws that affect citizens of all 50 states.

- The three branches of our national government are headed by the President, Congress, and the Supreme Court.

THINK ABOUT IT

1. How many Senators does New York have in the United States Senate?

2. How many representatives does New York have in the United States House of Representatives?

3. **FOCUS** What are the three parts of our national government?

4. **THINKING SKILL** *Decide* whether you would like to work in the government. If so, what would you do? Give reasons for your decision.

5. **WRITE** What qualities do you think are important in a senator or representative?

LOCAL CONNECTIONS
ELMIRA:
LEARNING FROM NEWSPAPERS

The students in Mr. Pappas's fourth-grade class were curious when they saw a stack of newspapers on their teacher's desk.

"Mr. Pappas, are we going to read newspapers today?" Jamal asked.

"Yes, Jamal. These are copies of the Elmira *Star-Gazette*, our daily newspaper. What can we learn by reading the newspaper?" he asked.

"My sister plays basketball at the high school. I look for stories about her team," said Maria.

"My mom and I read the paper to see what's playing at the movies," Malcolm responded.

"We read newspapers because we want to know what is happening in our community," Mr. Pappas said.

"The newspaper tells us about issues, problems, or events in our city. As a special project, we will look for stories about our city government. Then we will make a chart describing the activities of city officials."

Mr. Pappas explained that he had been saving the paper for several weeks. That way each group would have a different paper to read.

"Our paper has a great story about the new police chief!" exclaimed Jacintha. "His name is Michael L. Ciminelli."

"Our paper has a story about the city manager," Ruth said. "Mr. Iraci says that his job is to watch the city's budget. He tries to keep the streets repaired and the costs down."

Newspapers are an important way to learn about events in our community.

STAR-GAZETTE
Elmira, New York

PARTLY SUNNY
High: 53° Low: 30°
Details/2A

FRIDAY
October 4, 1996
N.Y. EDITION
first Gannett newspaper

40¢ stores/50¢ vending machines

New chief plans changes
Elmira likely to see more officers walking beats, volunteers in office

By JIM PFIFFER
Star-Gazette

Elmira's new police chief wants to see more officers walking beats, more community volunteers and more cooperation with other law enforcement agencies.

Michael Ciminelli, a former Rochester police sergeant, outlined his plans for the 83-member police force as he made his debut Thursday during a special Elmira City Council meeting at City Hall.

The 41-year-old Ciminelli is scheduled to start his $62,000-a-year police chief job on Nov. 2, said Elmira City Manager Samuel F. Iraci Jr., who appointed him to the post. The appointment does not need city council approval.

Ciminelli, who works in the criminal law section of the U.S. Drug Enforcement Administration in Washington, D.C., replaces former chief Joseph Michalko, who retired in May.

After Thursday's meeting, Ciminelli met with reporters to outline his plans. He said he hopes to:

■ Take more officers out of patrol cars and put them on walking beats, to get closer to the people they serve.

■ Develop a volunteer citizens program to use civilians to answer

SPENCER PLATT/Star-Gazette

"This paper has a story about a city council member, Mr. DiChiara. He wants to buy cellular phones for a group of people who are trying to reduce crime in their neighborhood," said Evelyn.

"This story says Councilman Richard Micelotta is on Elmira's Columbia Street Task Force. He and other citizens are going to Syracuse to speak about ways to make neighborhoods better places to live," said Hernando.

The students continued reading. They learned that the city manager must find ways to keep costs for city services such as police patrols and trash collection down. They also learned that the city council votes to buy things the city needs, like a new computer system. The students were surprised to discover that their city leaders had to do lots of homework and know all about the issues if they were going to make good decisions for the city. They were pleased to find out that their city leaders look for ways to make life better for the people in Elmira.

MAKE Your LOCAL CONNECTION

What can you learn from reading your local newspaper? Look for stories about your community's leaders. What are some of the problems they help solve? Make your own chart and share this information with others.

Students in Elmira made a chart (left) telling about the activities of the city's leaders. Millions of papers (below) are printed and read each day by New Yorkers.

Elmira City Government

Names of Officers

Mayor: Howard F. Townsend
City Council Members: Kenneth Brooks, John Corsi, Patsy DiChiara, Stephen Hughes, Terry McLaughlin, Richard Micelotta
City Manager: Samuel F. Iraci

Newspaper Articles

City Officer	Date	Event/Action
City Manager	Oct. 4	Appoints new Chief of Police.
Mayor and City Council	Oct. 14	Studying whether to sell old YMCA building for apartments for senior citizens.
Mayor and City Council	Oct. 18	Discuss buying new computer system for the city to improve service. Voted to replace worn-out computers in police department for $71,271.
Council Member	Nov. 3	Agrees with the new police chief's approaches to solving problems.
City Manager	Nov. 4	Preparing the city's budget for next year; trying not to raise taxes.
Council Member	Nov. 7	Asks for money for cellular phones for Neighborhood Watch.
Council Member	Nov. 21	Will present a plan for improving neighborhoods at a conference in Syracuse.

311

CHAPTER 12 REVIEW

THINKING ABOUT VOCABULARY

Number a sheet of paper from 1 to 10. Next to each number write the word or term from the list that best completes the sentence.

budget   legislative
Congress   municipal
elect   State Assembly
executive United States Supreme Court
judicial   veto

1. The governor has the power to _____ a bill if he or she is against it.

2. A _____ government is the government of a village, town, county, or city.

3. The highest court in our country is the _____.

4. To _____ means to choose a person for office by voting.

5. The courts in New York are part of the _____ branch of government.

6. The legislative branch of New York's government is made up of the State Senate and the _____.

7. The United States _____ has two parts, the Senate and the House of Representatives.

8. The governor of New York is the head of the _____ branch of government.

9. A plan for using money is a _____.

10. The _____ branch of government makes the laws.

THINKING ABOUT FACTS

1. How do the citizens of the United States take part in the government?

2. What kinds of services do municipal governments provide? What does a mayor do?

3. What is the purpose of the New York State Constitution?

4. What are checks and balances? Give an example of checks and balances.

5. In which city do the members of New York's government meet?

6. What is a budget? Where does the state government get money for its budget?

7. What branch of state government does the governor head? How is the governor chosen, and how long does he or she serve?

8. How are the members of the state legislature chosen? How long do they serve?

9. Who is the head of the executive branch of the United States government? Name two responsibilities of this person.

10. How many senators are elected by each state to the United States Senate? How many representatives does New York send to the United States House of Representatives?

THINK AND WRITE

WRITING A BILL ◄▤►
Suppose you are a senator in the New York Senate. Write a bill that would make our state a better place to live.

WRITING A POSTER ◄▤►
Create a poster showing the three branches of our state government. Label the branches and write captions explaining their responsibilities.

WRITING AN ARTICLE ◄▤►
Suppose you are the editor of a newspaper. Write an editorial encouraging people to vote in the next election. Explain why voting is an important responsibility for each citizen.

APPLYING STUDY SKILLS

READING NEWSPAPERS

1. What five questions should a well-written news article answer?

2. Look at the news article about Sleepy Hollow on page 305. Identify the headline, the byline, and the dateline.

3. What is an editorial? How does it differ from a news article?

4. Look again at the news article on page 305. How would you change the article to make it an editorial?

5. What can you learn from reading newspapers?

Summing Up the Chapter

Use the following table to organize information from the chapter. Copy the table on a sheet of paper. Then fill in the blank spaces on the table. When you have filled in the table, use it to write a paragraph that answers the question "What do local, state, and national governments have in common? How are they different?"

	EXECUTIVE BRANCH	LEGISLATIVE BRANCH	JUDICIAL BRANCH
Local			
State			
National			

CHAPTER 13

New Yorkers Today

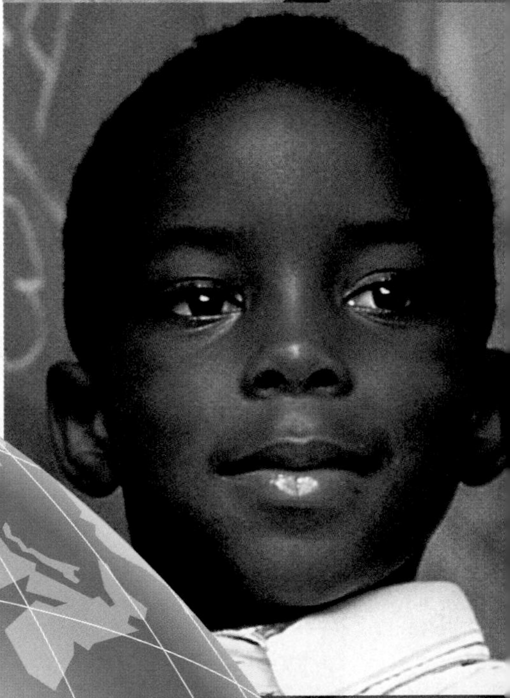

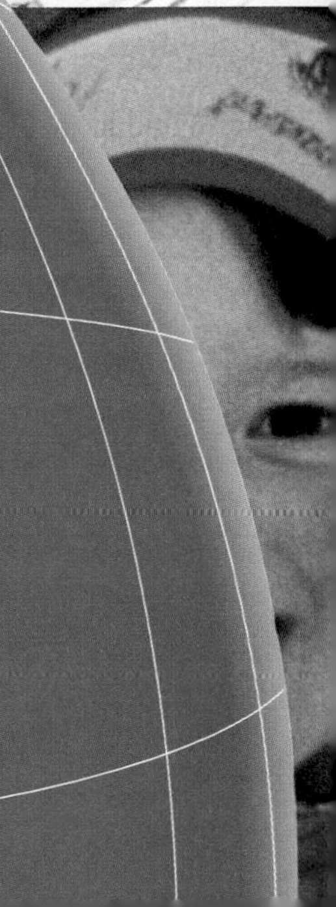

THINKING ABOUT ECONOMICS AND CITIZENSHIP

New York provides a home for people from many different backgrounds. This great mix of cultures makes New York an interesting and exciting place to live. Read on to find out more about how people live in New York today.

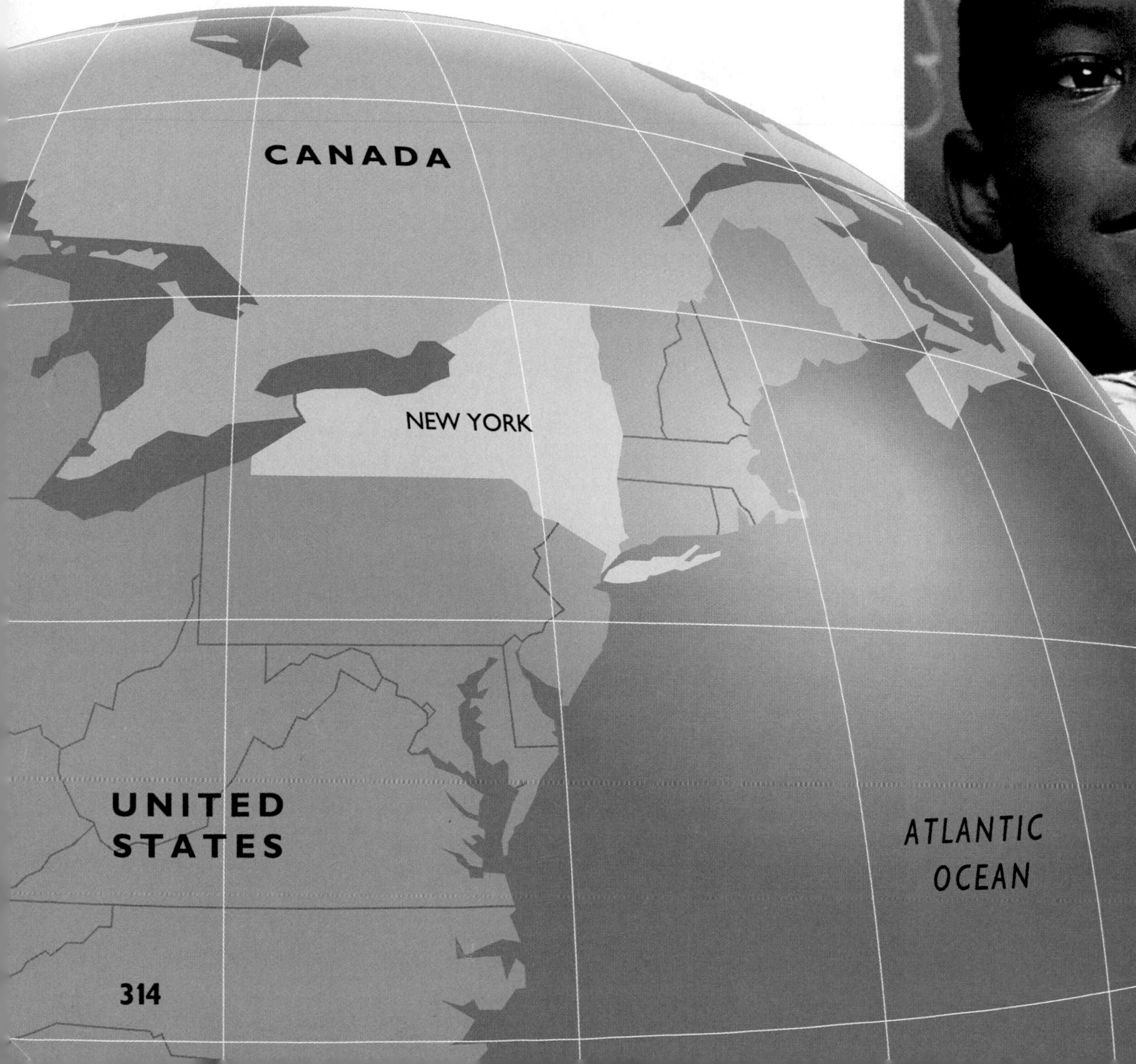

CANADA

NEW YORK

UNITED STATES

ATLANTIC OCEAN

THE PEOPLE OF NEW YORK

Focus Activity

READ TO LEARN
Who are New Yorkers?

VOCABULARY
culture
diversity
ethnic group
powwow
metropolitan area

READ ALOUD

Poet Arnold Adoff, who grew up in New York City, describes in a poem what he sees on the city streets:

> *People fill all the sidewalk space*
> *between open shops and parked cars.*
> *We slow walk through the crowds of*
> *languages and clouds of steam*
> *from carts of cooking foods*
> *. . . . We eat our way from country to country:*
> *souvlaki pizza falafel*
> *waffles hotdogs.*

THE BIG PICTURE

What did Adoff mean by "from country to country"? Each of the foods he mentioned was brought to the United States by immigrants from different countries. Souvlaki (soo VLAH kee) is a roasted-meat sandwich made by Greeks. Sandwiches of falafel (fuh LAH fuhl), a patty made from chickpeas, are eaten all over the Middle East. Immigrants from Northern Europe brought waffles, a kind of pastry with ridges. Do you know what groups brought pizza, egg rolls, and bagels to our country? The way of life that a group of people shares is its culture. Culture includes foods people eat, languages they speak, holidays they celebrate, and ideas they believe in. Culture even includes the jobs people do.

PEOPLE AND CULTURE

About 18 million people live in New York State today. Almost 3 million are recent immigrants. They come for freedom and for jobs. They come to start a new life.

Damir Lecek (duh MEER LEH chik) is an immigrant from Croatia who moved to Ithaca in 1988. He says, "I came to New York because my mother was living here. After she returned to Croatia, I stayed. . . . I saw that there were many opportunities here. I think that New York is a wonderful place to live."

Diverse New York

Diversity (di VUR si tee) means "many different kinds." New York has a great diversity of people. A neighborhood called Elmhurst in Queens may be the most diverse in our country! Immigrants from over 110 countries have settled there. Colombians, Dominicans, Pakistanis, and Koreans are only a few of the ethnic groups in Elmhurst. One church there offers services in English, Spanish, Korean, and Chinese.

New York's Ethnic Groups

You have read about Native Americans and African Americans who came to live in our state. You have also read about immigrant groups from the Netherlands, Great Britain, Germany, Ireland, Italy, and Poland who made New York home.

A group of people whose ancestors are from the same country or area form an ethnic group. Many ethnic groups in New York keep alive the customs, speak the language, or practice the religion of their ancestors. They celebrate culture at festivals such as the West Indian Day Parade in Brooklyn or the Italian Festival in Buffalo. Powwows are celebrations of Native American culture involving music and dance. More than 60,000 Native Americans live in New York today.

Honoring our ethnic heritage as well as our New York heritage is part of what it means to be a New Yorker. What cultural festivals are held in your area?

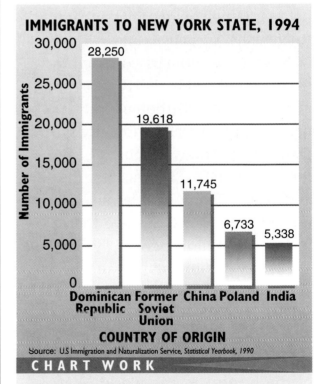

IMMIGRANTS TO NEW YORK STATE, 1994

Source: U.S Immigration and Naturalization Service, *Statistical Yearbook, 1990*

CHART WORK

Immigrants from all over the world come to live in New York.

1. Where did the largest immigrant group come from?
2. How many more Chinese than Polish immigrants came to New York in 1994?

WHERE DO NEW YORKERS LIVE?

New York State has 49,000 square miles of land and offers people a variety of places to live and work. Some people enjoy the exciting life of New York's big cities. Others like the quiet life of small villages. Some live in areas in between.

Cities and Suburbs

In our state eight out of ten people live in urban, or city, areas. New York City is the largest city in the state—and in the country! Over 7 million people live there. Buffalo is the second largest city in our state. Its population is over 300,000 people. Other large cities include Rochester, Syracuse, and Albany.

New York suburbs continue to grow in the 1990s. Forty years ago, many people with homes in the suburbs went to work in the city's downtown. Today, suburbs have their own shops, businesses, theaters, and parks. Many people now work in the suburbs as well as live there.

Twelve million people live in New York City's suburbs. These include Westchester County, Nassau and Suffolk counties, and nearby parts of New Jersey and Connecticut. The New York **metropolitan area** is one of the largest in the world. A metropolitan area is a city and its suburbs together. The metropolitan area of Buffalo includes suburbs such as Kenmore, Amherst, Williamsville, and Cheektowaga

Some New Yorkers live in the tree-filled **rural** areas of our state (above). Others live in the suburbs (right) just outside of cities.

(CHEEK tah wah gah). Albany, Schenectady, and Troy, which are close to each other, form a single metropolitan area.

Trees, If You Please . . .

Not everyone in New York State lives in cities or suburbs. They prefer a rural life, living in the countryside. Rural areas include farms and villages. There are also many forests in New York's rural areas. About one fourth of the state is covered with trees.

Compared to the noise and bustle of the city, life in New York's rural areas seems peaceful. Many people who live in rural areas enjoy living in a place where they know most of their neighbors in the community. They also like being close to beautiful lakes, rivers, forests, and wildlife.

Links to LANGUAGE ARTS

Names With Meaning

City and town names can tell us a lot about the people who once lived there. If you look at a map of the Hudson Valley, you will see many towns that end with "kill." These include Peekskill, Beaverkill, and Fishkill. These towns were named by the Dutch. "Kill" means "creek" in the Dutch language. Towns with names like Brockport, Middleport, and Lockport were founded along the Erie Canal. They were ports where boats could dock. Other town names are Nicholville, Franklinville, and Baldwinsville. Look up "ville" in a large dictionary to see what it means.

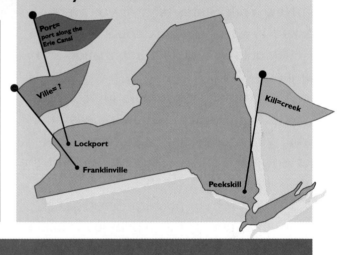

Port= port along the Erie Canal

Ville= ?

Kill=creek

Lockport

Franklinville

Peekskill

WHY IT MATTERS

Each day, people from many different places come to New York to start a new life. They settle in cities, suburbs, and the rural countryside. They celebrate their individual cultures with festivals and special events. You will learn about these in the next lesson.

✓ Reviewing Facts and Ideas

SUM IT UP

- Immigrants came from all over the world to make their homes in New York State.
- Many New Yorkers honor their ethnic heritage as well as their New York heritage.
- Some people live in cities and suburbs, while others live in rural areas of New York.

THINK ABOUT IT

1. What are some things that people share in a culture?

2. What is a metropolitan area?

3. **FOCUS** Who are New Yorkers?

4. **THINKING SKILL** _Predict_ some of the ways in which our state might be different if immigrants had not come here.

5. **WRITE** Describe the place where you live to someone who has never been there. Is it a city, a suburb, or a small village? What makes it a nice place to live?

STUDY SKILLS

Writing Notes and Outlines

VOCABULARY
outline

WHY THE SKILL MATTERS

You have just read about the different kinds of people who make their homes in New York State. What if you were asked to write a report about them? How would you collect information and organize it?

As you read, take notes in your own words. Write down the main ideas of what you are reading. You should also jot down important facts that support the main ideas.

Place a roman numeral beside each main idea, and put a capital letter beside each fact. Under each of your main ideas, group the facts that support it. A plan for organizing written information about a subject is called an outline.

USING NOTES AND OUTLINES

People from all over the world have moved to our country during this century. The following short article talks about immigration to New York City during the early 1900s. Try taking notes. Then study the outline below to see how it organizes the information.

In the early 1900s, large groups of immigrants arrived in New York City. Some, like many Jews from Eastern Europe, came so they could practice their religion freely. Others came to find new and better jobs, or to start their own businesses. Some came for both these reasons.

The immigrants came from many different places, although most came from Europe. Many immigrants were from southern and eastern European countries like Austria-Hungary, Russia, Italy, Greece and Poland. Many were from farms or small towns.

These new immigrants arrived by ship and landed at New York City's Ellis Island. Here they began their new life in a new country. A large number of these newcomers found jobs in New York City, and so they stayed there. They often settled in neighborhoods where other immigrants from the same country lived.

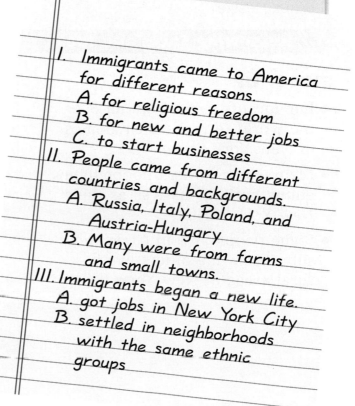

I. Immigrants came to America for different reasons.
   A. for religious freedom
   B. for new and better jobs
   C. to start businesses
II. People came from different countries and backgrounds.
   A. Russia, Italy, Poland, and Austria-Hungary
   B. Many were from farms and small towns.
III. Immigrants began a new life.
   A. got jobs in New York City
   B. settled in neighborhoods with the same ethnic groups

According to the outline, the first main idea is that large groups of immigrants came to New York City for different reasons. Three facts support this idea. What are the other main ideas?

TRYING THE SKILL

Read the article about foreign immigration to New York City today. Take notes as you read. Then write an outline. Use the Helping Yourself box for hints. What are your main ideas? What facts can you use to support them? Do main ideas or facts get roman numerals in your outline?

REVIEWING THE SKILL

1. How does writing outlines help you organize information? How could you use this information?

2. In your outline on New York State immigration, how would you classify the statement that Ellis Island has been turned into a museum. Is it a main idea or a supporting fact?

3. How did you decide which statements were main ideas and which were supporting facts?

4. How can taking notes and writing an outline help you to learn more about immigration in New York State?

Today immigrants continue to arrive in New York. Many still come from European countries, but large numbers also come from Puerto Rico and other countries like China, India, Korea, the Dominican Republic, and countries in Latin America.

By the 1950s, more and more immigrants began coming to the United States by plane. Instead of sailing to Ellis Island, many immigrants now fly into John F. Kennedy Airport in Queens. Like those who came before them, many decide to stay in New York City.

Ellis Island closed in 1954. It has been turned into a museum that honors the immigrants who passed through on their way to a new life.

Immigrants from many countries contribute to New York's diversity.

NEW YORK ARTS, RECREATION, AND SPORTS

Focus Activity

READ TO LEARN
How do New Yorkers have fun?

VOCABULARY
recreation
historical site

READ ALOUD

The Chautauqua Institution (shu TAH kwah in sti TOO shun) is located on Chautauqua Lake in Western New York. Since it was founded in 1874, it has been a gathering place for students, teachers, and artists. People come to discuss ideas and to enjoy theater, dance, and musical performances.

Theodore Roosevelt, a New Yorker and former President of the United States, called the Chautauqua Institution "The most American place in America."

THE BIG PICTURE

The Chautauqua Institution is just one of many places you can visit in New York State. New York has museums and art galleries that are world famous. The forests, mountains, lakes, and rivers in our state offer people many ways to get outside and enjoy the outdoor life. People also enjoy the many sports events held in our state. All of these provide people with recreation, which are the things we do for relaxation and enjoyment.

THE ARTS IN NEW YORK

New York has many places that celebrate the arts. The arts include painting, sculpture, dance, writing, theater, and music.

New York City is considered by many to be the arts capital of the world. It has hundreds of museums and theaters where you can see and hear works by great artists. But there are a lot of other places in our state where you can experience art.

New York's Museums

Most of New York's large cities have museums. They are great places to learn about different kinds of art.

The Canajoharie Library and Art Gallery has many beautiful paintings of the Erie Canal. The Frederic Remington Art Museum in Ogdensburg has a collection of this New York artist's paintings. Buffalo's Albright-Knox Art Gallery has works by famous artists including New Yorkers Andy Warhol and Jackson Pollock.

New York City has some of the largest museums in the country. The Metropolitan Museum and the Guggenheim (GOO gen him) Museum are just two of them. There are also many smaller museums that show work by new artists.

The Stage is Calling!

Do you dream of becoming an actor, musician, dancer, or writer? New York is the place for you! Each year millions of people come to our state to attend arts events. Many travel to New York City to see Broadway plays. These plays often include beautiful costumes, dancing, and singing.

Dance performances are also very popular. Ballet, modern, and tap are all types of dance. The Joyce Theater in Manhattan presents dance companies from all over the world.

Writers also like to present their work to audiences. Places like Writers & Books in Rochester, and Just Buffalo Literary Center in Buffalo, offer writers a place to read their work. New York is a great place for artists—like you!

You can see plays in theaters on Broadway (below) and art in the Guggenheim Museum (left).

HAVE SOME FUN!

New Yorkers find time for recreation on evenings, weekends, holidays, or summer vacations.

Sports in New York

New Yorkers love sports! Each year, thousands of people attend sporting events in our state. High school sports are very popular. Parents and students watch their teams play everything from lacrosse to tennis to softball.

Professional teams are made up of athletes who play the sport as a job, not just for fun. New York has nine professional teams that play hockey, basketball, baseball, and football. The Buffalo Bills have been a strong football team and the New York Yankees won the 1996 baseball World Series.

Lacrosse is a popular high school sport in New York.

New York is Wild!

Many New Yorkers enjoy the outdoor life. Anna Hammond likes to go fishing with her father in Lake Erie. She says "It's fun even when we don't catch anything. I just like being out on the water."

New York offers many ways to enjoy the winter. You can go skiing in Ellicottville, go ice skating at Rockefeller Center in the heart of Manhattan, or take a trip to Lake Placid to see the beautiful Adirondack Mountains capped with snow.

Christopher Shaw writes many songs about the Adirondacks. His fishing song on the next page tells about one of his pastimes, trying to catch a tricky fish named Walter.

Hockey's New York Islanders have won the Stanley Cup championship four times.

Walter

Words and Music by
Christopher Alden Shaw

Old Walter, he's a cag-ey trout, he's lived up here for years, by the

wat-er-fall, that's where you'll al-ways find him. He'll steal your bait and tack-le, break an

ang-ler down to tears, Leave a-noth-er year of per-il far be-hind him!

Rise! Rise! Feast your eyes on an A-di-ron-dack morn-ing!

Wa-ter's low and it's time to go to the pool where Wal-ter lives, you know!

Rise! Rise! Feast your eyes on an A-di-ron-dack morn-ing!

Wet a line in the clear sun-shine and take what na-ture gives!

Infographic

Places to Visit

Why not take a family vacation to these great New York spots!

Discovery Center, Syracuse

Learn about science from exhibits you make move.

Children's Museum of Manhattan, New York City

So you want to be a TV star? This museum has a TV studio for kids and other great exhibits.

Adirondack Scenic Railroad, Old Forge.

Take an old-fashioned train ride along the Moose River.

Howe Caverns, Howes Cave

Have you ever taken a boat ride underground? The caverns feature a lake that's 200 feet underground.

PLACES TO GO IN NEW YORK	
WHERE TO GO	**LOCATION**
American Museum of Natural History	New York City
ArtPark	Lewiston
Bronx Zoo	The Bronx
Chautauqua Institution	Chautauqua
Sainte Marie Among the Iroquois	Syracuse
Whaling Museum	Cold Spring Harbor
Rochester Museum & Science Center	Rochester
Vanderbilt Mansion, Marine Museum, Planetarium, and Park	Centerport

This sculpture is at the Women's Rights National Historical Park, a historical site in Seneca Falls.

PANDAS AND THE PAST

There are plenty of other exciting places to visit in New York. Some are wild, like the state's zoos. Others are places where important events took place. If you visit them you can take a journey to New York's past!

From Lions to Penguins

Most large cities in New York have zoos. The Bronx Zoo is famous for its large collection of animals which are kept in natural surroundings. The Utica Zoo has several endangered animals including a red panda, Siberian tiger, and snow leopard. There are also zoos in Binghamton, Syracuse, and on Staten Island.

Places of the Past

History comes alive at many of New York's historical sites. These are places that are protected because important or interesting things happened there in the past. If you visit Hyde Park, you can see the home of former President Franklin D. Roosevelt.

No matter where you go in New York State, you'll find something fun to do!

WHY IT MATTERS

From museums to sports to historical sites, New York provides many kinds of recreation. Thanks to our state's rich cultural heritage and natural resources, we have many ways to have fun in our great state.

✓ Reviewing Facts and Ideas

SUM IT UP

- Museums and other places preserve art that was created in the past and give new artists a place to express themselves.

- New York's parks, lakes, and rivers offer many recreational activities.

- Football, hockey, basketball, and baseball are some of the popular sports in New York.

- New York's zoos and historical sites offer great opportunities for learning.

THINK ABOUT IT

1. What are some outdoor activities New Yorkers enjoy?

2. Name two professional teams in New York.

3. **FOCUS** How do New Yorkers have fun?

4. **THINKING SKILLS** *Classify* into groups the different recreational activities New Yorkers enjoy.

5. **GEOGRAPHY** How does our state's geography affect recreation?

327

BASEBALL

Legend has it that the game of baseball was invented by Abner Doubleday, a West Point cadet, in Cooperstown, New York, in 1839. Historians today think Doubleday had little to do with baseball. But many people love the story of Abner Doubleday. To celebrate the 100th year of Doubleday's "invention," the Baseball Hall of Fame opened in Cooperstown in 1939.

In 1845, New Yorker Alexander Cartwright started the Knickerbocker Baseball Club of New York. He wrote a set of rules for the game that are still followed today. The game of baseball caught on. Soon, people everywhere were playing.

You can learn more about the history of baseball if you visit the Baseball Hall of Fame. You can learn more about the real legends of the game, like Babe Ruth, Willie Mays, and Jackie Robinson. Baseball and Cooperstown are New York's legacies to the world.

In 1947, Brooklyn Dodger first baseman Jackie Robinson (above) became the first African American to play in the major leagues. That year the Dodgers faced the Yankees in the World Series and the Yankees won 4 games to 3. Robinson was named Rookie of the Year. The 1996 New York Yankees (below) celebrate their World Series victory.

Shortstop Ray Ordõnez (above) of the New York Mets fires the ball to first base to turn a double play. Babe Ruth's bat (right) is on display in Cooperstown at the Baseball Hall of Fame.

GENUINE
George "Babe" Ruth
LOUISVILLE SLUGGER

Powerized

LOUISVILLE SLUGGER
125
HILLERICH & BRADSBY CO.
MADE IN U.S.A.

Baseball Hall of Fame Library, Milo Stewart, Jr., Cooperstown, N.Y.

329

LOCAL CONNECTIONS
MANHATTAN:
LEARNING FROM CUSTOMS

The students in Mrs. LaVelle's fourth-grade class in Manhattan were studying local customs.

"I like St. Patrick's day in March. My favorite part is the parade," said Shawn. "Everyone in my family wears something green! Last year we saw the mayor marching."

Michael explained that in December his family celebrates Kwanzaa. "It's a time when families and friends come together, think about the past, and plan for the new year," he said. "We have fun watching performances, dancing to African music, and eating African foods like yams."

"That sounds a lot like Chinese New Year," May said. "We also spend several days celebrating. We cook lots of special dishes, and watch the dragon parade," she added.

"A dragon parade! That sounds really exciting," said Nicole. "Mrs. LaVelle, can we learn more about Chinese New Year?" she asked. The students all agreed that learning about this custom would be interesting and fun.

The dragon is a symbol for goodness and strength. It is an important part of Chinese New Year.

330

May explained how her family prepares for the new year. "First we clean the house and decorate. We hang up banners that wish the family happiness in the new year." Fruits, such as oranges and apples, and flowers are placed around the house.

Orange and red are used in many decorations because the Chinese believe they are colors of joy and happiness. "We must think good thoughts and speak kind words," said May. "During the celebration, people greet each other by saying 'Gung-Hey-Fat-Choy.' That's Happy New Year in Cantonese Chinese!"

May also explained that families get together for a feast of fish, meats, vegetables, noodles, seaweed, and rice. After the feast, the adults give the children money in red envelopes for good luck.

May finished telling about the customs of Chinese New Year. Then the students researched the Dragon Parade so they could hold a celebration in class. They learned that the dragon is bright red, yellow, and green. Many people build the dragon out of papier-mâché and fabric, like silk. Then they carry it on sticks through noisy streets full of music and happy people. The dragon wishes everyone good luck, peace, and wealth.

As part of their New Year's celebration, the students made dragon masks to wear in their own dragon parade.

MAKE your LOCAL CONNECTION

What customs are celebrated by people in your community? Work with other students to find out more about these customs. Then hold a celebration and invite other classes to join in.

Students made dragon masks to wear during their celebration of Chinese New Year.

CHAPTER 13 REVIEW

THINKING ABOUT VOCABULARY

Number a sheet of paper from 1 to 5. Next to each number write the word or phrase from the list that best completes the sentence.

culture
ethnic group
historical site
metropolitan area
recreation

1. A _____ is a city and its suburbs together.

2. All the things we do for relaxation and enjoyment are called _____.

3. A _____ is a place where something important or interesting happened in the past.

4. People whose ancestors are from the same country or area are part of the same _____.

5. The way of life that a group of people shares is its _____.

THINKING ABOUT FACTS

1. About how many people live in New York today? About how many are recent immigrants?

2. How many Native Americans live in New York?

3. Name two metropolitan areas in New York.

4. Name three ethnic groups that make their homes in the Elmhurst neighborhood of Queens.

5. What are powwows?

6. What are some customs New Yorkers keep?

7. What do people in our state do for winter recreation?

8. What is a professional sports team?

9. What forms of art can be found in New York?

10. Why are historical sites important?

THINK AND WRITE

WRITING AN ARTICLE

Suppose you are a sports reporter for the local newspaper. You have been assigned to cover one of the sports teams from New York during the biggest game of the season. Write an article describing the game. Include a headline and a byline.

WRITING A RESEARCH REPORT

Choose a museum or historical site that you read about in Lesson 2. Do some research about when it was founded or what happened there. Include details about what can be found in the museum or at the site.

WRITING A DESCRIPTION

Suppose you have just attended the Italian Festival in Buffalo or a Native American powwow described in Lesson 1. Write a description of the event. Include as many details as you can think of.

APPLYING STUDY SKILLS

WRITING AN OUTLINE

1. What is an outline? How can writing an outline help you organize information?

2. What are the steps in writing an outline?

3. Read the section in Lesson 1 titled "Cities and Suburbs." Take notes as you read, and write an outline of the section.

4. Read the section in Lesson 2 titled "Sports in New York." Write an outline of the section.

5. How can taking notes and writing an outline help you to write a research report about recreation in our state?

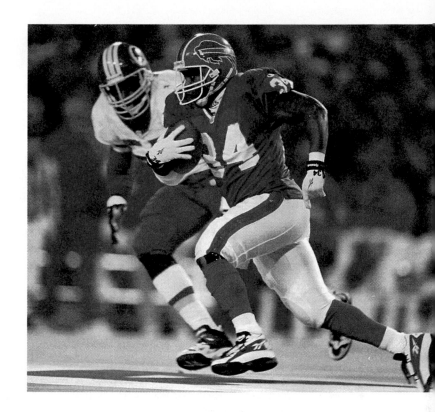

Summing Up the Chapter

Use the following main-idea chart to organize information from the chapter. Copy the headings on a sheet of paper. Then fill in the main ideas. When you have filled in the chart, use it to write a paragraph answering the question "How do people, sports, recreation, and art make New York a great place to live?"

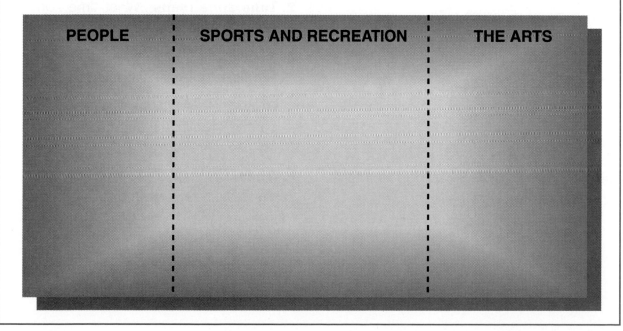

PEOPLE	SPORTS AND RECREATION	THE ARTS

UNIT 5 REVIEW

THINKING ABOUT VOCABULARY

Number a sheet of paper from 1 to 10. Beside each number, write the word or term from the list below that best completes each sentence.

agriculture
checks and balances
consumer
diversity
legislative branch

metropolitan area
municipal
recreation
services
veto

1. To _____ a bill is to reject it.

2. A _____ government takes care of the streets and sidewalks, and runs libraries, parks, police, and fire departments.

3. Swimming and hiking are two things people do for _____.

4. The business of growing crops and raising animals is known as _____.

5. The _____ of our state government makes the laws.

6. The many different cultures in New York show the state's _____.

7. Anyone who buys goods is a _____.

8. A city and all its suburbs make up a _____.

9. _____ are jobs people do that help other people.

10. The idea of limiting each government branch's power is called _____.

THINK AND WRITE ◀▬▬▶

WRITING AN EXPLANATION

Write a paragraph that explains the three branches of New York's government.

WRITING A REPORT

Find out more about a service industry that employs many people in your area. Write a report on what services this industry provides and how it helps people.

WRITING A LETTER

Suppose you are vacationing somewhere in New York. In a letter to a friend, describe some of the different activities you did for recreation.

BUILDING SKILLS

1. **Time zone maps** Use the map on page 287 to tell what time it is in Oregon when you wake up at 7:00 A.M. in New York.

2. **Time zone maps** What time zone is next to your time zone on the west?

3. **Newspapers** What five questions should a good news article answer?

4. **Outline** Read "Financial Services" on page 284. What main ideas would you list on your outline?

5. **Outline** Make an outline of New York's state government.

YESTERDAY, TODAY &
TOMORROW

In this unit you have read about changes in New York's economy. For many years New Yorkers have worked in agricultural industries. Today, however, they also use computers and other high-technology products to make work easier. How do you think New Yorkers will earn a living in the future?

READING ON YOUR OWN

These are some of the books you could find at the library to help you learn more.

THE LIFE AND TIMES OF THE APPLE
by Charles Micucci
This book tells all about apples—from seed, to flower, to fruit, to pie—and more!

MY NEW YORK
by Kathy Jacobsen
See New York City with 10-year-old Becky and her friend as they visit some of New York's famous and interesting sights.

RUTH BADER GINSBURG
by Jack L. Roberts
Read about the life of the second woman ever to serve on the United States Supreme Court.

UNIT PROJECT

Make a New York Wheel

1. Research several facts about famous people, places, or events in New York today.
2. Use a paper plate to trace a circle on a heavy piece of paper. Draw a second circle about an inch smaller.
3. Draw lines on the circles to divide them into six equal pie shapes.
4. Write a question about one of the facts you researched in each section of the smaller circle. Draw a picture to help illustrate each question.
5. Cut out the large circle. Decorate the outside edge. Write an answer in each section.
6. Cut the small circle along the lines into pie shapes. Tape each question to the outside edge of the large circle over the correct answer. You can then lift it like a flap to show the answer underneath.
7. Glue the wheel to a craft stick for a handle.
8. Take turns asking and answering each other's questions.

REFERENCE SECTION

The Reference Section has many parts,
each with a different type of information.
Use this section to look up people,
places, and events as you study.

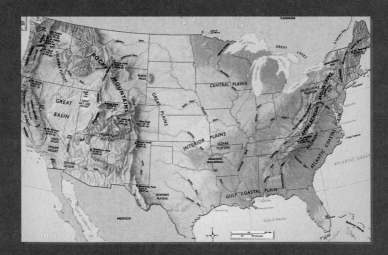

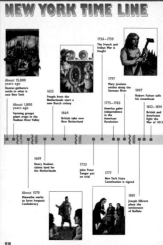

The Granger Collection, N.Y.

THE UNITED STATES: Political

RUSSIA

ALASKA

CANADA

ARCTIC OCEAN

70°N

180°

60°N

170°W

160°W

150°W

140°W

• Nome

• Fairbanks

• Anchorage

Juneau

Yukon

River

Arctic Circle

PACIFIC
OCEAN

0   250   500 Miles

0   250   500 Kilometers

CANADA

Seattle •

Spokane •

★ Olympia

WASHINGTON

River

40°N

• Portland

★ Salem

• Eugene

OREGON

Columbia

IDAHO

• Boise

Snake River

Great Falls •

Helena ★

MONTANA

• Billings

WYOMING

• Casper •

Cheyenne ★

Missouri River

• Pocatello

Great
Salt
Lake

• Ogden

★ Salt Lake City

• Provo

COLORADO

UTAH

Denver ★

Colorado
Springs •

Pueblo •

NEVADA

• Reno

★ Carson City

San Francisco •

• Oakland

• San Jose

★ Sacramento

CALIFORNIA

Las
Vegas •

30°N

PACIFIC OCEAN

130°W

• Los Angeles

• Long Beach

San Diego •

Colorado River

ARIZONA

★ Phoenix

Tucson •

NEW MEXICO

Albuquerque •

Santa
Fe ★

El Paso •

Rio Grande

160°W

PACIFIC
OCEAN

155°W

N

• Kauai

Niihau

★ Oahu

Honolulu

Molokai

Lanai   Maui

Kahoolawe

HAWAII

Hawaii   Hilo •

20°N

0   100   200 Miles

0   100   200 Kilometers

N

W   E

S

N

W   E

S

20°N

120°W

110°W

MEXICO

R4

CANADA

Lake Superior

NORTH DAKOTA
Grand Forks
★ Bismarck Fargo

Duluth

MICHIGAN

Lake Huron

MAINE
★ Augusta

MINNESOTA

WISCONSIN

Lake Michigan

Montpelier
Burlington **VERMONT** Portland
★ **NEW** ★
HAMPSHIRE ★ Concord

SOUTH DAKOTA
★ Pierre

Minneapolis ★ St. Paul

Green Bay

Madison Milwaukee

Grand Rapids Lansing

Detroit

Lake Erie

Lake Ontario

Buffalo **NEW YORK** Albany **MASSACHUSETTS** ★ Boston
★Providence
Hartford★ **RHODE**
CONNECTICUT **ISLAND**

Sioux Falls

Missouri

IOWA
Cedar Rapids Rockford

Chicago Gary Fort Wayne Toledo Cleveland

PENNSYLVANIA
Pittsburgh Harrisburg
Newark
Trenton New York
NEW JERSEY
Philadelphia

NEBRASKA

Omaha ★ Des Moines

Davenport

Peoria

OHIO Wheeling
★ Columbus

Dover

Baltimore **DELAWARE**
Washington, ★ Annapolis
D.C. **MARYLAND**

Platte River

Lincoln ★

Springfield
★ Indianapolis

INDIANA

Cincinnati

Ohio River

WEST
★Charleston
VIRGINIA

VIRGINIA
Richmond ★

Norfolk

Kansas City

MISSOURI

ILLINOIS

St. Louis Evansville

Frankfort

Topeka ★ Kansas City

Jefferson City

Louisville

KANSAS

Arkansas River

Wichita

KENTUCKY

NORTH CAROLINA
★ Raleigh

Nashville ★ Knoxville

Charlotte

Tulsa

River

TENNESSEE

Tennessee River

SOUTH CAROLINA
★ Columbia

ARKANSAS

Oklahoma City
Fort Smith Little Rock ★

Memphis

Charleston

OKLAHOMA

Red River

Mississippi River

Birmingham

GEORGIA

Atlanta

ATLANTIC OCEAN

MISSISSIPPI

ALABAMA

Columbus

Savannah

Fort Worth Dallas

Shreveport

Jackson ★

★ Montgomery

TEXAS

LOUISIANA

Austin

Biloxi Mobile

Tallahassee ★ Jacksonville

Baton Rouge ★

Houston

New Orleans

FLORIDA

San Antonio

Gulf of Mexico

Tampa

THE BAHAMAS

Laredo Corpus Christi

Miami

⊛ National capital   ★ State capital   • Other city

0   150   300 Miles

0   150   300 Kilometers

CUBA

100°W   90°W   80°W

50°N

40°N

70°W

30°N

R5

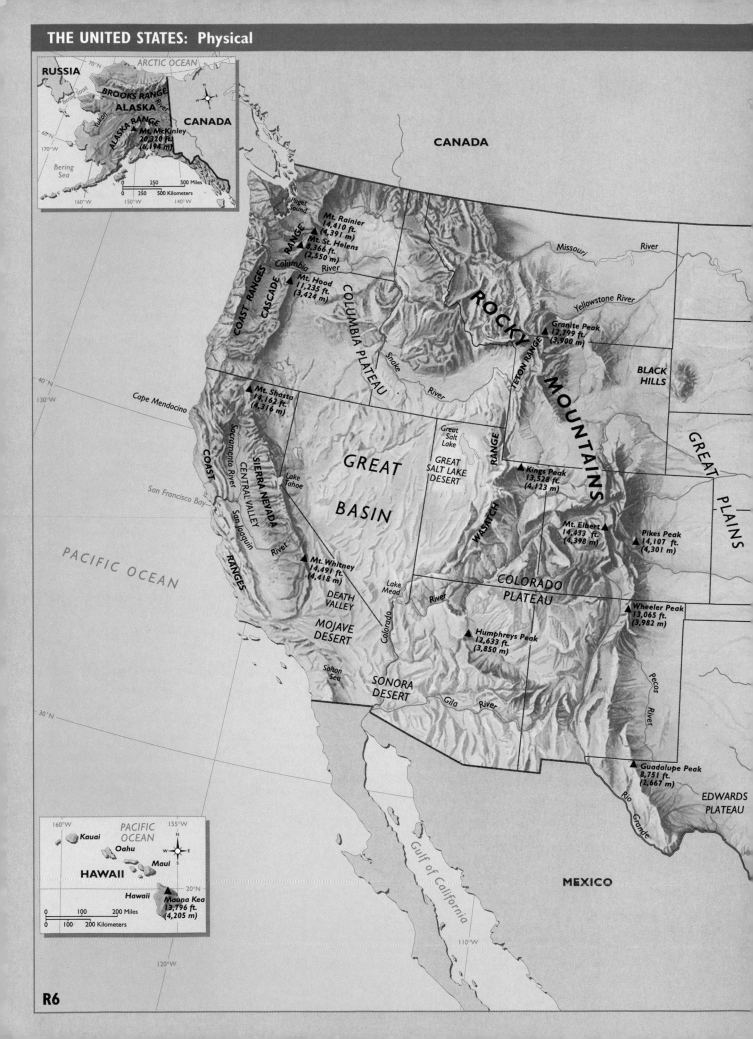

RUSSIA

ARCTIC OCEAN

BROOKS RANGE

ALASKA

CANADA

ALASKA RANGE

▲ Mt. McKinley
20,320 ft.
(6,194 m)

Yukon

Bering
Sea

250   500 Miles

250   500 Kilometers

CANADA

Puget
Sound

▲ Mt. Rainier
14,410 ft.
(4,391 m)

▲ Mt. St. Helens
8,366 ft.
(2,550 m)

COAST RANGES

CASCADE RANGE

Columbia   River

▲ Mt. Hood
11,235 ft.
(3,424 m)

COLUMBIA PLATEAU

Missouri   River

ROCKY MOUNTAINS

Yellowstone River

Snake

River

TETON RANGE

▲ Granite Peak
12,799 ft.
(3,900 m)

BLACK HILLS

Cape Mendocino

▲ Mt. Shasta
14,162 ft.
(4,316 m)

40°N

130°W

GREAT
BASIN

Great
Salt
Lake

GREAT
SALT LAKE
DESERT

RANGE

WASATCH

GREAT

PLAINS

Sacramento River

COAST

San Francisco Bay

SIERRA NEVADA

CENTRAL VALLEY

Lake
Tahoe

▲ Kings Peak
13,528 ft.
(4,123 m)

▲ Mt. Elbert
14,433 ft.
(4,398 m)

▲ Pikes Peak
14,107 ft.
(4,301 m)

San Joaquin

River

RANGES

▲ Mt. Whitney
14,491 ft.
(4,418 m)

DEATH
VALLEY

Lake
Mead

River

COLORADO
PLATEAU

▲ Wheeler Peak
13,065 ft.
(3,982 m)

PACIFIC OCEAN

MOJAVE
DESERT

Colorado

▲ Humphreys Peak
12,633 ft.
(3,850 m)

Pecos

River

Salton
Sea

SONORA
DESERT

Gila   River

30°N

▲ Guadalupe Peak
8,751 ft.
(2,667 m)

Rio

Grande

EDWARDS
PLATEAU

Gulf of California

MEXICO

110°W

PACIFIC
OCEAN

160°W   155°W

Kauai

Oahu

N

W   E

S

Maui

HAWAII

Hawaii

20°N

▲ Mauna Kea
13,796 ft.
(4,205 m)

100   200 Miles

100   200 Kilometers

120°W

R6

CANADA

Lake of
the Woods

MESABI RANGE

Lake Superior

GREAT

LAKES

St. Lawrence River

WHITE MTS.

Mt. Washington
6,288 ft.
(1,917 m)

GREEN MTS.

ADIRONDACK
MTS.

Cape Cod

Lake Huron

Lake Michigan

Mississippi

CENTRAL PLAINS

Lake Ontario

Lake Erie

ALLEGHENY
PLATEAU

APPALACHIAN MOUNTAINS

Hudson River

Long Island

40°N

70°W

Platte River

River

Susquehanna

River

Delaware Bay

Missouri

River

Wabash River

Ohio

River

ALLEGHENY MOUNTAINS

Potomac

River

ATLANTIC COASTAL PLAIN

Chesapeake Bay

Arkansas

River

INTERIOR PLAINS

OZARK
PLATEAU

River

Mt. Mitchell
6,684 ft.
(2,037 m)

PIEDMONT

Cape Hatteras

OUACHITA
MOUNTAINS

Mississippi

River

Tennessee

River

River

Savannah River

ATLANTIC OCEAN

Red

River

Alabama

River

Chattahoochee

30°N

Brazos

River

GULF COASTAL PLAIN

Mobile Bay

Colorado River

Galveston Bay

Mississippi Delta

Lake
Okeechobee

Bahama Islands

Gulf of Mexico

50°N

N
W E
S

0   150   300 Miles
0   150   300 Kilometers

Florida Keys

Straits of Florida

80°W

90°W

CUBA

R7

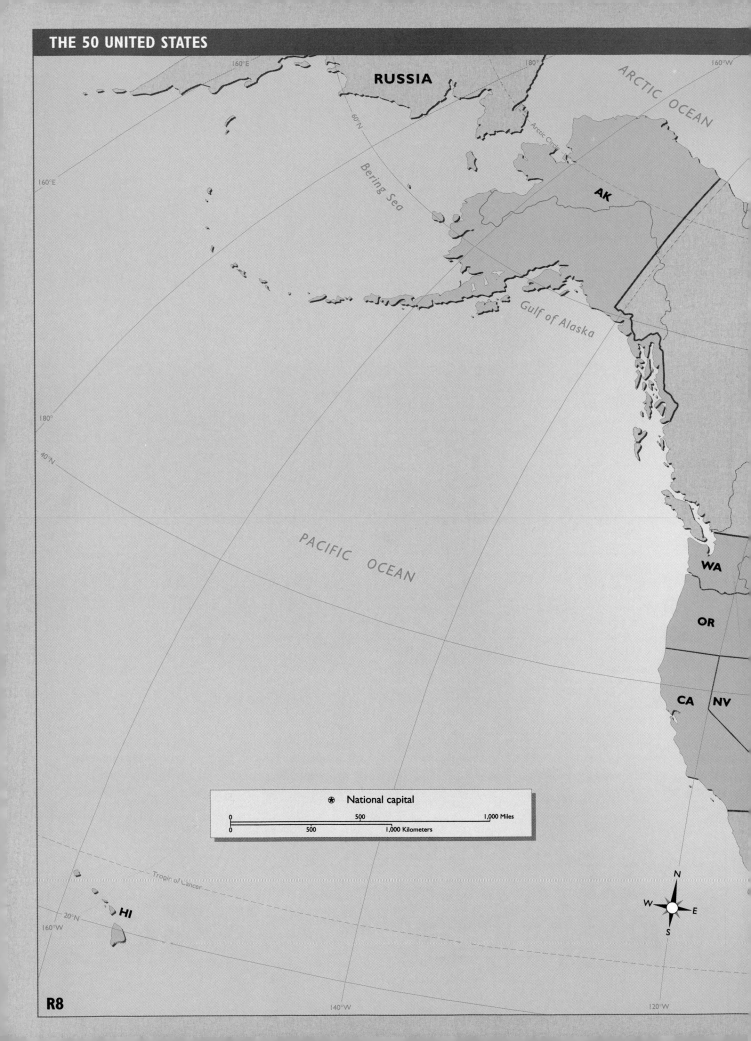

RUSSIA

ARCTIC OCEAN

Bering Sea

Arctic Circle

AK

Gulf of Alaska

PACIFIC OCEAN

WA

OR

CA   NV

⊛ National capital

0		500		1,000 Miles

0	500	1,000 Kilometers	

Tropic of Cancer

HI

20°N

160°W

160°E

160°E

180°

40°N

180°

160°W

60°N

N
W   E
S

140°W

120°W

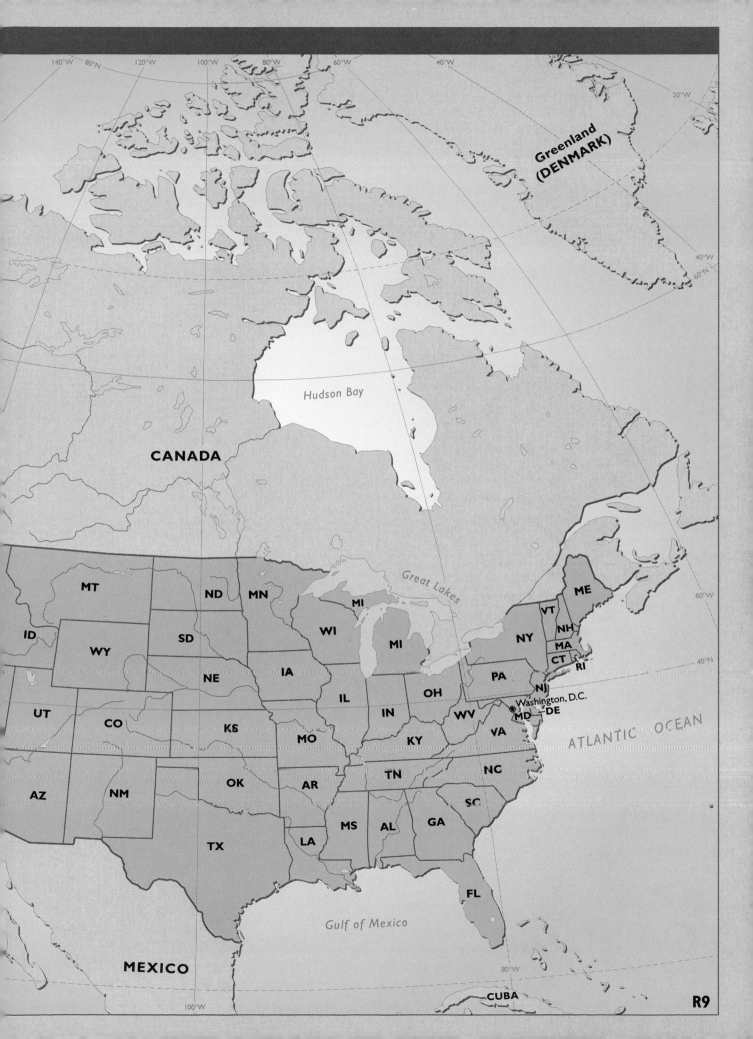

Greenland
(DENMARK)

Hudson Bay

CANADA

Great Lakes

MEXICO

Gulf of Mexico

ATLANTIC OCEAN

CUBA

MT
ND
MN
MI
ID
SD
WI
MI
WY
IA
ME
VT
NH
NY
MA
CT
RI
PA
NE
NJ
UT
IL
OH
Washington, D.C.
CO
KS
IN
WV
MD
DE
AZ
MO
KY
VA
NM
OK
AR
TN
NC
TX
MS
AL
GA
SC
LA
FL

140°W 80°N 120°W 100°W 80°W 60°W 40°W 20°W
40°W
60°N
60°W
40°N
80°W
100°W

R9

ARCTIC OCEAN

GREENLAND
(DENMARK)

ALASKA (U.S.)

CANADA

NORTH AMERICA

UNITED STATES

BERMUDA
(U.K.)

ATLANTIC OCEAN

MIDWAY ISLANDS
(U.S.)

Tropic of Cancer

MEXICO

See inset below

Caribbean Sea

HAWAII (U.S.)

PACIFIC OCEAN

VENEZUELA   GUYANA
             SURINAME

COLOMBIA

FRENCH GUIANA
(FRANCE)

GALÁPAGOS ISLANDS
(ECUADOR)

ECUADOR

SOUTH AMERICA

Equator

PERU

BRAZIL

WESTERN
SAMOA

AMERICAN SAMOA
(U.S.)

FRENCH POLYNESIA
(FRANCE)

BOLIVIA

TONGA

PARAGUAY

Tropic of Capricorn

URUGUAY

CHILE   ARGENTINA

FALKLAND ISLANDS
(U.K.)

Antarctic Circle

ANTARCTICA

Central America and West Indies

Gulf of Mexico

BAHAMAS

Tropic of Cancer

TURKS AND
CAICOS IS. (U.K.)

ATLANTIC OCEAN

CUBA

VIRGIN ISLANDS
(U.S. AND U.K.)

CAYMAN ISLANDS
(U.K.)

JAMAICA

HAITI   DOMINICAN
        REPUBLIC

ANTIGUA AND
BARBUDA

MEXICO

PUERTO RICO
(U.S.)

ST. KITTS
AND NEVIS

GUADELOUPE
(FRANCE)

BELIZE

DOMINICA

GUATEMALA

Caribbean Sea

MARTINIQUE
(FRANCE)

ST. LUCIA

HONDURAS

EL SALVADOR

ST. VINCENT AND
THE GRENADINES

ARUBA
(NETHERLANDS)

NETHERLANDS
ANTILLES
(NETHERLANDS)

BARBADOS

PACIFIC
OCEAN

NICARAGUA

GRENADA

TRINIDAD AND
TOBAGO

COSTA
RICA

PANAMA

VENEZUELA

0   250   500 Miles
0   250   500 Kilometers

COLOMBIA

GUYANA

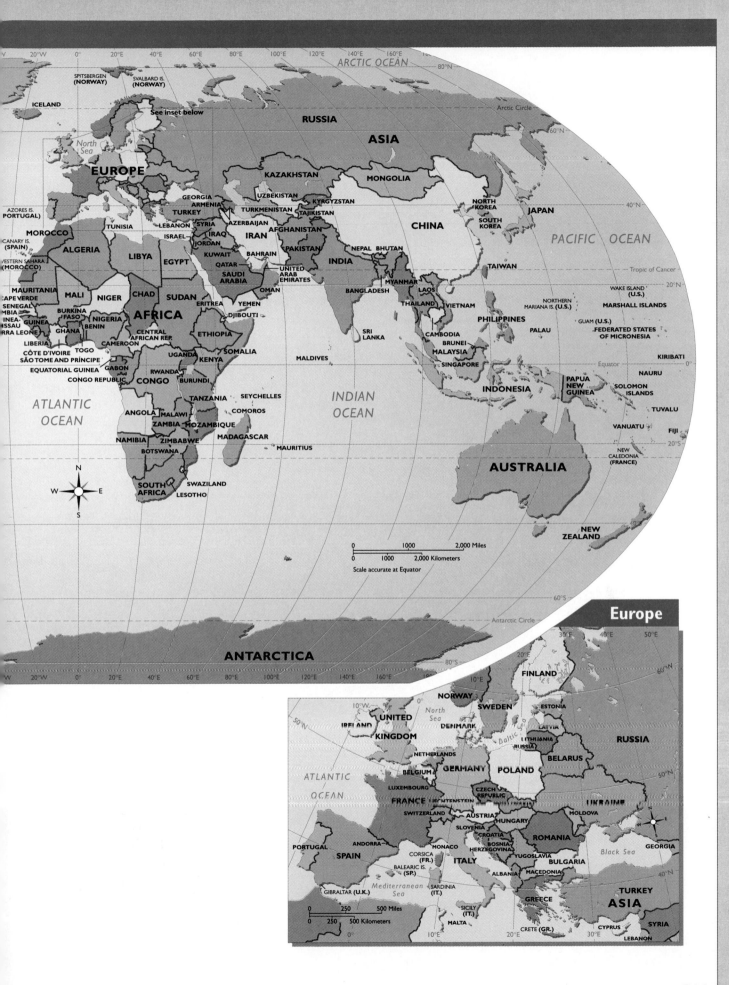

ARCTIC OCEAN

SPITSBERGEN
(NORWAY)
SVALBARD IS.
(NORWAY)

ICELAND

See inset below

North
Sea

RUSSIA

ASIA

EUROPE

KAZAKHSTAN

MONGOLIA

AZORES IS.
PORTUGAL)

GEORGIA
ARMENIA
TURKEY

UZBEKISTAN

KYRGYZSTAN

TAJIKISTAN

NORTH
KOREA

JAPAN

TURKMENISTAN

SOUTH
KOREA

PACIFIC OCEAN

CANARY IS.
(SPAIN)

MOROCCO

TUNISIA

LEBANON
SYRIA
ISRAEL
JORDAN
IRAQ

AZERBAIJAN

AFGHANISTAN

CHINA

ALGERIA

LIBYA

EGYPT

IRAN

PAKISTAN

NEPAL BHUTAN

TAIWAN

WESTERN SAHARA
(MOROCCO)

KUWAIT
BAHRAIN
QATAR
SAUDI
ARABIA

UNITED
ARAB
EMIRATES

INDIA

Tropic of Cancer

MAURITANIA
CAPE VERDE

MALI

NIGER

CHAD

SUDAN

OMAN

YEMEN

BANGLADESH

MYANMAR

LAOS

WAKE ISLAND
(U.S.)

SENEGAL
MBIA
NEA-
SSAU
RRA LEONE

BURKINA
FASO

NIGERIA

ERITREA

DJIBOUTI

AFRICA

THAILAND

VIETNAM

NORTHERN
MARIANA IS. (U.S.)

MARSHALL ISLANDS

GHANA

BENIN

CENTRAL
AFRICAN REP.

ETHIOPIA

GUAM (U.S.)

PHILIPPINES

PALAU

FEDERATED STATES
OF MICRONESIA

LIBERIA
CÔTE D'IVOIRE
SÃO TOME AND PRÍNCIPE

TOGO

CAMEROON

UGANDA

SOMALIA

SRI
LANKA

CAMBODIA

BRUNEI

KIRIBATI

EQUATORIAL GUINEA
CONGO REPUBLIC

GABON

RWANDA

KENYA

MALDIVES

MALAYSIA

SINGAPORE

Equator

NAURU

CONGO

BURUNDI

INDONESIA

PAPUA
NEW
GUINEA

SOLOMON
ISLANDS

ATLANTIC
OCEAN

ANGOLA

TANZANIA

SEYCHELLES

INDIAN
OCEAN

TUVALU

MALAWI

COMOROS

ZAMBIA

MOZAMBIQUE

VANUATU

FIJI

NAMIBIA

ZIMBABWE

MADAGASCAR

NEW
CALEDONIA
(FRANCE)

20°S

BOTSWANA

MAURITIUS

N

W   E

S

SOUTH
AFRICA

SWAZILAND

LESOTHO

AUSTRALIA

0   1000   2,000 Miles

0   1000   2,000 Kilometers

Scale accurate at Equator

NEW
ZEALAND

60°S

Antarctic Circle

ANTARCTICA

80°S

FINLAND

NORWAY

SWEDEN

ESTONIA

IRELAND

UNITED
KINGDOM

North
Sea

DENMARK

Baltic
Sea

LATVIA

LITHUANIA

RUSSIA

RUSSIA

ATLANTIC
OCEAN

NETHERLANDS

BELGIUM

GERMANY

POLAND

BELARUS

LUXEMBOURG

FRANCE

LIECHTENSTEIN

CZECH
REPUBLIC

UKRAINE

SWITZERLAND

AUSTRIA

HUNGARY

MOLDOVA

SLOVENIA

CROATIA

ROMANIA

PORTUGAL

SPAIN

ANDORRA

MONACO

CORSICA
(FR.)

BALEARIC IS.
(SP.)

ITALY

BOSNIA
HERZEGOVINA

YUGOSLAVIA

GEORGIA

Black Sea

BULGARIA

ALBANIA

MACEDONIA

TURKEY

GIBRALTAR (U.K.)

Mediterranean
Sea

SARDINIA
(IT.)

GREECE

ASIA

0   250   500 Miles

0   250   500 Kilometers

SICILY
(IT.)

MALTA

CRETE (GR.)

CYPRUS

SYRIA

LEBANON

ARCTIC OCEAN

80°N

60°N

Arctic Circle

Ob River

Volga River

URAL MTS.

EUROPE

ALPS

Mont Blanc
15,771 ft. (4,807 m)

Mt. Elbrus
18,510 ft. (5,642 m)

ASIA

GOBI

40°N

HINDU KUSH

HIMALAYAS

Ganges R.

Chang R.

Everest
29,028 ft.
(8,848 m)

SYRIAN
DESERT

SAHARA

Nile River

AFRICA

DECCAN
PLATEAU

Tropic of Cancer

20°N

PACIFIC OCEAN

Mt. Kilimanjaro
19,340 ft. (5,895 m)

Equator

0°

INDIAN OCEAN

ATLANTIC
OCEAN

NAMIB DESERT

KALAHARI
DESERT

GREAT
SANDY
DESERT

AUSTRALIA

20°S

Tropic of Capricorn

Cape of
Good Hope

Mt. Kosciusko
7,310 ft. (2,228 m)

N
W   E
S

0   1,000   2,000 Miles
0   1,000   2,000 Kilometers
Scale accurate at Equator

60°S

Antarctic Circle

ANTARCTICA

80°S

180°

20°W   0°   20°E   40°E   60°E   80°E   100°E   120°E   140°E   160°E   180°

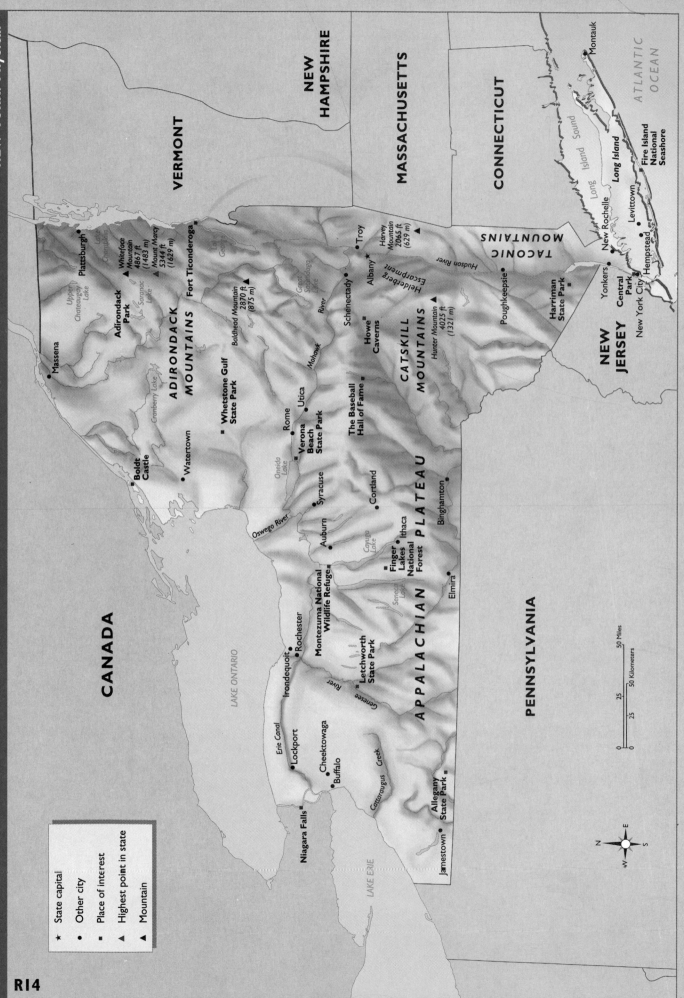

Legend

- ★ State capital
- ● Other city
- ■ Place of interest
- ▲ Highest point in state
- ▲ Mountain

CANADA

NEW HAMPSHIRE

VERMONT

MASSACHUSETTS

CONNECTICUT

NEW JERSEY

PENNSYLVANIA

ATLANTIC OCEAN

Montauk

Long Island Sound

Long Island

Fire Island National Seashore

New Rochelle

Levittown

Yonkers
Central Park
New York City
Hempstead

TACONIC MOUNTAINS

Poughkeepsie

Harriman State Park

Hudson River

Harvey Mountain 2065 ft (629 m) ▲

Troy

Albany ★

Schenectady

Helderberg Escarpment

Hunter Mountain 4025 ft (1321 m) ▲

Howe Caverns

CATSKILL MOUNTAINS

APPALACHIAN PLATEAU

Binghamton

Elmira

Cortland

Ithaca

Finger Lakes National Forest

Cayuga Lake

Seneca Lake

Auburn

Syracuse

The Baseball Hall of Fame

Utica

Rome

Verona Beach State Park

Oneida Lake

Mohawk River

Boldhead Mountain 2870 ft (875 m) ▲

Great Sacandaga Lake

Lake George

Mount Marcy 5344 ft (1629 m) ▲

Whiteface Mountain 4867 ft (1483 m) ▲

Fort Ticonderoga

ADIRONDACK MOUNTAINS

Adirondack Park

Whetstone Gulf State Park

Watertown

Saranac Lake

Lake Champlain

Upper Chateaugay Lake

Cranberry Lake

Plattsburgh

Massena

Boldt Castle

Oswego River

Montezuma National Wildlife Refuge

Letchworth State Park

Genesee River

Rochester

Irondequoit

Lockport

Erie Canal

Cheektowaga

Buffalo

Niagara Falls

Cattaraugus Creek

Allegany State Park

Jamestown

LAKE ONTARIO

LAKE ERIE

50 Miles
50 Kilometers
0   25   50
0   25   50

N
W   E
S

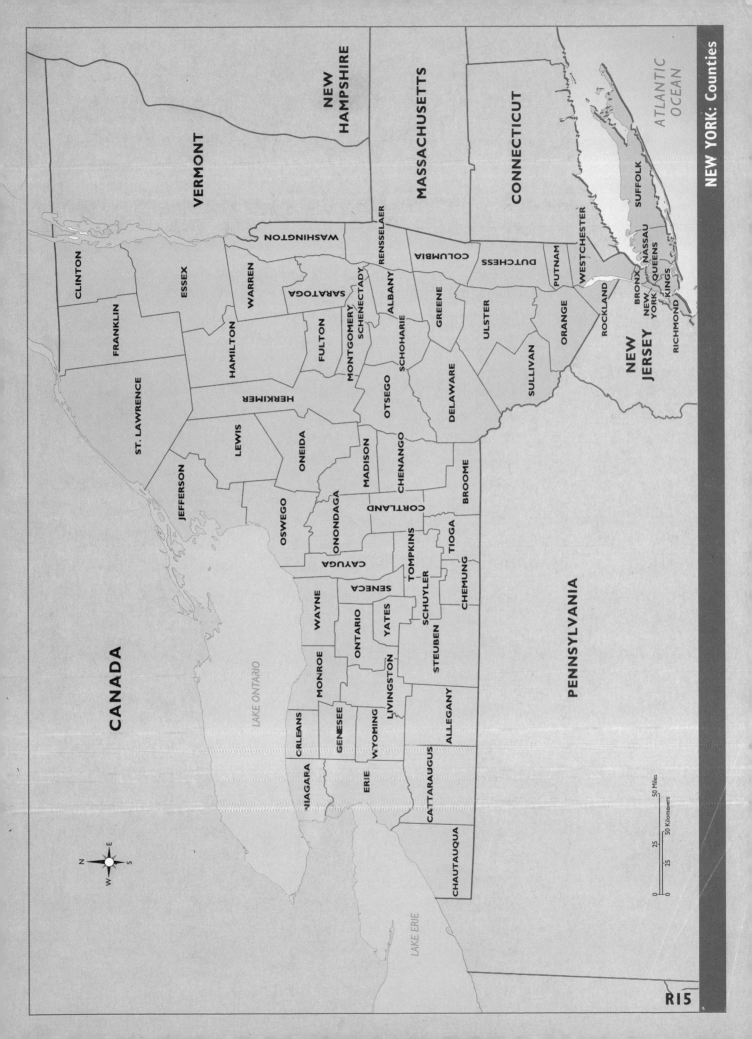

NEW YORK: Counties

ATLANTIC OCEAN

CANADA

VERMONT

NEW HAMPSHIRE

MASSACHUSETTS

CONNECTICUT

NEW JERSEY

PENNSYLVANIA

LAKE ONTARIO

LAKE ERIE

CLINTON
FRANKLIN
ESSEX
ST. LAWRENCE
HAMILTON
WARREN
WASHINGTON
SARATOGA
SCHENECTADY
RENSSELAER
FULTON
MONTGOMERY
ALBANY
COLUMBIA
HERKIMER
OTSEGO
SCHOHARIE
GREENE
LEWIS
ONEIDA
MADISON
CHENANGO
DELAWARE
ULSTER
JEFFERSON
OSWEGO
ONONDAGA
CORTLAND
BROOME
SULLIVAN
ORANGE
ROCKLAND
WESTCHESTER
PUTNAM
DUTCHESS
CAYUGA
TOMPKINS
TIOGA
SENECA
SCHUYLER
CHEMUNG
WAYNE
ONTARIO
YATES
STEUBEN
MONROE
LIVINGSTON
ALLEGANY
GENESEE
WYOMING
ORLEANS
NIAGARA
ERIE
CATTARAUGUS
CHAUTAUQUA
BRONX
NEW YORK
QUEENS
KINGS
RICHMOND
NASSAU
SUFFOLK

N
W E
S

50 Miles
25
0
25
50 Kilometers
0

R15

NEW YORK COUNTIES

COUNTY NAME	COUNTY SEAT	POPULATION (1990)	AREA (SQ. MILES)	YEAR FORMED
Albany	Albany	292,594	524	1683
Allegany	Belmont	50,470	1,032	1806
Bronx	Bronx	1,203,789	42	1912
Broome	Binghamton	212,160	712	1806
Cattaraugus	Little Valley	84,234	1,306	1808
Cayuga	Auburn	82,313	695	1799
Chautauqua	Mayville	141,895	1,064	1808
Chenango	Norwich	51,768	897	1798
Clinton	Plattsburgh	85,969	1,043	1788
Columbia	Hudson	62,982	638	1786
Cortland	Cortland	48,963	500	1808
Delaware	Delhi	47,225	1,440	1797
Dutchess	Poughkeepsie	259,462	804	1683
Erie	Buffalo	968,532	1,046	1821
Essex	Elizabethtown	37,152	1,806	1799
Genesee	Batavia	60,060	497	1802
Greene	Catskill	44,739	648	1800
Hamilton	Lake Pleasant	5,279	1,721	1816
Herkimer	Herkimer	65,797	1,416	1791
Jefferson	Watertown	110,943	1,273	1805
Kings	Brooklyn	2,300,664	70	1683
Lewis	Lowville	26,796	1,283	1805
Livingston	Geneseo	62,372	633	1821
Madison	Wampsville	69,120	656	1806
Monroe	Rochester	713,968	663	1821
Montgomery	Fonda	51,981	404	1784
Nassau	Mineola	1,287,348	287	1898
New York	Manhattan	1,487,536	22	1683
Niagara	Lockport	220,756	526	1808

COUNTY NAME	COUNTY SEAT	POPULATION (1990)	AREA (SQ. MILES)	YEAR FORMED
Oneida	Utica	250,836	1,219	1798
Onondaga	Syracuse	468,973	784	1794
Ontario	Canandaigua	95,101	644	1789
Orange	Goshen	307,647	826	1683
Orleans	Albion	41,846	391	1824
Oswego	Oswego	121,771	954	1816
Otsego	Cooperstown	60,517	1,004	1791
Putnam	Carmel	83,941	231	1812
Queens	Jamaica	1,951,598	109	1683
Rensselaer	Troy	154,429	655	1791
Richmond	Saint George	378,977	59	1683
Rockland	New City	265,475	175	1798
St. Lawrence	Canton	111,974	2,728	1802
Saratoga	Ballston Spa	181,276	810	1791
Schenectady	Schenectady	149,285	206	1809
Schoharie	Schoharie	31,859	624	1795
Schuyler	Watkins Glenn	18,622	329	1854
Seneca	Waterloo	32,638	327	1804
Steuben	Bath	99,088	1,396	1796
Suffolk	Riverhead	1,321,864	911	1683
Sullivan	Monticello	69,287	976	1809
Tioga	Owego	52,337	519	1791
Tompkins	Ithaca	94,097	477	1817
Ulster	Kingston	165,304	655	1683
Warren	Town of Queensbury	59,209	882	1813
Washington	Hudson Falls	59,330	836	1772
Wayne	Lyons	89,123	605	1823
Westchester	White Plains	874,866	438	1683
Wyoming	Warsaw	42,507	595	1841
Yates	Penn Yan	22,810	339	1823

Source: *New York Facts: Flying the Colors*

NEW YORK TIME LINE

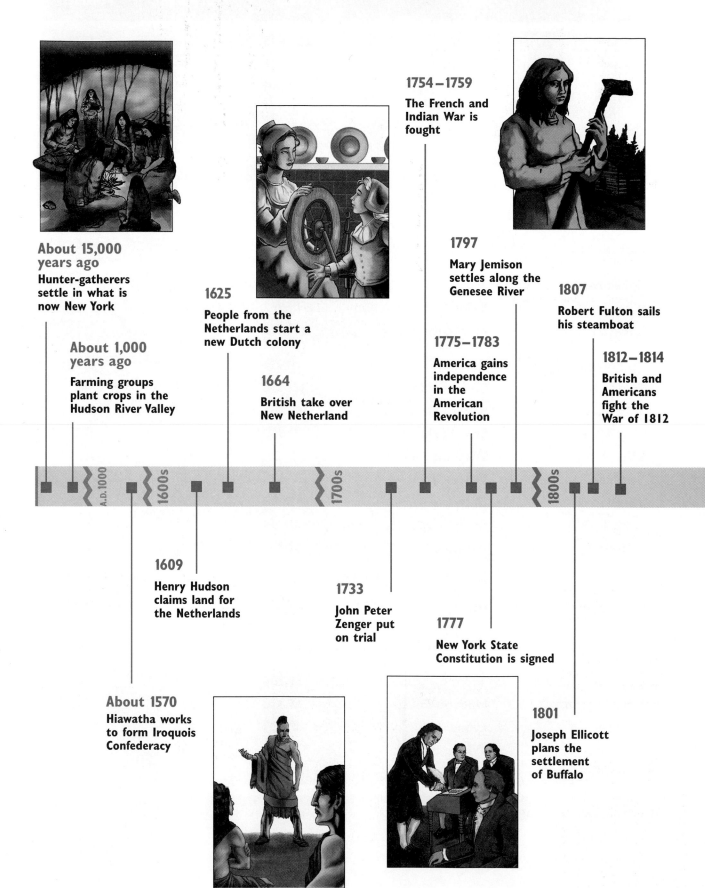

About 15,000 years ago
Hunter-gatherers settle in what is now New York

About 1,000 years ago
Farming groups plant crops in the Hudson River Valley

1625
People from the Netherlands start a new Dutch colony

1664
British take over New Netherland

1754–1759
The French and Indian War is fought

1797
Mary Jemison settles along the Genesee River

1775–1783
America gains independence in the American Revolution

1807
Robert Fulton sails his steamboat

1812–1814
British and Americans fight the War of 1812

A.D. 1000   1600s   1700s   1800s

1609
Henry Hudson claims land for the Netherlands

1733
John Peter Zenger put on trial

1777
New York State Constitution is signed

About 1570
Hiawatha works to form Iroquois Confederacy

1801
Joseph Ellicott plans the settlement of Buffalo

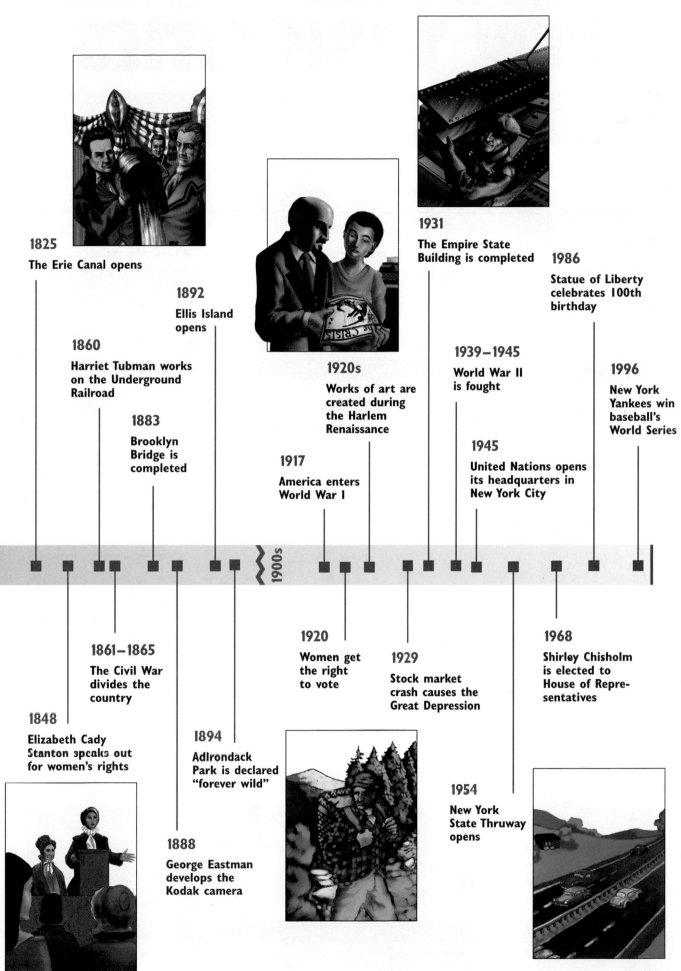

1825
The Erie Canal opens

1860
Harriet Tubman works on the Underground Railroad

1892
Ellis Island opens

1883
Brooklyn Bridge is completed

1931
The Empire State Building is completed

1986
Statue of Liberty celebrates 100th birthday

1920s
Works of art are created during the Harlem Renaissance

1939–1945
World War II is fought

1996
New York Yankees win baseball's World Series

1917
America enters World War I

1945
United Nations opens its headquarters in New York City

1900s

1861–1865
The Civil War divides the country

1920
Women get the right to vote

1929
Stock market crash causes the Great Depression

1968
Shirley Chisholm is elected to House of Representatives

1848
Elizabeth Cady Stanton speaks out for women's rights

1894
Adirondack Park is declared "forever wild"

1954
New York State Thruway opens

1888
George Eastman develops the Kodak camera

NEW YORK CITIES

CITY NAME	CITY POPULATION	COUNTY	POPULATION RANK
Albany	101,082	Albany	6
Binghamton	53,008	Broome	15
Brentwood	45,218	Suffolk	20
Buffalo	328,123	Erie	2
Cheektowaga	84,387	Erie	7
Commack	36,124	Suffolk	26
East Meadow	36,909	Nassau	25
Freeport	39,894	Nassau	24
Hempstead	49,453	Nassau	17
Hicksville	40,174	Nassau	23
Irondequoit	52,322	Monroe	16
Levittown	53,286	Nassau	14
Mount Vernon	67,153	Westchester	10
New Rochelle	67,265	Westchester	9
New York	7,322,564	Bronx, Kings, New York, Queens, Richmond	1
Niagara Falls	61,840	Niagara	12
Rochester	231,636	Monroe	3
Rome	44,350	Oneida	21
Schenectady	65,566	Schenectady	11
Syracuse	163,860	Onondaga	5
Troy	54,269	Rensselaer	13
Utica	68,637	Oneida	8
West Babylon	42,410	Suffolk	22
West Seneca	47,866	Erie	19
White Plains	48,718	Westchester	18
Yonkers	188,082	Westchester	4

All cities with a population greater than 35,000 in the 1990 census have been listed.

Source: *The American Tally*, 1993

ANNUAL EVENTS IN NEW YORK

SPRING

MARCH
Ringling Brothers & Barnum & Bailey Circus, Uniondale
Saint Patrick's Day Parade, New York City
Winter Carnival, Buffalo

APRIL
Central New York Maple Festival, Marathon
Dingus Day, Buffalo
Kite Weekend, East Meadow
Pet Expo, Suffern

MAY
Discovery Week, Howes Cave
Dutch Festival, Hempstead
Tulip Festival, Albany
Lucille Ball Festival of New Comedy, Jamestown
May Merriment Shakespearean Renaissance Faire, Annandale-on-Hudson
Telegrapher's Weekend, Poughkeepsie

SUMMER

JUNE
Art in the Sky Kite Festival, Cazenovia
Chocolate Festival, Fulton
Columbia County Carriage Days, Kinderhook
Hong Kong Dragon Board Festival, Glen Cove
Ithaca Festival, Ithaca
Juneteenth Festival, Buffalo
Kidrific Weekend, Alexandria Bay
Market Fair, Johnstown
Mohawk Frontier Festival, Johnstown
Tour de Dutchess, Pleasant Valley

JULY
Blueberry Festival, Nichols
Bluegrass Festival, Shinhopple
Canal Fest of the Tonawandas, Tonawanda
Convention Days, Seneca Falls
Cowboy Roundup, Pulaski
Lincoln Center Festival, New York City
Erie Canal Canoe Classic, Marcy
Willard Hanmer Guideboat and Canoe Race, Saranac Lake

AUGUST
Coxsackie Riverside Festival, Cocksackie
The Great New York State Fair, Syracuse
Green Corn Festival, Nedrow
Independence Day Celebration, Old Bethpage
Iroquois Indian Festival, Howes Cave
Polish American Arts Festival, Buffalo
Run for the Roses, Grafton

FALL

SEPTEMBER
Adirondack Balloon Festival, Glens Falls
Appleumpkin Festival, Wyoming
Civil War Weekend, Monroe
Festival by the Sea, Lido Beach
Festival of Grapes, Silver Creek
Long Island Fiddle and Folk Music Festival, Stony Brook
War of 1812 Encampment, Youngstown
Wild About the Hudson Valley, Wappingers Falls

OCTOBER
Applefest, Warwick
Giant Pumpkin Party and Children's Parade, Grahamsville
Great Escape Oktoberfest, Wilmington
Haunted Fort, Ticonderoga
Portage, Little Falls

NOVEMBER
A Festival of Lights, Niagara Falls
Festival of Nations, Syracuse
Macy's Thanksgiving Day Parade, New York City
New York City Marathon, New York City

WINTER

DECEMBER
Christmas Open House, Johnstown
Eglevsky Ballet's Nutcracker, Greenvale
First Night New Year's Eve, Buffalo
Reindeer Round-up Ski Races, Northville

JANUARY
Fulton County Winter Festival, Fulton County
New Year's Day Polar Bear Swim, Lake George
Winter Arts Festival, Bethpage State Park
Winterfest, Syracuse

FEBRUARY
Hague Winter Carnival, Hague
Natural Ice Bridge, Niagara Falls
Rockland County Kennel Club Dog Show, Suffern

Famous New Yorkers

Mariah Carey
Born in Huntington in 1970; singer; received two Grammy awards as Best New Artist and Best Pop Vocal Female (1990); Adult Contemporary Artist of the Year (1991)

Oscar Hijuelos
Born in Manhattan in 1951; author; won a Pulitzer Prize for Fiction for The Mambo Kings Play Songs of Love (1990)

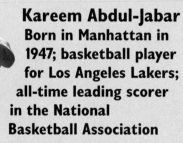

Christopher Reeve
Born in Manhattan in 1952; actor; known for his starring role in the Superman movies and as a spokesperson for the rights of people with disabilities

Kareem Abdul-Jabar
Born in Manhattan in 1947; basketball player for Los Angeles Lakers; all-time leading scorer in the National Basketball Association

Maya Lin
Born in Athens, Ohio, in 1959; lives in New York City; sculptor and architect; best known for Vietnam Veterans Memorial in Washington, D.C. (1982)

Mary Cleave
Born in Southampton in 1947; astronaut; spent 262 hours in space as a missions specialist and flight engineer

Joseph Bruchac III
Born in Saratoga Springs in 1942; poet, author; best known for founding the Greenfield Review Press, which publishes Native American authors

Colin Powell
Born in the Bronx in 1937; four-star general, former Chairman of the Joint Chiefs of Staff; led American Forces in the Persian Gulf War (1991)

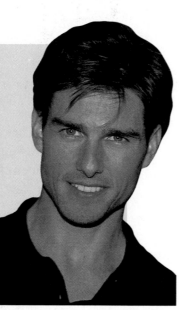

Tom Cruise
Born in Syracuse in 1962; actor; known for his roles in the movies *Rain Man* (1988) and *Mission: Impossible* (1996)

Rosie Perez
Born in Puerto Rico in 1968; raised in Brooklyn; actor, dancer, choreographer; known for her films *Do the Right Thing* (1989) and *Fearless* (1993)

Geraldine Ferraro
Born in Newburgh in 1935; teacher, attorney, member of Congress; first woman nominated by a major political party to run for vice president (1984)

Helen Frankenthaler
Born in Manhattan In 1928; painter; invented the "soak-stain" technique for painting; best known for her colorful abstract paintings

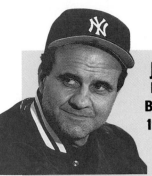

Joe Torre
Born in Brooklyn in 1940; baseball player and manager; played on All Star teams 5 years in a row; manager of New York Yankees team that won 1996 World Series

Jay Leno
Born in New Rochelle in 1950; comedian; known for hosting television's "The Tonight Show"

Nydia M. Velazquez
Born in Puerto Rico in 1953; first Hispanic to serve on New York City Council (1984), member of Congress from New York's 12th District in New York City

Toni Morrison
Born in Lorain, Ohio, in 1931; moved to Syracuse in 1966; writer, professor; won Pulitzer Prize for *Beloved* (1987); first African American to win Nobel Prize for Literature (1993)

Tommy Hilfiger
Born in Elmira in 1952; head designer and founder of Tommy Hilfiger Corporation; awarded Men's Wear Designer of the Year (1995)

Connie Chung
Born in Washington, D.C., in 1946; broadcast journalist in New York City; first Asian American to co-anchor nightly news on a major network

Shirley Chisholm
Born in Brooklyn in 1924; member of Congress, author; first African American woman elected to the U.S. House of Representatives (1969)

Barbra Streisand
Born in Brooklyn in 1942; singer, actor, movie writer, director; known for the movies *Funny Girl* (1968) and *The Mirror Has Two Faces* (1996)

Maurice Sendak
Born in Brooklyn in 1928; author, illustrator; known for his books *Where the Wild Things Are* (1963) and *We Are All in the Dumps With Jack and Guy* (1993)

Denzel Washington
Born in Mount Vernon in 1954; actor; won an Academy Award for his role in the movie *Glory* (1989)

Elizabeth Peña
Born in Elizabeth, New Jersey; moved to Manhattan in 1969; actor; known for her film *La Bamba*

Maurice Kenny
Born in the Akwesasne region, St. Regis Reservation, in 1929; poet, editor, professor; won the American Book Award for *The Mama Poems* (1984)

ANIMALS AND PLANTS
OF NEW YORK

R26

1. Gray squirrel
2. Woodpecker
3. Opossum
4. Great gray owl
5. Wood duck
6. Bass
7. Brown trout
8. River otter
9. Mallard
10. Common loon
11. Gray fox
12. White-tailed deer
13. Balsam fir
14. Eastern white pine
15. American goldfinch
16. Black spruce
17. Red-tailed hawk
18. Moose
19. Lynx
20. Skunk
21. Sundew
22. Great blue heron
23. Pond lily
24. Timber rattlesnake
25. Black racer
26. Eastern cottontail
27. Porcupine
28. White oak
29. Fisher
30. Crow
31. Black bear
32. Poison ivy
33. May apple
34. Five-lined skink
35. Northern pitcher plant
36. Beaver
37. Ring-necked pheasant
38. Snowshoe hare
39. Gray goldenrod
40. Eastern bluebird
41. Humpback whale
42. Great black-backed gull
43. Sea oats
44. Sanderling
45. Loggerhead turtle
46. Lobster
47. Oyster

NEW YORK FUN FACTS

America's most famous pirate, Captain William Kidd, collected treasure from robbing merchant ships. Some people believe he buried this treasure near the eastern end of Long Island, but it has never been found.

Traveling jazz musicians used to call any town or city an "apple." They started calling New York City, the largest city of all, "The Big Apple."

The geographic center of New York is located in Madison County, about 12 miles south of Oneida and 26 miles southwest of Utica.

New York is known for its foods! Buffalo wings are spicy chicken wings that were first made in Buffalo. Coney dogs got their start at Coney Island Amusement Park. And Thousand Island dressing is named after the Thousand Islands.

Allan Hershell of North Tonawanda made the first steam-powered merry-go-round in 1883. Later, his company became the largest maker of carousels in the world.

GOVERNORS of NEW YORK

GOVERNORS OF THE STATE OF NEW YORK	TERM
George Clinton	1777–1795
John Jay	1795–1801
George Clinton	1801–1804
Morgan Lewis	1804–1807
Daniel D. Tompkins	1807–1817
John Taylor (acting)	1817
DeWitt Clinton	1817–1822
Joseph C. Yates	1823–1824
DeWitt Clinton	1825–1828
Nathaniel Pitcher (acting)	1828
Martin Van Buren	1829
Enos T. Throop (acting)	1829–1830
Enos T. Throop	1831–1832
William L. Marcy	1833–1838
William H. Seward	1839–1842
William C. Bouck	1843–1844
Silas Wright	1845–1846
John Young	1847–1848
Hamilton Fish	1849–1850
Washington Hunt	1851–1852
Horatio Seymour	1853–1854
Myron H. Clark	1855–1856
John A. King	1857–1858
Edwin D. Morgan	1859–1862
Horatio Seymour	1863–1864
Reuben E. Fenton	1865–1868
John T. Hoffman	1869–1872
John Adams Dix	1873–1874
Samuel J. Tilden	1875–1876
Lucius Robinson	1877–1879
Alonzo B. Cornell	1880–1882
Grover Cleveland	1883–1885
David B. Hill (acting)	1885
David B. Hill	1886–1891
Roswell P. Flower	1892–1894
Levi P. Morton	1895–1896
Frank S. Black	1897–1898
Theodore Roosevelt	1899–1900
Benjamin B. Ordell, Jr.	1901–1904
Frank W. Higgins	1905–1906
Charles Evans Hughes	1907–1910
Horace White (acting)	1910
John Alden Dix	1911–1912
William Sulzer	1913
Martin Glynn (acting)	1913–1914
Charles S. Whitman	1915–1918
Alfred E. Smith	1919–1920
Nathan L. Miller	1921–1922
Alfred E. Smith	1923–1928
Franklin D. Roosevelt	1929–1932
Herbert H. Lehman	1933–1942
Charles Poletti (acting)	1942
Thomas E. Dewey	1943–1954
W. Averell Harriman	1955–1958
Nelson Rockefeller	1959–1973
Malcolm Wilson (acting)	1973–1974
Hugh J. Carey	1975–1982
Mario M. Cuomo	1983–1994
George E. Pataki	1995–

The New York State Seal carved on a fireplace in the State Capitol

OUR FIFTY STATES

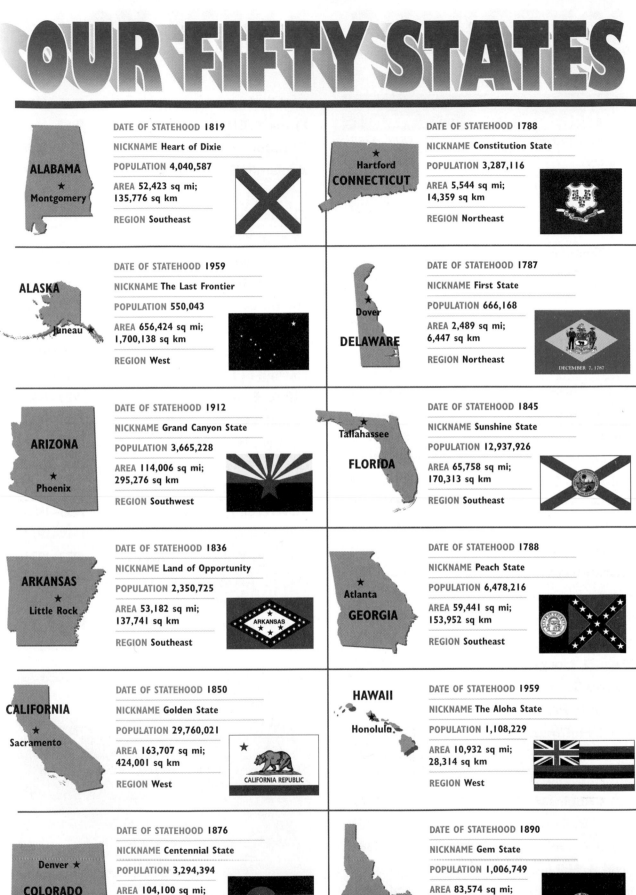

ALABAMA
★ Montgomery

DATE OF STATEHOOD 1819

NICKNAME Heart of Dixie

POPULATION 4,040,587

AREA 52,423 sq mi; 135,776 sq km

REGION Southeast

Hartford ★
CONNECTICUT

DATE OF STATEHOOD 1788

NICKNAME Constitution State

POPULATION 3,287,116

AREA 5,544 sq mi; 14,359 sq km

REGION Northeast

ALASKA
Juneau ★

DATE OF STATEHOOD 1959

NICKNAME The Last Frontier

POPULATION 550,043

AREA 656,424 sq mi; 1,700,138 sq km

REGION West

Dover ★
DELAWARE

DATE OF STATEHOOD 1787

NICKNAME First State

POPULATION 666,168

AREA 2,489 sq mi; 6,447 sq km

REGION Northeast

DECEMBER 7, 1787

ARIZONA
★ Phoenix

DATE OF STATEHOOD 1912

NICKNAME Grand Canyon State

POPULATION 3,665,228

AREA 114,006 sq mi; 295,276 sq km

REGION Southwest

Tallahassee ★
FLORIDA

DATE OF STATEHOOD 1845

NICKNAME Sunshine State

POPULATION 12,937,926

AREA 65,758 sq mi; 170,313 sq km

REGION Southeast

ARKANSAS
★ Little Rock

DATE OF STATEHOOD 1836

NICKNAME Land of Opportunity

POPULATION 2,350,725

AREA 53,182 sq mi; 137,741 sq km

REGION Southeast

ARKANSAS

★ Atlanta
GEORGIA

DATE OF STATEHOOD 1788

NICKNAME Peach State

POPULATION 6,478,216

AREA 59,441 sq mi; 153,952 sq km

REGION Southeast

CALIFORNIA
★ Sacramento

DATE OF STATEHOOD 1850

NICKNAME Golden State

POPULATION 29,760,021

AREA 163,707 sq mi; 424,001 sq km

REGION West

CALIFORNIA REPUBLIC

HAWAII
Honolulu

DATE OF STATEHOOD 1959

NICKNAME The Aloha State

POPULATION 1,108,229

AREA 10,932 sq mi; 28,314 sq km

REGION West

Denver ★
COLORADO

DATE OF STATEHOOD 1876

NICKNAME Centennial State

POPULATION 3,294,394

AREA 104,100 sq mi; 269,619 sq km

REGION West

★ Boise
IDAHO

DATE OF STATEHOOD 1890

NICKNAME Gem State

POPULATION 1,006,749

AREA 83,574 sq mi; 216,457 sq km

REGION West

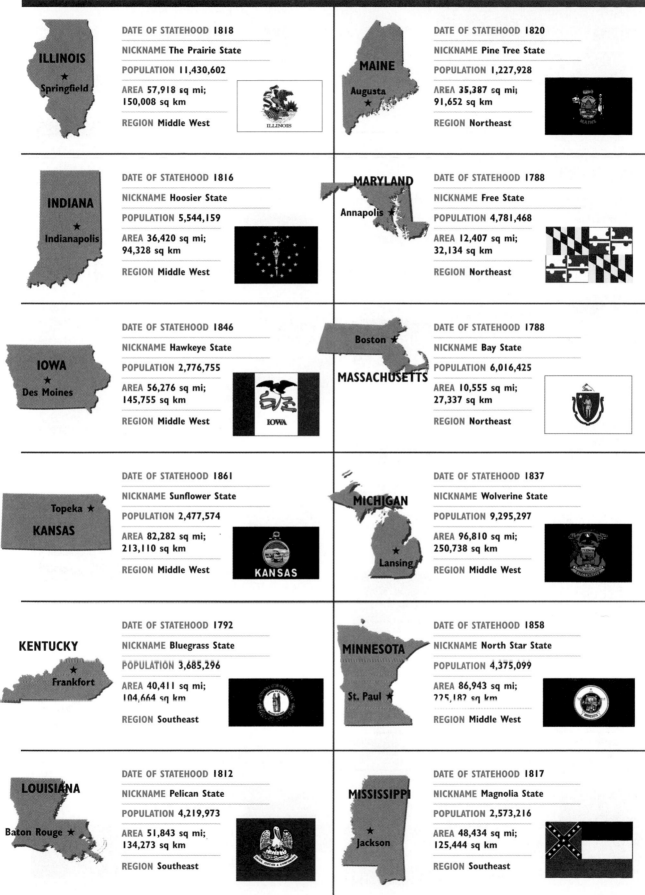

ILLINOIS
★
Springfield

DATE OF STATEHOOD 1818

NICKNAME The Prairie State

POPULATION 11,430,602

AREA 57,918 sq mi;
150,008 sq km

REGION Middle West

MAINE
Augusta
★

DATE OF STATEHOOD 1820

NICKNAME Pine Tree State

POPULATION 1,227,928

AREA 35,387 sq mi;
91,652 sq km

REGION Northeast

INDIANA
★
Indianapolis

DATE OF STATEHOOD 1816

NICKNAME Hoosier State

POPULATION 5,544,159

AREA 36,420 sq mi;
94,328 sq km

REGION Middle West

MARYLAND
Annapolis ★

DATE OF STATEHOOD 1788

NICKNAME Free State

POPULATION 4,781,468

AREA 12,407 sq mi;
32,134 sq km

REGION Northeast

IOWA
★
Des Moines

DATE OF STATEHOOD 1846

NICKNAME Hawkeye State

POPULATION 2,776,755

AREA 56,276 sq mi;
145,755 sq km

REGION Middle West

Boston ★

MASSACHUSETTS

DATE OF STATEHOOD 1788

NICKNAME Bay State

POPULATION 6,016,425

AREA 10,555 sq mi;
27,337 sq km

REGION Northeast

Topeka ★

KANSAS

DATE OF STATEHOOD 1861

NICKNAME Sunflower State

POPULATION 2,477,574

AREA 82,282 sq mi;
213,110 sq km

REGION Middle West

MICHIGAN
★
Lansing

DATE OF STATEHOOD 1837

NICKNAME Wolverine State

POPULATION 9,295,297

AREA 96,810 sq mi;
250,738 sq km

REGION Middle West

KENTUCKY
★
Frankfort

DATE OF STATEHOOD 1792

NICKNAME Bluegrass State

POPULATION 3,685,296

AREA 40,411 sq mi;
104,664 sq km

REGION Southeast

MINNESOTA
St. Paul ★

DATE OF STATEHOOD 1858

NICKNAME North Star State

POPULATION 4,375,099

AREA 86,943 sq mi;
225,182 sq km

REGION Middle West

LOUISIANA
Baton Rouge ★

DATE OF STATEHOOD 1812

NICKNAME Pelican State

POPULATION 4,219,973

AREA 51,843 sq mi;
134,273 sq km

REGION Southeast

MISSISSIPPI
★
Jackson

DATE OF STATEHOOD 1817

NICKNAME Magnolia State

POPULATION 2,573,216

AREA 48,434 sq mi;
125,444 sq km

REGION Southeast

OUR FIFTY STATES

MISSOURI
Jefferson City ★

DATE OF STATEHOOD 1821

NICKNAME Show Me State

POPULATION 5,117,073

AREA 69,709 sq mi;
180,546 sq km

REGION Middle West

MONTANA
★ Helena

DATE OF STATEHOOD 1889

NICKNAME Treasure State

POPULATION 799,065

AREA 147,046 sq mi;
380,849 sq km

REGION West

NEBRASKA
Lincoln ★

DATE OF STATEHOOD 1867

NICKNAME Cornhusker State

POPULATION 1,578,385

AREA 77,358 sq mi;
200,357 sq km

REGION Middle West

NEVADA
★ Carson City

DATE OF STATEHOOD 1864

NICKNAME Silver State

POPULATION 1,201,833

AREA 110,567 sq mi;
286,369 sq km

REGION West

NEW HAMPSHIRE
Concord ★

DATE OF STATEHOOD 1788

NICKNAME Granite State

POPULATION 1,109,252

AREA 9,351 sq mi;
24,219 sq km

REGION Northeast

NEW JERSEY
Trenton ★

DATE OF STATEHOOD 1787

NICKNAME Garden State

POPULATION 7,730,188

AREA 8,722 sq mi;
22,590 sq km

REGION Northeast

NEW MEXICO
Santa Fe ★

DATE OF STATEHOOD 1912

NICKNAME Land of Enchantment

POPULATION 1,515,069

AREA 121,598 sq mi;
314,939 sq km

REGION Southwest

NEW YORK
Albany ★

DATE OF STATEHOOD 1788

NICKNAME Empire State

POPULATION 17,990,455

AREA 54,475 sq mi;
141,090 sq km

REGION Northeast

NORTH CAROLINA
Raleigh ★

DATE OF STATEHOOD 1789

NICKNAME Tar Heel State

POPULATION 6,628,637

AREA 53,821 sq mi;
139,396 sq km

REGION Southeast

NORTH DAKOTA
Bismarck ★

DATE OF STATEHOOD 1889

NICKNAME Peace Garden State

POPULATION 638,800

AREA 70,704 sq mi;
183,123 sq km

REGION Middle West

OHIO
★ Columbus

DATE OF STATEHOOD 1803

NICKNAME Buckeye State

POPULATION 10,847,115

AREA 44,828 sq mi;
116,105 sq km

REGION Middle West

OKLAHOMA
★ Oklahoma City

DATE OF STATEHOOD 1907

NICKNAME Sooner State

POPULATION 3,145,585

AREA 69,903 sq mi;
181,049 sq km

REGION Southwest

OREGON
★ Salem

DATE OF STATEHOOD 1859

NICKNAME Beaver State

POPULATION 2,842,321

AREA 98,386 sq mi;
254,820 sq km

REGION West

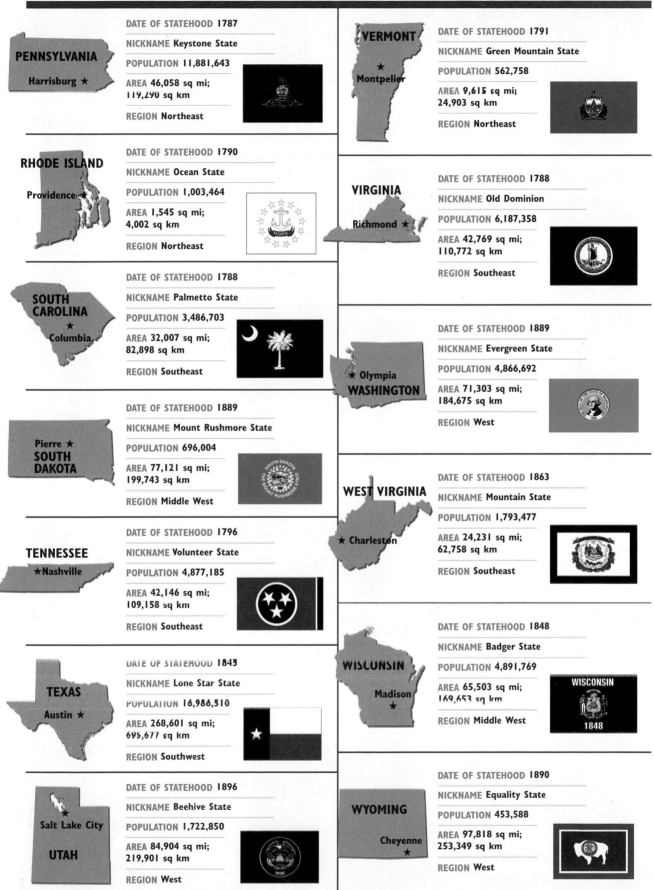

PENNSYLVANIA
Harrisburg ★

DATE OF STATEHOOD 1787

NICKNAME Keystone State

POPULATION 11,881,643

AREA 46,058 sq mi; 119,290 sq km

REGION Northeast

RHODE ISLAND
Providence ★

DATE OF STATEHOOD 1790

NICKNAME Ocean State

POPULATION 1,003,464

AREA 1,545 sq mi; 4,002 sq km

REGION Northeast

SOUTH CAROLINA
★ Columbia

DATE OF STATEHOOD 1788

NICKNAME Palmetto State

POPULATION 3,486,703

AREA 32,007 sq mi; 82,898 sq km

REGION Southeast

SOUTH DAKOTA
Pierre ★

DATE OF STATEHOOD 1889

NICKNAME Mount Rushmore State

POPULATION 696,004

AREA 77,121 sq mi; 199,743 sq km

REGION Middle West

TENNESSEE
★Nashville

DATE OF STATEHOOD 1796

NICKNAME Volunteer State

POPULATION 4,877,185

AREA 42,146 sq mi; 109,158 sq km

REGION Southeast

TEXAS
Austin ★

DATE OF STATEHOOD 1845

NICKNAME Lone Star State

POPULATION 16,986,510

AREA 268,601 sq mi; 695,677 sq km

REGION Southwest

UTAH
Salt Lake City ★

DATE OF STATEHOOD 1896

NICKNAME Beehive State

POPULATION 1,722,850

AREA 84,904 sq mi; 219,901 sq km

REGION West

VERMONT
★ Montpelier

DATE OF STATEHOOD 1791

NICKNAME Green Mountain State

POPULATION 562,758

AREA 9,615 sq mi; 24,903 sq km

REGION Northeast

VIRGINIA
Richmond ★

DATE OF STATEHOOD 1788

NICKNAME Old Dominion

POPULATION 6,187,358

AREA 42,769 sq mi; 110,772 sq km

REGION Southeast

WASHINGTON
★ Olympia

DATE OF STATEHOOD 1889

NICKNAME Evergreen State

POPULATION 4,866,692

AREA 71,303 sq mi; 184,675 sq km

REGION West

WEST VIRGINIA
★ Charleston

DATE OF STATEHOOD 1863

NICKNAME Mountain State

POPULATION 1,793,477

AREA 24,231 sq mi; 62,758 sq km

REGION Southeast

WISCONSIN
Madison ★

DATE OF STATEHOOD 1848

NICKNAME Badger State

POPULATION 4,891,769

AREA 65,503 sq mi; 169,653 sq km

REGION Middle West

WYOMING
Cheyenne ★

DATE OF STATEHOOD 1890

NICKNAME Equality State

POPULATION 453,588

AREA 97,818 sq mi; 253,349 sq km

REGION West

Sources: population—U.S. Bureau of Census, 1990; area—U.S. Bureau of Census, 1991; capital—World Almanac, 1995.

Dictionary of GEOGRAPHIC TERMS

GULF (gulf) Part of an ocean that extends into the land; larger than a bay.

PLATEAU (pla tō´) A high, flat area that rises steeply above the surrounding land.

DAM (dam) A wall built across a river, creating a lake that stores water.

RESERVOIR (rez´ər vwär) A natural or artificial lake used to store water.

ESCARPMENT (e skärp´mənt) A steep cliff.

CANYON (kan´yən) A deep, narrow valley with steep sides.

MESA (mā´sə) A hill with a flat top; smaller than a plateau.

HILL (hil) A rounded, raised landform; not as high as a mountain.

BUTTE (būt) A small, flat-topped hill; smaller than a mesa or plateau.

VALLEY (val´ē) An area of low land between hills or mountains.

DESERT (dez´ərt) A dry environment with few plants and animals.

COAST (cōst) The land along an ocean.

BAY (bā) Part of an ocean or lake that extends deeply into the land.

ISLAND (ī´lənd) A body of land completely surrounded by water.

PENINSULA (pə nin´sə lə) A body of land nearly surrounded by water.

VOLCANO (vol kā′nō) An opening in Earth's surface through which hot rock and ash are forced out.

MOUNTAIN (moun′tən) A high landform with steep sides; higher than a hill.

PEAK (pēk) The top of a mountain.

HARBOR (här′bər) A sheltered place along a coast where boats dock safely.

GLACIER (glā′shər) A huge sheet of ice that moves slowly across the land.

CANAL (kə nal′) A channel built to carry water for irrigation or transportation.

LAKE (lāk) A body of water completely surrounded by land.

PORT (pôrt) A place where ships load and unload their goods.

TRIBUTARY (trib′yə ter ē) A smaller river that flows into a larger river.

SOURCE (sôrs) The starting point of a river.

TIMBERLINE (tim′bər līn) A line beyond which trees do not grow.

RIVER BASIN (riv′ər bā′sin) All the land that is drained by a river and its tributaries.

WATERFALL (wô′tər fôl) A flow of water falling vertically.

MOUNTAIN RANGE (moun′tən rānj) A row or chain of mountains.

RIVER (riv′ər) A stream of water that flows across the land and empties into another body of water.

PLAIN (plān) A large area of nearly flat land.

BASIN (bā′sin) A bowl-shaped landform surrounded by higher land.

DELTA (del′tə) Land made of soil left behind as a river drains into a larger body of water.

MOUTH (mouth) The place where a river empties into a larger body of water.

BARRIER ISLAND (bar′ē ər ī′lənd) A narrow island between the mainland and the ocean.

OCEAN (ō′shən) A large body of salt water; oceans cover much of Earth's surface.

R35

Gazetteer

Gazetteer

This Gazetteer is a geographical dictionary that will help you to pronounce and locate the places discussed in this book. Latitude and longitude are given for cities and some other places. The page numbers tell you where each place first appears on a map or in the text.

A

Adirondack Mountains (ad ə rän'dak moun'tənz) Mountain range in northeastern New York. (m. 11, t. 10)

Albany (ôl'bə nē) City on the Hudson River; capital of New York State; 43°N, 74°W. (m. G6, t. 144)

Allegany State Park (al ə gā'nē stāt pärk) Largest New York state park, located in the southwestern part of the state. (t. 14)

Appalachian Plateau (ap ə lā'chən pla tō') Plateau of rolling hills that covers nearly half the state. (m. 11, t.12)

Auburn (ô'bərn) City in the Finger Lakes Region; home of Harriet Tubman; 43°N, 77°W. (m. 194)

B

Buffalo (buf'ə lō) City and port on Lake Erie; endpoint of the Erie Canal; 43°N, 79°W. (m. G6, t. 163)

C

Canandaigua (kan ən dā'gwə) City in the Finger Lakes Region at the north end of Canandaigua Lake; 43°N, 77°W. (t. 196)

Catskill Mountains (kat'skil moun'tənz) Mountain range in southeastern New York. (m. 11, t. 12)

Central New York (sen'trəl nü yôrk) Region of New York State around the joining of the Mohawk and Hudson Rivers; includes the cities of Albany, Schenectady, and Troy. (m. 46, t. 45)

Central Park (sen'trəl pärk) Large public park in New York City built between 1857 and 1876. (m. G11, t. 183)

Corning (kôr'ning) City in the Finger Lakes Region; center of New York's glass industry; 42°N, 77°W. (t. 278)

D

Dutchess Quarry Caves (duch'əs kwôr'ē kāvz) A series of caves located in southeastern New York, near present-day Middletown. (m. 59, t. 61)

E

Ellis Island (el'əs ī'lənd) Island in New York Bay; served as an immigration center from 1892 to 1954. (t. 223)

Elmira (el mī'rə) City in the Finger Lakes Region; an important stopping point on the Underground Railroad; 42°N, 77°W. (m. 194)

Empire State Building (em'pīr stāt bil'ding) New York City's most famous skyscraper, completed in 1931. (t. 245)

Erie Canal (ir'ē kə nal') Canal that runs over 350 miles from Buffalo on Lake Erie to Albany on the Hudson River. (m. 168, t. 168)

Etna (et'nə) Town in the Finger Lakes Region; a stopping point on the Underground Railroad; 43°N, 76°W. (m. 194)

pronunciation key

a	at	ī	ice	u	up	th	thin
ā	ape	îr	pierce	ū	use	th	this
ä	far	o	hot	ü	rule	zh	measure
âr	care	ō	old	ù	pull	ə	about, taken,
e	end	ô	fork	ûr	turn		pencil, lemon,
ē	me	oi	oil	hw	white		circus
i	it	ou	out	ng	song		

F

Finger Lakes (fin′gər lāks) Group of long narrow lakes arranged like the fingers of a hand; located in the Finger Lakes Region. (m. G6, t. 12)

Finger Lakes Region (fin′gər lākz rē′jən) Region of New York State where the Finger Lakes and Rochester are found. (m. 46, t. 44)

Fort Niagara (fôrt nī ag′rə) Fort at the mouth of the Niagara River; first built by the French in 1725. (m. 113, t. 113)

Fort Orange (fôrt är′inj) First Dutch settlement in New York; the location is now Albany. (m. G11, t. 91)

Fort Ticonderoga (fôrt tī kän dər ō′gä) Fort built on the waterway linking Lake George and Lake Champlain; named Fort Ticonderoga in 1759. (m. 113, t. 113)

Freeport (frē′pôrt) Town on the south shore of Long Island; 41°N 74°W. (t. 24)

G

Genesee River (jen ə sē′ ri′vər) River that flows across Western New York into Lake Ontario. (m. 20, t. 12)

Geneseo (jen ə sē′ō) Village on the Genesee River; location of the Big Tree Treaty in 1797; 43°N, 78°W. (m. 161, t. 162)

Gloversville (gluv′ərz vil) City in Central New York; a glovemaking center of the United States; 43°N, 74°W. (t. 179)

Grand Central Terminal (grand sen′trəl tərm′nəl) Large train station built in New York City. (t. 215)

H

Harlem (här′ləm) Part of Manhattan; by 1920, it was the largest African American community in the United States. (t. 242)

Helderberg Escarpment (hel′dər bərg e skärp′mənt) A line of steep cliffs southwest of Albany. (t. 45)

Hudson River (hud′sən ri′vər) River in eastern New York that flows into New York Bay. (m. 17, t. 18)

Hudson River Valley (hud′sən ri′vər va′lē) Valley that runs north and south between the Catskill Mountains and the Taconic Mountains. (t. 12)

Hudson River Valley and Catskill Mountains Region (hud′sən ri′vər va′lē and kat′skil moun′tənz) Region of New York State where the lower Hudson River Valley, Catskill Mountains, and Taconic Mountains are located. (m. 47, t. 45)

I

Ilion (il′ē ən) Village on the Mohawk River; location of the Remington Company; 43°N, 75°W. (t. 198)

Ithaca (ith′i kə) City in the Finger Lakes Region at the south end of Cayuga Lake; 42°N, 77°W. (m. 194)

K

Kingston (king′stən) City on the Hudson River; meeting place of the first state government in 1777; 42°N, 74°W. (t. 143)

L

Lake Champlain (lāk sham plān′) Long, narrow lake in northern New York; forms part of the border with Vermont. (m. 20, t. 20)

Lake Erie (lāk îr′ē) The most southern of the five Great Lakes; forms part of the border between the United States and Canada. (m. 11, t. 20)

Lake George (lāk jôrj) Lake in Northern New York; linked to Lake Champlain. (m. 20, t. 113)

Lake Oneida (lāk ō nīd′ ə) Large lake in Central New York. (m. 20, t. 14)

Lake Ontario (lāk on târ′ē ō) The smallest of the five Great Lakes; forms part of the border between the United States and Canada. (m. 11, t. 20)

Levittown (lev′ət taun) Long Island community, suburb of New York City built in 1946; 41°N, 74°W. (t. 255)

Lockport (lok′pôrt) City on the Erie Canal; a series of five locks were built there to allow boats to pass a 60-foot drop in elevation; 43°N, 79°W. (t. 172)

Gazetteer

Long Island (lông ī'lənd) Island in the Atlantic Ocean with 280 miles of coastline; the borough of Brooklyn lies on its southern end. (m. 11, t. 12)

Long Island Sound (lông ī'lənd sound) A narrow part of the Atlantic Ocean that lies between the Connecticut and New York shores to the north and Long Island to the south. (m. 20, t. 13)

Love Canal (luv kə nal') Town near Niagara Falls; location of environmental cleanup in the 1970s; 43°N, 79°W. (t. 257)

M

Mohawk River (mō'hôk ri'vər) Largest tributary of the Hudson River, located in Central New York. (m. 17, t. 19)

Montauk Point (mon'tôk point) Tip of Long Island that is the easternmost place in New York. (t. 13)

N

New Amsterdam (nü am'stər dam) Dutch settlement started in 1625 on Manhattan Island, which became New York City. (m. G11, t. 91)

New Netherland (nü neth'ər lənd) Dutch colony in North America (1624–1664) that included parts of present-day New York, New Jersey, and Delaware. (m. G11, t. 91)

New Paltz (nü pôlts) Village in the Hudson River Valley first settled by Huguenot immigrants; 42°N, 74°W. (m. 101, t. 101)

New Rochelle (nû rō shel') City on Long Island Sound; first settled in 1688 by Huguenots; 41°N, 74°W. (m. 101, t. 101)

New York Bay (nü yôrk bā) Bay in southern New York at the mouth of the Hudson River, where it flows into the Atlantic Ocean. (m. 20, t. 21)

New York City (nü yôrk si'tē) City at the mouth of the Hudson River; largest city in the country and an important port and business center; 41°N, 74°W. (m. G6, t. 97)

New York City and Long Island Region (nü yôrk si'tē and lông ī'lənd) Region that includes the most southern and most eastern parts of New York State. (m. 47, t. 45)

Niagara Falls (nī ag'rə fôls) Great falls on the Niagara River; up to 184 feet high. (m. G7, t. 20)

Niagara River (nī ag'rə ri'vər) River in Western New York that connects Lake Erie with Lake Ontario. (m. 20, t. 20)

Northern New York (nor'thərn nü yôrk) Region of New York State where the Adirondack Mountains and Lake Champlain are located. (m. 46, t. 44)

O

Olana (ō la'nə) Home of painter Frederic Edwin Church, located near the town of Hudson; 42°N, 74°W. (t. 181)

Oriskany (ô ris'kə nē) Village on the Mohawk River; location of American Revolution battlefield; 43°N, 75°W. (m. 125, t. 125)

P

Plattsburgh (plats'bərg) City in Northern New York on the western shore of Lake Champlain; 45°N, 74°W. (mG6, t. 164)

Q

Quebec (kwi bek') City in Canada on the north bank of the St. Lawrence River; 47°N, 72°W. (m. 83, t. 84)

R

Rhinebeck (rīn'bek) Village on the east bank of the Hudson River in southeastern New York; 42°N, 74°W. (m. 101, t. 101)

Rochester (roch'ə stər) City on the Genessee River and port on the Erie Canal; major New York center for industry; 43°N, 78°W. (m. G6, t. 163)

S

St. Lawrence River (sānt lär'əns ri'vər) River on the border of the United States and Canada that connects the Great Lakes with the Atlantic Ocean. (m. 20, t. 20)

Saratoga (sar ə tō'gə) Village on the west bank of the Hudson River; now called Schuylerville. Location of British surrender in 1777 after the Battle of Saratoga; 43°N, 74°W. (m. 125, t. 125)

Seneca Falls (sen'i kə fôls) Village in Finger Lakes Region; location of first women's rights convention in 1848; 43°N, 77°W. (t. 191)

Syracuse (sir'ə kyüs) City in the Finger Lakes Region; an important port on the Erie Canal; 43°N, 76°W. (m. G6, t. 179)

T

Taconic Mountains (tə kän'ik moun'tənz) Mountain range along the eastern border of New York. (m. 11, t. 12)

Thousand Islands (thouz'ənd ī länds) Group of about 1,700 islands located where the St. Lawrence River meets Lake Ontario. (t. 45)

Troy (troi) City in Central New York on the Hudson River; 43°N, 74°W. (t. 198)

U

Utica (yü'ti kə) City on the Mohawk River, important starting point for settlers moving west in the early 1800s; 43°N, 75°W. (m. G6, t. 161)

W

Wall Street (wôl strēt) Street on the southern tip of Manhattan Island; became the business center of New York State and the United States. (t. 151)

Washington, D.C. (wä'shing tən dē sē) Capital of the United States; 39°N, 77°W. (m. G9, t. 308)

Watertown (wôt'ər taûn) City in Northern New York; 44°N, 76°W. (m. G6, t. 288)

Watkins Glen Gorge (wät'kinz glen gorj) A beautiful, 2-mile long gorge, 300 feet deep in places, located in the Finger Lakes Region. (t. 44)

Western New York (wes'tərn nü yôrk) Westernmost region of New York State that borders Lake Erie, where Buffalo and Niagara Falls are found. (m. 46, t. 44)

Whiteface Mountain (hwīt'fās moun'tən) Peak in the Adirondack Mountains over 4,800 feet high. (t. 24)

Biographical Dictionary

The Biographical Dictionary tells you about the people you have learned about in this book. The Pronunciation Key tells you how to say their names. The page numbers tell you where each person first appears in the text.

A

Allen, Ethan (al'ən), 1738–1789 Leader of the Green Mountain Boys, who captured Fort Ticonderoga from the British in the American Revolution. (p. 116)

Anthony, Susan B. (an'thə nē), 1820–1906 Abolitionist and women's rights leader. (p. 191)

B

Badillo, Herman (bə dē'yō), 1929– Politician; the first Puerto Rican person to be elected to the United States House of Representatives. (p. 256)

Bartholdi, Frederic-Auguste (bär täl'dē), 1834–1904 French sculptor who designed the Statue of Liberty. (p. 227)

Bethune, Mary McLeod (be thün'), 1875–1955 Educator who worked to get fair treatment for African Americans. (p. 251)

Blackwell, Elizabeth (blak'wel), 1821–1910 First woman doctor in America. (p. 198)

Blatch, Harriot Stanton (blach), 1856–1940 Leader in the women's rights movement, like her mother, Elizabeth Cady Stanton. (p. 241)

Brace, Charles Loring (brās), 1826–1890 Reformer who started the Children's Aid Society in New York City in 1853. (p. 218)

Brant, Joseph (brant), 1772–1807 Mohawk leader who sided with the British in the American Revolution. He fought at the Battle of Oriskany. (p. 125)

Burgoyne, John (bər gôyn'), 1722–1792 British general whose defeat at the Battle of Saratoga in 1777 helped to convince France to aid the Americans during the American Revolution. (p. 124)

C

Cartier, Jacques (kär tē ā' zhäk), 1491–1557 French explorer who traveled from the Atlantic up the St. Lawrence River. (p. 84)

Catt, Carrie Chapman (kat), 1859–1947 A leader in the women's rights movement. (p. 241)

Champlain, Samuel de (sham plān'), 1567–1635 French explorer who founded Quebec in 1608 and discovered Lake Champlain in 1609. (p. 84)

Chisholm, Shirley (chiz'əm), 1924– Politician; the first African American woman to be elected to the United States House of Representatives. (p. 256)

Church, Frederic Edwin (chərch), 1826–1900 Landscape painter associated with the Hudson River School. (p. 181)

Clinton, De Witt (klin'tən), 1769–1828 New York governor who supported the building of the Erie Canal. (p. 168)

Clinton, George (klin'tən), 1739–1812 Lawyer and general in the Continental Army who was elected governor of New York in 1777. He became Vice President of the United States in 1805. (p. 144)

Cole, Thomas (kōl), 1801–1848 Painter associated with the Hudson River School. (p. 181)

Columbus, Christopher (kə lum'bəs), 1451?–1506 Italian sea captain and explorer. Sailing under the flag of Spain, he reached the Americas in search of a sea route to Asia in 1492. (p. 82)

pronunciation key

a	at	i	ice	u	up	th	thin
ā	ape	îr	pierce	ū	use	th	this
ä	far	o	hot	ü	rule	zh	measure
âr	care	ō	old	ù	pull	ə	about, taken,
e	end	ô	fork	ûr	turn		pencil, lemon,
ē	me	oi	oil	hw	white		circus
i	it	ou	out	ng	song		

Cooper, James Fenimore (kü′pər), 1789–1851 New York writer of stories about the frontier. (p. 180)

Cornish, Samuel (kôr′nish), 1793–1858 African American abolitionist who, together with John Russwurm, started the first African American newspaper, *Freedom's Journal*. (p. 192)

D

Deganawida (dā gän ə wē′də), 1500s Leader of the Iroquois who helped organize the Iroquois Confederacy. (p. 71)

Douglass, Frederick (dug′ləs), 1817-1895 Abolitionist who escaped from slavery and spoke out against slavery. He founded an anti-slavery newspaper in Rochester called the *North Star*. (p. 190)

DuBois, W.E.B. (dü boyz′), 1868–1963 African American leader who helped to start a magazine called *The Crisis* and helped encourage the Harlem Renaissance. (p. 242)

E

Eastman, George (ēst′mən), 1854–1932 Inventor of a new kind of film that made it easier to take photographs. (p. 216)

Ellicott, Joseph (e′lə kət), 1760–1826 Mapmaker for the Holland Land Company; founder of the settlement of Buffalo in 1801. (p. 163)

Ellington, Duke (el′ing tən), 1899–1974 Songwriter, jazz musician, and bandleader whose music was popular during and after the Harlem Renaissance, and is still popular today. (p. 242)

F

Friedan, Bettty (frē dan′), 1921– Leader in the women's rights movement. (p. 256)

Fulton, Robert (fŭl′tən), 1765–1815 Builder of the first successful steamboat in 1807. (p. 167)

G

Garrison, William Lloyd (gar′ə sən), 1805–1879 Abolitionist who started the American Anti-Slavery Society in 1833. (p. 192)

Gates, Horatio (gāts), 1728–1806 American general who defeated the British at the Battle of Saratoga in the American Revolution. (p. 125)

Ginsburg, Ruth Bader (gins′bərg), 1933– Judge; the second woman to serve on the United States Supreme Court. (p. 309)

Gompers, Samuel (gom′pərs), 1850–1924 Labor union leader from New York City who helped form one of the first labor unions in 1873. (p. 218)

Grant, Ulysses S. (grant), 1822–1885 Leader of the Union Army during the Civil War. He was the 18th President of the United States, 1869–1877. (p. 199)

Green, Hetty (grēn), 1834–1916 Businessperson who made her fortune by buying and selling stocks and land. (p. 218)

H

Hamilton, Alexander (ham′əl tən), 1755–1804 New York representative who signed the United States Constitution and helped to start the Bank of New York. He was the first United States Secretary of the Treasury. (p. 144)

Hiawatha (hī ə wä′thə), 1500s Mohawk leader who, with Deganawida, helped organize the Iroquois Confederacy. (p. 71)

Hudson, Henry (hud′sən), ?–1611 English sea captain and explorer. Working for a Dutch trading company, he sailed up the Hudson River in 1609 as far north as present-day Albany. (p. 84)

Hughes, Langston (hūz), 1902–1967 Writer and poet who first became famous during the Harlem Renaissance. (p. 242)

I

Irving, Washington (ûr′ving), 1783–1859 New York writer whose works include *The Sketch Book*. (p. 180)

J

Jay, John (jā), 1745–1829 Lawmaker who helped write the New York Constitution. He became the first Chief Justice of the United States Supreme Court. (p. 116)

Jay, Sarah (jā), 1756–1802 Patriot; wife of John Jay. (p. 123)

Biographical Dictionary

Thomas Jefferson • Franklin Delano Roosevelt

Jefferson, Thomas (jef´ər sən), 1743–1826 A Virginian who drafted the Declaration of Independence. He became the third President of the United States, 1801–1809. (p. 116)

Jemison, Mary (jem´ə sən) 1743–1833 Settler in the Genesee River Valley after the American Revolution; received land on Gardeau Flats from the Big Tree Treaty. (p. 162)

Johnson, William (jon´sən), 1715–1774 British leader who convinced the Iroquois not to take sides in the French and Indian War. (p. 113)

L

Latimer, Lewis (lat´i mər), 1848–1928 African American inventor who improved the light bulb by making it last longer. He helped put in the country's first electric power station in Manhattan. (p. 216)

Lincoln, Abraham (ling´kən), 1809–1865 The 16th President of the United States, 1861–1865. He led the country during the Civil War. (p. 196)

Livingston, Robert (liv´ing stən), 1654–1728 Powerful landowner who owned a 160,000-acre manor in the Hudson River Valley. (p. 103)

Ludington, Sybil (lud´ing tən), 1761–1839 Daughter of a colonel in the New York militia; she warned militia members that the British had arrived in Danbury. (p. 124)

M

Marshall, Thurgood (mar´shəl), 1908–1991 Lawyer who was the first African American to serve as a justice on the United States Supreme Court, 1967–1991. (p. 256)

Minuit, Peter (min´yə wət), 1580–1638 Dutch colonial governor of New Netherland who bought Manhattan Island from the Lenni Lenape. (p. 91)

Morgan, J. P. (môr´gən), 1837–1913 A banker who made millions of dollars and helped some big businesses grow by lending them money. (p. 218)

N

Nicolls, Richard (nik´əls), 1624–1672 First British governor of New York, 1664–1668. (p. 98)

P

Parker, Ely S. (pär´kər), 1828–1895 Union officer and Seneca chief. (p. 199)

Philipse, Frederick (fil´ips), 1626–1702 A wealthy landowner in New York. He and his wife, Margaret, set up Philipsburg Manor. (p. 102)

Philipse, Margaret Hardenbroeck (fil´ips), ?–1690 A successful fur trader and ship owner who began a shipping line between New Amsterdam and Europe. She and her husband, Frederick, set up Philipsburg Manor. (p. 102)

R

Red Jacket (red ja´kət) 1758?–1830 Seneca leader who did not want to sell Iroquois land to the Holland Land Company. (p. 162)

Riis, Jacob (rēs), 1849–1914 A newspaper reporter who wrote about and took photographs of immigrants to show that their living conditions needed to be improved. (p. 224)

Rochester, Nathaniel (ro´chəs tər), 1752–1831 Founder of the settlement of Rochester on the Genessee River in 1803. (p. 163)

Rockefeller, John D., Jr. (rok´ə fel ər), 1874–1960 A wealthy New York businessperson who gave the United Nations $8.5 million to buy land for its buildings. (p. 253)

Rockefeller, Nelson (rok´ə fel ər), 1908–1979 Governor of New York from 1959 to 1973. He was appointed Vice President of the United States in 1974. (p. 254)

Roebling, Emily (rōb´ ling), 18??–1903 Wife of Washington Roebling; she assisted in building the Brooklyn Bridge. (p. 229)

Roebling, John (rōb´ling), 1806–1869 The bridge builder who prepared the plans for the Brooklyn Bridge in 1867. (p. 229)

Roosevelt, Eleanor (rō´zə velt), 1884–1962 The wife of Franklin Delano Roosevelt, she worked for the rights of all Americans. (p. 251)

Roosevelt, Franklin Delano (rō´zə velt), 1882–1945 The 32nd President of the United States from 1933 to 1945. He was governor of New York from 1928 to 1932. (p. 249)

Roosevelt, Theodore (rō´zə vəlt), 1858–1919 The 26th President of the United States from 1901 to 1909. He was governor of New York from 1899 to 1900. (p. 219)

Russwurm, John (rus´wərm) 1799–1851 Abolitionist who, together with Samuel Cornish, started the first African American newspaper, *Freedom's Journal.* (p. 192)

S

Singer, Isaac (sing´ər), 1811–1875 Inventor of the Singer sewing machine. (p. 179)

Smith, Martha Turnstall (smith), 1700s Owner and manager of a whaling company on Long Island. (p. 99)

Stanton, Elizabeth Cady (stan´tən), 1815–1902 Abolitionist and women's rights leader. (p. 191)

Stuyvesant, Peter (stī´və sənt), 1610–1672 Governor of New Netherland from 1647 until 1664, when Great Britain took over. (p. 94)

T

Tesla, Nikola (tes´lə), 1856–1943 Inventor who developed a system to send electric power over long distances. (p. 231)

Townsend, Samuel (toun´sənd), 1717–1790 Long Island trader who sold items in New York City. (p. 99)

Truth, Sojourner (trüth), 1797?–1883 Abolitionist who escaped from slavery in 1827 and spoke out for abolition of slavery and for women's rights. (p. 193)

Tubman, Harriet (tub´mən), 1820?–1913 Abolitionist who escaped from slavery in 1849. She became a conductor on the Underground Railroad and made 19 trips to slave states to free others. (p. 193)

V

Vanderbilt, Cornelius (van´dər bilt), 1794–1877 Businessperson who began the New York Central Railroad. (p. 215)

Verrazano, Giovanni da (ver ə zän´ō jō vä´nē də), 1485(?)–1528(?) Italian sea captain and explorer. Sailing under the flag of France, he arrived in New York in 1524. (p. 83)

W

Wald, Lillian (wäld), 1867–1940 Nurse who made life better for immigrants by starting a program that provided basic health care. (p. 224)

Washington, George (wä´shing tən), 1732–1799 First President of the United States from 1789 to 1797. He fought in the French and Indian War and led the Continental Army during the American Revolution. (p. 113)

Washington, Martha (wä´shing tən), 1731–1802 Wife of George Washington. She was the first First Lady. (p. 147)

Watson, Elkanah (wät´sən), 1758–1842 Businessperson who started Albany's first bank. (p. 152)

Westinghouse, George (wes´ting hous), 1846–1914 Inventor who helped Nikola Tesla develop a system to send electric power over long distances. (p. 233)

Z

Zenger, John Peter (zen´gər), 1697–1746 Newspaper printer whose trial in 1731 was an important step toward freedom of the press. (p. 98)

pronunciation key

a **at**; ā **ape**; ä **far**; âr **care**; e **end**; ē **me**; i **it**; ī **ice**; îr **pierce**; o **hot**; ō **old**; ô **fork**; oi **oil**; ou **out**; u **up**; ū **use**; ü **rule**; ù **pull**; ûr **turn**; hw **white**; ng **song**; th **thin**; th **this**; zh **measure**; ə **about, taken, pencil, lemon, circus**

Glossary

Glossary

A

abolition (ab ə lish′ən) Ending or doing away with completely. (p. 192)

agriculture (ag′ri kul chər) The business of growing crops and raising animals. (p. 272)

Allied Powers (al′lĭd pou′ərz) The name given to the forces led by Great Britain, France, Russia, and the United States during World War I. (p. 240)

Allies (al′lĭz) The name given to the countries allied against the Axis Powers in World War II, including the United States, Great Britain, and France. (p. 251)

ally (a′ lĭ) A friend with whom one is united for a common purpose. (p. 84)

amendment (ə mend′ment) An addition to the constitution. (p. 241)

American Revolution (ə mer′i kən rev ə lü′shən) The war fought by the American colonies to end British rule, 1775–1783. (p. 115)

ancestor (an′ses tər) A person in your family, starting with your parents, who was born before you. (p. 69)

archaeologist (är kē äl′ ə jist) A scientist who studies artifacts to learn about the past. (p. 61)

artifact (är′tə fakt) An object made by people who lived in the past. (p. 61)

Axis Powers (ak′sis pou′ərz) The name given to the countries that fought the Allies in World War II, including Germany, Italy, and Japan. (p. 251)

B

bank (bank) A business that helps people save and borrow money. (p. 151)

Battle of Saratoga (ba′təl uv sar ə tō′gə) A Revolutionary War battle fought in 1777. It was an important victory for the Americans because it helped convince France that the Americans could win the war. (p. 125)

Battle of Yorktown (ba′təl uv yôrk′toun) The final battle of the American Revolution. (p. 127)

bay (bā) A part of an ocean or lake that cuts deeply into the land. (p. 21)

Big Tree Treaty (big trē trē′tē) Agreement in which the Senecas sold nearly all their land to the Holland Land Company. (p. 162)

bill (bil) A written idea for a law. (p. 301)

blizzard (bli′zərd) A snowstorm with very strong winds. (p. 24)

broadcasting (brôd kast ing) To send news and information between people, often using the latest technology. (p. 281)

budget (buj′ət) A plan for using money. (p. 299)

Buttonwood Agreement (but′ən wůd ə grē′mənt) An agreement signed under a buttonwood tree on Wall Street in 1792 that laid out rules for buying and selling stocks. (p. 153)

byline (bī′lin) A line at the beginning of a newspaper article that names the writer. (p. 304)

C

canal (kə nal′) An inland waterway built for transportation or irrigation. (p. 168)

capital (ka′pə təl) A place where the government meets. (p. 143)

cardinal directions (kär′də nəl di rek′shənz) The main directions of the globe: north, south, east, and west. (p. G6)

cause (kôz) An event that makes something else happen. (p. 64)

CD-ROM (sē dē rom′) A reference source used with a computer that may include writing, pictures, sounds, or short movies. (p. 220)

Central Powers (sen′trəl pou′ərz) The name given to the forces led by Germany, Austria-Hungary, and Turkey in World War I. (p. 240)

checks and balances (cheks and bal′ən səz) The system in which the power of each branch of government is balanced by the powers of the other branches. (p. 298)

circle graph (sûr′kəl graf) A graph in the shape of a circle that shows the sizes of different parts of a whole; also called a pie graph. (p. 176)

pronunciation key

a	at	ī	ice	u	up	th	thin
ā	ape	îr	pierce	ū	use	th	this
ä	far	o	hot	ù	rule	zh	measure
âr	care	ō	old	ü	pull	ə	about, taken,
e	end	ô	fork	ûr	turn		pencil, lemon,
ē	me	oi	oil	hw	white		circus
i	it	ou	out	ng	song		

citizen (sit′ə zən) A person who is born in a country or who has earned the right to become a member of the country by law. (p. 191)

city council (si′tē koun′səl) A group of people who meet to talk and make decisions. (p. 296)

city manager (si′tē man′ə gər) A person hired to run the city's daily business. (p. 296)

civil rights (siv′əl rīts) The rights of all citizens to be treated equally under the law. (p. 256)

Civil War (siv′əl wôr) The war in the United States between the Union states of the North and the Confederate states of the South, 1861–1865. (p. 196)

clan (klan) A group of Native American families who share the same ancestor. (p. 73)

clan mother (klan mə thər) The head of a clan. (p. 73)

climate (klī′mit) The pattern of weather of a certain place over many years. (p. 22)

coast (kōst) The land next to an ocean. (p. 21)

colonist (kol′ə nist) A person who lives in a colony. (p. 90)

colony (kol′ə nē) A place that is ruled by another country. (p. 90)

communications (kə mū ni kā′shənz) The exchange of information between people, often using the latest technology. (p. 281)

commute (kə mūt′) To travel a distance each day from one's home to one's workplace. (p. 255)

compass rose (kum′pəs rōz) A small drawing on a map that shows directions. (p. G6)

conclusion (kən klü′zhən) A statement that pulls together several pieces of information and gives them a meaning. (p. 200)

Confederacy (kən fed′ər ə sē) The government formed by 11 Southern states that seceded from the United States, 1861–1865. (p. 197)

Congress (kong′ris) The legislative branch of the United States government. (p. 308)

conservation (kon sər vā′shən) The careful use of a natural resource. (p. 36)

constitution (kon sti tü′shən) A document that has the basic rules to govern a state or country. (p. 143)

consumer (kun sü′mər) A person who buys a product or uses a service. (p. 277)

continent (kon′tə nənt) One of Earth's seven great bodies of land—Africa, Antarctica, Asia, Australia, Europe, North America, and South America. (p. G4)

Continental Congress (kon tə nen′təl kong′ris) A group of colonists who met in Philadelphia in 1775 to discuss how the colonies should deal with Great Britain. (p. 116)

convention (kən ven′shən) A formal meeting held for a special purpose. (p. 142)

council (koun′səl) A group of people who meet to talk and make decisions. (p. 73)

county (coun′tē) One of the areas into which a state is divided. (p. 296)

Croton Aqueduct (krō′tən ak′wə dukt) A pipeline that brings water from the Croton River to New York City. (p. 182)

culture (kul′chər) The way of life shared by a group of people, including language, beliefs, music, foods, and holidays. (p. 101)

D

dateline (dāt′lin) The lead-in to a newspaper article, telling when and where the story was written. (p. 304)

decision (di sizh′ən) A choice that helps you reach a goal. (p. 40)

Declaration of Independence (dek lə rā′shən uv in di pen′dəns) A document written by Thomas Jefferson in 1776 explaining why the 13 colonies should be free of British rule. (p. 116)

degree (di grē′) A unit for measuring distance on Earth's surface; also a unit for measuring temperature. Represented by the symbol °. (p. 86)

democratic republic (dem ə krat′ik re pub′lik) A government in which citizens elect representatives to make decisions for them. (p. 306)

dictionary (dik′shə ner ē) A book that explains the meanings of words and shows how to pronounce and spell them. (p. 220)

discrimination (di skrim′ə nā shən) An unfair difference in the treatment of people. (p. 256)

diversity (di vûr′si tē) Variety; differences. (p. 317)

double house (du′bəl hous) A house with a business on the ground floor and a home upstairs. (p. 105)

draft (draft) A plan to select people to serve in the military. (p. 198)

drumlin (drum′lən) A smoothly rounded hill formed by a melting glacier. (p. 15)

Dutch West India Company (duch west in′dē ə kump′ə nē) The Dutch trading company that set up the colony of New Netherland. (p. 90)

---

pronunciation key

a **at**; ā **ape**; ä **far**; âr **care**; e **end**; ē **me**; i **it**; ī **ice**; îr **pierce**; o **hot**; ō **old**; ô **fork**; oi **oil**; ou **out**; u **up**; ū **use**; ü **rule**; ú **pull**; ûr **turn**; hw **white**; ng **song**; th **thin**; th **this**; zh **measure**; ə **about, taken, pencil, lemon, circus**

E

economy (i kon′ə mē) The way a country or other place uses or produces natural resources, goods, and services. (p. 34)

editorial (ed i tôr′ē əl) A newspaper article that gives opinions, rather than facts. (p. 304)

effect (i fekt′) An event that happens as a result of another event. (p. 64)

elect (ē lekt′) To choose by voting. (p. 295)

elevation (el ə vā′shən) The height of land above sea level. (p. 16)

Emancipation Proclamation (i man sə pā′shən prok lə mā′shən) The announcement by President Lincoln in 1863 that all enslaved people living in Confederate states were free. (p. 198)

encyclopedia (en sī klə pē′dē ə) A book or set of books that gives facts about people, places, things, and events. (p. 220)

entrepreneur (än trə prə nûr′) Someone who starts and runs his or her own business. (p. 150)

environment (en vī′rən mənt) The surroundings in which people, plants, or animals live. (p. 32)

equator (i kwā′tər) An imaginary line that lies halfway between the North Pole and the South Pole, at 0° latitude. (p. G4)

ethnic group (eth′nik grüp) Group of people whose ancestors are from the same country or area. (p. 317)

executive branch (eg zek′ū tiv branch) The branch of government that carries out laws. (p. 299)

export (ek′spôrt) Something sold or traded to another country. (p. 277)

F

fact (fakt) A statement that can be checked and proven true. (p. 148)

factory (fak′trē) Business where goods are made in large numbers. (p. 179)

famine (fa′mən) A time when there is a shortage of food and many people go hungry. (p. 182)

feature article (fē′chər är′ti kəl) A newspaper story that takes a detailed look at a person, subject, or event. (p. 304)

fertilizer (fûr′ti lī zər) Chemicals added to soil to help plants grow. (p. 33)

financial service (fī nan′shəl sər′vəs) Industry involved with managing money. (p. 284)

free enterprise (frē en′tər prīz) The economic system that allows people to own and run their own businesses. (p. 150)

freedom of the press (frē dəm uv thə pres) The right of people to print or tell the news. (p. 99)

French and Indian War (french and in′dē ən wôr) A war between Great Britain and France, and its Native American allies. 1754–1759. (p. 113)

frontier (frun tēr′) The edge of a settled area. (p. 160)

G

geography (jē og′rə fē) The study of Earth and the way people, plants, and animals live on and use it. (p. 10)

glacier (glā′shər) A huge sheet of ice that moves slowly across the land. (p. 14)

global grid (glō′bəl grid) The crisscrossing lines of latitude and longitude on a map or globe. (p. 88)

gorge (gôrj) A narrow, deep valley with steep, rocky sides. (p. 44)

government (guv′ərn mənt) The laws and people that run a country, state, county, city, or town. (p. 112)

governor (guv′ər nər) A person who runs a colony or state. (p. 91)

graph (graf) A diagram that shows information in a picture. (p. 176)

Great Depression (grāt di presh′ən) The period of widespread economic hardship in the 1930s. (p. 248)

Great Migration (grāt mī grā′shən) The movement of many African Americans in the early and middle 1900s from rural areas of the Southeast to urban areas of the Northeast and Middle West. (p. 242)

gristmill (grist′mil) A place where grain is ground into flour. (p. 103)

guide word (gīd wûrd) Words at the top of each page of a reference book that show the first and last entries on that page. (p. 220)

H

harbor (här′bər) A sheltered place along a coast where boats can dock. (p. 21)

Harlem Renaissance (här′ləm ren′ə säns) A time in the 1920s in Harlem when many important works of art and learning were created. (p. 242)

headline (hed′lin) A title printed in large letters at the beginning of a newspaper article. (p. 304)

hemisphere (hem′i sfēr) Half a sphere; one of the four hemispheres of Earth—Northern, Southern, Eastern, and Western hemispheres. (p. G5)

heritage (her′i tij) The history and traditions that a group of people share. (p. 66)

high technology (hī tek nol′ə jē) The use of scientific ideas and special tools, such as those used in electronics and computers. (p. 278)

historical map (hi stôr′i kəl map) A map that shows information about past events and where they occurred. (p. G11)

historical site (hi stôr′i kəl sīt) A place where something interesting or important happened in the past. (p. 327)

history (his′tə rē) The story of what happened in the past. (p. 43)

House of Representatives (hous uv rep rē sen′tə tivs) The house of Congress in which each state's number of representatives is determined according to its population. (p. 308)

Hudson River School (hud′sən riv′ər skül) A group of artists who became known for their paintings of the Hudson River. (p. 181)

hunter-gatherer (hun′tər ga′thər ər) A person who found food by both hunting animals and gathering plants, fruit, and nuts. (p. 62)

hurricane (hûr′i kān) A storm with very strong winds and heavy rains. (p. 24)

hydroelectric power (hī drō i lek′trik pou′ər) Electricity made from flowing water in rivers. (p. 230)

I

Ice Age (īs āj) A period of time when Earth was much colder than it is today. (p. 14)

immigrant (im′i grənt) A person who comes to a new country to live. (p. 182)

import (im′pôrt) Something brought in from another country for sale or use. (p. 277)

indentured servant (in den′shərd sər′vənt) A person who works for an employer for a period of time in return for payment of travel expenses. (p. 100)

Industrial Revolution (in dus′trē əl rev ə lü′shən) The major change, starting in the 1800s, in which power-driven machines replaced hand tools. (p. 179)

industry (in′dus trē) All the businesses that make one kind of goods or provide one kind of service. (p. 179)

insurance (in shûr əns) Something people buy to protect things like their house, health, or cars. (p. 284)

intermediate directions (in tər mē′dē it di rek′shəns) The directions between the cardinal directions—northeast, southeast, southwest, northwest. (p. G6)

interstate highway (in′tər stāt hī′wā) A road that connects cities in two or more states with at least two lanes of traffic in each direction. (p. 255)

Iroquois Confederacy (ēr′ə koi kən fed′ər ə sē) A political union of six Native American groups (Cayuga, Mohawk, Oneida, Onondaga, Seneca, and Tuscarora) founded around 1570. (p. 70)

J

judicial branch (jü dish′əl branch) The branch of government that makes sure laws are obeyed. (p. 302)

L

labor union (lā′bər ūn′yən) A group of workers organized to get better working conditions. (p. 218)

landform (land′fôrm) Any of the shapes that make up Earth's surface. (p. 10)

landform map (land′fôrm map) A map that shows the landforms of the area. (p. G10)

landscape (land′skāp) A painting that shows a view of the outdoors. (p. 181)

latitude (lat′i tüd) A measure of distance on Earth north or south of the equator. (p. 86)

legislative branch (lej′is lā tiv branch) The branch of government that makes laws. (p. 301)

line graph (līn graf) A graph that shows how a piece of information changes over time. (p. 176)

livestock (līv′stok) Animals kept on a farm, such as cattle, hogs, and chickens. (p. 273)

locator (lō′kā tər) A small map or globe set onto another map that shows where the main map is located. (p. G8)

lock (lok) A kind of water elevator that moves boats within a canal to higher or lower levels. (p. 169)

longhouse (lông′hous) A long wooden building in an Iroquois village that housed many families. (p. 67)

longitude (lon′ji tüd) A measure of distance on Earth east or west of the prime meridian. (p. 87)

Loyalist (loi′ə list) A colonist who remained loyal to Britain. (p. 114)

M

manor (man′ər) A large piece of land that the owner rents in smaller plots to a number of farmers. (p. 102)

manufacturing (man yə fak′chər ing) Making large amounts of goods in factories. (p. 276)

map key (map kē) An explanation of what the symbols on a map represent. (p. G7)

mayor (mā′ər) The head of a municipal government. (p. 296)

merchant (mər′chənt) A person who buys and sells goods. (p. 104)

meridian (mə rid′ē ən) A line of longitude. (p. 87)

pronunciation key

a at; ā ape; ä far; âr care; e end; ē me; i it; ī ice; îr pierce; o hot; ō old; ô fork; oi oil; ou out; u up; ū use; ü rule; ù pull; ûr turn; hw white; ng song; th thin; th this; zh measure; ə about, taken, pencil, lemon, circus

metropolitan area (me trə po′li tən ār′ē ə) A city and its suburbs together. (p. 318)

moraine (mə rān′) A line of low hills formed by the rocks pushed at the front of a glacier. (p. 14)

mouth (mouth) The place where a river empties into an ocean, a lake, or a larger river. (p. 19)

municipal government (mū nis′ə pəl guv′ərn mənt) Government of a village, town, county, or city. (p. 295)

N

natural resource (nach′ər əl rē′sôrs) Something found in the environment that people can use. (p. 32)

neutral (nü′trəl) Not taking sides. (p. 240)

New Deal (nü dēl) Government programs started by President Franklin D. Roosevelt in the 1930s to aid people during the Great Depression. (p. 250)

New York Stock Exchange (nü yôrk stok eks′chānj) A building on Wall Street where stocks are bought and sold. (p. 153)

news article (nüz är′ti kəl) A newspaper story that contains facts about recent events. (p. 304)

nonrenewable resource (non ri nü′ə bəl rē′sôrs) A natural resource that cannot be replaced. (p. 33)

O

ocean (o shən) One of Earth's four largest bodies of water—the Arctic, Atlantic, Indian, and Pacific oceans. (p. G4)

opinion (ə pin′yən) A personal feeling or belief. (p. 148)

outline (out′līn) A plan for organizing written information about a subject. (p. 320)

P

parallel (par′ə lel) A line of latitude. (p. 86)

Patriot (pā′trē ət) A colonist who was opposed to British rule. (p. 114)

patroon (pə trün′) A land owner in New Netherland who had to bring 50 settlers to the colony to help settle his land. (p. 94)

physical map (fiz′i kəl map) A map that shows natural features of Earth. (p. G10)

plain (plān) A large area of flat or nearly flat land. (p. 10)

plateau (pla tō′) A large area that rises steeply above the surrounding land. (p. 12)

political map (pə lit′i kəl map) A map that shows information such as cities, capitals, states, and countries. (p. G9)

pollution (pə lü′shən) Anything that dirties the air, soil, or water. (p. 257)

population (pop yə lā′shən) The number of people who live in a place or area. (p. 33)

port (pôrt) A place where ships load and unload their goods. (p. 44)

powwow (pow′wow) A celebration of Native American culture involving music, dance, and other Native American traditions. (p. 317)

precipitation (pri sip i tā′shən) The moisture that falls to the ground as rain, snow, sleet, or hail. (p. 23)

prehistory (prē his′tə rē) The time before written records. (p. 61)

prime meridian (prīm mə rid′ē ən) The line of longitude, marked 0°, from which other meridians are numbered. (p. 87)

profit (prof′it) The money a business earns after it pays for tools, salaries, and other costs. (p. 277)

publishing (pub′lish ing) The business of writing and printing books, newspapers, and magazines. (p. 278)

Q

quarry (kwôr′ē) A place where stone is cut out and removed from the ground. (p. 34)

R

ratify (ra′tə fī) To formally approve. (p. 145)

ration (ra′shən) To use less of something. (p. 252)

recreation (rek rē ā′shən) Things people do for relaxation and enjoyment. (p. 322)

reference source (ref′ər əns sôrs) A book or any form of information that contains facts about many different subjects. (p. 220)

reform (rē fôrm′) A change to make things better. (p. 190)

region (rē′jən) An area with common features that set it apart from other areas. (p. 43)

renewable resource (ri nü′ə bəl rē′sôrs) A natural resource that can be replaced. (p. 33)

representative (re pri zen′tə tiv) A person chosen to speak or vote for others. (p. 143)

retreat (ri trēt′) To turn back. (p. 124)

rural (rûr′əl) Of the countryside; including farms, small villages, or unsettled land. (p. 214)

S

sachem (sā′chəm) A council member of the Iroquois Confederacy. (p. 74)

scale (skāl) The relationship between the distance shown on a map and the distance on Earth. (p. G8)

secede (sə sēd′) To withdraw or formally leave an organization such as a government. (p. 196)

Senate (sen′it) The house of Congress in which each state has two members, regardless of its population. (p. 308)

service (sûr′vis) A job people do to help others, rather that to make things. (p. 280)

sheriff (she′rif) The person in charge of making sure the laws are obeyed in a county. (p. 296)

skyscraper (skī′skrā pər) A tall building, usually one supported by a steel frame. (p. 211)

slavery (slā′və rē) The practice of making one person the property of another. (p. 101)

source (sôrs) The place where a river begins. (p. 19)

Stamp Act (stamp akt) An act passed by Great Britain in 1765 that placed taxes on newspapers and pamphlets. (p. 114)

State Assembly (stāt ə sem′blē) One of the two branches that make up the New York State legislature. (p. 301)

State Senate (stāt sen′it) One of the two branches that make up the New York State legislature. (p. 301)

stock (stok) A share of ownership in a business. (p. 152)

strike (strīk) A refusal of all the workers in a business to work until the owners meet their demands. (p. 218)

suburb (sub′ûrb) A community outside of but near a larger city. (p. 254)

subway (sub′wā) A network of trains that run through tunnels under New York City. (p. 246)

suffrage (suf′rij) The right to vote. (p. 191)

Supreme Court (sə prēm′ côrt) The highest court in the United States. (p. 309)

surrender (sə ren′dər) To give up. (p. 123)

suspension bridge (sə spen′shən brij) A bridge that hangs, or is suspended, over the water. (p. 229)

sweatshop (swet′shop) A factory where workers are paid low wages and work in unhealthy conditions. (p. 224)

symbol (sim′bəl) Anything that stands for something else. (p. G7)

tanning (tan′ing) A method of scraping and soaking animal skins to make leather. (p. 179)

tax (taks) Money people pay to the government so that it can perform public services. (p. 98)

technology (tek nol′ə gē) Use of scientific ideas and special tools to meet people's needs. (p. 278)

temperature (tem′pər ə chər) A measurement of how hot or cold something is, often the air. (p. 23)

tenant farmer (te′nənt fär′mər) A farmer who works land owned by someone else and pays rent in either cash or shares of produce. (p. 103)

tenement (ten′ə mənt) A crowded, poorly maintained apartment building. (p. 224)

till (til) Soil and rocks dropped by a glacier. (p. 15)

time line (tīm līn) A diagram that shows a series of events in the order in which they happened. (p. 120)

time zone (tīm zōn) A region in which all the clocks are set to the same time. (p. 286)

toll (tōl) A small fee people pay to use a canal, bridge, or road. (p. 170)

tourism (tûr i zəm) Services for tourists. (p. 283)

trade (trād) The buying and selling of goods. (p. 150)

transportation (trans pôr tā′shən) The moving of goods or people from one place to another. (p. 19)

transportation map (trans pôr tā′shən map) A map that shows how to travel from one place to another (p. G11)

Treaty of Ghent (trē′tē uv gent) The treaty signed in 1814 by the United States and Great Britain that ended the War of 1812. (p. 164)

tributary (trib′yū ter ē) Any river that flows into another, larger river. (p. 19)

Underground Railroad (un′dər ground rāl′rōd) A group of people who helped enslaved African Americans escape to freedom along secret routes before and during the Civil War. (p. 193)

Union (ūn′yən) The states that remained in the United States after the Confederacy formed. (p. 196)

urban (ûr′bən) Of a city. (p. 214)

valley (va′lē) The low land between hills or mountains, often with a river at the bottom. (p. 12)

veto (vē′tō) To refuse to approve. (p. 299)

wampum (wom′pəm) Polished beads used in ceremonies by Iroquois and other Native Americans to represent certain ideas; also used in gift-giving and trading. (p. 75)

War of 1812 (wôr uv a′teen twelv) A war between the United States and Great Britain, 1812–1814. (p. 164)

weather (weth′ər) The condition of the air at a certain time in a certain place, including temperature, precipitation, and wind. (p. 22)

pronunciation key

a **at**; ā **ape**; ä **far**; âr **care**; e **end**; ē **me**; i **it**; ī **ice**; îr **pierce**; o **hot**; ō **old**; ô **fork**; oi **oil**; ou **out**; u **up**; ū **use**; ü **rule**, ů **pull**; ûr **turn**; hw **white**; ng **song**; th **thin**; <u>th</u> **this**; zh **measure**; ə **about, taken, pencil, lemon, circus**

index

This Index lists many topics that appear in the book, along with the pages on which they are found. Page numbers after an *m* refer you to a map. Page numbers after a *p* indicate photographs, artwork, or charts.

CREDITS

COVER PHOTOGRAPHY: Macmillan/McGraw-Hill School Division

Maps: Geosystems

Chapter Opener Globes: Greg Wakabayashi

PHOTOGRAPHY CREDITS: All photographs are by the Macmillan/McGraw-Hill School Division (MMSD) except as noted below.

Table of Contents: iii: t.l.: Lori Adamski Peek, Tony Stone Images; b.l.: Richard Laird, FPG International; b.r.: Superstock. iv: t.l.: Thaw Collection, Fenimore House Museum, Cooperstown, N.Y., Photo by John Bigelow Taylor, NYC; b.l.: Guy Gillette, Photo Researchers, Inc.; b.r.: Albany Institute of History and Art. v: t.l.: Sophia Smith Collection, Smith College; b.l.: Library of Congress, LC-B8171-7035; b.r.: Griffith Bailey Coale, *On the Erie Canal*, Canajoharie Library and Art

Gallery, Canajoharie, N.Y. vi. c.l.: The Bettmann Archive; b.l.: Lewis W. Hine, Courtesy of George Eastman House; b.r.: Corbis-Bettmann. vii: t.l.: David Young Wolff, Tony Stone Images; c.l.: Gary Gold; b.l.: Superstock; b.r.: Robert E. Daemmrich, Tony Stone Images. ix: t.l.: I♥NY used with permission. I♥NY (the "Mark") is a registered trademark and service mark of the New York State Department of Economic Development (the "Department") and is licensed to the publisher of this document. Inclusion of the Mark in this publication does not constitute an endorsement. The Department makes no representation, express or implied, about the accuracy of the contents of this publication. Neither the State of New York nor the Department shall be liable to any person for any loss incurred in connection with the use of or reliance upon any information contained in or derived from this publication; b.r.: New York State Department of Economic Development. **Front Matter:** G: t.: Steve Wall; b.: Cosmo Condina, Tony Stone Images. G2: bkgd: Elizabeth Wolf ; t.: Jodi Cobb; b.: National Baseball Hall of Fame & Museum, Inc. G3: Sylvain Grandadam, Tony Stone Images. G4: Macmillan. **Chapter 1:** 2: t.l.: Don Mason, The Stock Market; t.r.: Greg Miller; b.l.: Courtesy of *Star-Gazette*, Elmira, N.Y.; b.r.: Seneca-Iroquois National Museum. 3.: l.: Jose L. Pelaez, The Stock Market; r.: Ken Lax. 4. t.l.: Cosmo Condina, Tony Stone Images; t.r.: Ken Fisher, Tony Stone Images; c.: Richard Laird, FPG International; b.l.: Lori Adamski Peek, Tony Stone Images; b.r.: SuperStock. 5.: SuperStock; r.: Jerry Irwin, Photo Researchers, Inc. 6: bkgd: Roger Tully, Tony Stone Images; r.: Sam Abell; b.l.: Kenneth Garrett; b.r.: Hub Willson, H. Armstrong Roberts. 7: James P. Blair. 9: Nancie Battaglia; c.t.: New York State Department of Economic Development; c.b.: James Blank, FPG International; b.: John Pinderhughes, The Stock Market. 10: Nancie Battaglia. 11: SuperStock. 12: l.: Ariel Skelley, The Stock Market; r.: Nancie

Battaglia. 13: t.l.: Joseph Sohm, Tony Stone Images; t.r.: Karen Tweedy-Holmes, New York, N.Y.; b.l.: New York State Department of Economic Development; b.r.: Dennis Hallinan, FPG International. 14: l. & r.: Dave Spier, Clifton Springs, N.Y. 16: Uniphoto Picture Company. 18: Copyright 1996 Carl E. Heilman II. 19: l.: New York State Department of Economic Development; r.: Nancie Battaglia. 21: l.: Nava Swan, FPG International; r.: Dennis Hallinan, FPG International. 22: Art Tilley, FPG International. 23: Telegraph Colour Library, FPG International. 24: l.: Nancie Battaglia; r.: Ohio Department of Natural Resources. 25: Leland Bobbe, Tony Stone Images. 26: New York State Department of Economic Development. 27: l.: Richard T. Nowitz, Photo Researchers, Inc.; r.: Greg Miller. **Chapter 2:** 31: t.: New York State Department of Economic Development; c.t.: Nancie Battaglia; c.b.: Rafael Macia, Photo Researchers, Inc.; b.: Jack Kidd, The Fingerlakes Association. 32: Ohio Department of Natural Resources. 33: l.: David Noble, FPG International; r.: Charles Gupton, The Stock Market. 34: Guy Gillette, Photo Researchers, Inc. 35: t.: Karen Tweedy-Holmes, New York, N.Y.; b.: Pete Saloutos, The Stock Market. 36: Russel Muson, The Stock Market. 37: t.: George Ancona, Santa Fe, N.M.; b.: John Cronin. 38: t.: Copyright 1996 Carl E. Heilman II; b.: Stan Sholik, FPG International. 39: b.: Dale Kakkak from *Ininitig's Gift of Sugar* by Laura Waterman Wittstock, Copyright 1993, by Lerner Publications Co., All Rights Reserved; t.: Grandma Moses: *Sugaring Off*. Copyright 1991, Grandma Moses Properties Co., N.Y. 41: l.: William Taufic, The Stock Market; r.: Stephen J. Krasemann, Photo Researchers, Inc. 42: t.: Nancie Battaglia; b.: New York State Department of Economic Development. 44: b.: New York State Department of Economic Development; t.: David Doody, FPG International. 45: Clifford Oliver Mealy, New York State Parks. 46: t.l.: Bill Banaszewski, Finger Lake Images; b.l.: New York State Department of Economic Development; b.r.: Copyright 1996 Carl E. Heilman II. 47: t. & c.: New York State Department of Economic Development; b.l.: I♥NY used with permission; see above page ix, t.l. b.r.: Chad Slattery, Tony Stone Images. 48: t. & c.: Nicholas Lisi, Syracuse, N.Y.; b.: Courtesy of Mrs. Lillie Fields, Principal of Nate Perry Elementary School. 51: New York State Department of Economic Development. 53: Greg Miller. **Chapter 3:** 54: t.l.: U.S. Army Center of Military History; t.r. Collection of The New-York Historical Society; c.l.: Thaw Collection, Fenimore House Museum, Cooperstown, N.Y., Photo by John Bigelow Taylor, NYC; c.r.: Albany Institute of History and Art; b.l.: Clinton County Historical Museum, Plattsburgh, N.Y.; b.r.: North Wind Pictures. 55: t.: Guy Gillette, Photo Researchers, Inc.; b.: Thaw Collection, Fenimore House Museum, Cooperstown, N.Y., Photo by John Bigelow Taylor, NYC. 56: bkgd: Painting by Howard Smith, Continental Insurance Company; b.l.: Saratoga National Historical Park, Stillwater, N.Y. 57: Emory Kristof. 60: t.: Courtesy of the New York State Museum, Albany, N.Y.; b.: Clinton County Historical Museum, Plattsburgh, N.Y. 61: Clinton County Historical Museum, Plattsburgh, N.Y. 62: Courtesy of the New York State Museum, Albany, N.Y. 63: Courtesy of the New York State Museum, Albany, N.Y. 64: t.: North Wind Pictures; b.: SuperStock/Four by Five, Inc. 65: Cleveland Museum of Natural History. 66: Iroquois Indian Museum, Howes Cave, N.Y. 67: l.: Thaw Collection, Fenimore House Museum, Cooperstown, N.Y., Photo by John Bigelow Taylor, NYC; r.: Courtesy of the New York State Museum, Albany, N.Y. 70: Detail from *Ki-on-twog-ky the Seneca Chief known as Cornplanter* by E. Bartoli, Collection of The New-York Historical Society. 71: t.r.: Courtesy of the New York State Museum, Albany, N.Y.; c.: The Granger Collection, N.Y.; b.l.: The Buffalo and Erie County Historical Society. 73: t.: Courtesy of the Artist: Arnold Jacobs/IROQUOIS; b.: Iroquois Indian Museum, Howes Cave, N.Y. 74: l.: Cranbrook Institute of Science ; c.: Detail from *TeeYee Neen Ho Ga Row* by John Verelst, National Archives of Canada/CO92414; r.: The Buffalo and Erie County Historical Society. 76: t. & b.: Seneca-Iroquois National Museum. 77: Greg Miller. **Chapter 4:** 82: The Granger Collection, N.Y. 83: Scala, Art Resource, N.Y. 84: t.: Photo by Blaire & Webber Photography, Courtesy of Clinton County Historical Society; b.: Fort Ticonderoga Museum. 85: t.: The Granger Collection, N.Y.; c.: North Wind Pictures; b.: Photo by Gilbert W. Hagerty, Courtesy of Doris and Thomas H. Hagerty, Whitesboro, N.Y. 90: The Granger Collection, N.Y. 91: t.: L.F. Tantillo, Nassau, N.Y.; b.: Museum of the City of New York. 92: t.: Columbia County Historical Society, Kinderhook, N.Y., Michael Fredericks, Photographer; c.l.: Museum of the City of New York; c.r.: Columbia County Historical Society, Kinderhook, N.Y., Michael Fredericks, Photographer; b.l.: Courtesy of the Brooklyn Museum; b.r.: Courtesy of the Henry Francis du Pont Winterthur Museum. 93: l.: Museum of the City of New York; r.: Collection of The New-York Historical Society. 94: Detail from *Governor Peter Suyvesant* attributed to Henri Couturier, Collection of The New-York Historical Society. 96: Corbis-Bettmann. 97: Collection of The New-York Historical Society. 98: Corbis-Bettmann. 100: Historic Hudson Valley, Tarrytown, N.Y. 101: l.: Museum of the City of New York; r.: Courtesy of the Henry Francis du Pont Winterthur Museum. 102: Historic Hudson Valley, Tarrytown, N.Y. 103: t.: Historic Hudson Valley, Tarrytown, N.Y.; b.: Courtesy Bronck Museum. 104: l.: *Portrait of Mrs. Roger Morris* by John Singleton Copley ca. 1771, Courtesy of the Henry Francis du Pont Winterthur Museum; r.: Teapot by Nicholas Roosevelt ca. 1755-65, Yale University Art Gallery, The Mabel Brady Garvan Collection. 105: Corbis-Bettmann. 106: Ken Lax. 107: Ken Lax. **Chapter 5:** 112: Detail from *Johnson Hall* by Edward Lamson Henry, Collection of the Albany Institute of History and Art. 113: t.: McCord Museum of Canadian History; b.: Thaw Collection, Fenimore House Museum, Cooperstown, N.Y., Photo by John Bigelow Taylor, NYC. 114: t.: The Granger Collection, N.Y.; b.: *The American Revolution: A Picture Sourcebook*, Dover Publications, Inc. 115: Chemung County Historical Society. 116: Fort Ticonderoga Museum. 117: The Granger Collection, N.Y. 118: The Granger Collection, N.Y. 119: t.: The Granger Collection, N.Y.; c. & b.: Courtesy of Westchester County Historical Society. 122: New York State Department of Economic Development. 123: The Granger Collection, N.Y. 124: l.: New York State Department of Economic Development; r.: United States Postal Service. 125: Chemung County Historical Society. 126: t.r.: Detail from *General John Burgoyne* by Reynolds, Copyright The Frick Collection, N.Y.; b.l.: Independence National Historical Park. 127: The Granger Collection, N.Y. 128: t. & b.: U.S. Army Photo, U.S. Military Academy, West Point, N.Y. 129: t.l., t.r., & b.r.: U.S. Army Photo, U.S. Military Academy, West Point, N.Y. 130: Photo by Richard Freer, Courtesy of National Park Service. 131: Photo by Richard Freer, Courtesy of National Park Service. 135: Greg Miller. **Chapter 6:** 136: t.l.: The Metropolitan Museum of Art, Bequest of Maria DeWitt Jesup, from the collection of her husband, Morris K. Jesup, 1914 (15.30.59); t.r.e.: The Granger Collection, N.Y.; c.: Library of Congress, LC-B8171-7035; b.l.: Sophia Smith Collection, Smith College; b.r.: Griffith Bailey Coale, *On the Erie Canal*, Canajoharie Library and Art Gallery, Canajoharie, NY. 137: l.: The Granger Collection, N.Y.; r.: Detail from *The Entrance of the Highlands*, by Currier & Ives, 1864, the Harry T. Peters Collection, Museum of the City of New York. 138: bkgd & l.: Bob Sacha. 139: t.l.: Bob Sacha; b.l.: Sam Abell. 142: The Granger Collection, N.Y. 143: l. & r.: Courtesy of Senate House State Historic Site, New York State Office of Parks, Recreation, and Historic Preservation. 144: Collection of The New-York Historical Society. 146: t.r.: The Independence National Historical Park; c.t., c.b., b.l., & b.r.: The Granger Collection, N.Y. 147: r.: The Granger Collection, N.Y. e.: Charles Peale Polk, SuperStock. 148: The Granger Collection, N.Y. 149: The Granger Collection, N.Y. 150: The New York Public Library. 151: The New York Public Library, Astor, Lenox, and Tilden Foundations. 152: l.: Corbis-Bettmann; r.: Courtesy of The Bank of New York Archives. 154: Jose L. Pelaez, The Stock Market. 155: Buffalo and Erie County Historical Society. **Chapter 7:** 160: Detail from *Schenectady Harbor, 1814*, Painting by L.F. Tantillo, Nassau, N.Y. 161: The Granger Collection, N.Y. 162: l.: Detail from *Portrait of Sa-go-ye-wat-hg or Red Jacket* by Robert Weir, Collection of the New-York Historical Society; r.: New York State Office of Parks, Recreation and Historic Presevation-Letchworth State Park. 163: t.: Rochester Public Library; b.: Courtesy of Rochester Historical Society. 164: Detail from McDonough's Victory on Lake Champlain by N. Currier, 1846. The Harry T Peters Collection, Museum of the City of New York. 165: t. & b.: Courtesy of Joyce Plembleto. 166: The Bettmann Archive. 167: The New York Public Library, Astor, Lenox, and Tilden Foundations. 168: Erie Canal Museum, Syracuse, New York. 169: Anthony Mario, Margo Studio/Erie Canal Village. 170: l.: Collection of The New-York Historical Society; r.: National Portrait Gallery, Smithsonian Institution/Art Resource, N.Y. 171: Canal Society of New York State. 172: t.: Erie Canal Museum, Syracuse, N.Y.; b.: Detail from *The First Railroad Train* by E.L. Henry, Collection of the Albany Institute of History and Art, Gift of Friends of the Institute. 174: t.: Renee Lynn, Photo Researchers, Inc.; b.: Erie Canal Museum, Syracuse, N.Y. 175: t.: John Meuser/Finger Lake Images; c.: New York State Department of Economic Development; b.: A. Wadsworth Thompson, *Life on the Towpath*, Canajoharie Library and Art Gallery, Canajoharie, N.Y. 178: t.: Carl Purcell, Photo Researchers; b.: Paul Steel, The Stock Market. 179: t. & b.: Corbis-Bettmann. 180: Collection of the New-York Historical Society. 181: l.: Gift of Martha C. Karolik for the M. and M. Karolik Collection of American Paintings, 1815-1865, Courtesy of the Museum of Fine Arts, Boston; r.: Otto Rogge, The Stock Market. 183: Shinichi Kanno, FPG International. 184: The Granger Collection, N.Y. 185: l.: Greg Miller; r.: The Bettmann Archive. **Chapter 8:** 190: The Granger Collection, N.Y. 191: t.l.: Smithsonian Institution, (74.847); c.: Bettmann; b.r.: Smithsonian Institution, (74.847). 192: The J. Paul Getty Museum, Los Angeles, California. 193: t.: The Granger Collection, N.Y.; b.: Oberlin College Archives. 194: t.l.: The Granger Collection, N.Y.; t.r.: Onondaga Historical Association, Syracuse, New York; b.r.: UPI/Corbis-Bettmann. 196: Library of Congress, LC-B8171-7095. 198: t.: Radcliffe College; b.: Courtesy of Broome County Historical Society. 199: Library of Congress, LC-B8171-7514. 200: Schomburg Center for Research in Black Culture, New York Public Library. 201: Library of Congress, LC-B8184-B46. 202: Bob Collier. 203: l.: Greg Miller; r.: Bob Collier. 207: Greg Miller. **Chapter 9:** 208: t.l.: Corbis-Bettmann; t.r.: Bettmann; c.: Lewis W. Hine, Courtesy of George Eastman House; b.l.: Library of Congress, LC-USF34-25924D; b.r.: Courtesy of the New York Stock Exchange, Inc. 209: l.: Charles Sheeler, *Rolling Power*, Smith College Museum of Art, Drayton, Hillyer Fund; r.: The Bettmann Archive. 210: bkgd: David Ball, Tony Stone Images; l.: Richard T. Nowitz. 211: t.: UPI/Bettmann; b.: Cosmo Condina, Tony Stone Images. 214: The Granger Collection, N.Y. 215: From the Collections of Henry Ford Museum & Greenfield Village. 216: t.: Courtesy of George Eastman House; b.: Corbis-Bettmann. 217: t.l.: The Granger Collection, N.Y.; t.r.: Collection of The Corning Museum of Glass, Corning, N.Y., Gift of Jerry E. Wright; c.l.: Chris Rogers, The Stock Market; c.r.: The Granger Collection, N.Y.; b.l.: The Bettmann Archive; b.r.: Courtesy of Carrier Corporation. 218: Corbis-Bettmann. 221: Copyright 1990 Macmillan Publishing Company. 222: Corbis-Bettmann. 223: The Collection of Walter and Naomi Rosenblum. 224: Jacob A. Riis, Museum of the City of New York. 225: The Collection of Walter and Naomi Rosenblum. 226: t.: UPI/Bettmann; b.: FPG International. 227: t.: Edward Moran, Museum of the City of New York; b.: Corbis-Bettmann. 228: t. & b.: Gary Gold. 229: t.: Corbis-Bettmann; b.: Spencer Grant, FPG International. 230: New York State Department of Economic Development. 232: Nancie Battaglia. 233: t.: Peter Bauer; b.: Courtesy of Adirondack Park Agency, Photo by Mike Storey; c.: Michael R. Martin. 234: t.: Rochester Public Library; b.: Don Mason, The Stock Market. 235: t.l.: Rochester Public Library; t.r.: Michael Hagar, Museum Photographics; c.: Courtesy of Rochester City Photographer; b.l.: Courtesy of Rochester Fire Department; b.r.: Rochester Public Library. **Chapter 10:** 240: Buffalo and Erie County Historical Society. 241: Corbis-Bettmann. 242: l.: National Portrait Gallery, Smithsonian Institution/Art Resource, New York; r.: National Museum of American Art, Smithsonian Institution, Gift of Benjamin and Olya Margolin/Art Resource, New York. 243: Photo World, FPG International. 244: The Bettman Archive. 245: Avery Library, Columbia University. 246: The Collection of Walter and Naomi Rosenblum. 247: t.l. & t.r.: Photograph by Berenice Abbott, Museum of the City of New York; c.: James VanDerZee, The Metropolitan Museum of Art (1970.539.7); b.l.: Lewis W. Hine, Courtesy George Eastman House; b.r.: Donna VanDerZee. 248: FPG International. 249: t.: UPI/Bettman; b.: Library of Congress, LC-USF33-11402-M4. 250: l.: Library of Congress, LC-USF-34-25908D; r.: FPG International. 251: l.: FPG International; r.: UPI/Corbis-Bettmann. 252: l.: Library of Congress, LC-USW3-26094-D; r.: Cradle of Aviation Museum. 253: Fergus O'Brien, FPG International. 254: Tadder/Baltimore, Archive Photos. 255: l.: Corbis-Bettmann; r.: UPI/Corbis-Bettmann. 256: t.l.: Archive Photos; c.l. & r.: UPI/Corbis-Bettmann; b.l.: Frank Leonardo, Archive Photos.260: UPI/Corbis-Bettmann. 261: Greg Miller; 265: Greg Miller. **Chapter 11:** 266: t.l.: New York State Department of Economic Development; t.c.: SuperStock; t.r.: Steve Elmore, Tony Stone Images; c.: Courtesy of Rochester City Photographer; b.l.: New York State Department of Economic Development; b.r.: David Young Wolff, Tony Stone Images. 267: t.: Gary Gold; b.: Robert E. Daemmrich, Tony Stone Images. 268: bkgd: Joseph Pobereskin, Tony Stone Images; t.: Kathleen Campbell, Tony Stone Images; b.: Will & Deni McIntyre, Tony Stone Images. 269: t.: Jon Riley, Tony Stone Images; b.: Jose Azel. 271: t.: Lance Coleman Photography, Elmira, N.Y.; c.t.: Nancie Battaglia; c.b.: Courtesy of S/N Precision Enterprises; b.: Uniphoto Picture Agency.272: t.: Lance Coleman Photography, Elmira, N.Y.; b.: Burwell, Folio, Inc. 274: t. & b.: Lance Coleman Photography, Elmira, N.Y. 276: David Joel, Tony Stone Images. 277: Jack Manning, *New York Times*. 278: Courtesy of S/N Precision Enterprises. 279: International Stock Photo. 280: t.: Nancy J. Parisi, Buffalo, N.Y.; b.: Rob Gage, FPG International. 283: Michael A. Keller, The Stock Market. 284: Just Buffalo Literacy Center, Inc. 285: Photo by Chris Lee, Courtesy of the New York Philharmonic. 288: Courtesy of Champion International Corporation. 289: l.: Courtesy of La Fave, White, and McGivern, L. S., P.C.; r.: Courtesy of the Department of the Army, Fort Drum. 291: Richard Laird, FPG International. **Chapter 12:** 293: Gary Gold. 294: Office of the Mayor of the City of Salamanca. 295: t.r.: John R. Patton; b.l.: Viviane Moos, The Stock Market; b.c.: SuperStock; b.r.: The Stock Market. 297: Charles Gupton, Stock Boston. 298: State of New York. 300: Nancie Battaglia. 302: Uniphoto Picture Agency. 303: t. & b.: Courtesy of Nora Gross. 306: t.: SuperStock; b.: UPI/Corbis-Bettmann. 307: t.: Reuters/Corbis-Bettmann; b.: Brownie Harris, The Stock Market. 309: t.: Collection, The Supreme Court of The United States, Courtesy of The Supreme Court Historical Society; b.l.: Courtesy of the United States Senate. b.r.: AFP/Corbis. 310: Courtesy of *Star-Gazette*, Elmira, N.Y. 311: Michael Hayman, Photo Researchers, Inc. **Chapter 13:** 314: t.: Uniphoto Picture Agency; c.: The Stock Market; b.: Mike Timo, Tony Stone Images. 315: t.l.: Rob Gage, FPG International; t.r.: Roy Morsch, The Stock Market; c.l.: Rob Gage, FPG International; c.r.: Robert Vega, Vega Design; b.l.: Stephen Simpson, FPG International; b.r.: Uniphoto Picture Agency. 316: Rafael Macia, Photo Researchers, Inc. 318: New York State Department of Economic Development. 319: H. Dratch, The Image Works. 321: Bonnie Freer, Photo Researchers, Inc. 322: Photo by T. Wolf, Courtesy of Chautauqua Institution. 323: l.: David Heald, The Solomon R. Guggenheim Foundation, N.Y.; r.: Hirouvki Matsumoto, Tony Stone Images. 324: t.: Richard Pasley, Stock Boston; b.: John Dunn, AP/Wide World Photos. 325: James Randkley, Tony Stone Images. 326: t.l.: Time Warner Media Center, Photo by Mark Avers, Courtesy of Children's Museum of Manhattan; t.r.: Courtesy of Milton J. Rubenstein Museum of Science & Technology; b.l.: Howe Caverns, Inc., N.Y.; b.r.: Courtesy of Adirondack Scenic Railroad. 327: B Weir/Don Franklin 1997, Rochester, N.Y. 328: Mark Lennihan, AP/Wide World Photos. 329: l.: Baseball Hall of Fame Library, Milo Stewart, Jr., Cooperstown, N.Y.; t.r.: UPI/Bettmann Newsphotos; b.r.: Adam Nadel/AP Wide World Photos. 330: William S. Helsel, Tony Stone Images. 331: Greg Miller. 333: Charles Agel, AP/Wide World Photos. 335: Greg Miller **Reference Section:** R3: The Granger Collection, N.Y. R22: t.l.: AP/Wide World Photos; t.r.: Copyright Miriam Berkley; c.l.: Reuters/Gary Hershorn/Archive Photos; c.r. & b.l.: AP/Wide World Photos; b.r.: Courtesy of NASA. R23: t.l.: Courtesy of Greenfield Review Press; t.r.: AP/Wide World Photos; c.l.: Jean Cummings/Archive Photos; c.r.: Popperfoto/Archive Photos; b.l.: AP/Wide World Photos; b.r.: Chris Felver, Archive Photos. R24: t.l.: Saga '90/G. Asakawa, Archive Photos; t.c.: Reuters/Ray Stubblebine/Archive Photos; t.r.: Courtesy of United States House of Representatives; b.l.: Eric R. Michelson/Archive Newsphotos; b.c.: Horst Tappe/Archive Photos, b.r.: Archive Photos/fotos international. R25: t.l.: AP/Wide World Photos; t.r.: Archive Photos/fotos international; c.l.: A. Kachatorian/Saga, Archive Photos; c.r.: Peter Iovino/Saga/Archive Photos; b.l.: Scott R. Sutton, Archive Photos; b.r.: Julian Block/White Pine Press. R29: Gary Gold.

The Princeton Review
— Handbook of —
Test-Taking Strategies

READ QUESTIONS CAREFULLY

The most common mistake students make when they take a test is to answer the questions too quickly. Rushing through a test causes careless mistakes. Don't rush. Read each question carefully. Make sure you understand the question BEFORE you try to answer it.

Use the map to answer questions 1 through 3.

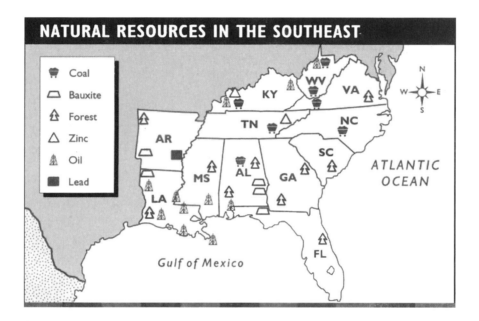

1 In which state is oil an important natural resource?

   A Georgia   **C** Louisiana

   B North Carolina   **D** Tennessee

2 South Carolina's natural resources include

   F bauxite   **H** coal

   G zinc   **J** forest

3 In which state would a lead miner be most likely to find a job?

   A Arkansas   **C** Florida

   B West Virginia   **D** Alabama

TIME LINES

Historical information is sometimes presented in the form of a time line. A time line shows events in the order in which they happened. Time lines are usually read from left to right, like a sentence. If the time line is drawn vertically, it is usually read from top to bottom.

If you read carefully, you should do very well on time line questions.

Look at the time line below. Then answer questions 1 and 2.

Groups Arrive in Hawaii, 500–1900

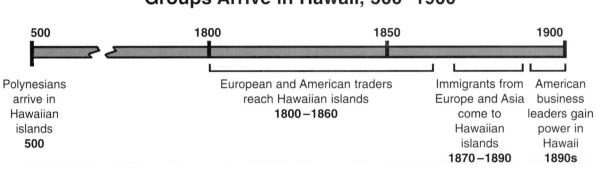

1 Which group was the first to reach the Hawaiian islands?

   A Europeans   **C** Asians

   B Americans   **D** Polynesians

2 Which of the following most likely occurred in 1845?

   F Traders from Europe and America came to the Hawaiian islands.

   G The first Polynesians arrived in the Hawaiian islands.

   H American business leaders gained power in Hawaii.

   J Asian immigrants came to the Hawaiian islands.

                    Remember: Do not write in your textbook.

LOOK AT THE DETAILS BEFORE YOU START

Some test questions contain lots of details. These questions may use:

- charts
- graphs
- flow charts

- time lines
- word webs
- maps

Before you try to answer questions like these, take a few moments to study the information that the charts, graphs, maps, or other visuals contain. The questions will be much easier to answer, because you will know exactly where to look for information!

Study the bar graph. Then do questions 1 and 2.

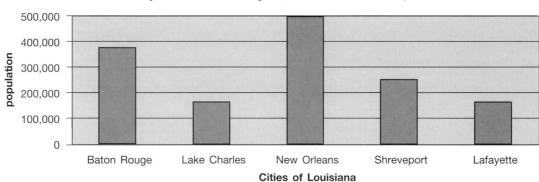

Population of Major Louisiana Cities, 1990

1 In 1990, which Louisiana city had a population of about 380,000?

A Lake Charles
B New Orleans
C Shreveport
D Baton Rouge

2 In 1990, which two Louisiana cities had approximately the same population?

F Baton Rouge and New Orleans
G Lake Charles and Lafayette
H Shreveport and Baton Rouge
J New Orleans and Lake Charles

Remember: Do not write in your textbook.

DIFFERENT TYPES OF GRAPHS

Different types of graphs are used to present numerical information. A **line graph** shows how something changes over time. A line graph might be used to show how the population of the United States has grown over the years. A **bar graph** compares amounts. A bar graph might show the population of different United States cities. A **circle graph** shows how a whole is divided into smaller parts. For example, a circle graph might show how the government divides its budget to pay for roads, education, and other services.

Sometimes you will see a set of questions accompanied by more than one graph. Each question will contain clues to tell you which graph you should read to find the answer. Take the extra time to make sure you are looking at the correct graph. This will help you avoid careless mistakes.

Use the graphs below to answer questions 1 and 2.

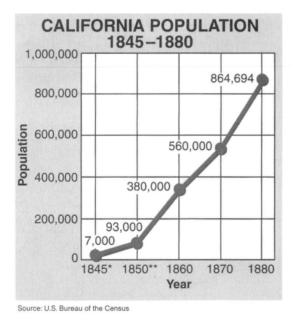

Source: U.S. Bureau of the Census

Source: United States Census, 1860

1 In what year did the population of California reach 380,000?

   A 1840

   B 1850

   C 1860

   D 1870

2 How many people were working as professionals in California in 1860?

   F 10,304

   G 17,175

   H 59,583

   J 82,573

Remember: Do not write in your textbook.

PROCESS OF ELIMINATION

Sometimes when you read a test question, you will not know the answer right away. If you don't know the answer, don't give up. You may be able to find the correct answer another way.

On a multiple-choice test, you can look at the answer choices. One of the answers will be the best answer. The others will be wrong, or not as good. Look at the choices and see if there are any that you know are definitely wrong. If there are, you can ELIMINATE, or ignore, those answers.

Sometimes you will be able to eliminate all of the answers except one. When that happens, it means that you have found the best answer by the PROCESS OF ELIMINATION.

Try using the process of elimination to answer this question:

1 The largest city in South Dakota is

    A   Los Angeles

    B   Dallas

    C   Sioux Falls

    D   Mexico City

Were you able to eliminate any *wrong* answers? How many?

Now try using the process of elimination to answer this question:

2 The section of the United States Constitution that protects the freedom of Americans is called the

    F   Declaration of Independence

    G   Bill of Rights

    H   Civil War

    J   Star Spangled Banner

Remember: Do not write in your textbook.

OUTSIDE KNOWLEDGE

Many questions on multiple-choice tests ask you to look at a map, a chart, a graph, or a drawing. Then you are asked to choose the correct answer based on what you see. On these questions, the information you need to answer the question will be in the map, chart, graph, or drawing.

Sometimes, however, multiple-choice tests will ask you to remember a fact that you learned in social studies class. You won't be able to find the correct answer on a map, chart, graph, or drawing; the correct answer will be in your memory. We call these OUTSIDE KNOWLEDGE questions.

If you are sure you know the answer to an OUTSIDE KNOWLEDGE question, choose the correct answer. It's that simple! When you're NOT sure what the correct answer is, use the PROCESS OF ELIMINATION to answer the question.

1 Which of these books would probably provide the most information about the life of Martin Luther King, Jr.?

   A   an atlas

   B   an encyclopedia

   C   a novel about the South during the Civil War

   D   a collection of poetry

2 Which of the following statements about the southern portion of the United States is true?

   F   The South does not have many farms.

   G   The South is home to the largest cities in the United States.

   H   The South is the most mountainous region in the United States.

   J   The South has a warmer climate than the northern United States.

Remember: Do not write in your textbook.

FLOW CHARTS

A flow chart shows the sequence of steps used to complete an activity. It shows the steps In the order they happen. A flow chart usually uses arrows to show which step happens next.

The first thing to do when you look at a flow chart is to see if it has a title. The title will tell you what the flow chart is about. The next thing you should do is find the arrows. The arrows tell you the order in which to read the chart.

Read flow charts carefully. Don't just look at the illustrations. Make sure to read any text beneath the illustrations.

Study the flow chart. Then do questions 1 and 2.

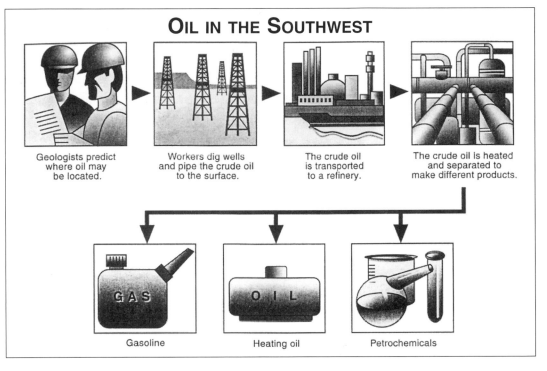

OIL IN THE SOUTHWEST

Geologists predict where oil may be located.

Workers dig wells and pipe the crude oil to the surface.

The crude oil is transported to a refinery.

The crude oil Is heated and separated to make different products.

Gasoline

Heating oil

Petrochemicals

---

1 Which of these questions is answered by the flow chart?

   A What are some of the products that can be made from crude oil?

   B How much does it cost to produce heating oil?

   C Where in the United States is the most crude oil found?

   D How many automobiles are there in the United States?

2 The crude oil Is probably transported to the oil refinery in

   F automobiles

   G large ships

   H helicopters

   J tractors

Remember: Do not write in your textbook.

MAPS

The ability to read and understand maps is an important skill in social studies. Many of the multiple-choice tests you take will require you to read a map.

Look carefully at all the parts of a map. Maps contain a lot of information. Whenever you see a map, you should ask yourself questions like these:

- What does the title of the map tell you?
- Where is the map key?
- What symbols are on the map key? What do they stand for?
- Where is the compass rose?
- What does the compass rose tell you?
- Is there a map scale?

Use the map of Pennsylvania to answer questions 1 and 2.

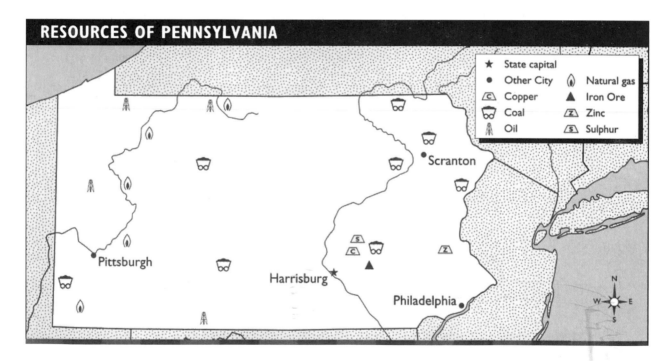

RESOURCES OF PENNSYLVANIA

1 Which natural resource is found only in the western part of Pennsylvania?

    A zinc

    B natural gas

    C coal

    D iron ore

2 Which of these people would be most likely to find a job near Scranton?

    F a driller of oil wells

    G a coal miner

    H a miner of iron ore

    J a zinc miner

Remember: Do not write in your textbook.